FROM THE FIFTY JĀTAKA

FROM THE FIFTY JĀTAKA

SELECTIONS FROM THE THAI PAÑÑĀSA JĀTAKA

Translated and introduced by

Chris Baker and Pasuk Phongpaichit

Silkworm Books

ISBN: 978-616-215-127-9

First published in 2019 by
Silkworm Books
430/58 M. 7, T. Mae Hia, A. Mueang, Chiang Mai, Thailand 50100
info@silkwormbooks.com
www.silkwormbooks.com

Cover: Sudhana crossing the caustic river on the back of a giant python;
from murals in the ordination hall of Wat Suthat Thepwararam, Bangkok.
Photo courtesy of Peerapat Sumran.

Typeset in Gentium Book Basic 10.5 pt. by Silk Type

Printed and bound in the United States by Lightning Source

CONTENTS

Preface *vii*
Acknowledgments *ix*
Introduction *xi*

THE GREAT QUESTS
Sudhana
1
Suvaṇṇasaṅkha: The Golden Conch
27
Rathasena
57
Samuddaghosa
75
Prince Pācitta
87
Subhamitta
99
Sirasā
111

SELF-SACRIFICE
Ratanapajjota: The Shining Gem
141
Bahalāgāvī
151
Suvaṇṇa Kacchapa: The Golden Turtle
155

Siri Cuḍāmaṇi
159

Dulaka Paṇḍita
165

Dhammasoṇḍaka
175

GOOD WORKS FOR THE RELIGION
King Kanakavaṇṇa
183

King Vaṭṭaṅgulī
189

MORAL TALES
Dukammānika
203

The King of Bārāṇasī
213

Sisora
221

TEACHING BY STORIES AND RIDDLES
Bhaṇḍāgāra: The Treasurer
249

STORY CYCLE
Sabbasiddhi
265

COMPLEX QUEST
Varanujja
277

Appendix I: Collections of the Fifty Jātaka *327*
Appendix II: Summaries of All Sixty-One Tales *330*
Glossary *361*
Bibliography *367*

PREFACE

Many of the best-known and best-loved stories from Asia are in the form of a *jātaka*, an account of one of the Buddha's former lives. The earliest originated in India. Later many appeared in Southeast Asia and were gathered in collections, often entitled the Fifty Jātaka.

In Siam one such collection of sixty-one stories was translated from Pali to Thai and published in the 1920s. It has remained in print ever since. The collection includes many of the country's best-known stories, still taught in schools, performed as dance and drama, and continually adapted to new forms of expression.

The stories come in many forms. Some are romantic quest stories. Others are vignettes illustrating a Buddhist virtue. The narratives flow between the human world, the heavens, and the great forest populated by mythical creatures including ogres, serpents, demons, and enticing bird-women. While containing moral messages, they are often designed to be exciting, romantic, and fun in order to succeed as popular teaching.

In this book we present the first English translations of a selection of twenty-one of these stories. The selection has been designed to include the best known of the tales as well as a representative sample of the whole collection. We also include summaries of all sixty-one stories.

Until recently, these stories were considered a minor part of the literary and religious heritage. That judgment has changed. They are now considered the lifeblood of Siam's literature over several centuries. In this collection's introduction, we summarize the new academic literature recognizing their importance and tracing their antecedents.

These stories have been part of mass teaching and popular entertainment over centuries. They offer a window into a part of the Thai cultural heritage that is often overlooked.

ACKNOWLEDGMENTS

Thanks to the two ladies who suggested we undertake this project to counter the great demerit we must have accumulated. Special thanks to Niyada Lausunthorn for her scholarship and encouragement; all references to Thai literary adaptations of these stories come from her pioneering work. Thanks to the Government Savings Bank for providing us with their splendid edition of both the Thai and Pali versions of these tales. Thanks to Peerapat Sumran for the cover photo from the rarely seen murals in the ordination hall of Wat Suthat. Thanks to Peter Skilling, Naomi Appleton, Justin McDaniel, and Arthid Sheravanichkul for necessary guidance. Thanks to Trasvin Jittidecharak and Joel Akins of Silkworm Books.

INTRODUCTION

In the 1920s, the great administrator, historian, and litterateur Prince Damrong Rajanubhab launched a project to translate a Siamese collection of *jātaka* tales into Thai. This collection, now known as the Thailand National Library collection, has sixty-one stories. This book contains a selection from that collection, here published in English translation for the first time.

Jātaka are accounts of a previous life of a Buddha as remembered by him and related to his followers.[1] A collection of 547 stories is preserved in the Khuddaka Nikaya, part of the main Buddhist scriptures, sometimes called the Pali Canon, compiled in South Asia after the Buddha's death. Many other more fragmentary collections exist. These stories vary from an aphorism of a few lines to complex tales, the longest running to ninety pages in English translation.[2] In these past lives, the Buddha was born in many stations in life, including king, merchant, pauper, and various animals. The last ten tales have special prominence as they are believed to show how Gotama Buddha achieved the ten "perfections," which prepared him to achieve enlightenment as the Buddha of our era.[3]

From the early years of Buddhism, these tales have played a large role in popular religious teaching because they combine moral lessons with entertainment.[4] They have spread throughout the Buddhist world, crossing

1. For general introduction to the *jātaka* tradition, see Skilling, "*Jātaka* and *Paññāsa-jātaka*"; Appleton, *Jātaka Stories*, esp. ch. 3; and the introduction in Appleton and Shaw, *Ten Great Birth Stories*.
2. Cowell, *Jātaka*. The longest is J546 Mahā-ummagga (Mahosadha).
3. Appleton and Shaw, *Ten Great Birth Stories*.
4. In surveys of texts found in temple libraries, *jātaka* texts always dominate; see Skilling, "*Jātaka* and *Paññāsa-jātaka*,", 127–28; McDaniel, *Gathering Leaves*, 192.

boundaries of sect and language. They have been adapted to sermons, recited at festivals, depicted in sculpture and painting on religious buildings, performed as dance and drama, and continually adapted to new forms of expression. By the seventh or eighth century CE, the Indian *jātaka* had spread into Southeast Asia as attested by depictions in sculpture.[5]

In mainland Southeast Asia, several other *jātaka* appeared that are not known in India. These are written in Pali, the scriptural language of Theravada Buddhism,[6] or a mixture of Pali and a local language. They are sometimes called the noncanonical or apocryphal *jātaka*. Some have been gathered into collections that are known in various languages as something like the "fifty birth stories." In Pali this is Paññāsa Jātaka. Some of these collections have fifty stories, but most do not. "Fifty Jātaka" has become a conventional title.

When were these stories composed and assembled into these collections? In his preface to the Thai translations of the stories published in 1924, Prince Damrong gave this view:

> The Fifty Jātaka is a collection of fifty tales told in Siam from olden times. A Chiang Mai monk collected and composed them as *jātaka* tales in Pali around 2000–2200 BE [1457–1657 CE]. This was an era when the monks of that country had learned from Sri Lanka. They knew Pali well. They had imported the Sri Lankan model of monkhood. They composed works in Pali, some in the style of commentaries, such as the Mangala Dīpanī, some as histories of the religion, such as Jinakālamāli, following the model of the Mahāvaṁsa chronicle of Lanka, some as *jātaka* tales, such as the Fifty Jātaka, following the model of the Nipāta Jātaka. They intended to make the religion strong and permanent and to create texts that were weighty because they were in the same language as the Tipiṭaka. However, the Fifty Jātaka seems to have been composed toward the end of this period, as the knowledge of Pali had deteriorated from the level found in earlier works. The

5. The earliest are probably at the Phra Pathom Chedi in Nakhon Pathom.

6. Theravada, the way or school of the elders, meaning the original senior monk disciples of the Buddha, is the modern term of choice for the form of Buddhism that predominates in Sri Lanka and Southeast Asia. On the evolution of the tradition, see Skilling, *How Theravada is Theravada?*; Crosby, *Theravada Buddhism*.

> original of the Fifty Jātaka was in the form of palm leaves in fifty bundles. Currently this form exists only in Siam, Luang Prabang, and Cambodia.[7]

In the most thorough study of the Thai collection, Niyada Lausunthorn concluded that "the Fifty Jātaka must have been composed before 1808 BE [1265 CE]."[8] She based this judgment on references to individual stories in inscriptions and other early literary works. One of the stories is mentioned in a Burmese inscription dated 1265.[9] Another story is referenced in the *Chiang Mai Chronicle* in 1288/89.[10] Three are mentioned in the *Traiphum phra ruang*, a cosmological text attributed to King Lithai of Sukhothai in 1345.[11] A Burmese monk rendered two of the stories in verse, probably in the 1480s or 1490s.[12] A monk (who might be the well-known monk-author Ratanapañña Thera) recorded that he rendered one of the stories into Lanna Thai, possibly in the 1510s.[13] Five of the stories are alluded to in two early Thai literary works, *Nirat hariphunchai* and *Thawathotsamat*, which probably date to the late fifteenth or early sixteenth century.[14]

More recently scholars have pointed out that while individual stories may indeed be of early origin, these are only a fraction of the total, they are not necessarily in *jātaka* form in this era, and there is no documentary evidence of *collections* or the term "Fifty Jātaka" until much later. Peter Skilling reckons the first explicit mentions of such collections appeared in both Siam and Burma in the late eighteenth century, and still had no details of the contents.[15] The earliest tables of contents date to the later

7. This preface appears in all editions of these Thai translations.

8. Niyada, *Panyat chadok*, 33. This work originated as a doctoral thesis at the Faculty of Arts, Chulalongkorn University, in 1981 and was first published in 1995.

9. P9 Subhamitta ("Thombamik") in the Kusa-samuti inscription from Pwazaw.

10. P20 King Vaṭṭaṅgulī; see Wyatt and Aroonrat, *Chiang Mai Chronicle*, 34–35.

11. P17 Viriya Paṇḍita, P25 Narajiva, and P27 Mahāpaduma; see Reynolds and Reynolds, *Traiphum*, 266; Niyada, *Panyat chadok*, 176.

12. P2 Sudhana and P3 Sudhanu, by Shin Agga in *Thanhmya Pyistan Pyo*.

13. P1 Samuddaghosa; see Niyada, *Panyat chadok*, 31.

14. P1 Samuddaghosa, P2 Sudhana, P3 Sudhanu, and P39 Prince Pācitta in *Thawathotsamat*; P42 Rathasena, P3 Sudhanu, and P1 Samuddaghosa in *Nirat hariphunchai*; see Niyada, *Panyat chadok*, 36–38; Trongjai, *Upathawathotsamat*, 129–32.

15. In Siam in the *Traibhumilokavinicchayakatha*, a revised version of the Three Worlds cosmology commissioned by King Rama I; see Skilling, "*Jātaka* and *Paññāsa-jātaka*," 164.

nineteenth century. A "traditional catalogue of Pali scriptures" from a manuscript at Wat Pa Duea, Chiang Mai, dated to CS 1234 (1876 CE), includes a list of fifty "Paññāsa-jātaka."[16] The process by which these stories were composed, circulated, and eventually assembled into collections probably extended over a long period of time and involved many different people in several different places.[17] The process also flowed back and forth between the *jātaka* format in Pali and other literary forms in local languages (see below).

Several collections are now known. Earlier they were labeled as Thai, Cambodian, Burmese, and Lao "national" collections, but they should more appositely be assigned to the particular *wat* or archive where the collection resides. As shown in the appendix table comparing collections, several stories recur across several of these collections and there is some parallelism in the numbering and sequencing, but there is also a lot of difference. By Dorothy Fickle's count, there is a total of around 105 tales in these major collections.[18] The total number of *jātaka*-type stories circulating in Southeast Asia either singly or in various collections runs to several hundred.[19]

Moreover, the stories changed as they moved. In the milieu of literary reproduction by manuscript writers in the Southeast Asian past, there was no concept of an original story that had to be preserved intact. Rather, the writers felt they had a duty to improve the story, particularly when preparing it for a new audience.[20] So when the same story appears in two collections, the two versions may vary. At one extreme, these differences may be only minor details, perhaps resulting from errors in copying. By comparing the Burmese and Cambodian versions of the Samuddaghosa story in Pali language, Ginette Terral found nineteen changes of minor

16. A similar manuscript from Wat Sung Men, Phrae, dated to CS 1244, also lists Paññāsa-jātaka; see Santi, *Piṭakamālā*, xli–l, 173–80.

17. Skilling ("Romance and Riddle," 167) notes, "We have no information whatsoever about authorship, and I only venture to *suggest* that the stories were not composed by solitary authors working in isolation, but that they were produced collectively within communities that shared like-minded ideals and ideologies, as well as similar sermon and storytelling practices."

18. Fickle, "Historical and Structural Study," 192.

19. Hundius counted two hundred stories, including those circulating outside collections, in northern Thailand alone; see Skilling, "*Jātaka* and *Paññāsa-jātaka*," 131–33.

20. Justin McDaniel describes this milieu very well, see *Gathering Leaves*, especially chs. 5 and 6.

details, such as the size of the Chaddanta Lake, the number of elephants at the lake, and the height of a certain pavilion.[21] The Pali text of this story from Thailand differs from both the Burmese and Cambodian to a slightly greater extent by omitting some of the verses and several minor details. Whether such variations are slips in copying or editorial choices, they do not seriously change the tale.

In other cases, the changes are more substantial. Sometimes, the names of places and characters are changed, perhaps to be more familiar. In some cases, the plot is the same but the didactic passages are not, perhaps drawing a different moral from the tale. In several stories that appear in both the Thai and Burmese collections, the overall plot is the same and the details of many scenes are the same, but there is not a single sentence in the Pali that is identical in both versions.[22] Possibly these stories traveled in a compressed form used by storytellers and thus differed when they were expanded and written down. Other ways of transmission can be imagined. Clearly they did not always travel as Pali texts.

Comparing the Burmese and Thai versions of one story, Dorothy Fickle noted that in the Thai version the beginning was much more compressed, so the plot moved along more quickly, while the ending was padded with more elaborate teaching.[23] These stories were teaching tools, not tablets of stone.

The Thailand National Library Collection

To create this collection, Prince Damrong Rajanubhab sought texts from the Capital Library (the old Palace Library), and the libraries of Wat Arun, Wat Rakhang, and Wat Pathum Khongkha.[24] He recruited a team of at least seven translators, most of whom had worked earlier with him on translations of the classical *jātaka*.[25] The first two stories, Samuddaghosa

21. Terral, "Samuddaghosajātaka."

22. See for example P4 Ratanapajjota, P13 Dukamannika, P20 King Vaṭṭaṅgulī, P28 Bhaṇḍāgāra, P29 Bahalāgāvi, P32 King of Bārāṇasī, and P60 Sirasā in the Pali GSB version and the equivalent tales in Jaini, *Paññāsa-jātaka or Zimmè Paṇṇāsa*. The Burmese versions tend to be longer because of both more detail in the storytelling and more verses of moral instruction.

23. Fickle, "Historical and Structural Study," 8.

24. Damrong, "Kham athibai."

25. Prince Sammata Amornphan, 1 story; Luang Thamrong Jediyarat (Thet Viriyarat), 26; Phra Ratchaphirom (Jaem Burananon), 15; Phrayanwichit (Sithi

and Sudhana, were published in a single volume by the Capital Library in 1924, and a total of sixty-one stories were published in twenty-seven volumes between then and 1935. The collection was republished in two volumes (one with fifty stories, the other with eleven stories and three other texts) by the Fine Arts Department in 2000, and also by commercial publishers. In 2011 the Government Savings Bank (GSB) published a four-volume edition containing both the Thai translations and transcriptions of the original Pali.[26]

Damrong wrote only a short preface with no details on the translation. Niyada Lausunthorn learned from a surviving member of the translation team that there was no editing or correction of the text, and any amendments were inserted in footnotes.[27] However, Padmanabh Jaini, who had helped translate several of the same stories found in Burma into English, called Damrong's set an "abridged Siamese translation."[28] Which of these is true? With the GSB publication of the Pali transcriptions, it is possible to track in detail what the Thai translators did. The Thai translations vary from the Pali originals in only minor ways.

First, the translators sometimes sped up the story slightly, particularly in the early stages. The tales consist of narrative rendered in prose, and verses that are mostly but not always didactic. The translators sometimes omitted verses that do not form part of the narrative, or rendered them in more compressed prose. Where a verse has been dropped, it often repeats material present in the prose portion of the text or is a commentary on the action. Where the verse is compressed into prose, nothing significant seems to have been lost.

Second, the translators sometimes lengthened didactic passages by adding extra explanation or emphasis to make the message clearer in Thai.

Third, in passages where the Pali mentions flora, fauna, or cultural items such as food and dress, the Thai translators sometimes replaced the Pali originals with items that would be more familiar to a Thai reader.

Lojananon), 11; Nai Bui Saengchai, 2; Nai Yim Wat Mahathat, 1 Nai Phrom Khomala, 1; unknown, 4.

26. In the GSB publication, the Thai translations were checked against the first publications in the 1920s. The Pali was transcribed from Khom to Thai characters, using a set of 50 bundles of *bailan* manuscripts held in the National Library, presumably the collection assembled by Prince Damrong. See the preface in each of the GSB volumes.

27. Niyada, *Panyat chadok*, 40–41.

28. Jaini, "The Story of Sudhana and Manoharā," 535 n. 11; Jaini, *Paññāsa-jātaka or Zimmè Paṇṇāsa*, 2: xi, footnote.

Fourth, and very rarely, the translators imported details that are present in the folk version of the story but not in the Pali. For instance in the Thai translation of the tale of Prince Pācitta, an astrologer predicts that the prince will find his future wife's mother sheltered by an umbrella invisible to ordinary humans. The Pali original has neither the astrologer nor this prediction. The translator seems to have imported them from the folk version.[29] Where we have identified such importations, we flag them in the footnotes.

None of these modifications make any significant change in either the plot or the teachings. Beyond these changes, the translations follow the Pali very closely.[30] While there were over seven translators, the variation in their approaches is slight. Perhaps they were conforming to a policy, but possibly they were following the standard practice of the time. The difference that Padmanabh Jaini detected between the Thai and Burmese tales is present in the respective Pali versions; it is not a product of the translation from Pali to Thai.

Origins of the stories

Padmanabh Jaini, Niyada Lausunthorn, Toshiya Unebe, and Dorothy Fickle have traced where various of these stories came from.[31] By origin, they can be classified into four groups.

First, some are based on old tales that have been adapted into the format of a *jātaka*. Eight can be traced back to northern India in the early-to-mid-first millennium CE.[32] One or two can be found in old Chinese collections, and one may have come from Persia.[33] One is adapted from a collection of much-reproduced tales about a legendary Indian king, Vikrama.[34] Some

29. See GSB, *Panyat chadok*, 2:236; on the folk versions, see *Wannakam samai thonburi lem 2*, esp. 284.

30. The one partial exception to this assertion is P47 Rathasena; see the introduction to the tale below.

31. Jaini, *Paññāsa Jātaka*, 2:xi–xliii; Niyada, *Panyat chadok*, esp. chapter 4; Fickle, "An Historical and Structural Study"; Unebe, "Three Stories from the Thai Recension."

32. P2 Sudhana, P16 King Kamakavaṇṇa, P18 Dhammasoṇḍaka, P20 King Vattaṅgulī, P26 Surūpa, P40 Sabbasiddhi, P43 Suvaṇṇa Kacchapa, P46 Arindama.

33. P47 Rathasena has echoes of an old Persian tale that appears in Richard Burton's supplements to the Arabian Nights as "Histoire de Mohammed l'Avisé." See the introduction to the tale below.

34. P40 Sabbasiddhi.

others possibly have early origins that have not been identified.[35] These old tales are found in most of the known collections. They spread widely because they were great stories. Besides their appearance as *jātaka*, most of these popular tales have had a parallel life in an oral tradition of storytelling and have been adapted into new forms of literature and performance that developed in Siam from the seventeenth century onwards.

Second, a handful are found in the legends of specific places. An example is Rathasena from Luang Prabang, where the tale is associated with the foundation of the city, and sites around the city are named after incidents in the plot. Some of such stories are claimed by more than one location.[36] Whether the *jātaka* was developed from a local tale or the local tale was borrowed from a *jātaka* is difficult to determine.

Third, several others seem to be original moral tales, as no precursor can be found, though they may have themes and plot elements derived from the classical *jātaka*, from other tales, or from folklore. Several of these stories probably originated as sermons or some form of teaching, as they have a simple plot designed to dramatize a particular moral message.

Fourth, a dozen stories, which mostly appear toward the end of the collection, are long and complex tales that have clearly borrowed incidents and plot elements from others in the collection and from the classical *jātaka*, but also add something new and distinctive. These tales seem to have emerged from the process that Justin McDaniel called "the creative anthologizing of stories," whereby "a great number of new *jātaka*-type narratives were being composed in this region, many including random bits of information, tropes, characters, plot elements, morals and so forth."[37]

In sum, the stories are either old stories from India or specific localities in mainland Southeast Asia that have been *converted* into *jātaka*; or original tales, probably composed for teaching; or tales, probably of more recent origin, written in imitation of the old tales (and classical *jātaka*) and often borrowing elements from them.

35. Skilling ("Romance and Riddle," 172) wonders whether some may have come from the Mon-language culture that preceded the arrival of Thai in the Chao Phraya Basin.

36. P39 Prince Pācitta (Phimai), P45 Varavaṃsa (Surat Thani), P47 Rathasena (Luang Prabang, Mong Nai, Kampong Chhang), P53 Suvaṇṇasaṅkha (Uttaradit, Takua Pa, Nakhon Sawan), P60 Sirasā (middle Mekong).

37. McDaniel, *Gathering Leaves*, 214–15.

An analogous collection of thirty-four nonclassical *jātaka* was compiled by the poet Haribhaṭṭa in Kashmir around 400 CE. Peter Khoroche notes, "In varying degrees each of these works in a literary reworking of widely known stories, not all of them Buddhist in origin, intended at least as much to entertain as to edify."[38] The *jātaka* was a form of preservation. In oral tradition, stories are easily lost. Becoming a *jātaka* was a way that stories were preserved by being written down by monks, stored in *wat* libraries, and regularly recopied.

The *jātaka* form

As Naomi Appleton has shown, the concept of a *jātaka* tale originates from the account of the Buddha's enlightenment when he acquired the ability to remember his previous lives and realized the potential of these narratives for moral instruction.[39] Several stories are found in early Buddhist texts, and the idea of *jātaka* as a category of text was known by the second century BCE, but the early tales are very diverse in form. The structure of *jātaka* as known in the Theravada tradition today emerged with a collection known as the *Jātakatthavaṇṇanā*, compiled around the fifth century CE. Key to this structure is the central role of a bodhisatta, or Buddha-to-be, engaged in a long progression through multiple lives towards his ultimate enlightenment. With the emergence of this structure, as Appleton notes, "almost any story could become a *jātaka* with the simple association of one character (or even a totally silent and uninvolved witness) with the Bodhisatta, and the placing of the story within the teaching career of the Buddha. The result is that this rather motley collection of predominantly secular stories is firmly established as Buddhist."[40] In this respect, the Southeast Asian stories are no different from the Indian ones.

Most of the Fifty Jātaka have adopted the structure found in the *Jātakapāli*. The Southeast Asian authors seem to have clung closely to this format in order to claim authenticity.[41] Only eight of the sixty-one Thai tales diverge from the model.[42] This structure has five parts.

38. Khoroche, *Once a Peacock*, 4.
39. The account is in the Majjhima Nikāya, 36; see Appleton, *Jātaka Stories*, 44–45.
40. Appleton, *Jātaka Stories*, 61.
41. "One of the functions of the literary use of Pāli is to invoke authority." Skilling, "Romance and Riddle," 165.
42. By having no tale of the present: P11 Dulakapaṇḍita, P17 Viriyapaṇḍita, P18

1. Opening. In most of the stories, the opening phrase quotes the first line of the first verse (or the first verse containing teaching rather than narrative). In the Pali this quotation is not explained, but in six stories the Thai translator added that this phrase was used to identify or define this *jātaka* by the *phra sangkhitikajan*, meaning the monks who participated in a Buddhist Council.[43] This seems to be an attempt to claim authenticity by suggesting the story was recorded in the early councils, which collected the teachings now considered to be canonical. Three of the stories[44] begin with "evaṃ me sutaṃ" (thus have I heard), a Pali phrase found at the start of almost all the canonical texts and meaning that the Buddha's close disciple Ānanda had heard these words from the Buddha and related them at the first council after the Buddha's death.

2. Nidāna or Paccuppannavatthu. The opening preamble or "story of the present" is set in the lifetime of Gotama Buddha, usually when he is staying at the Jeta Grove (Jetavana) in Sāvatthi or the Bamboo Grove (Veluvana) near Rājagaha. His monk-followers talk among themselves about some quality of Gotama Buddha or some event in his life. The Buddha overhears this through his supernormal hearing, joins the meeting, asks what the monks are talking about, and then remarks that the same quality or a similar event had also been present in a previous life. The monks beg him to tell the tale. As Appleton notes, this device establishes the following "story of the past" as words spoken by the Buddha himself, and allows the authors to present a moral purpose of the story that may not in fact be present in the "story of the past."[45]

3. Atītavatthu. The main part of the story is thus the "story of the past" as related by the Buddha himself.

4. Gāthā. The classical *jātaka* consist of passages in verse, considered to be the words of the Buddha, and passages in prose added later to complete the narrative. The verses generally but not always contain moral teachings. The Fifty Jātaka have passages of verse in the same way. Some of these

---

Dhammasoṇḍaka, P19 Sudassana, P32 King of Bārāṇasī, P33 King Brahmaghosa, P45 Varavaṃsa, P47 Rathasena. In two others, P16 King Kanakavaṇṇa and P21 King of Old Kapila, the stories of the present and the past are merged together. In two others, P20 King Vattaṅgulī and P23 Cāgadāna, the story of the present is exceptionally long.

43. P22 King Dhammika Paṇḍita, P38 King Atideva, P42 Candasena, P44 Sisora, P49 Vanāvana, P50 Bākula. These were all translated by Phra Ratchaphirom.

44. P20 King Vattaṅgulī, P21 King of Old Kapila, P56 Devandha.

45. Appleton, *Jātaka Stories*, 60.

passages are moral teachings explicitly presented as the words of the Buddha, but others are part of the storytelling. In Prince Damrong's Thai translations, the verses are given in both the original Pali and a Thai prose translation.

5. Samodhāna. At the close of the story, the narrative returns to Gotama Buddha and the gathering of monks, where the Buddha summarizes the story's message, pronounces the Four Noble Truths, and finally, in the samodhāna (connection), identifies the main characters in the *jātaka* as previous lives of individuals in his own entourage and history—particularly his family members and early disciples.[46]

The proper names found in the stories also stake a claim to authenticity. Most of the stories are set in cities of northern India known from the life of the Buddha. Bārāṇasī is the primary setting for sixteen stories, and around twenty cities from northern India are mentioned. A few tales, however, are set in cities that have names that sound similar to these known Indian cities yet seem to be fictional. Examples are Purinda, Kutara, Suciravati, and Theyya. The same is true for the names of kings, queens, and princes.

This selection

This selection aims to include the best-known tales and a sampling of the whole collection. Scholars have classified these tales according to several principles, including the occasion in the story of the past, the main moral message, and the role of the Bodhisatta (king, pauper, mouse, etc.). Fickle applied a universal typology of storytelling. Here our classification has no other purpose than making a reasonably representative selection. The categories are not discrete. Several stories would fit in two or more categories.

46. Those that appear repeatedly in this collection are Tathāgata, the Buddha; Suddhodana and Mahāmāyā, his father and mother; Yasodharā Bimbā, his wife; Rāhula, his son; Mahāpajāpati Gotamī, his aunt, foster-mother, and the first nun; Devadatta, his cousin and rival, who attempted to kill him; Nanda, a half-brother and Janapada Kalyānī, a half-sister; Sāriputta and Moggallāna, his two chief disciples; Ānanda and Anuruddha, first cousins and leading disciples; Uppalavaṇṇā, chief female disciple (along with Khemā); Aṅgulimāla, a multiple killer who became a follower and *arahant*; Ciñcā Maṇāvikā, a beautiful woman persuaded to feign pregnancy in a failed plot to discredit the Buddha; and (Mahā) Kassapa, a brahman convert. Others who appear only once are identified in footnotes.

Quests. In these tales, the Bodhisatta overcomes obstacle upon obstacle in order to achieve some goal. One of the oldest stories, and perhaps the model for others, is Sudhana, where a human prince is separated from his beloved *kinnari* wife and crosses from the human to the supernatural world in order to be reunited. All of the stories in this category are old and have been reproduced in many forms other than *jātaka*.

Self-sacrifice. These come in three subtypes. In the first, the Bodhisatta gives his own life in order to save that of his mother or father.[47] In a slight variant, the Bodhisatta in the form of a giant turtle gives his life for a group of merchants.[48] In the second subtype, the Bodhisatta wishes to go beyond the normal limits of charity by giving away his wife, his kingdom, and his own life.[49] Some of these tales clearly take their inspiration from the Vessantara Jātaka, the 547th and last of the classical *jātaka*, in which the king gives away everything he has, including his kingdom, possessions, wife, and children. Others go beyond this famous tale by dwelling on the sacrifice of flesh.[50] In the third subtype, the Bodhisatta sacrifices himself for the benefit of the religion.

Giving for the religion. A distinctive feature of early Indian Buddhism was that monks and nuns were dependent on the daily support of the laity for food and other necessities, a practice still observed in the living Theravāda Buddhism of Sri Lanka and Southeast Asia. The physical fabric of temples, images, and texts also depends on patronage. The stories in this category reinforce these practices by promising rewards for feeding monks, creating and repairing images, and ensuring the scriptures are preserved for posterity.

Single moral lesson. A number of stories illustrate one moral teaching through a simple and single-minded story, followed by a sermon. Three

47. P29 Bahalāgāvi, P5 Sirivipulakitti, P4 Ratanapajjota, P25 Narajīva, P27 Mahāpaduma.

48. P43 Suvaṇṇakacchapa.

49. P30 Setapaṇḍita, P7 Siricuḍāmaṇi, P14 Mahāsurasena, P46 Arindama, P11 Dulakapaṇḍita, P17 Viriyapaṇdita, P18 Dhammasoṇḍaka, P26 Surūpa.

50. Arthid ("Self-Sacrifice of the Bodhisatta") points out that self-sacrifice is explicitly discouraged in the Buddha's words and the Vinaya code and appears in only seven of the 547 classical *jātaka*, but figures in fourteen of the sixty-one stories in this collection. Arthid shows that in later Buddhist teaching, especially the Buddhavaṃsa, extreme sacrifice, including self-sacrifice, is a "complete" form of giving, combined with a release from attachment to this world. Stories of sacrifice are also prominent in Haribhaṭṭa's *Jātakamālā* (Khoroche, *Once a Peacock*, Nos. 3–9).

presented here emphasize respectively the importance of good judgment, friendship, and sympathy for animals. A fourth is a longer dramatization of the consequences of karma made in a prior life. In two other tales (not selected here), the Bodhisatta is taken on a tour of the heavens in order to display the rewards of a good and righteous life.[51] This theme is similar to the popular tales in which Phra Malai visits not only the heavens but also the hells.

Teaching through questions. From the brainteasers of Zen to the lucid exposition of the *Questions of Milinda*, a framework of question-and-answer is prominent in Buddhist teaching texts. In four stories in the collection, a king is required to answer a series of questions but only the Bodhisatta can do this correctly. This framework provides an opportunity for moral instruction while also highlighting the wisdom of the Bodhisatta.

Story cycle. Two of the tales are in fact story cycles or collections. In Sabbasiddhi, an old tale, a prince tells a series of stories, which are also like riddles, in order to provoke a princess into responding and thereby win her hand. Surabha is more complex. The main frame story emboxes four substories, each of which frames several further stories. In one of these frames, a dancing girl tells stories all night long, echoing part of the famous *Thousand and One Nights*. The model for such story cycles is perhaps Mahosadha, one of the last ten classical *jātaka*, in which around a hundred and fifty tales and riddles are told around one central character.[52]

Complex quests. These generally long tales reuse story elements, subplots, vignettes, and teachings that are found in other *jātaka*, particularly in the great quest stories in this collection and in the most famous of the classical *jātaka*. Perhaps the origin of this type is Sudhanu. The name of the bodhisatta differs from another story, Sudhana, in only the final vowel, and the story borrows the archery scene from Sudhana's climax, along with the shipwreck scene from Mahājanaka, the mural pavilion from Samuddaghosa, and the ogre's doting sister from Rathasena. Most tales of this type are in the form of a quest, often begun because of a wrongful exile. The most complex, the sixty-first and last in the collection, is divided into thirteen chapters, has two leading males and half a dozen leading females,

51. P22 King Dhammika Paṇḍita, P24 Dhammarāja.
52. Appleton and Shaw, *Ten Great Birth Stories*, 187–333.

shuttles between four main locations, and delves briefly backward into the hero's previous life and forward to that of his son.

Many classical *jātaka* stories illustrate one of the ten "perfections" (pāramī) achieved by the Buddha. Although some of these stories can be interpreted in this way, this theme is not prominent in the collection, and the term scarcely appears.

These translations

In her doctoral thesis, the late Dorothy Fickle made an English translation of three of the stories: Sudhana, Dhammasoṇḍaka, and King Kannakavanna. We have used her translations but have checked them and substantially revised them to match our style and conventions.

In the republications of Prince Damrong's collection, the first fifty stories are numbered sequentially, and the final eleven stories are numbered in a new sequence from one to eleven. We have followed others in numbering them all in one sequence from 1 to 61. The heading for each story shows this number, the title in Pali as it appears in the GSB edition, and the title in Thai.

In footnotes, stories in the Thai Paññāsa Jātaka are referenced with their number and title, such as "P2 Sudhana," while stories from the classic Indian collection are referenced in the form "J547 Vessantara."

In a few cases, the Thai translators invented a story of the present because none was present in the Pali original. We have omitted these.

We present full translations of the stories, with nothing knowingly omitted.

THE GREAT QUESTS

SUDHANA

P2 *Sudhanajātaka*

สุธนชาดก

INTRODUCTION

Several of the best-known stories among the Fifty Jātaka are quests in which the Bodhisatta overcomes many obstacles in the pursuit of some goal. Most of these are old stories that are also known as folk tales outside the *jātaka* format.

The story of Sudhana and Manoharā (known as Suthon-Manora in Thai) is very old. It is found in the *Mahāvastu* ("great stories") and *Divyāvadāna* ("divine narratives"), two Sanskrit anthologies of Buddhist tales that may date to the second century CE, and Haribhaṭṭa's *Jātakamālā* dating to 400 CE. Over the centuries, it was translated into Chinese, Tibetan, and Khotanese. In a form very close to the way it is told here, the tale was depicted on twenty panels of the bas-reliefs at the Borobudur temple in Java, built in the eighth or ninth century.[1] The theme of romance between a human hero and a bird princess turns up all over the world, including *Swan Lake*.

The subplot of a minister scheming to hold a sacrifice to remove a rival has echoes in J542 Canda (Kaṇḍahāla).[2]

The tale is one of the best known and most reproduced throughout Southeast Asia, partly because it adapts so well to recitation, dance, and drama. Performance versions are recorded in Siam, Cambodia, and Burma since at least the seventeenth century. The *nora* dance drama from southern Thailand, which also features a bird-princess and seems to echo the name of Manoharā, is often associated with this story but may have separate origins.

1. Jaini, "The Story of Sudhana and Manoharā"; Khoroche, *Once a Peacock*, 147–75.
2. Jaini, *Paññāsa Jātaka*, 1:xviii; Appleton and Shaw, *Ten Great Birth Stories*, 404–22.

Sudhana's great quest—overcoming great obstacles and crossing from the human to the divine world—seems to be the model for several other tales in the collection. In Thailand, the Sudhana-Manoharā story continues to be adapted and reproduced in dance, drama, film, and television.

This translation has benefited from the earlier unpublished translation by Dorothy Fickle ("Historical and Structural Study," appendix B).

> When the Great Teacher was living in the Jeta Grove, he spoke of a monk who was lovesick, and for that reason gave this sermon, beginning, "Where did you come from?" with the story of the present as follows.
>
> As has been heard, a monk on almsround saw a beautiful woman and fell in love. On return from almsround, he hung up his alms bowl without eating any food. Seeing his mood, his fellow monks asked, "Are you unwell?"
>
> "O friend,[3] it's nothing. This morning on almsround I saw a woman and fell in love, so I'm feeling very lovesick over her."
>
> The other monks took him to see the Great Teacher, who asked about his lovesickness. The monk told the truth. The Buddha said, "O monk, you are devout. You have renounced and been ordained in my religion, yet you have succumbed to desire for women. Desire for women is the cause of evils that are hard to prevent. Sages in the past have had problems as a result of desire for women, causing them to neglect their wealth, their parents, and even their own life, causing great hardship, on account of sensual feelings like this." Because the monks wished to know the story, they invited the Buddha to tell a story from the past as follows.

One time in the past a king named Ādiccavaṃsa ruled in North Pañcāla City (Uttarapañcāla). His chief queen, who was exceedingly beautiful, was named Canda Devī. At that time our Bodhisatta was conceived in the womb of this queen, and after ten months she gave birth to a royal son. At birth,

3. Pali: āvuso, friend or brother, term of address used by monks in Pali texts. In modern Thai, the word has come to mean "senior" or "elder," and is rendered that way by several of the translators in this collection, but the context seems to indicate the original Pali meaning.

he was as beautiful as a golden statue, and gold mines appeared at the four corners of the palace. Seeing these, the royal father said, "My son possesses great merit and power, rivaling the Thousand-Eyed One." He made worship and gave him the name Prince Sudhana [great wealth].

The prince grew up to be handsome, to the satisfaction of the people. He was superior to ordinary folk, and studied to have unmatched expertise in the arts and disciplines.

As has been heard, in the east of the capital of North Pañcāla lay a pond of crystal-clear water filled with great lotuses, red lotuses, and white lotuses. On its banks were flowering trees with various kinds of fruit. It was a truly refreshing place. A *nāga* king named Jambucitra lived in that pond, and because of his power the city had an abundance of food every day. The people came every year to worship the *nāga* king and to beg him to continue to provide their city with an abundance of food.

To the east of North Pañcāla lay Great Pañcāla City. Food there became scarce, and the troubled citizens began to migrate and settle in North Pañcāla. Soon almost all the population had trickled away. When the ruler of this city, King Nanda, saw how few were left, he asked his courtiers, "Where have all my people gone?"

"Your Majesty, to North Pañcāla."

"Why?"

"Because it is easy to find food there."

"And why is it easier to find food there?"

"Because the *nāga* king Jambucitra looks after them. The happiness and prosperity of the people is due to his power."

King Nanda decided to kill the *nāga* king. He asked people, "How can I kill this *nāga* king?"

"Sire, ordinary people cannot kill that *nāga* king by whatever means, but a brahman skilled in mantras could kill him."

The king summoned five hundred brahmans and selected one who knew how to recite mantras. He said, "Brahman, if you bring the *nāga* king back, dead or alive, I will give you half my kingdom."

"Very well, sire, I shall bring him back to you."

"Then do it quickly, brahman, without delay!"

The brahman took leave of the king and hastened to the pond. He thought, "I will sleep first and perform the ceremony to capture the *nāga* king at dawn." That evening, he rehearsed the ceremony to test the power of the mantra. He rinsed his mouth and dressed in white lower and upper cloths. Holding a bundle of *lalang* grass in his left hand and stretching out his right hand, he recited the mantra on the bank of the pond. Immediately the pure water became cloudy and smoke began to rise. The brahman was pleased. He stopped reciting the mantra, and went to sleep. At dawn he went to find medicines in the forest. The *nāga* king emerged from the water, changed his form into a brahman, and stood concealed at the bank of the pond.

Just then a hunter named Puṇḍarika [white lotus] came by on some business of his own and encountered the *nāga* disguised as a brahman. The brahman addressed him in a verse, saying:

> "*Where did you come from? I am waiting to see a brahman*
> *recite a mantra. Hear my question.*
> *What business brought you here?*"

"Good sir, I am a forest hunter, with no business other than hunting game."

"Hunter, are you from North Pañcāla or somewhere else?"

"From North Pañcāla."

"Is it easy or difficult to find food there?"

"Easy."

"Why is that?"

"Because of the power of the *nāga* Lord Jambucitra, who looks after us."

"If someone did harm to Lord Jambucitra, what would you do to him?"

"I would cut off the head of anyone doing harm to the *nāga* king."

"Really, hunter?"

"Really."

Jambucitra told the hunter the truth, saying, "I am that *nāga* king. Right now a brahman has come to do me harm. You must help kill him. If you do not protect my life, I will die by this brahman's hand."

The *nāga* gave instructions: "Hide at the edge of the forest. When the brahman comes back, recites a mantra, and scatters a potion from the bank of the pond, you will see the water become cloudy and smoke rise. Shoot the brahman but do not kill him. Rush out from the woods, grab his head, raise your sword as if to slash him, and threaten him, saying, 'You evil brahman, relax the mantra or I will kill you now.'"

"But, *nāga* king, how will I know when he has relaxed the mantra?"

"Hunter, you must watch when the water is calm as normal. Once you know he has relaxed the mantra, cut off his head." With that, Jambucitra returned to the *nāga* world.

Soon, the brahman came back, carrying offerings. He recited the mantra and cast a potion on the water. Instantly the water gave off smoke and burst into flames. When Puṇḍarika saw this from his hiding place, he shot an arrow and the brahman fell to the ground. The hunter rushed out, grabbed the brahman's head, and raised his sword as if to slash him, with the threat, "See here, wicked brahman, the *nāga* king Jambucitra is our guardian deity. Why have you come to harm him? Relax the mantra immediately, or I'll cut off your head with this sword." The wicked brahman, fearing death, immediately relaxed the mantra. When the hunter saw that the waters had become calm as normal, he cut off the brahman's head. The brahman died.

The *nāga* king felt relieved. He came up to take Puṇḍarika back down to the *nāga* world, where he honored him for seven days. Then he gave him a jewel of great value and led him back up to the bank of the pond, saying, "If you wish to see me for any reason, find the *nāga* who guards the entrance, and he will lead you to me." Then he spoke a verse:

> "*Friend, walk straight along this road. Your home is on this way.*
> *Go this way, meet your wife, children, relatives, and friends, and live happily.*"

The hunter Puṇḍarika returned home safely.

One day some time later, when Puṇḍarika was roaming in the forest looking for game, he came upon the hermitage of the ascetic Kassapa. He lay down his bow and arrows and entered to pay respect. The hermit inquired in a verse:

> "*You have come a long way to this forest with no friend.*
> *What business or desire do you have here?*"

"Honorable sage, I am not afraid. Like a lord of the lions, I have come alone into the forest seeking game." After paying homage, the hunter continued on his way, looking for deer. He saw a shady garden with many beautiful *khae foi* trees.[4] In the center was a square pond filled with bright, clear water strewn with lotuses of five colors and rimmed by banks covered

4. แคฝอย, *Stereospermum fimbriatum* and related species, sometimes called snake tree.

with many flowers, such as champaka and jasmine. The hunter retraced his steps and asked the rishi about the garden in a verse:

"Over there is a beautiful garden with a lotus pond in the center,
a delightful place adorned with many kinds of trees, such as champaka.
I wonder, has this garden been made by humans or by the gods? Please tell me."

Kassapa replied, "Hunter, I do not know who made that garden. It was like this before I came. A group of *kinnari* comes to play in that pond. If you wish to see them, hide near the bank and you'll see them playing—a lovely sight."

Puṇḍarika happily concealed himself in bushes by the bank. That day was a full moon on the fifteenth waxing, a holy day, when the *kinnari* usually came to play.

At that time, seven *kinnari*, the daughters of King Duma from Mount Kelāsa, came flying through the air with a thousand retainers. On arrival at the pond in the garden, they went down to play in the water. Some swam, some dived, some merrily sang and danced. In the afternoon they flew away again. Puṇḍarika was enraptured because he had never seen them before. He thought, "These *kinnari* are very beautiful. How can I catch one to present to Prince Sudhana as his principal wife?" He returned to the hermit and asked in a verse:

"Reverend sir, I saw many kinnari playing in the water.
I would like one of them. How can that be done?"

Kassapa replied in a verse:

"Listen, I'll tell you the way I have devised.
To catch a kinnari, you must use a nāga-noose and perform ceremonies.
Don't think you can find a nāga-noose to get the kinnari.
It's like hoping for the moon and stars. No chance! Waste of effort."

Puṇḍarika the hunter asked, "How can I find out where there is a *nāga*-noose, so I can get one somehow? Please tell me"

"Only in the *nāga* world. If you can get a *nāga*-noose, you may get the *kinnari* you want."

The hunter was very happy to hear this. Thinking of the *nāga* king, he took leave of the rishi and hastened to the big pond. When the gatekeeper knew what the hunter wanted, he took him down to the *nāga* king, who asked in a verse:

> *"Why have you come to see me? What is your desire?*
> *Tell me, and I shall grant your wish."*

Puṇḍarika explained, "Valiant *nāga* king, I came to ask for a *nāga*-noose."

"O friend, ask for something else. If I give you the *nāga*-noose, my lifesaver, the *garuḍa* will come and capture me.[5] If I'm holding the *nāga*-noose, the *garuḍa* will not approach but flee away. So I cannot give it."

"Please, *nāga* king. I beg you, let me borrow it. I will bring it back."

The *nāga* king thought, "This hunter saved my life. I am in his debt. Whether I live or die, it's not fitting to refuse." He handed the *nāga*-noose to the hunter, who praised him profusely. The *nāga* king took the hunter back to the human world, saying a verse:

> *"Dear friend, if there is something else, come to me at this pond.*
> *Think of me, and I will help to achieve what you want."*

The joyful hunter hastened back to the rishi, concealed himself in bushes near the pond, and waited for the *kinnari* to come flying back.

The seven *kinnari* daughters of the *vijjādhara*,[6] wearing wings and tails and ornaments and accompanied by their retinue, came flying from Kelāsa to the lotus pond. They took off their ornaments and their wings and tails, lay them aside, and went down to play in the water. The hunter crept stealthily out from the bushes and threw the *nāga*-noose into the midst of the group of *kinnari*. The loop caught the hand of Manoharā [captivating]. Seeing the hunter, the other *kinnari* scrambled out of the water in alarm, dressed, and flew off into the air, crying, "We have always come to play in this pond without any danger. Why is there danger now? Let's go and tell the king that a hunter has captured his daughter. Her mother the queen will weep and probably come to die with her daughter here."

5. The rivalry between *garuḍa* and *nāga*, bird and snake, is found in Hindu mythology and may symbolize rivalry between mountain dwellers and plains dwellers. "Whenever a *garuda* snatches a *naga* from the middle of the ocean, the splash extends for 100 *yojana* in every direction. He grasps the tail of the *naga* tightly in his talons, flies away through the air leaving its head dangling down below, and takes it to his dwelling place where he eats it" (Reynolds and Reynolds, *Three Worlds*, 88–89).

6. Duma is king of the *vijjādhara* yet has *kinnari* as his daughters.

The *kinnari* flew back to Mount Kelāsa. They let down their hair, took off their ornaments, and fell at the feet of the *vijjādhara*, King Duma. Weeping, they told him, "A disaster has happened! Manoharā has been captured by a hunter, like a tiger catching a deer in the forest."

The queen raised her two hands into the air, beat her breast in sorrow, and lamented in a verse:

> *"O Manoharā, mother's beloved child! I will not see you anymore.*
> *Thinking of you, I feel my heart is breaking, as if pierced by the hunter's arrow.*
> *I will not see Manoharā. Dying is better than living on.*
> *There is no point in living further without my daughter. I must die right now."*

She addressed her husband, "Grant me leave to follow Manoharā."

"That is good. Hurry!"

With her retinue she set off flying through the air to search for her daughter.

When the hunter Puṇḍarika saw that the *nāga*-noose had caught the hand of Manoharā, he rushed to grasp her hand. She cried, "Don't touch me or I will die! Set me loose and I will go along with you."

The hunter took the noose off her hand and said, "Take off your ornaments, wings, and tail, and give them to me." She took them off,[7] handed them to the hunter, then knelt on the earth facing toward the north and paid homage to her parents, saying, "This is the end. Your child will never return to this sacred pond. Forgive me. I must go with this hunter. Mother and father, what else can I do? Through my carelessness I have fallen under someone's power."

As she walked with the hunter through a mountain pass, she turned around and sat down. She removed her jeweled breast chain, buried it, and entrusted it to the care of the lord of the Himavanta Mountain, saying, "If my mother follows me to this point, please give her this jeweled breast chain and tell her that a hunter has taken me this way." She continued to lament in a verse:

> *"Mother, I used to see you morning and evening, now I see neither hand nor foot.*
> *You were my refuge, but now I will never see you again however hard I search,*

7. Above she took off everything before entering the water.

not knowing whether you live or die. By nature nothing in the world is constant.
Togetherness and separation are common everywhere.
All beings born in the world face change by nature.
There is youth, and there is sorrow. There is parting all the time.
Mothers and children love yet change and decline as a matter of course."

After this lament, Manoharā walked along with the hunter. He did not even think of taking her hand, as he was not auspicious or fitting for such a beauty. He could not taste joy with her. He thought, "I shall present this *kinnari* as a consort for Prince Sudhana."

Here there is a belief that any woman who has the merit to be big in the world will be born with a beautiful appearance and should live in the abode of a man of fine appearance; hence the hunter Puṇḍarika thought that he should present Manoharā to Prince Sudhana.

Before long they arrived at the city of North Pañcāla.

On that day the Bodhisatta was riding on an elephant to the royal park, accompanied by his retainers. He saw the hunter passing by accompanied by Manoharā and was smitten with love because of some attachment from a past life. He sent a man to bring the woodsman and woman and asked, "What are your names? Where are you from? Why have you come?"

The hunter replied, "My name is Puṇḍarika, and I have come from the Himavanta Forest to present Your Majesty with this royal daughter of a *vijjādhara*."

The Bodhisatta was pleased. He rewarded the hunter with a thousand pieces of gold, a diamond ring, and other treasures. Then he sent an officer to inform his parents, King Ādiccavaṃsa and Queen Canda, who were delighted. A drummer was sent to proclaim that all the people should prepare presents and go out to welcome Manoharā, the daughter of the king of the *vijjādhara*, his new daughter-in-law. The citizens did as instructed. King Ādiccavaṃsa had the city decorated as beautifully as the Tāvatiṁsa Heaven and invited Manoharā to come from the park into the royal palace. There he made arrangements for three auspicious ceremonies: entering the palace, marriage, and royal anointment.[8] After these ceremonies, the

8. *Pāsādamaṅgala* (entering the palace), *vivāhamaṅgala* (wedding), and the

great being made love with Manoharā alone, not thinking of other palace women, and enjoying great contentment.

Meanwhile the mother of Manoharā traveled in search of her daughter. Arriving at the lotus pond, she descended from the sky and saw some jeweled earrings and garlands scattered and abandoned at the landing. She fell to the ground, like the peak of a palace tower breaking and tumbling down. She wept for her child, saying, "I see only the beautiful pond, not the face of Manoharā. I don't know whom to ask because no one is around. Oh, our separation must be due to karma. How can I see her face?" She wept on and on as if she were mad.

The queen lifted her hands to loosen her hair. Filled with misery, she followed a trail of footprints into the Himavanta Forest. When she spied the bundle of ornaments in the fork of a tree,[9] she fainted to the ground. Upon reviving, she wept again, thinking, "Manoharā must have passed this way. I cannot find my daughter, only this bundle of ornaments." She held them to her breast and stumbled onward. Not finding her daughter, she returned to Mount Kelāsa and went to see her husband, King Duma. When he saw that she had come back, he asked in a verse:

> *"My queen, you have been searching in the mountains and forests.*
> *As you have returned, have you found our daughter or not?"*

She replied, "Your Majesty, I have looked everywhere but have not found Manoharā—only these ornaments in the fork of a tree. I could go no further so I returned." The six *kinnari* sisters sat close around their mother and wept.

For several months, the Bodhisatta ruled the realm happily. There was a brahman, learned in the Vedas, who served him faithfully every day. The Bodhisatta observed his skill and commented, "You work very hard on my behalf. Do you have any wish?"

"Your Majesty, when your father dies and you become ruler, may I request the post of priest-counselor?" The Bodhisatta accepted this request.

abhisekamaṅgala (consecration).

9. In the Thai, Manoharā buried her jeweled breast chain, and here it is found in the fork of a tree. In the Pali, the items are simply abandoned and found, with no locations mentioned.

When the incumbent priest-counselor found out about this, he felt vengeful against the Bodhisatta. He provoked King Ādiccavaṃsa by saying, "Prince Sudhana is plotting treason. He is planning to kill you so that he can become the king." The royal father did not believe the priest-counselor.

One day enemy troops attacked the outer territories of North Pañcāla. King Ādiccavaṃsa thought that he would go himself to subdue the enemy but feared that he might not succeed, and so consulted his priest-counselor, saying, "Who should go to confront this enemy?"

"Your Majesty, send the prince."

"But my son is still young and not skilled in war. If I send him, he won't succeed."

"Your Majesty, your son is a vigorous youth, more skilled in fighting than his elders."

The king agreed with the priest-counselor. He sent for the prince and said, "Sudhana, you must go out to fight this enemy in the outer territories."

The Great Being accepted the order, took his leave, informed his mother, and then told Manoharā. She begged him not to go. After consoling her, he hastened off to ready the army.

At an auspicious time, Prince Sudhana rode out of the city on an elephant, accompanied by the four-limbed army in a procession of close ranks, covering the earth. The elephants trumpeted loudly. The well-trained cavalry and the bold foot soldiers, all surrounded by their followers, made the earth shake. The spirits came to offer them protection. Swiftly the column moved in stages up to the outer territories. Through the power of the Bodhisatta, the enemy forces did not wait to fight but fled.

During the night after the Bodhisatta had left with the army, King Ādiccavaṃsa dreamed that his innards flowed out of his chest, circled three times around the entire Jambu Continent, and then shrank back into his chest. He started awake in fright. At dawn he sent for the priest-counselor and asked him the meaning of the dream. The priest-counselor was delighted, thinking, "What I planned will succeed! Today I will see the back of my enemy, Sudhana."

Addressing the king, he said, "Your Majesty, this dream is not good."

"In what way, brahman?"

"Your Majesty, the manual states that both you and the realm are in great danger."

"How can I avert this danger?"

"You must perform a rite of sacrifice."

"What kind of sacrifice?"

"You must sacrifice two-footed and four-footed creatures to change this bad omen into good." The brahman priest-counselor added a verse:

> *"Your Majesty, the manuals of knowledge predict that*
> *if someone who had a bad dream performs a rite of sacrifice, the bad turns to good.*
> *Hence, if Your Majesty performs a great sacrifice, there will be no danger.*
> *You and the queen will reign happily as before."*

The king ordered his courtiers to round up all two-footed and four-footed creatures for the sacrifice. The courtiers passed the order on to hunters to find the creatures, including a man and woman, and bring them to the sacrificial ground. On being informed, the king commanded the priest-counselor, "All the beings have been prepared. Carry out the sacrifice immediately."

"Your Majesty, one creature is still missing. The sacrifice cannot be done."

"What is still missing, brahman?"

"A *kinnara*."

"But a *kinnara* is very hard to find."

"Not difficult at all. There is a *kinnara* living in this city—Manoharā."

"But Manoharā is the life partner of Sudhana. It is not fitting for her to be sacrificed."

"Your Majesty, you must consider carefully what is fitting and what not. You, your queen, and your kingdom are in grave danger."

"Priest-counselor, I cannot kill the chief wife of my son Prince Sudhana as you say."

"Your Majesty, listen to my words. People do sometimes sacrifice their beloved wives and children. Those wives and children agree to help the one making the sacrifice succeed, and they receive the praise of wise men. If a burning ember were to fall on your head and your child was close by, would you ask your child to help, or would you ask someone else's child to put out the fire? While you are still alive, it's fitting and correct for you to think how to escape suffering. For this reason, you must immediately look after yourself. Of what concern is Manoharā to you? If you are still alive, you can find another woman for Sudhana—someone equal to Manoharā or even better. Wise men praise those who know how to protect themselves from danger."

The king fell silent, offering no opposition. The brahman knew the king had agreed. He ordered the officiants of the sacrifice to capture Manoharā to be killed.

Word spread throughout the city and soon reached the ears of the slaves and servants of Manoharā. Feeling as if her heart would break into seven pieces, Manoharā hastened to the Bodhisatta's mother. She lowered her face onto her mother-in-law's feet and said, sobbing, "Mother, have you heard? At this very moment the king, believing the word of the priest-counselor, is planning to capture me to kill in a sacrifice. Help me, mother! Please go and ask the king to delay until my husband returns. Then I can pay homage at his feet, ask his forgiveness for my wrongdoings, and take leave to go to my death in accordance with karma."

Accompanied by her retainers, Queen Canda hastened to attend on King Ādiccavaṃsa. The king told his servants not to allow her into audience. She returned to Manoharā's palace, embraced her daughter-in-law, and wept. Manoharā said, "Mother, since you were not able to see the king, then I shall surely die. Though we have a fine king, he does not offer shelter I can rely upon. At this very moment, people are coming to capture me and take me to sacrifice today. My husband is not here to be my refuge. He will surely die to follow me. Dear mother, please give me my ornaments so that I may pay respect and go to my death dressed in my finery."

Queen Canda gave her back her ornaments, including her wings and tail. She adorned herself and danced for her mother-in-law. Queen Canda caressed her and said sorrowfully, with breaking heart, "When my son Sudhana returns and does not see Manoharā, he will search everywhere. When he does not find you, he will surely die to follow you."

"Mother, when my husband Sudhana comes back, please tell him in these words that I, Manoharā, bow at my husband's feet and ask his forgiveness for all my misdeeds. Tell him that I now bid him farewell and go to my death in accordance with karma." She faced to the east, prostrated to the Bodhisatta's mother, and spoke a verse:

> *"Mother, please tell my fine husband that I pay respect to his feet.*
> *I bow my head to him every morning and evening.*

I pay respect now for the last time. There will be no more.
Togetherness and separation are natural for beings of this world."

She bowed her head at the feet of her mother-in-law, begging her for forgiveness. The queen embraced her and sobbed, saying, "We separated young animals or birds from their mothers in a past life, and fruit of that karma has caught up with us, causing me to part from you and you from your husband. From now on I will wander in the mountains and forests, like a mother deer searching for her lost fawn. Why do the spirits who reside in the forests, mountains, and sky, all of them, let me be separated from my daughter? When my son returns to the city and does not see you, he will be as lonely as a mother bird finding her nest empty."

As Queen Canda continued to weep, royal servants came crowding up into the palace to capture Manoharā for the sacrifice. Putting the two wings on her arms, Manoharā bade farewell to her mother-in-law and flew up into the air and away to the Himavanta Forest. She landed at the rishi Kassapa's hermitage, paid her respect, and related everything that had happened. "Reverend sir, if my husband Sudhana should come searching for me, please give him this piece of woolen cloth and this diamond ring, and tell him that I forbid him to follow me for these reasons: the way ahead is very difficult, it is not a route for humans but a land of nonhumans alone. Let him go back and not follow me any further." Again she raised her clasped hands to pay homage to her husband and spoke a verse:

"I beg your forgiveness and I bid you farewell.
If I have done any wrong to you in word or deed in the past,
please pardon me with a pure heart."

She turned her face to the south, raised her hands to pay respect to the Bodhisatta, and spoke another verse:

"I had intended to live with you until the end of my life,
but now that cannot be as wished. Perhaps in a past life
you made some sin or bad karma, and its fruit
has brought my wishes to this sad conclusion."

She said to the ascetic, "Reverend sir, if my husband will not go back but follows me, tell him to go to the north, taking this powder instilled with a mantra. When he has traveled far beyond the realm of humans he will arrive first at a forest where the trees have poison. He should capture a young monkey, which can taste the fruit before he eats any. Next he will come to a great rattan forest. He should wrap this piece of red woolen cloth tightly around his body and lie down quietly on the ground. A *hatthaliṅga* bird, looking for food, will think he is the meat of a hog deer and will swoop down, grasp him in his talons, and carry him beyond the rattan forest. When the bird reaches his nest in a huge tree, he should clap his hands, and the bird will flee in fright.

"After that he will meet a pair of fighting elephants who will bar his way. He must spread this powder all over his body down to his feet and recite a mantra. Then he can walk safely between the legs of the elephants. Next he will come to a twin-peaked mountain that, as if it had the mind of a spirit, will bend down to bar his path. He must cast a mantra upon the entire mountain, from the top all the way to the base. The mountain will split open to make a passage through which he must quickly escape. Next he will come to a group of water spirits. He must say a mantra and then go on. After another *yojana,* he will reach a forest of *lalang* grass and then a golden mountain and a silver mountain, then a forest of sharp grass, then a bamboo forest, then a thicket of reeds. About three *yojana* further, he will reach a thick jungle where the trees are closely packed together, the bushes are thorny, the ponds are deep, and this wild place swarms with various snakes. Also there is a river with mountains along the banks and no level places. Passage will be extremely difficult.

"After that he will come to a great upland forest, where he will meet a giant ogre, as tall as seven sugar-palm trees, looming over the heart of that forest. He must sprinkle some powder on an arrow and shoot at the chest of the great ogre, who will fall down, and Sudhana will have to walk over his head. A hundred *yojana* further, he will come to another river, where a python with a huge, long body will lie stretched across the river from bank to bank like a bridge. He should sprinkle powder on the soles of his feet and walk across on the back of the snake. At the opposite bank he must quickly jump over the snake's head.

"Another one hundred *yojana* ahead, he will come to a dense rattan forest where no passage can be found. Many birds live in that forest. At the edge of the forest there is a huge tree with a nest of some enormous birds with bodies as big as houses. My husband must climb up, lie hidden in a nest of chicks, and watch when one of the birds is flying off to look for food in the capital city. Then he must hide in among the wing feathers and hold on tightly. The bird will carry him across the forest. When the bird swoops down to the ground, Sudhana must let go and cry out to frighten the bird to fly away. Then my husband will have arrived at Mount Kelāsa, as wished."

When Manoharā had finished giving all these instructions to the hermit, she wrote a mantra on a leaf, which she gave to him along with the piece of red woolen cloth, the diamond ring, and the powder, saying, "Please give these to my husband when he follows me here." She bowed in homage to her husband, saluted the rishi, and flew off to Mount Kelāsa, the capital city of her royal parents.

When King Duma learned that Manoharā had returned, he thought, "Our daughter Manoharā has lived with humans for a long while. She can no longer live among us as she used to do. We shall build a new golden residence where she may live with a separate group of *kinnari*." And thus he ordered a new residence built for Manoharā.

Meanwhile, Sudhana had marched an army to subdue the enemy in the outer territories. He returned with the army to the capital of North Pañcāla, attended on his father, King Ādiccavaṃsa, to report government business, and went to pay respect to his mother. She came out to receive him and embraced him in great distress.

The Great Being asked, "Why are you crying like this, mother?"

"O son, your wife Manoharā has gone away." She told him everything from the beginning.

His heart trembled as if it was about to break apart. He returned to his own dwelling, which was still and quiet as a graveyard. He could not avoid falling down in a faint as if someone had cut off both his feet. Queen Canda brought perfumed water to bathe his whole body. He revived and went into his bedroom. Seeing the bed with its cover and withered flowers scattered everywhere, he felt sick and sorrowful. He spoke a verse:

"My heart will break apart as if shot with a poisoned arrow.
Where has Manoharā gone? I do not see her face.
Mother, let me take leave to search for her.
If I cannot find her, I will not return but die in the great forest.
If I find my wife I will bring her back to my mother's house.
If I do not find her, I will surely die in the forest."

In hope of helping her son overcome his sorrow, she spoke a verse:

> *"Don't grieve over Manoharā, son. There are many other noble ladies*
> *who are as beautiful as apsara. Find happiness with them.*
> *Later you will rule the kingdom. Don't follow after Manoharā."*

The Bodhisatta replied, "Mother, if I will not see Manoharā again, let me live no longer."

Unable to stop him, Queen Canda fell silent. Sudhana paid respect to his mother, went down from the palace, and left the city. Seeing him leave, she felt her heart would break apart immediately. She hastened after him, begging him with a verse:

> *"Come back, son. Don't leave your mother with no refuge.*
> *If I no longer see my son, my life must surely end."*

She stood on the spot, gazing after him.

The Bodhisatta left the city, traveled to the house of the forest hunter, and asked him, "Where does Manoharā live? Do you know?"

"I do not know, sire. She has great supernormal power and can travel through the air. By this time she may have reached the world of the *vijjādhara*. If you wish to follow her, go to ask the hermit Kassapa. He might know where Manoharā lives."

Sudhana strapped on his sword and dagger, picked up his bow and arrows, and set off for the hermitage, accompanied by the hunter. He turned back once more to look at the capital of North Pañcāla, saying a verse:

> *"If I find Manoharā, then I will see this beautiful place again.*
> *If I do not find Manoharā, then I will not return."*

Uttering a powerful roar like a lord of the lions, he turned his face toward the Himavanta Forest. He journeyed in stages until he reached the dwelling of the rishi Kassapa. There he sent the hunter back home. He took off his ornaments and weapons, laid them aside, and entered the hermitage. He paid respect to the rishi, sat in an appropriate place, and made conversation. Finally, again folding his hands in respect to the rishi, he asked in a verse:

> *"I ask you with the greatest respect,*
> *have you seen Manoharā, my most beloved, or not?"*

Kassapa replied in a verse:

"Yes, Prince Sudhana, I did see your Manoharā.
She left word that you should return home from here.
'The way ahead is extremely difficult, a path for nonhumans alone,
so tell him to go back.' That was Manoharā's order."

Kassapa said, "Manoharā left three things for me to give you: a diamond ring, a red woolen cloth, and a small ring for the little finger." He placed them in the Bodhisatta's hand. Seeing them, Sudhana beat his breast with his two hands and wept, feeling as if Manoharā had appeared before his eyes.

Kassapa asked, "Will you go back or go ahead?"

"Most reverend sir, I would rather die than turn back."

The ascetic realized that Sudhana truly loved Manoharā, so he relayed to him all of her instructions, saying, "Manoharā left instructions that, if you come after her, you must follow the directions I now give you, and take this powdered medicine and this mantra to instill in the powder. Catch a little monkey to be your guide. Set off in this direction." He relayed every word just as she had spoken, without any mistake. Sudhana listened, tied the rings to his chest, paid homage to the rishi, and declared in a verse:

"If I find my beloved, I will return to my own city.
But if I do not find her, I must die in the forest.
If I have been of assistance to any beings
and not consorted with another's wife in the past, may I find Manoharā."

He caught a small young monkey as a guide, bade a respectful farewell to the hermit, and set off as Manoharā had instructed, toward the north. The hermit accompanied him for a short distance and then returned to the hermitage.

The Bodhisatta traveled for seven years, seven months, and seven days. He encountered many dangers before reaching the dense forest with a fearsome ogre as tall as seven sugar-palm trees, with eyes as red as fire and skin as green as Mount Añjana.[10] The ogre stood blocking the path with an iron pestle in his left hand and an iron axe in his right. Seeing him, Sudhana was not startled or afraid but acted as bold as a lord of the lions. He smeared the powder instilled with a mantra on the tip of an arrow and

10. Site of a deer park where the Buddha stayed.

shot it at the chest of the great ogre, who fell to the earth. The Bodhisatta walked along his body and over his head.

He traveled further to a caustic[11] river, where he sprinkled the powder on his feet and walked on the back of a python. Next he came to the rattan forest with thorns sharper than acid. He managed to get through by swinging on vines like a monkey and climbing up a big tree among the rattan. The sun was setting. He did not know how to go further. He grieved and reproached himself, "I lived with a woman who had left her mother and father and suffered great hardship. Which way should I go now?" He felt low in spirits.

At that moment a great flock of birds with bodies as large as houses gathered in the tree to sleep. They chatted together about where they should go the following day to find food. One said, "On Mount Kelāsa is the capital city of King Duma. He has a daughter, Manoharā, who was captured by humans but has returned home. Tomorrow is the seventh anniversary of her return. There is going to be a great festival and a ceremony to cleanse her of the odor of humans. Let's go there to eat the offerings made to the spirits. There will be lots." Hearing these plans, the Bodhisatta crept quietly in among the wing feathers of one of the birds and fastened himself securely to the wing with rope. In the morning the bird summoned his friends, and they all flew across the thick rattan forest, descending at the edge of a large pond outside a golden city. The Bodhisatta quietly untied himself and hid beside the pond.

The seven daughters of the *vijjādhara* discussed together, "Let us fetch water from the pond to bathe Manoharā today." Each took a golden pot. At the bank of the pond, they stopped to talk. The Bodhisatta overheard them and thought, "My effort will end in success. Hearing about Manoharā, all that struggling through forest, thicket, rapids, streams, and mountains has borne fruit. But how shall I let Manoharā know that I have come? The only way is to make a prayer that my wish be granted."

In truth, prayers are always successful for all bodhisatta, beginning from the prediction of a certain Buddha.[12] Hence Sudhana made a prayer: "If I am

11. Pali: khāra, meaning pungent, saline, caustic.
12. This refers to a vow to become a Buddha made by the Bodhisatta Sumedha in the presence of the Dīpaṅkara Buddha. This story is the starting point of the bodhisatta tradition. See Appleton, *Jātaka Stories*, 77, 87, 91–93.

to be joined in love with Manoharā, let one girl be unable to lift her pot." He came out of the bushes and sat down under a large tree.

The *kinnari* were dipping water from the pond, lifting their pots, and leaving. One *kinnari* was unable to lift her pot. She looked about, saw the Bodhisatta sitting under the tree, and begged him, "Please, sir, help lift this pot for me."

"Why are you fetching water?"

The *kinnari* explained everything. As the Bodhisatta lifted the pot for her, he slipped a ring into the pot.

Each of the *kinnari* poured water over Manoharā. When the last one poured water over her head, the Bodhisatta's wish, aided by merit, was fulfilled: in the stream of water, the diamond ring fell from the golden pot onto Manoharā's little finger. Her heart leapt at the realization that her husband had arrived. She felt great concern for the effort he had made to follow her to that place.

As soon as the bathing was finished, Manoharā went into the bedroom to find that last *kinnari* and asked, "Why did you return after the others?" The *kinnari* told her everything that had happened. Manoharā said, "Those words you repeat are the words of my husband, Prince Sudhana! Where is he now? Please tell me."

"He is sitting beneath a tree on the bank of the lotus pond."

"Don't say anything about this to anyone. Please take these ornaments, this perfume, and these celestial clothes to him. Tell him to bathe in the pond and adorn himself with these."

The *kinnari* took the clothing and ornaments to Sudhana and relayed Manoharā's instructions. He bathed, dressed himself in the clean apparel, and sat down to wait at the edge of the pond.

Manoharā thought, "I should tell my mother that he has come." When she did so, her mother said, "You must also go and tell your father." Manoharā went to her royal father, paid him homage, and sat to one side, fearing his authority.

When King Duma noticed his daughter, he said, "Manoharā, you lived for a long time with a human. What sort of man was your husband? Was he a warrior or a brahman or a trader? I still don't know."

"Noble father, my husband was no ordinary man, perfect, as strong as seven Lord Vishnus, the foremost ruler in all the Jambu Continent, with 101 kings as his retinue."

"If so, why did you leave him and come back here?"

Manoharā told him the whole story from beginning to end. The king asked, "If your husband has as much strength and perseverance as you say, then why has he not followed you here? If he were to arrive here, I could appreciate his strength and perseverance and give you to him as his queen."

Manoharā was overjoyed to hear these words. She said, "Sire, is what you just said true or not?"

"Manoharā, true, of course."

"Sire, my husband, named Prince Sudhana, has followed me here."

"Is that true?"

"It is true, sire."

"Where is he now?"

"Outside the city."

"You must have him summoned here!"

She sent a maidservant to fetch him to audience. Sudhana entered the city like a lord of the lions. He went up to the royal throne hall, where the king was seated on a jeweled lion-throne. Kneeling respectfully, Sudhana rendered homage to the king and then sat in an appropriate place.

When all the *vijjādhara* saw the Bodhisatta, they stared at him with hardly a blink of their eyes. The king was happy the moment that he saw him. He asked, "How long did it take you to cross the mountains, forests, and rivers to reach this city?"

"Your Majesty, I have been traveling for seven years, seven months, and seven days. After I had passed through many difficulties, I shot an arrow at a giant ogre, killed him, and walked over his head. Next I arrived at a caustic river, where I dusted my feet with enchanted powder and crossed over walking on the back of a giant python that was stretched across the river, head on one bank, tail on the other, like a wooden bridge. I jumped across. Right after that I arrived at a dense, impassable rattan thicket, where I had to duck through, breaking branches, and swing across, bit by bit, until I reached a large tree in the middle of the forest. It was dusk, so I stayed in a fork of the tree. That night, a flock of enormous birds slept there. They were talking about coming to the city this morning to find food. I hid myself among the wing feathers of one of the birds and tied myself on firmly. The bird flew across that dense thicket and landed on the bank of the lotus pond outside the city. I hid near the pond. There I met the *kinnari* who had come to fetch water. Manoharā thus learnt that I had arrived."

The king clapped his hands and said, "Wonderful!" He asked the Bodhisatta, "Your name is Sudhana, is it not?"

"Yes, Your Majesty, my name is Prince Sudhana."

"Are you skilled in archery?"

"There is nothing about archery that I do not know."

"Good! Let us see your skill."

"Your Majesty, have officials set up seven palm trees in a row, each one fathom apart. In the spaces between the palm trees, erect seven planks of fig wood, each three cubits thick and one fathom wide. Next erect seven stone pillars in front of the fig-wood planks, and then seven sheets of iron and seven sheets of copper, each four cubits thick, one fathom wide, and one fathom long, interspersed in front of the stone pillars. In front, have a row of seven bullock carts filled with sand. I will shoot an arrow through all of that."

"You can shoot through all that?"

"Have no doubt, sire."

King Duma instructed his ministers to prepare everything as Sudhana had directed, and had drummers summon the *vijjādhara* to assemble. Prince Sudhana stood in the palace courtyard, calm and unafraid, bold as the king of the gods fighting with the *asura*. He lifted his bow, notched an arrow in place, and let fly. The seven sugar-palm trees, seven planks of fig wood, seven stone pillars, seven iron sheets, seven copper sheets, and seven bullock carts filled with sand were all shattered. The arrow, like a flaming discus, flew on through the surface of the ocean and through the belly of Mount Cakkavāḷa,[13] then turned and flew back to the right hand of the Bodhisatta.

The *vijjādhara*, including King Duma, and all the gods in the sky, shouted their praise of the Bodhisatta, and spoke a verse:

> "*Be praised, be praised! Great strength. Be praised, be praised! Great wisdom.*
> *Before long you will surely become a Buddha.*"

King Duma descended from his throne, embraced the Great Being, and said, "In this city there is a stone throne which requires a thousand people to lift. Can you lift it?"

13. "Mount Universe," meaning Mount Meru/Sineru at the center of the universe.

"Your Majesty, I can lift it through the power of your merit and that of the gods gathered here."

He stood up and stretched his body like a lord of the lions. He approached the stone throne, walked around it three times, stroked the stone with his right hand, and spoke this prayer: "If in the future I will sit on the diamond throne and defeat Māra and his demon troops, if I will persevere until I attain full enlightenment and omniscience under the bodhi tree, and if I will tear down the great mountain that weighs on the hearts of all creatures in this world, now let this stone throne be so light that I can lift it."

He lifted the throne as if it were made of leaves, raised it high, and walked back and forth for the king to see.

In amazement, King Duma watched this feat that had never been done before. He descended from his lion throne, embraced the Great Being, and asked his forgiveness. All the *vijjādhara* cheered, waving hundreds of thousands of flags.

The king then asked the Great Being, "Can you remember your wife?"

"I can, sire."

The king returned to the palace in a joyful mood. He gave orders for his seven daughters to adorn themselves to look beautiful in their finery, to behave in a similar fashion, and to sit in a row with Manoharā among them. He called Sudhana and asked, "Prince Sudhana, my seven daughters are all sitting here. Is your wife here? If so, take her by the hand."

The Great Being could not recognize Manoharā. He tried to think of a way to do so: "Usually a bodhisatta uses a prayer. Right now I will make a prayer of merit to take the hand of Manoharā as wished." He spoke a verse:

> "*If I have been of assistance to any beings,*
> *and if I have truly not consorted with another man's wife in the past,*
> *let me recognize Manoharā as I wish. May the gods help show me.*"

At that moment the realm of Lord Sakka, king of the gods, felt hot. The Thousand-Eyed Lord considered the reason, then flew through the air to land near the Great Being, saying, "Great Being, I shall change myself into a golden fly and circle one lady's head so you may recognize that she is your wife."

When the golden fly circled her head, the Bodhisatta went straight to Manoharā, took her by the hand, and said to the king, "Sire, this is my wife."

King Duma was happy to see this amazing feat. He gave orders to have an anointing pavilion with a heap of gold and gems erected in the royal courtyard. He anointed Sudhana and Manoharā to rule the realm. The Bodhisatta made love with Manoharā as he wished.

One night soon after, the Bodhisatta became mournful thinking about his parents and reproached himself, "I have forgotten the merit of my parents. I was born because of them. My parents have virtue so great that the earth, the rivers, and Mount Cakkavāḷa, even if five times as deep, tall, and wide, cannot compare. Yet I have abandoned them. I must go to see them." Reproaching himself thus, he wept and spoke a verse:

> "*I do not know how my mother is now. What must I do to see her*
> *and my other kin? If I do not see them, I shall die here for certain.*"

He closed his eyes and lay sadly upon the bed. When Manoharā awoke and saw her husband lying there looking so sad, she asked him several times if he was sick. He could not restrain his tears and began to cry, saying, "Manoharā, I have been thinking about my mother. When I left home, my mother wept like this."

"What do you wish to do?"

"Without my mother I may not live on. I must return home."

"Let me go with you. Wherever you go, I will follow." However much he objected, Manoharā insisted on following him, so he said, "It's good if you come too."

At dawn, he went in to see his father-in-law to take leave for going to see his mother. Pleased at the proposal, King Duma said, "Prince Sudhana, I will go to the human world with you." He ordered his officials to make ready the troops, and he set a day for the departure. On that day, King Duma, surrounded by a retinue of *vijjādhara*, led the Bodhisatta and Manoharā out from the capital, with a great following. Using their own powers, the *vijjādhara* conducted the troops through the air, and in a very brief time they arrived in the human world outside the capital of North Pañcāla. In a single night they erected a royal pavilion and a camp for the army that looked like a new city. The people of North Pañcāla were so alarmed that they prepared the defenses of their city.

When King Ādiccavaṃsa opened his window in the morning and peered into the distance, he saw the new city with walls and forts made of fresh wood. Not knowing what to do, he moped in his palace.

Meanwhile Prince Sudhana thought, "My royal father will be alarmed and fearful. He may think that an enemy has discovered that I am not there and has brought an army to seize the realm." Surrounded by a resplendent retinue of *vijjādhara*, he left the royal pavilion and entered the precincts of the palace. He explained the matter to officials, then attended on his father and mother and related to them all that had happened from the beginning of his wanderings until now, when he had returned home with Manoharā.

King Ādiccavaṃsa and Queen Canda Devī welcomed their beloved son with joy, kissed and embraced him, and said, "Since the day you left, we have both only wept and cried." They talked over several matters with the Bodhisatta. They came out from the city with a great retinue and approached the royal encampment. King Duma came out to receive them, and they exchanged greetings and joyful conversation. They all stayed there in the encampment for seven days. Then King Duma presented royal gifts including jewels to the parents of the Bodhisatta, took leave, and returned to his own capital.

Manoharā stayed with the Bodhisatta. King Ādiccavaṃsa ordered his officials to decorate the city and anointed the Bodhisatta to rule the kingdom of North Pañcāla. King Ādiccavaṃsa renounced the world and became a hermit. In a short time he attained higher knowledge through meditation and upon his death entered the Brahma realms.

The Bodhisatta ruled the kingdom justly, looked after his father and mother, and made merit, including giving of alms. When he passed away, he was reborn in Tusita Heaven. The people who followed the teachings of the Bodhisatta, on passing away were reborn in the heavens.

After finishing this sermon, the Great Teacher said, "O monks, sages in the past sacrificed their own life and left their parents because of the strong power of love." He gave the Four Noble Truths. Monks inspired by the sermon on a past life attained the eye of wisdom of an *arahant*.

The Great Teacher explained the birth connections: "King Ādiccavaṃsa at that time was reborn as King Suddhodana; Queen Canda as Queen Mahāmāyā; King Duma as Sāriputta; the rishi Kassapa as Kassapa; the *nāga* king as Moggallāna; the hunter Puṇḍarika as Ānanda; Lord Sakka, king of the gods, as Anuruddha; the priest-counselor as Devadatta; Manoharā as the mother of Rāhula; the people as the followers of Buddhism; and Prince Sudhana as the Tathāgata."

SUVAṆṆASAṄKHA: THE GOLDEN CONCH

P53 *Suvaṇṇasaṅkhajātaka*

สุวรรณสังขชาดก

INTRODUCTION

Stories of a beautiful boy born from a conch are found in Tibet, the Shan country, Bengal, and Sri Lanka, but other elements of the story are specific to Southeast Asia.[1] The story is claimed as a local story in Thung Yang (Uttaradit), Takua Pa, and Nakhon Sawan. There are murals on the tale at Wat Phra Borommathat, Thung Yang, probably dating to the late Ayutthaya era, and also at Wat Phra Sing, Chiang Mai. The story, known in Thai as *Sangthong*, had probably been passed down in oral tradition for a long time and has been adapted in many forms. There is a fragment of a drama version, which Prince Damrong dated to the Borommakot reign (1733–58), two poetic versions from early Bangkok, and a famous drama version composed in the Second Reign court, partly by the king himself. All of these acknowledge the *jātaka* and have the same outline story but also differ in many details, possibly drawn from versions in oral tradition.[2] The story remains almost universally known due to teaching in school and constant reproduction in film, cartoons, and other media. Elements of this story appear in *Sang Sinchai*, a well-known tale in Mon, Lao, and Thai.

The opening part is similar to several other tales, with a strange birth, a jealous queen, exile on a raft, separation, a quest through ogre country, and a doting ogress. The ending part is also similar to others, with an armed attack by a rival king countered with supernormal devices. The central section, beginning when the Bodhisatta finds the disguise and ending when he discards the disguise, is very distinctive. Like P52 Sihanada, this tale has no verses.

1. Ingersoll, *Sang Thong*, 21–24.
2. Niyada, *Panyat chadok*, 161–62, 179–80.

When the Great Teacher was staying at the Jeta Grove, the monastery of the layman Anāthapiṇḍika, he spoke of the monk Devadatta, who was intent on ending the Buddha's life. For this reason, he gave this sermon, beginning with "These words are surely true" and telling this story.

The monk Devadatta, a son of King Suppabuddha Sakya, was ordained as a Buddhist monk and tried to kill the Blessed One. One time, monks gathered to talk in the teaching hall, saying, "O friends, Devadatta was a very bad fellow, trying to kill our Blessed One." In his fragrant quarters the Great Teacher heard this through his divine hearing. He left the quarters, came to sit on the great pulpit, and asked, "Monks, what are you all talking about?" The monks paid respect and said, "About Devadatta trying to kill you." The Buddha said, "Devadatta has tried to kill me not only now but in past time also." He then told a tale that has been hidden in realms large and small, as follows.

O monks, in a time long ago, there was a king named Brahmadatta ruling at Brahmapura.[3] He had two primary queens, of the left and right. The queen of the right was called Candā Devī [shining, moon], but the name of the queen of the left is unknown. These two were the king's favorites above all others. At that time, a bodhisatta who was still traveling in the cycle of birth passed from the world of the gods and was conceived in the womb of King Brahmadatta's queen of the right.

On the day the Bodhisatta was conceived, Queen Candā Devī was sleeping on her bed. Near daybreak, she dreamed that the rays of the sun, shining in every direction, circled Mount Meru three times and struck her breast, startling her awake. Once it was light, she bathed, went to audience, paid respect, and related the dream to the king. On the same night, the queen of the left was asleep on her bed. Near daybreak, she dreamed that Lord Vāsava (Indra) of Tāvatiṁsa Heaven presented her with a golden champaka flower and then left. The queen accepted the flower and admired it with

3. Here called Brahmanagara, but later Brahmapura. Brahmavati here in the Pali.

joy. When she awoke, she bathed, went to audience, paid respect, and related the dream.

The king sent for a seer. After he had heard the two dreams, the seer predicted that Candā Devī's dream meant she would have a son of incomparable beauty while the queen of the left's dream meant she would have a daughter of incomparable beauty. From that time, the queen of the left was given the name Suvaṇṇa Campāka Devī [golden champaka flower].

The king was happy. He gave each of them a comfortable palace in the wish they would look after their wombs well. The king wanted to make the five regalia items for the royal anointing of the son. He thought, "This son to be born will carry on the family line." He gave orders for making the regalia.

After hearing the prediction that she would have a daughter, Queen Suvaṇṇa Campāka Devī, queen of the left, lay thinking, "How can I make the king expel Candā Devī? I don't have any friend to help think up the means." She went to find Minister Pālaka [guardian] and told him, "According to the seer, Candā Devī is pregnant with a son and I with a daughter. If this is true, the king will love her more than me by a hundred times, a thousand times. I won't bathe him in joy. What can I do to become part of the royal clan and enjoy the royal wealth? If I gain high rank, you will become chief minister. You must help think up a plan to make the king drive Candā Devī out of the palace. Once I have power in the royal clan, I will help you gain the highest rank and greatest wealth."

Minister Pālaka replied, "Don't fret. I will find a way. It's not difficult. This is a job for me." With this agreement, Queen Suvaṇṇa Campāka Devī returned to her quarters.

One day Minister Pālaka went to attend on the king, paid respect, and said, "Sire, Queen Candā Devī is not loyal to you. She has made love with a low-born fellow. She does not behave properly. Behind your back, she behaves immorally in the same fashion as some young women and some widows, with no fear of your power. She should not remain in the palace."

After stirring things up in this way, the minister left, and Queen Suvaṇṇa Campāka Devī entered audience. She paid respect and stirred things up some more by adding, "Sire, the minister's words are true. Queen Candā Devī is not serving you properly. She has been having a dirty affair with a man. Her pregnancy did not arise from your power alone. She goes around in public everywhere with men of the city."

Without examining the truth of these accusations, the king flew into a rage and ordered that Queen Candā Devī be driven out of the palace.

Queen Candā Devī had nobody to turn to. She wept along the way, "In the past I must have done some bad deed to have this great hardship now." Consorts and lady servants heard her lamenting as she walked away from her beloved palace. They wept, collapsed down, and writhed around like sal trees that, hit by the era-ending wind and dashed by rain, topple over on top of one another.

Queen Candā Devī raised her clasped hands to the guardian gods of the palace and said to her female relatives, "May you all stay well, eat well, and have no fear. I beg to take my leave of you all and go to face great difficulty according to the karma I have made." She lamented in this way as she left on her own without friend or patron.

Her plight was pitiful. When in the palace, there were many pleasures. She was used to wearing golden slippers, riding in a fine palanquin, bathing her body with scented water and floral powder, washing her hair with scented water, and dressing beautifully. After she was driven out, she had no scents, her body stank, sweat flowed everywhere, and she was smothered in dust. She walked along until coming across an old couple, who approached and asked her, "Where are you from? Why are you on your own? Where are you going?"

She answered, "I am the queen of the right of King Brahmadatta. He used to favor me greatly. Queen Suvaṇṇa Campāka Devī saw this and had me driven out of the palace." The old couple had pity on her and took her home. She stayed there until her pregnancy reached the sixth month.

While in the womb, the Bodhisatta realized his mother was facing hardship. He thought, "She has had to leave the city on her own without friends or relatives to take care of her. If I am born with a golden body, she will have a hundred thousand times the trouble. I should transform my body into a conch." He pronounced a prayer and turned into a conch. After ten months, her womb gave forth a beautiful golden conch. She washed him in a stream and looked after him for a long time.

One day when she was away in the forest, the Bodhisatta emerged from the golden conch, swept the house, made his mother's bed, and went back into the shell. When she came back from the forest and saw the house had been swept, she felt happy but kept the matter to herself and told nobody. When she went into the forest next time, he emerged from the shell, cleaned up the bed and house, put things scattered around in order, and returned to the shell. When she returned and saw, she was astonished. Not knowing that he had done this, she thought, "This is a miracle. What is happening?" She told nobody. One day she pretended to go into the forest, leaving the door a little ajar, and circled back to peek and find out what was happening. She saw him emerge from the shell and sweep the house. He was incomparably beautiful. In joy, she rushed in, hugged and kissed her son, saying, "Prince of the Golden Conch, you are my son with the king. He has two wives. The other was jealous of me and had me driven out of the palace."

Then she thought, "If my son is a conch, we will speak in different ways." So she smashed the shell and burned the pieces.

He said, "Mother, why did you smash the conch? There was celestial matter inside. If I'm in danger, whom can I turn to?"

She said, "My most beloved son, your body has an appearance of great merit. Nobody will threaten you. Do you know why? When you were first conceived, I had a dream." She told him the story and consoled him, "With such a beautiful appearance, no human can triumph over you." She resolved to look after him with great care.

When people saw his appearance, they acclaimed him as the most beautiful being in the world. His reputation spread to King Brahmadatta, who ordered his officials, "Take horses with fine tack along with troops, and bring back my son and the queen right now." The officials did so. Queen Candā Devī returned to live in the palace as before. The king commanded the Prince of the Golden Conch to attend in audience, embraced him, sat him on his lap, kissed his head, and admired him greatly.

Seeing the king's joy over the prince, Queen Suvaṇṇa Campāka Devī was jealous. She sought a way to have him and Queen Candā Devī come to a bad end. One day she found out that he had been born in a conch shell, and thought, "That gives me an idea" She went to attend on the king and said, "Queen Candā Devī will bring bad luck. She gave birth to the child as a conch." Minister Pālaka repeated the accusation in the throne hall.

King Brahmadatta was not clever. He believed them, flew into a rage, and ordered his officials, "Make a big raft. Put Queen Candā Devī and her son on the raft and float them down the river." Queen Candā Devī and the city folk heard about this and set up a great weeping and wailing.

After the Great Teacher had attained enlightenment, he used this story to teach Sāriputta in the Cariyā Piṭaka,[4] saying, "O Sāriputta, minister of the dhamma, in the past, while I was still seeking enlightenment, I was born as the son of King Brahmadatta in Brahmapura. This king believed the words of an evil-hearted queen and floated me and my mother down the river on a raft."

The officials and people held a meeting in the royal courtyard and petitioned the king to spare the Bodhisatta, but he would not listen. The people wept and collapsed to the ground like sal trees blown down by the era-ending wind. A great and amazing commotion arose. The surface of the earth 240,000 *yojana* thick trembled as if feeling grief. Mount Meru, the support of the world, swayed back and forth like the tip of a cane plant. Rain fell from above. Thunder rolled like a drunken elephant, and living beings were greatly concerned.

The raft floated along the river for a long time. Through the old karma of the queen and the Bodhisatta, a great storm wind smashed the raft. The queen floated away, clutching onto one piece of the broken raft. Near the bank she saw a tree with the tip of a branch close to the surface of the water. She tried to swim with all her strength, grasped the tip of the branch firmly, and gradually raised herself into a fork of the tree. She sat thinking sadly of her son.

That tree was close to Maddarāja City. In the city at that time, there was a rich man with much property called Dhanañjaya. One of his female slaves who was walking along the riverbank came across Candā Devī weeping in the fork of the tree. She approached and called out, "What are you doing there?"

"I am the queen of King Brahmadatta of Brahmapura." She told the story. The servant girl took her to Maddarāja and told the story to her master. Dhanañjaya welcomed her warmly and invited her to stay with him. She thanked him and accepted. Dhanañjaya made her his cook, and she lived there happily from then on.

Meanwhile the Bodhisatta floated away on the raft broken by the gale, separated from his mother, out to the great ocean. Through his great merit,

4. "The basket of actions," the fifteenth division of the Khuddaka Nikāya, containing thirty-four stories of the Buddha's previous births, mainly compressed versions of classical *jātaka* tales.

the world of the *nāga* felt hot. The lord of the *nāga* world came up to the surface, conjured up a golden raft, and decorated it with seven peaked pavilions along the center. He brought this raft close to the Bodhisatta, lifted him into a pavilion, and let the golden boat float to an island that had trees full of refreshing flowers and fruit and that resounded with the melodious and captivating cries of peacocks—able to drive away the sadness of all who saw them.

The Bodhisatta left the boat and walked ahead, admiring the various trees, until he saw a lake full of red and white lotuses with masses of fish and turtles swimming among them. After admiring these flowers, he walked on and came upon a rishi sitting cultivating the four sublime states of mind[5] in front of his retreat. He approached, raised his clasped hands in greeting, and sat down.

The rishi, happy to see him, asked, "On what matter have you come here alone?"

The Bodhisatta replied, "I am a son of King Brahmadatta of Brahmapura. The king floated me and my mother away down the river on a raft. When the raft was broken by a gale, we were separated. The lord of the *nāga* helped by lifting me into the golden boat in which I arrived here. If my mother, who was traveling to the city, is still alive, please tell me the way there."

The rishi said, "If you're going to Bārāṇasī, there is a way but there are ogres living along it."

"O rishi, if there is any way at all, please tell me."

"You must go down the river first and you will come across the city of the ogresses on the way. The ogresses will try to catch you, but they should be no danger to you."

The rishi accompanied the Bodhisatta to the golden boat moored at the landing, helped him to board, and pushed him off down the river. Before long, he reached the city of the ogres. The chief of the ogres in this country had already died, and his lady ogress was looking after the city with her female retinue. These ogresses saw the Bodhisatta and plunged into the water, intending to catch him to eat, but failed because the great river rose up in great waves that swamped the ogresses and scattered them far away, causing many to die. Those that survived were alarmed. They went

5. จตุพรหมวิหาร, *jatu phrommawihan*, catu brahmavihāra.

to the residence of the lady ogress and told her, "Mistress, a golden boy in a golden boat came floating down the river. We rushed into the water to catch him to give to you, but the water in the river rose up in great waves, and many ogresses drowned in the current."

The lady ogress thought, "When my husband was ruling, there was nothing amazing, but now he has gone, there is. I must go to the landing and see what is happening." She saw the Bodhisatta sitting in the boat, looking splendid like no other being. She felt love for him as for a child born of her own womb. She jumped into the water and brought the Bodhisatta up to her palace, where he stayed for a long time.

One day when she was caressing her adopted son, who was sitting on top of her, she said, "Beloved son, I have given you these ornaments, and I will give you a thousand ladies to serve you in the palace all the time. I don't want you to go elsewhere."

She gathered all the property in the palace and hid it away. She gave him her golden bracelet and a little-finger ring and said, "May you prosper in the city of the ogres until you are 120 years old. I don't see anyone else to take care of my corpse.[6] Do not go out of the palace on the road to the park to the north. Do not go off to play in the palace above." She summoned the ladies and gave orders. "I'm going into the forest. You stay behind and look after my son well." She went off into the forest to hunt for animals to eat.

After she had left, he wondered, "Why doesn't she want me to go to the upper palace or the park?" In the evening, he went to look at the park. Everywhere there were piles of bones from which the ogres had eaten the flesh. Seeing them, he felt dismayed. He went to the upper palace and saw wells of silver and gold all full of celestial water, a pair of golden shoes, armor in the shape of a forest dweller, ugly and fearful, and a short sword with a jeweled haft. He thought, "The ornaments I'm wearing are very ordinary." He put on the suit of the forest negrito,[7] stuck the sword in his waist, put his feet in the golden shoes, and flew around inside the palace. On return, he took everything off, and walked back the way he had come. When he dipped his little finger in the well of golden water,

6. Meaning she is hoping he will arrange her cremation when she dies, as would a son.

7. Here the Thai changes from คนป่า, *khon pa*, a forest person, to เงาะป่า, *ngo pa*, a "forest rambutan," where rambutan is a metaphor for a spiky-haired negrito. In the Pali, the term is vananara, forest person, throughout.

the finger turned gold, and no amount of rubbing could remove the gold but only made it shine brighter. He bound the little finger in a scrap of cloth so people would not know, and returned from the upper palace to his residence.

In the evening, when the lady ogress came back from the forest, she asked the ladies, "While I was away, did my son go anywhere?"

"He's very bold. As soon as you left, he went off here and there."

"He's very brave. A one-off. However much we tried to stop him, he didn't listen."

She summoned him and saw his bound finger. "Why is your finger bound up? Did you cut it with a knife? Let me see how bad it is." She unwound the cloth and saw the gold color. She spat on the finger and the gold disappeared.

From then on she watched over him constantly to make sure he obeyed her advice, but her body wasted away because she had no fresh meat to eat. One day she summoned him and said, "Son, I'm going to the forest to hunt. You stay here and don't go sneaking off anywhere."

When she had left, the Bodhisatta thought, "What's the use of staying here? Should I put on those celestial trappings and run away from her?" He went to the upper palace and bathed in the well of golden water, making his whole body shine with gold. He put on the suit of the forest negrito, the sword, and the golden shoes. He flew out through a chink in a window and through the air to Takkasilā City. He saw a leaf hut outside the city beside a river and flew across to stay there.

The lady ogress hunted until evening and then returned to her palace and found her adopted son was missing. She asked the servant girls, who said they knew nothing. She was so angry she could not control herself. She went off to shout for him in the park, and then to the upper palace. "It looks like he's run away." She went to check on the negrito suit, golden shoes, and sword with a jeweled haft and found them missing. "My beloved son has really run away." She wept from both love and resentment. She flew after him to the river and saw him from afar in the hut on the other side at Takkasilā. She could not fly across. She stayed on her side and appealed to him with the words, "O son beloved as my own heart, come back to mother. What made you angry enough to run away? I'm intent on you taking care of my corpse, and ready to give you all my wealth and servant girls so you can continue the customs of my lineage in the future."

Here there is a question. The lady ogress had great power. Why could she not fly across the river? The answer is this: She could fly only in her own territory, not outside it. Hence she sat crying on her side of the river.

Hearing her pleading, he shouted in reply, "I cannot stay with you, mother. Go home. I just came to be your son, that's all. If I go back there, I'll feel ashamed among the servant girls. Go home and enjoy the treasure of ruling so the people of your realm are content. I'm truly not coming back."

"Beloved son, if you don't come back, I'll die here. Come and study sacred mantras. I'll teach you. You'll be able to rely on them in the future."

Interested in being taught sacred mantras, he asked, "What use are these mantras?"

"O son, they have supernormal powers. If you want fish or meat, just pronounce a mantra and blow it. Any being, fish or animal, anything on land or in the water, if they have made any karma, will come to you. If they have made no karma and should not die, they will escape."

He could study mantras elsewhere, so he called out a farewell, "Mother, go back to the city. May you live long. I'm leaving you. I won't come back for a long time." He flew away.

She was so sad that she died right there and was reborn in the Tāvatiṁsā Heaven.[8]

Here there is a question. As she had killed animals to eat all her life, why was she reborn in the heavens? The answer of the Great Teacher is this: She had made merit in past lives, and she had befriended the Bodhisatta, a person of great accumulated merit. She was greatly attached to the Bodhisatta up to the day she died. For these reasons, when she died from the world of the ogres she was reborn in Tāvatiṁsā Heaven.

The Bodhisatta saw her die and went back to see whether she was truly dead. He collected wood to make a fire, lifted her on top, and cremated her corpse. He made three circuits of the pyre and flew away. He inspected cities big and small and saw that Bārāṇasī was content with good food, so he descended by a village near the city and went in to see the village headman. Seeing him looking like a forest negrito, the headman asked, "Where are you from, lad? I'm the village head."

"I have no patron and I'm looking for a way to make a living."

8. This scene of the Bodhisatta taking leave of the doting ogress, the two separated by a river, and her dying from grief is also found in P47 Rathasena.

"Fine, lad. Don't go anywhere else. Please stay with me and I'll look after you."

The headman gave him a packet of rice to eat and set him to looking after cows every day with other cowherds. These boys thought he looked strange, like a forest negrito. Some mocked him. Some called him an ugly fellow. But when they invited him to play dice,[9] not one of them could beat him. When they returned home in the evening, they asked him to play dice again so they might win, but none could beat the Bodhisatta, and all felt very peeved.

One day, the boys said to him, "Clever dice player, please teach us to play well. From now on we'll give you a packet of rice every day when we go to look after the cows." The Bodhisatta agreed. From then on, the cowherds all divided their rice packets and gave him one part.

At that time, a king with a higher rank and larger retinue than all others was ruling in Bārāṇasī. He had seven beautiful daughters. The six elder daughters had husbands—but not the youngest, Gandha [fragrance]. The king thought, "I will arrange a contest among the men of the city so there can be no gossip." He commanded the high officials, princes, princesses, and lords from around the realm to gather together and said, "Each of you is to dress the same. Bring all your officers and people from your cities to gather at the royal courtyard here so my daughter can choose."

People, including princes, were keen to have the princess as queen. They adorned themselves and attended the gathering at the royal courtyard. The king invited Princess Gandha and her retinue and told her to choose a husband she liked. She did not see anyone she liked, and told her father, "None of them appeals to me." He flew into a rage. "You low-life black girl. I want to have you married. I've summoned all these people, including good-looking princes, here. Can't you choose one?"

He asked the city folk, "Have you seen or heard about any man who has come from elsewhere to our city?"

"Sire, there is one with an appearance unlike a normal human, with a strange and odious body like a forest negrito. Now he's staying with the village headman and making a living as a cowherd."

9. The Pali, akkha, meaning "with eyes," can mean either a ball or dice. The Thai translator interpreted it here as ball, but it is clearly dice.

The king said, "Gandha, if you don't like others, I will have this strange and odious-looking forest negrito brought to become your husband. Alright?"

This order made Princess Gandha fall in love with the Bodhisatta, so she replied, "Please bring him, sire."

"Courtiers! Bring this forest negrito here right now."

While the courtiers were going to fetch him, that night nearing dawn the Bodhisatta dreamed that he went to bathe in Anotatta Lake. He awoke thinking, "This dream is a very good omen." The courtiers arrived at the house and told the headman, "The king has ordered us to fetch this forest negrito who is working for you because the princess had chosen him alone over all the city folk, lords, and princes."

Overhearing this, the Bodhisatta spoke to the courtiers: "I am alone and without a patron, with no father, mother, or blood relatives. My appearance is stranger than a human outcaste. It's not fitting to take me to attend on the king. Just look at my awful appearance."

"Ugly fellow, the king has frightful authority. You cannot refuse on grounds you're an outcaste in this way. Come along with us."

The Bodhisatta remembered the dream and thought, "I should not be in any danger." He agreed to go.

The headman cried out, "Ugly fellow, if you go with them you'll be no use to me. If you stay, you can make a happy living as a cowherd." The Bodhisatta paid no attention and left for the city with the courtiers.

That night, Princes Gandha dreamed that a god brought her a heavenly fruit with a strong aroma that people did not like. She split it with a knife and found the seven jewels, which she used to adorn her body. After she woke, bathed her face, and ate breakfast, she thought of the dream. "Amazing! This dream will have some good result for me for sure." She looked out of the window and saw the forest negrito walking behind the official to the palace courtyard. She smiled slightly as she felt greatly attracted to the Bodhisatta.

The Bodhisatta glanced up at the palace, saw the princess, and smiled as love captured his heart. In truth, in a past time the Bodhisatta had made great merit with Princess Gandha, so when they saw each other again, their hearts responded. She thought, "Last night I dreamed I would have a husband with incomparable knowledge."

The Bodhisatta walked to the royal courtyard and paid homage to the king who said, "Tomorrow morning come here to receive the garland."

Then he asked, "Where are you from, young man? How many days did it take you to reach our city?"

"Sire, from far away; about a month." He paid respect and left.

The king ordered his courtiers, "Send out drummers to announce that tomorrow Princess Gandha will throw a garland to find a husband by chance. Whichever man it lands on, the king will marry to his daughter as a royal husband."

Next morning all the city folk including courtiers dressed up well and went to the gathering at the royal courtyard. The king sent for his daughter and said, "Beloved daughter, you must throw the garland up in the air. Any man who has made merit with you in the past, let the garland land around his hand, and I will marry you to him." She saluted him to accept and sat in a fitting place.

The Bodhisatta, looking like a forest negrito, came and sat down. People shouted at him, "You can't sit there. This is where we'll sit for the princess to throw the garland. If she sees you, she will laugh and not make the proper prayer. Go and sit somewhere else." Though they grumbled at him, the Bodhisatta remained sitting there.

The princess made a prayer at the courtyard in front of all the nobles. "All you gods, *gandhabba*, *nāga*, *garuḍa*, Lord Kosiya and Lord Mahābrahma, guardians of the earth and of the city, come to hear my prayer. With this garland, I will choose a husband by chance. If any man here has made merit with me in the past, may the garland fly to circle his hand."

She raised the garland above her head and threw it up in the air. The garland made three clockwise circuits and dropped down around the right hand of the Bodhisatta. People came and fought to take it away, without success. They scoffed at the princess, "She has karma from past lives that gave her this ugly husband."

The king said, "Let it be according to the karma she has made." He had them prepare a royal anointing ceremony following past practice. The king ordered the Bodhisatta to undergo the anointing.

The Bodhisatta thought, "If I do this, people will see my body is golden and know I have great merit." He refused to undergo anointing, however much the king begged. In a fury, the king banished the couple.

The princess and the Bodhisatta could not disobey this order. They left the city without any servants and went to live on their own. Nobody from the city came to look for them. They lived alone as a lonely couple without a patron.

The husbands of the other six princesses complained, “People don’t like this fellow with the awful, strange body. This brings criticism on us too. If the neighboring lords, who bring gold and silver flowers to offer to our king, see this awful fellow, they will disapprove. The reputation will spread. Even the city will face ruin.” They went to attend on the king and said, “Princess Gandha’s husband is awful, strange, not like a citizen of this city. He will bring ruin on this city.”

The king of Bārāṇasī said, “I’ll think what to do about it.”

“Sire, please send this couple far away.”

The king consented. The couple went to live a long way away, in great difficulty and hardship. The Bodhisatta consoled the princess, “Don’t be sad and resentful. This hardship is a result of karma made in the past. I am not an evil and low person, but have great merit. The people don’t know me.”

When the king of Bārāṇasī thought about the Bodhisatta he felt ashamed. “When that terrible, evil fellow was here, we felt ashamed in front of people. If we quietly have him killed, we will be criticized. We must arrange to have him condemned for some misdeed and then kill him.” He consulted with the six sons-in-law on how to do this.

They replied, “Sire, you must treat all of us without mercy in the same way you treat the negrito, then you will escape criticism.”

The king gave orders to have the negrito found and brought to audience, and then said to all seven sons-in-law, “I’d like to eat venison. Go and catch me one deer apiece, all of you. Anyone who fails will be killed.”

The six other sons-in-law met at their residence. “We have lots of servants and weapons to find the deer.” They went into the forest to hunt but by evening had not found a single deer and were very tired. They ate and then talked. “If we don’t find a deer, how are we going to avoid being killed?”

The Bodhisatta returned from the audience, thinking, “I’ll find deer to present to the king.” Arriving at his residence, he told Princess Gandha, “Just now the king summoned me to audience and ordered me to find a deer to present to him, and he will give a reward, but if I don’t find a deer he will execute me. I’m leaving you to go into the forest to hunt a deer for the king.”

“O husband, why are you going alone? The forest is full of tigers, elephants, and dangerous spirits. Let me go along too.”

"Don't come with me. I'm not afraid of tigers, elephants, and spirits."

He put on the negrito suit and the golden shoes, picked up the jeweled sword, and flew up into the sky like a golden swan. He descended to sit on a white stone slab in the forest and took off his negrito suit. His body shone like gold, the rays lighting up the whole forest. He pronounced a mantra that the lady ogress had taught him to call all the deer to gather there, and then uttered a prayer: "Any deer that has not yet come to its time for death, please run away, but any that has, please die right now." Through the power of his merit and prayer, some deer died right in front of the Bodhisatta.

The six sons-in-law had still not come across a single deer. Traveling north, they met the Bodhisatta sitting on the white stone slab and emitting rays of golden light. In surprise and alarm, they talked together: "This fellow is not human but a god for sure." They approached the Bodhisatta, paid respect, and asked, "Are you a brahma, *garuḍa*, *nāga*, or *gandhabba*? What are you doing here? Please give each of us one deer apiece that we can present to the king and be given great rewards in the court. If you are not kind enough to give us the deer, we will die for certain."

The Bodhisatta said, "I am not Lord Sakka or a *gandhabba*, but a human from Bārāṇasī. I'll give you the deer you want. What will you give me in worship?"

"We will offer you seven jewels, cattle, and buffalo."

"I don't want these things. I just want a little piece of each of your ears."

"You want us to cut a piece from our ears to give you?"

"We couldn't stand the pain."

"If you can't do it, I cannot give you the deer either."

The six sons-in-law discussed together. "Unless we give him the ears, he won't give us the deer, so we should give him the ears." Each of them cut off a piece of his ear and gave it to the Bodhisatta. He allowed the six of them to take one of the deer each to present to the king.

Seeing the six sons-in-law approaching with the deer, the king asked, "Where did you get the deer?"

"We went hunting in the forest to the north and came upon Lord Indra sitting on a white stone slab. He gave us a deer each." The king was happy and praised them in many ways.

The Bodhisatta thought to himself, "Those six will go to attend on the king. I should go too." He put on the golden shoes and the negrito suit, stuck the sword in his waist, and chanted a mantra to call the herd of deer to go along to his house. He chose one of the deer, tied it securely, led it into the city, tethered it near the palace, and went to address the king. "Sire, I've brought a deer. It's tethered close by." The king sent an official to make sure it was securely tethered. The Bodhisatta paid respect and went home.

As he was surprised, the king sent officials to inspect the deer that the Bodhisatta had brought. The deer was frightened by the mass of people because it had not seen humans before. It sprang up with great force, snapping the rope, and ran off into the forest.

The king could not find fault with the Bodhisatta, so he gave thought to another trick. "I'll kill this forest negrito by having him bring a pig." He summoned the six sons-in-law. "Each of you go and bring me one pig. If you fail, you will be punished." He instructed them to convey this message to the Bodhisatta too. They sent for their retainers, armed themselves, and went into the forest but could not find a single pig.

The Bodhisatta thought it was time to go to the forest, so he put on the shoes and jeweled sword and flew to descend on the white stone slab in the forest. Looking as beautiful as an image cast from a whole bar of gold, he uttered the mantra named gem-jewel to summon a herd of pigs. He separated them into living and dead pigs in the same way as before.

The six sons-in-law came upon the Bodhisatta sitting on the white stone slab and emitting rays of golden light and begged him to give them some pigs. He asked, "What do you want pigs for?"

"O god, we have to give them to the king. He wants to kill the forest negrito, so he asked all of us, including the negrito, to bring him a pig. If we fail, he will kill us."

"If you want pigs, I can give them to you. What will you offer me in worship?"

"Whatever you want, we'll offer that."

"I want a finger from each of you."

They discussed and consented. Each cut off a finger and offered it to the Bodhisatta, who gave them a pig apiece. They went back and gave the pigs to the king.

After that, the Bodhisatta took one of the dead pigs to offer to the king.

"Why are you bringing me a pig?"

"I found it in the forest so I brought it to offer you." He paid respect and took his leave.

Here there is a question. Why does the Bodhisatta pay respect to the king so easily like this? The answer is this: he does so to show the king what great merit he has.

The king of Bārāṇasī ruminated, "I've thought up two tricks for killing the forest negrito without success. Now I'll make him find some fish. This time I'll succeed because he does not know how to fish."

Next morning at audience, the king told the six sons-in-law, "Today, each of you must go and bring me a lot of fish. If you fail, you will be punished." He told them to convey this order to the Bodhisatta as before. They went off with their retainers to a spot on the river and fished in all directions but at the end of the day had caught nothing. They met up and made a plea to the gods, "Please give us some fish, O gods."

The Bodhisatta heard the king's command. At a good time he put on all the gear, flew along the riverbank, and came down on a stone wharf near the six sons-in-law. He chanted the great jewel mantra to summon fish and prayed for those fish not near their death to flee away and others to stay. The six sons-in-law came downstream along the bank and found the Bodhisatta sitting on the stone wharf and emitting beautiful golden rays. They thought, "This fellow is surely Lord Indra. He gave us the deer and pig before, so we should ask him for fish."

When they asked him, the Bodhisatta said, "I'll give you the fish but what will you offer me?"

"Whatever you want."

"A bit of each of your noses."

They agreed, cut off a bit of the ends of their noses, and took the fish back to offer to the king. The king asked them, "Where did you get the fish?"

"From Lord Indra, the same as with the deer and the pigs. Three times now."

The king praised them, "You must have great merit to meet this god three times."

The six daughters noticed that their husbands were all missing a bit of the ear, one finger, and the end of the nose. They did not ask their husbands directly but asked the courtiers who went with them. The courtiers related the story: "When they went for the deer, the ear was cut; for the pig, the finger was cut; and for the fish, the nose was cut. We saw this happen all three times, but we don't know why this happened."

After the six sons-in-law had returned with the fish, the Bodhisatta brought a load of fish to present to the king and returned home. The king consulted his courtiers. "He brought the deer and the pig and the fish. What trick can we use to kill him?" The courtiers did not know what to say.

At that time, the Paṇḍukambalasilā throne of Lord Sakka, king of the gods, became unusually warm. The god reflected and, knowing the reason, thought to himself, "The king of Bārāṇasī is looking for a way to kill the Bodhisatta. I should go to the human world, threaten the king, praise the Bodhisatta, and return to the heavens." He went down, stood in the sky near the king's lion-window, and said, "I am Lord Indra and I have two questions for the king. First, what in this world has the brightest light? Second, what in this world is the darkest dark? Please answer within seven days. On the seventh, come and play polo with me in the sky. If you cannot answer the questions and cannot play polo in the sky, please find someone else to do so. Otherwise, at noon on the seventh day, I will cut off your head with an iron hammer." Lord Sakka returned to his abode.

The king was very alarmed. Next morning he summoned the six sons-in-law and his ministers to audience, told them the story, and asked who could answer the questions and play polo in the sky. "Nobody, sire. Because everyone still has so much sinful desire and material desire. Only a monk with exceptional insight can answer these questions and fly in the sky. All of us can serve you only on the ground, sire."

Hearing this, the king was as angry as if singed by fire. He ordered the courtiers to take the matter to the city folk and villagers; anyone who could answer the questions and play polo in the sky with Lord Indra would be given the whole realm. But no volunteer could be found. Upset to learn this, the king went to find solace with the queen, lamenting, "If I can't find someone by the seventh day, I'll die."

She said, "Why are you so upset? It's not fitting. Send for the forest negrito. He has real powers of merit. When you demanded deer and pigs and fish, only he could find them. He's smart, has all the tricks. He can answer the questions and compete with Lord Indra."

The six sons-in-law and officials laughed at this and voiced their objections in the audience hall. "Your Majesty, this forest negrito is like a human puppet. He can't answer the questions and compete with Indra."

The queen retorted, "O courtiers, this forest negrito is very powerful. Don't stand in the way. Hurry and bring him here right now."

The king added, "Bring both him and Princess Gandha." The courtiers rushed off to fetch the couple.

When they arrived, the king said to the Bodhisatta, "My beloved son, I'm distressed. Lord Indra came with these questions and a challenge to play polo in the sky. On the seventh day he'll come to split my head with an iron hammer." He outlined the questions. "If you can help get me out of this, I'll hand over the realm to you." The king still looked down on the Bodhisatta and only went along with this out of deference to the queen.

The Bodhisatta said, "Sire, if nobody else can do this, I may be able to solve the questions and fly to play the polo with Indra to repay your goodness. Please do not worry at all."

It was then the sixth day in the evening, so the Bodhisatta paid respect and left. The six sons-in-law and people including courtiers talked together: "It's amazing the forest negrito dares do this!" They showered the Bodhisatta with praise.

On the morning of the appointed day, the king felt anxious enough to shatter into seven pieces. He sent off a courtier to fetch the forest negrito. The Bodhisatta brought Princess Gandha along too and sat in a suitable spot in the audience hall. The king saw them and said, "Please answer the questions and play the polo. If you're late by even a little, I'm dead."

The Bodhisatta said, "Sire, if you wish for me to answer the questions and play polo, tell the courtiers and people to come and gather here." The king sent out drummers to make the announcement. When all had gathered, the Bodhisatta called out, "As nobody else will undertake this task, the king has asked me to help stand in for him. If Lord Indra loses, the king will hand over the realm to me. People, please be my witnesses."

He took off the forest negrito suit, put on the golden shoes, grasped the jeweled sword in his right hand, flew up as elegantly as a golden swan, and floated in mid air. Seeing this, the courtiers and people raised their clasped hands in salute and uttered their praise.

Lord Maghavā approached the Bodhisatta and said, "Now, sage, what makes darkness in this world and the next world? Answer this question clearly for the gods and the humans who have gathered on the earth and in the sky."

"Lord Sakka, king of the gods, anyone who accuses someone else who has done no wrong, who causes quarrels between people, or who commits one of the five gravest sins,[10] such as killing his mother, or who does not listen to the teachings of the sages because of an evil mind, that person makes for darkness in this world and the next world. O king of the gods, that's the heart of the matter."

All the gods including Lord Sakka made worship to the Bodhisatta with popped rice and flowers. The sound of their praise was deafening.

The Thousand-Eyed Lord asked the second question. "O sage, what gives light in this world and the next world?"

"Lord Sakka, king of the gods, anyone who practices the five precepts and eight precepts, gives alms to beggars, diligently listens to the teachings of the sages, is compassionate and kind toward all living beings, upholds the virtue of the Three Baskets to the day of his death, that person is a brilliant light in this world and the next world. Anyone who practices the four sublime states of mind continually and does not kill any living being, that person is a brilliant light in this world and the next world."

The gods and humans saluted and worshiped him as before.

Having answered the two questions, the Bodhisatta played polo with Lord Indra in the sky. The aura of both Lord Indra and the Bodhisatta shone brightly throughout the sky like a teardrop falling from an eye. Seeing this, all the gods and humans offered their praises to the Bodhisatta in an uproar. The praises went right up to the utmost Brahma worlds. Lord Indra lost the game of polo and fled back to the heavens. The Bodhisatta followed him for a while then returned to pay respect to the king.

The people, courtiers, and six sons-in-law saw the beautiful appearance of the Bodhisatta, brilliant like an image cast from a whole bar of gold. They said to one another, "The forest negrito with the awful ugly body has turned out to have great power of merit!"

"He fooled us to get the realm from the king."

The Bodhisatta heard the six sons-in-law and said, "After the king asked us to present him with a deer, you met me at the white stone slab and asked

10. อนันตริยกรรม, *anantriyakam*, anantariya-kamma, killing one's mother, killing one's father, killing an *arahant*, causing a Buddha to suffer contusion or bleeding, causing a schism in the sangha.

for a deer each, and I made you cut a piece from your ear. Then the pigs and your fingers, and the fish and the tips of your noses. Is this true or not?"

They conceded the truth. He brought out the pieces of ear, finger, and nose to show to the king, officials, and sons-in-law. The king looked at the pieces and flew into a rage at the six sons-in-law. "You told me Lord Indra gave you the deer, pigs, and fish. You're shameless!"

Hearing the Bodhisatta's words, the six princesses felt ashamed and raged at their husbands, saying, "You villains, deceiving us in several ways! How can you do this without any shame?" The six sons-in-law felt even more ashamed. They prostrated at the feet of the Bodhisatta and begged his forgiveness.

The Bodhisatta, full of mercy, gave teaching to the people, including the queen, king, and courtiers gathered there: "All of you, set your mind to perform good deeds such as almsgiving and upholding the precepts. Pay respect to the elders of your families that deserve respect, such as your mothers and fathers. The merit of good deeds will bear fruit in this world and the next world. People who practice the five precepts will enter heaven in the future." The people, including the king and courtiers, felt joy and devotion and raised their hands in praise.

The king ordered the ministers and royal priest-counselors to gather at the palace. He invited the Bodhisatta and Princess Gandha to sit on a jeweled throne, anointed them with sacred water, presented the realm, and gave a blessing: "You two of great merit, may you have power throughout the continents of the world, may you have long life without disease. Your father and mother beg to depend happily on your patronage from now on."

The Bodhisatta ruled in Bārāṇasī as King Suvaṇṇasaṅkha, King of the Golden Conch. His glory and reputation spread through the world. From that time, the city of Bārāṇasī was abundant with material treasures, abundant with rice shoots, and abundant with the seven jewels. Rain fell according to the season. The people blossomed with happiness. There were entertainments every night and day.

The Bodhisatta thought back to his mother. "We have been parted for a long time. I no longer know whether she is alive or dead. I should go to make enquiries in the cities and villages. If I find her, I shall bring her back and continue ruling happily here." He told his thoughts to Princess Gandha, saying, "You stay here and rule the realm while I go to find her."

He informed the king, left the city, and traveled to Maddarāja City. He made enquiries without result and so traveled on to the house of the rich man, Dhanañjaya.

Surprised to see such a beautiful figure, Dhanañjaya asked, "Where have you come from? What do you want from my house?"

"I am looking for Candā Devī, my mother. Do you know of her?"

Dhanañjaya thought, "This is a very fine looking fellow. He must come from a good family." He ordered his kitchen staff to prepare food for him. The staff, headed by Candā Devī, prepared the food and brought it out. When the Bodhisatta ate, the taste and aroma was like divine food. He speculated, "My mother must be the cook in this rich man's house." He asked Dhanañjaya, "Who prepares the food here? Food of this kind with such taste must be made on the command of someone with power."

"A woman who came from elsewhere has lived with me as cook, making the food."

"I'd like to see your cook."

Dhanañjaya had her fetched for him to see.

The Bodhisatta could not recognize her because they had been separated for so long since he was a small child. He asked, "What city are you from?"

"I am from Brahmapura. I am the queen of King Brahmadatta and have a son named the Golden Conch." She told the story of being expelled from the city, floating down the river on the raft, being separated from her son, and finding her way to the rich man's house. "Whether my son is dead or alive, I do not know."

"Mother, I am your son called the Golden Conch." She embraced him, asked about his travails, and wept in lamentation. After their sorrow diminished, the Bodhisatta addressed Dhanañjaya: "May I take leave and bring my mother back to Bārāṇasī?"

"When she came here, I did not know she was your mother. Please take her as you wish."

The king of Bārāṇasī saw the Bodhisatta returning with his mother. He happily assembled his courtiers, ministers, and priest-counselors and said, "We will have a ceremony of anointing Candā Devī as the queen mother." The ceremony was held.

The King of the Golden Conch ruled happily. He taught the nobles, including ministers, to practice the pure dhamma. They followed his advice to practice the four sublime states of mind and to pay respect to people worthy of respect. He was finer than any other king in the Jambu Continent. Bārāṇasī was a joyful place, abundant with jewels and wealth on par with the heavens. All the people praised the virtue of the king. His reputation spread to Brahmapura, the city of King Brahmadatta, his father.

The people of Brahmapura discussed together, saying, "The Prince of the Golden Conch is still alive. It turns out he is ruling at Bārāṇasī. If we stay here, we will face ruin for certain because our king does not follow the royal virtues. He even floated his own beloved daughter away on a raft. Let's leave." They all agreed together and took their wives and children off to Bārāṇasī, where they were happy every night and day living under the patronage of the Bodhisatta.

While making an inspection of the city, a courtier of King Brahmadatta noticed that the population was dropping and thought, "Why is our city not content? Because the king believed the minister and Suvaṇṇa Campāka Devī that the Golden Conch would bring misfortune and so had him and his mother floated away on a raft. Since then the city has deteriorated. There are fewer people than before. The city faces ruin for sure. I should tell the king to bring his son back to rule here so the place prospers as before."

He went to attend on the king. "Sire, from my inspection I find that the city faces ruin. Why? Because you floated your son away on a raft. He is still alive and ruling in Bārāṇasī. As a ruler, he has no equal. Many of our people have migrated there and it has become very well populated. Please go to Bārāṇasī and bring your son back to rule here. Through his merit, your city will be famous, joyful, and glorious."

To induce the king to agree, the courtier added, "Sire, without your son, your fame will not spread everywhere—like a river without water that provides no support for the people. Without your son, your power will not be known—like a leaderless herd of elephants that cannot overcome enemies. If you do not follow this advice, this city will disappear and you will not remain a ruler or will die without a successor to continue the royal line. The Prince of the Golden Conch was born from the womb of Queen Candā Devī alone. Consider the original cause. At first you wished to have a son in order to pass on the realm to him. When no son was born as hoped, you and Queen Candā Devī practiced the eight precepts and prayed for a son. One night she dreamed the sun struck her body. A seer predicted she would have the most excellent son in the world. Yet the king was wrongly led to believe this son would bring misfortune."

Hearing this stirred King Brahmadatta's old feelings for his son into a great sorrow. When his sadness subsided, he responded to the courtier, "I owe you incomparable thanks for coming to speak in this way. I will fetch back my son to rule here as you suggest."

Next morning he summoned his courtiers and priest-counselors and told them, "I will send a senior minister to Bārāṇasī to request my son and his queen to return to rule in Brahmapura."

All were happy to hear this. The king sent out drummers to announce the news to the people and had servants muster the troops, prepare the materials for an anointing ceremony, and assemble gifts to offer to the king of Bārāṇasī. The people and courtiers happily carried out these tasks.

On the appointed day, the king sent for a seer to calculate an auspicious time, and put a minister in charge. The minister arranged for people to carry gifts to Bārāṇasī. He attended on the king of Bārāṇasī and presented the gifts. After a customary exchange of speeches, the king sent for the Bodhisatta and his queen and asked, "What is the purpose of this visit?"

"King Brahmadatta has commanded me to bring his son and the son's mother back to rule in Brahmapura. Please give your permission, sire."

"But they were driven out because they brought ill fortune. Why does he want them back? We cannot let them go. We wish them to rule here."

The minister was clever at negotiation. "Sire, if you do not agree and the king sees me return on my own, he will be so afflicted with sorrow that his heart will break in two and he will die. Should he die for the love of his son in this way, you will carry the karma into the next world for certain."

These words made the king of Bārāṇasī feel compassion for King Brahmadatta. "In that case I will allow them to go."

The Bodhisatta asked, "Is my father still in good health? Do the people prosper?"

"Your father is well, but he misses you sorrowfully every day without pause."

The two agreed to go with the minister.

The king of Bārāṇasī gave orders to arrange transport, including elephants and horses. The three of them, Queen Candā Devī, the Prince of the Golden Conch, and Princess Gandha, went together to pay respect and take leave of the king. He did not wish them to leave and would miss them greatly but offered a blessing: "Son, rule the realm for the happiness of your people, and uphold the royal traditions with honesty."

The three took their leave of the people and retainers. At an auspicious time calculated by the seer, they ascended to their royal seats and left in procession with troops ahead and behind. Arriving at Brahmapura, they waited while citizens made a royal pavilion for them to stay in.

The minister attended on King Brahmadatta and informed him of the arrival. The king sent out drummers to announce that he would welcome his son to rule the realm. Beside the road along which they would come, people gathered with flowers, gold, silver, and garlands. Along both sides of the road were flags, sheets of cloth, banana trees, and sugarcane plants, tied, trimmed, and placed at intervals. The king and his retinue went out to welcome the three at a royal pavilion.

King Brahmadatta, the Prince of the Golden Conch, Queen Candā Devī, and Princess Gandha met together and wept. After recovering, they entered the palace. The king sent out drummers to summon courtiers and people to attend the anointment of the prince and princess to rule the realm. After the people had gathered, the king anointed them at an auspicious time and invited them to rule in his stead.

After the ceremony, Queen Candā Devī addressed her husband, "May I have permission to live alone with my son? Do not anoint me. I do not wish to be your queen any longer."

"What have I done wrong? I can't see it. Don't be angry at me. From now on, I won't do anything wrong for sure."

"Your merit is great. Even so, were I to die today, that would be better than again being called a cause of misfortune."

King Brahmadatta heard about this and asked Queen Suvaṇṇa Campāka Devī of the left, "Is there something wrong with the Prince of the Golden Conch or Queen Candā Devī."

"Yes, with Queen Candā Devī. She is a cause of misfortune."

Queen Candā Devī heard about this and felt very upset. She spoke with the king, "I am not a cause of misfortune. Whoever says this has bad intentions toward me. If the king sees fault in anyone, let it be tested by an ordeal of fire."

The king ordered officials to prepare a fire in the courtyard. The king told Queen Candā Devī, "You must make a prayer and enter the fire for the people to see."

She paid respect at the feet of her husband, and made a prayer to the gods. "O gods who protect the white umbrella, and gods who stay in the trees and grass, hear my words. If I am truly a cause of misfortune as Queen Campāka says, do not protect my life, let me die in the fire ordeal. If I am not a cause of misfortune, protect my life from danger." She went and sat in the fire. Immediately, a golden lotus poked up to support her so that her body was not burned by the flames, as if she was sitting talking in a palace. The courtiers were amazed. The king happily called her out from the fire. Bad karma impelled Queen Campāka to want to undergo the ordeal by fire. She made a prayer in the same way, entered the fire, and was burned to death. She was reborn in the Avīci hell. Her misdeeds were exposed to the eyes of the people, while Queen Candā Devī was absolved of any guilt.

For this reason, the Ancient Teacher states that anyone who speaks untruth, especially to cause the death of another, will come to ruin and suffer pitifully in Avīci hell as the fruit of their dishonesty, like Queen Campāka.

The king established Candā Devī to be the major queen. The Prince of the Golden Conch and Queen Candā Devī ruled in Bārāṇasī in health and happiness. The Prince of the Golden Conch told his father the long story of their troubles: "Sire, after you floated me and my mother away on a raft on the river, the raft broke up in a storm, and we were separated. Clinging onto a log, mother floated to the shore at Maddarāja, where she became cook for the rich man Dhanañjaya. After help from a rishi, I floated to another shore, where an ogress raised me as her stepson. I ran away from her and became a cowherd in a headman's house for a long time. Then I got the daughter of the king of Bārāṇasī as a wife and was very happy until I thought of my mother, tracked her down at the house of Dhanañjaya, and brought her to be happy in Bārāṇasī. Then you sent the minister for me. These were all our troubles. I must still have some merit from the past that caused me to find my father again."

The king said, "I wrongly believed the words of a villainous person and have done you great wrong, while you have done no wrong to me."

The Bodhisatta forgave him. From then on he ruled as a supreme king, upholding the ten virtues and encouraging the people to do good deeds and observe the five precepts.

As for Minister Pālaka, after the Prince of the Golden Conch returned to Brahmapura, Pālaka was worried that the prince would punish him. He had the idea of fleeing elsewhere and returning with an army to capture and kill the prince and his mother. He went to Pañcālaḍanī City, attended on the king, and told him that the Prince of the Golden Conch was preparing to attack his city with a large army in order to partition the realm.

King Pañcāla believed this. He sent out drummers to summon the people to assemble in the royal courtyard and told them this story. He appointed Pālaka to command a vanguard to go on ahead first, and put his own commander in charge of the main army following later. They marched to Brahmapura and laid siege to the city in seven circles. The shouting of the troops echoed around as if the earth and city would soon collapse.

Some soldiers cried, "We'll break through these walls!"

Others cried, "We'll capture and kill the king and prince!"

Hearing this, the people of Brahmapura were scared. "How can we escape such a large enemy force?"

The prince was also disheartened. He remembered the lady ogress. "Where has she been reborn now?" He chanted a mantra that she had taught him, and found that she had been reborn in the Cātumahārajika Heaven.[11] He put on his golden shoes, flew up to the heavens, paid respect to her, and said, "Mother, enemies are besieging our city. I cannot see anyone to turn to except you. Please help me and the city folk."

She had compassion for the Prince of the Golden Conch. "Take up this jeweled sword with divine power which I give you here. If an enemy threatens to seize your realm, fly into the air, and wave the jeweled sword over your head. The enemy will be defeated and return home as a result of the power of this jeweled sword. Do as I say."

He took up the sword, made his farewell, and returned home. Along with his troops, he left the city, flew into the air, and waved the sword as she had instructed. Rays from the jeweled sword struck the earth with sounds like thunder as if the whole enemy army would die together. The seven brigade leaders, feeling their heads would split open, loudly begged the Bodhisatta for their lives: "Sire, we will not think of attacking you again. Please spare our lives!"

Minister Pālaka could not withstand the power of the jeweled sword. He fell from his elephant's neck down onto the ground. As a result of his bad deeds and ingratitude, the earth 240,000 *yojana* thick gaped open. Minister Pālaka fell through and was burned in the fires of the Avīci hell.

11. After death the ogress was reborn in the Tāvatiṁsā Heaven. This discrepancy is found in the Pali.

For this reason, the Ancient Teacher taught that anyone who tells lies to condemn another person, whether a relation or friend, or to accuse a teacher or someone who has been good to him, when that person dies, he will be reborn in the Avīci hell like Minister Pālaka.

As the Bodhisatta had great compassion toward people, he said to the army commanders, "King Pañcāla believed Minister Pālaka's tricky words and thus sent an army against us who had done him no wrong. These were evil misdeeds. Do not make such evil karma in the future."

He gave further teaching, "Anyone who kills a living being, steals property, takes another's wife, tells lies, or drinks liquor will come to ruin like Minister Pālaka. Good works such as keeping the precepts, almsgiving, listening to the dhamma, cultivating friendship, and paying due respect to elders of the clan have great virtue. Anyone who is heedful of my teaching, on death will be reborn in the heavens due to these good works." He sent the army officers back to Pañcāla City and returned to his own city.

On their return to Pañcāla City, the army officers attended on the king and said, "Sire, we besieged the city in seven circles. The Prince of the Golden Conch has great merit. He flew into the air and waved his jeweled sword, which emitted light like a thunderclap, blinding and stunning us. We were defeated. Minister Pālaka fell from his elephant and was swallowed up by the earth because he was disloyal to his master. The Prince of the Golden Conch came down from the sky, gave teaching to us, and sent us home." King Pañcāla praised the Prince of the Golden Conch and arranged to send him tribute of many kinds.

Having defeated the enemies, the Prince of the Golden Conch entered the city and had the people established in the teachings. He ruled with integrity. His power and reputation spread to other lands. Other kings regularly sent him tribute. The people, including the king, were established in the royal advice, faced no dangers, made merit such as through almsgiving, and after death were reborn in the heavens. The Bodhisatta made merit, including almsgiving, and at death was reborn in the heavens.

> The Buddha finished this sermon. When telling the monks of the karma he had made in past lives, he said, "When I was still traveling in the cycle of birth and was born as the Golden Conch, son of King Brahmadatta, I suffered great hardships because my father believed the tricky words of Minister Pālaka and floated me away

on a raft, all as a result of bad deeds done in past lives." The monks did not know about this other past life and begged him to tell them the tale. The Buddha related an unknown story, as follows.

"In a past life a long time ago, I was born as a son in a poor family. I had no kin. One day that boy went down to bathe at a river landing. He saw a crab hole, put in his hand, and pulled out the crab. He scooped up a lump of mud, made a hole in the lump, and put the crab in there. He placed the lump on a raft, and let it float down to the ocean. After five days, the crab was still alive. The raft came aground on the shore of the ocean. Water dissolved the lump of mud, and the crab went up on the shore. As the fruit of this karma, I was born in a conch shell. See, you monks, King Brahmadatta, who believed Queen Campāka and Minister Pālaka, put me on a raft to float down to the ocean because of the karma of catching that crab and floating it away. As the crab did not die, so I did not have to die, yet I suffered pitiful hardship. The fact I was happy in the form of the conch shell and the forest negrito came from the karma made by putting the crab in the hollowed mud. The fact that the six sons-in-law of the king of Bārāṇasī criticized me in the form of the forest negrito was the result of karma made in a past life, as follows.

"O monks, in a past life, I was born as the king of Bārāṇasī. This king wanted to offer cloth to the monks. He knew that merchants had brought good-quality cloth to sell in his city. He sent a courtier to buy from the merchants. The price was 100,000 *kahāpaṇa* per piece. When the king saw the cloth, he offered a price of one weight of gold. The merchants discussed together, 'The price the king offers is not right for this cloth. We will ask the king for a price appropriate to the cloth.' When the king heard this, he was very angry at the merchants. The merchants heard he was angry and knew they could not ask for another price for the cloth. They returned to their home city. The king of Bārāṇasī died from this world and was reborn as the Golden Conch, who became the son-in-law of the king of Bārāṇasī. Those merchants died from this world and were reborn as the six sons-in-law who inveigled the king to kill the Bodhisatta. This was the result of the karma made by forcing them to reduce the price of the cloth."

After the Buddha gave this sermon, he made the birth connections: "The lord of the *nāga* who put the Golden Conch on a boat was reborn as Angulimāla; the rishi who helped the Golden Conch as Sāriputta; the lady ogress, stepmother of the Golden Conch, as Uppalavannā; Lord Sakka, king of the gods, who helped the Golden Conch, as Anuruddha; the king who invited Candā Devī and the Golden Conch to rule in Brahmapura, as Moggallāna; the rich man Dhanañjaya, who let Candā Devī stay with him, as Sīvalī;[12] Suvaṇṇa Campāka Devī, who wrongly accused Candā Devī, as Ciñcā Mahāvikā; Minister Pālaka, who was vengeful toward the Golden Conch, as Devadatta; King Brahmadatta, his father, as King Suddhodana, the father of the Buddha; Candā Devī as Siri Mahāmāyā, mother of the Buddha; Princess Gandha, queen of the Golden Conch, as Yasodharā Bimbā; those loyal to the Bodhisatta as those loyal to the Buddha; and the Prince of the Golden Conch as I, the Tathāgata." The words of the Buddha end here.

12. An early follower of the Buddha.

RATHASENA

P47 *Rathasenajātaka*

รถเสนชาดก

INTRODUCTION

This story is one of the most widely known in the collection under various names including *Phra rot* (Rathasena), *Phra rot meri* (Rathasena and Kaṅrī), and *Nang sipsong* (twelve sisters). Since the late Ayutthaya era, the tale has been adapted into various literary forms including verse, recitation texts, and dramas, especially in the mid-nineteenth century. It continues to be adapted today.

The story is strongly associated with Luang Prabang. In local tellings there, the ogress's daughter Nang Kwang Hi is the founder-queen of Luang Prabang, and Rathasena is called Buddhasena. At the end, Buddhasena misses Nang Kwang Hi, returns to find her dead body, dies of grief, and their bodies become the hills known as Phu Thao and Phu Nang (Lord Hill and Lady Hill) outside Luang Prabang. Several other locations in the vicinity are named after incidents in the story. Other places also claim the tale. At Mong Nai in the Shan States and Kampong Chhang in Cambodia, there are caves, cliffs, and mountains identified with incidents in the tale. At Phanat Nikhom in Chonburi there is a cave and shrine, and at Ban Mung in Phitsanulok there is a shrine, probably established by migrants brought forcibly from Laos in the nineteenth century.[1] Urangkathat, the chronicle of the That Phanom shrine, refers to the story, calling the hero Sud(dh)asena. A ruined ancient city in eastern Thailand has been dubbed Mueang Phrarot.

The story is also found further afield in India, Persia, and Sri Lanka. The story possibly draws on an old Persian tale, which appears in Richard Burton's supplements to the Arabian Nights as "Histoire de Mohammed

1. Rattanaphon, "The Journey of Nang Sip Song."

l'Avisé." A jealous queen has the king's forty other women blinded and imprisoned; they all give birth to children that they share as food, except for one son who performs various quests and recovers their eyes, after which the jealous queen dies.[2]

Rathasena does not appear in any other collections of the Fifty Jātaka. It seems to have been converted from the local tale into the *jātaka*, with the addition of passages of teaching, but also several clumsy omissions. There is no preamble or story of the present.

The *jātaka* differs from the folktale in ways that make it "more Buddhist." The Bodhisatta does not kill the evil ogress; instead she dies of a broken heart. He himself does not die with his ogress-lover in his arms. Perhaps for the same reason, the rishi's role in rewriting the letter has been changed—but rather clumsily, so this crucial part of the plot is unclear.

The *jātaka* also has many passages not found in the folktale. Some of these are passages of straightforward teaching or stories about accumulating karma in past lives, but others are simply episodes of a kind that are characteristic of other *jātaka*: a slave girl fetching water; hiding in the stomachs of animals; salutations by the gods; an army of demons, complete with description of the troops; a visit to a royal park, complete with a description of the flora and fauna; an intervention by Sakka; and the Bodhisatta lamenting over his mother. The role of the horse has also been enlarged to become the Bodhisatta's trusty companion, as in other *jātaka*.

Verses have been added. As in other stories, several lines or phrases have been taken from famous passages in the classical *jātaka*, particularly J547 Vessantara. Here, however, some of these borrowings are very clumsy. Some lines taken from Maddi's famous verse are inserted in contexts where they are totally irrelevant.

The translator from Pali to Thai seems to have had misgivings about some of these additions. He dropped six sets of verses, including those with the irrelevant passages from Maddi, the description of the army, a standard description of the forest, the Bodhisatta addressing the gods, and a comment by the Buddha that only repeats the preceding passage. He also dropped four short passages from the text: one giving the horse a retinue; one extending the salutations of the gods; one extending the account of the demon army; and one describing the decoration of the city. None of these

2. See *Arabian Nights in Sixteen Volumes: Vol. 16* (New York: Cosimo, 2008), 300–301.

dropped passages appear in the folktale. They are typical *jātaka* passages, and add nothing to the story. Other than these (quite understandable) omissions, the translation is very faithful to the Pali. The translator has not added anything from the folktale.

As has been heard, at one time during the religion of the fully enlightened Kassapa Buddha, there was a rich man named Nanda living in Samiddhagāma village. He had great wealth but no son or daughter.

Nanda put twelve bananas on his head and went to the temple, wishing to offer them to the Lord Buddha, thinking to himself, "I will worship the fully enlightened Kassapa Buddha. I will make a wish to have children in the future, many sons and daughters." At the temple he paid respect to the Blessed One, raised the twelve bananas as offering to the Kassapa Buddha, and made the wish as he had been thinking. On returning home, he told his wife, who was very happy. Later she became pregnant, time after time, and before long had given birth to twelve daughters. Over the time when the daughters were still playful infants and at later times, the wealth such as gold and silver in the rich man's house diminished. Male and female slaves fell dead. Nanda and his wife became poor. He still needed food such as boiled and plain rice to feed his daughters, but none remained. He was so angry that he put the twelve daughters in a cart, drove the cart into the forest, left them there, and drove the cart home.

At one time in the past, Nanda had taken wealth such as gold and silver away from his daughters while they were eating and had not returned it to them. The consequence of this old karma was now attached to him. For this reason he became destitute because of his twelve daughters. The fruit of bad actions is karma that surely matters in the future. For this reason, the Blessed One spoke a verse:

> *Impermanent indeed are bodies. By nature they arise and disappear.*
> *Having arisen, they pass way. Happy is the peace when they cease forever.*[3]
> *Those who make karma own that karma and must inherit its fruit.*

3. According to the Mahāparinibbāna Sutta, this verse was spoken by the god Sakka after the passing away of the Buddha (suttacentral.net/pi/dn16). It is chanted in funeral rites.

The twelve daughters searched for their father in the forest. Before long they arrived at the garden of an ogress, Sandhāmāra. The ogress came to the garden and saw them. With a loving heart, she took all twelve to raise as her own sisters.

One time, the eldest of the sisters saw the ogress eating human flesh and went to tell her sisters, "We've gotten ourselves into the lair of an ogress!"

All twelve thought of making an escape. Later the ogress went into the garden, could not find the twelve, and searched around. The twelve had entered into an elephant's stomach not far away. Not seeing the sisters, the ogress asked the elephant, "Have you seen twelve girls coming this way?"

The elephant said, "No, I haven't."

The ogress went home. The twelve came out from the elephant's stomach. When the ogress came after them again, they went into a horse's belly. Not seeing them, the ogress asked the horse, "Have you seen twelve girls?"

The horse answered, "No, I haven't"

The ogress went home. The girls came out from the horse's stomach. The ogress came after them again. The twelve went into a cow's stomach. The ogress asked the cow, "Have you seen twelve girls?"

The cow answered, "No, I haven't."

The ogress went back to the garden.

In the past, when these twelve girls had been playful children, they took twelve little puppies and left them in the forest. This bad karma had fruit for the twelve for five hundred lives. As a result of this karma, the twelve wandered around the country until they reached Kutāra City. On the bank of the city lake they saw a banyan tree and went up to sit there.

At that time, King Rathasiddha ruled in Kutāra City. He gave a gold water pot to a hunchbacked slave woman for fetching water for him. When the slave woman took this pot to the lake, she saw an aura from the twelve sisters shining on her and making the water appear like golden light. She thought to herself, "Why is someone as beautiful as me coming to fetch water?" She grew angry, smashed the golden pot, and went home. Not seeing the golden pot, King Rathasiddha gave her a silver pot. She went back with the silver pot, had the same feeling, angrily smashed the silver pot, and went home. Not seeing the silver pot, the king gave her a pot made of leather. She went back to the lake, had the same feeling, and angrily smashed the pot again, but it did not break because it was made of leather. The slave woman went back and forth, fetching water. The twelve sisters laughed and clapped their hands. The slave woman heard them clapping, looked up, and saw them up in the banyan with a beautiful aura. She rushed back and told the king, "Your Majesty, I've seen angels up in the banyan tree!"

King Rathasiddha came out from the city with his four-limbed army, saw the twelve sisters, liked them, and called out to them. The twelve climbed down from the banyan, paid respect, and stood there. The king had them sit in a palanquin and took them back to his palace with music, drums, dancing, and singing. He established them all as his queens and loved all twelve very much.

After a time, Sandhāmāra the ogress learned that the twelve had become queens of King Rathasiddha. She quickly left Gajapura City, went to Kutāra, saw the banyan tree by the lake, and went to sit up there, looking as beautiful as a full moon.

The hunchbacked slave woman came to fetch water from the lake, saw the water made beautiful by the light of the ogress, looked up and saw a beautiful lady at the very top of the tree. She rushed to inform the king, "Your Majesty, there's a beautiful lady like an angel in the banyan!"

The king took all his retinue and troops out from the city. When he saw the ogress, he was so pleased he called out to her with a verse:

"O my angel, like a crafted golden image with no likeness,
come down from the banyan. Up there, you will find no refuge."

The ogress came down and paid respect to King Rathasiddha. He put her in a golden palanquin, took her back to his palace, and made her his major queen. Queen Sandhāmāra was the beloved that made the king blissfully happy. In truth, she was more beautiful than the other queens, the twelve sisters, as a consequence of their old karma.

One time, Queen Sandhāmāra pretended to lie sick with a fever. People informed the king, who rushed to her bedside and asked, "What should I do?" He summoned brahmans and astrologers and ordered them, "Invite the potent gods to come and tend to her. Make medicines and mantras to treat her. Have brahmans and astrologers look after her."

Queen Sandhāmāra continued to pretend to be badly sick. She told the king, "Your Majesty, I am in a terribly bad way. If you have the eyes of the twelve sisters plucked out, it will make me much better."

The king summoned the twelve sisters to audience and had them sit in a row according to Sandhāmāra's instruction. The ogress got up from her bed and plucked out the eyes of the twelve sisters. While blood was flowing, she sent the eyes to the wind division[4] with an order, "Send these eyes to Kaṅrī, my daughter." Feeling very pleased with herself, she ate a meal.

When King Rathasiddha no longer saw the twelve sisters, he felt sad and troubled. The twelve were in great hardship as fruit of the karma made in the past. The eleven eldest were in great difficulty, but the youngest could still see through one eye. They said prayers that all life is impermanent, with hardship and without refuge. Before long, the eleven elder sisters became pregnant, but not the youngest.

At that time, the realm of Lord Sakka, king of the gods, seemed hot. He found out the reason and thought, "These twelve sisters are in trouble without any refuge. This should not be. I will give a son to the youngest, who has no refuge." He gave thought to which son would be appropriate for her. He found a bodhisatta who had reached his time and wanted to be reborn in a higher divine world. Lord Sakka went to this Bodhisatta and told him, "O troubled one, you should be born in the human world."

The Great Being asked, "What will be the beneficial result of my being born in the human world?"

Lord Sakka answered, "You will accrue merit by being the refuge of the people."

The Great Being accepted Lord Sakka's invitation, saying, "My being born in the human world will have the beneficial result that I accrue merit and become a refuge of the people. That will be of benefit for my achievement."

The Bodhisatta passed from the heavens and was conceived in the womb of the youngest sister. King Rathasiddha ordered courtiers to dig a cave, placed the twelve sisters there, and closed it up. From the time when the Bodhisatta was born, it helped diminish the sadness of the twelve.

It is said that in a previous life, when these twelve were children playing on the bank of a lake, they caught twelve fish and laid them on the ground. The youngest sister pierced only one eye of a fish, but the eleven others pierced both eyes. The fish were then released. As a consequence of this

4. กองลม, *kong lom*. In other versions of the story, Phra Phai, god of the wind, transports the eyes. Perhaps that is what is meant here. In Pali, kāyavāta, body-wind.

karma, Sandhāmāra plucked out both eyes of the eleven eldest but only one eye of the youngest. The bad karma followed the twelve without relief.

At the tenth month, the eleven gave birth. As there was no food, they tore flesh from the children to share as food. They ate the flesh of their children like that every day, like ogresses. Soon after, when the youngest reached the tenth month, she gave birth to the Great Being, who had a body that shone like gold.[5] She thus named him Rathasena.

One time the Great Being asked, "Mother, what is this place?"

She replied, "It's a cave. King Rathasiddha had it dug for me and my kin to stay in."

The Great Being felt troubled thinking that his mother and her kin were in great difficulty, abandoned to destitution. The Omniscient One, through the power of his merit, emitted an aura that lit up the whole cave like the light of the sun. He was happy to see this. The guardian deities of the cave door closed the door to the cave.

The Great Being rose up into the air above the door of the cave, looked up to the sky, and made a prayer in verse:

> "*My wish has been fulfilled. May Lord Sakka, king of the gods,*
> *greatest of deities, bring cloth for us, and give praise.*"

Lord Sakka, king of the gods, looked down and saw with his thousand eyes that a bodhisatta had been born in the human world. He sent down ornaments, cloth with beautiful colors, celestial flower garlands, and gave his praise. He also taught the Bodhisatta various tricks in gambling.

When the Bodhisatta returned to the cave, bringing the ornaments and celestial cloth, and paid respect to his mother, she asked him questions, so he bowed his head on his mother's feet and spoke a verse:

> "*We live together, just the two of us. Why do you treat me like another person?*"

She answered, "Beloved son, I love you like my own heart."

The Great Being took leave of his mother, left the cave, and looked in all directions. He saw a hut and humans gambling. He approached and saw

5. In the folktale, the children of the eleven sisters are born dead, and the younger sister hides Rathasena so that he is not eaten.

they were merchants who kept cows. They invited the Great Being to play with them. He asked, "Where shall we play?"

"Let's go to the cockfighting arena." The merchants took him there.

The Great Being said, "If I lose to any of you, I'll give you gold and gems. If you lose to me, please give me twelve packets of rice."

They gambled on cockfighting, and the merchants lost to him several times and so gave him twelve packets of rice. The Great Being was like the great Usubharāja [lord of cows]. He took the twelve packets of rice down into the cave, paid respect to his mother, placed the packets of rice on his head and spoke a verse:

> *"Mother, please kindly take these packets of rice to eat.*
> *Please take these packets of rice to eat with our kinfolk."*

He served his mother. She ate and then lamented. The kinfolk all ate the food and at nightfall were contented. The mother then kissed her son's head, stroked his back, and said, "O son, only you can help your mother and kin escape this hardship."

Rathasena spoke a verse to teach his mother:

> *"Mother, let me teach you. All you kinfolk, come and listen to the teaching.*
> *There is no happiness like the teaching, no treasure like the teaching,*
> *no world like the teaching. Worldly beings who uphold this supreme teaching are happy."*

After this teaching, Rathasena described the many great virtues of the Buddha. His mother and kin, feeling joyful, made salutations to show their respect for the teaching. The Great Being asked his mother, "What is my father's name?" She replied, "King Rathasiddha."

Seeing the difficulties of his kin, Rathasena took leave of his mother and went to see the cow herders. He gambled on cockfighting and won. This fact became generally known. King Rathasiddha heard about this and sent courtiers to bring Rathasena to audience. The courtiers quickly brought him. He paid respect and spoke like a lord of the lions. King Rathasiddha said, "Son, play dice with me."

The Great Being replied, "Your Majesty, if I lose, I will offer myself to you. If you lose, please give me twelve packets of rice."

In the first round of dice, the king lost. In the second round, he lost, and so gave Rathasena twelve packets of rice, and placed him on the same level as himself. Rathasena paid respect to take leave, returned to his mother, paid respect to her, and spoke a verse:

> *"Your son has played dice with the king and brought back twelve packets of rice.*
> *This is delicious food. Please take it to eat."*

Next morning King Rathasiddha thought about Rathasena. He summoned courtiers and said, "Bring the boy to me." The courtiers carried out the order. The Great Being took leave of his mother, went to attend on the king, and stood in the royal courtyard. The king called him over, saying, "Son, today we will go into the palace."

Rathasena heard and went up into the palace. The king saw the boy's appearance was as beautiful, lovable, and attractive as a golden palace. He asked, "Son, what is your mother's name? What is your father's name?"

"Your Majesty, my mother and her kin are twelve sisters. Our father's name is King Rathasiddha." He said the mother and her kin were queens.

The king kissed his son's head and spoke a verse:

> *"Beloved son, like your father's own heart or own right arm,*
> *help to free your father from sorrow and lack of protection."*

Hearing this, Queen Sandhāmāra knew that she would die and felt very unhappy. She pretended to be badly sick with a fever. She thought to herself, "What device can I use?" She went to the king's bedroom, saw the boy, and felt even worse. She summoned a courtier and said, "Go and tell the king that the queen has a severe fever."

The courtier informed the king. As he loved the queen greatly, the king was very upset. He thought to himself, "What shall I do?" He ordered courtiers, "Bring doctors to treat the queen with medicines."

Queen Sandhāmāra the ogress took the medicines that the doctors brought, but still felt as upset as if she were being stabbed, knowing she would die. She sent courtiers to inform the king that her illness had not eased.

The king sent for doctors from the city to treat her, but she did not recover and did not eat. Neither did the king. She told him, "Your Majesty, there is medicine to treat this illness in Gajapura City."

The king had drums beaten to call the city folk to a meeting in the royal courtyard. He announced, "Who of you will volunteer to bring the medicine from Gajapura City? If you want gold, I will give gold; if silver, I will give silver. Whoever makes the effort to bring the medicine from Gajapura, I will appoint as a senior minister."

A minister paid respect and said, "Your Majesty, Gajapura is very far away. No human can reach there."

Queen Sandhāmāra said, "Your Majesty, please allow Rathasena, your royal son, to go and get it." The king sent for him and said, "Beloved son, please bring the medicine from Gajapura to cure the queen."

Rathasena replied, "Your Majesty, I look after my mother and her kin every day to keep them alive. I will go to Gajapura City, but please have someone look after my mother and her kin while I am away fetching the medicine."

"Beloved son, I will have people look after your mother and her kin. Don't worry."

Rathasena accepted the king's words, saying "It is good." He asked, "By what means shall I go to Gajapura? If I go by sea, I will need a ship, if by land, a carriage, if through the air, a horse. By which means do you want me to go, Your Majesty?"

"Beloved son, if you want to go through the air, choose which you like from among my thousand horses." The Great Being took leave of the king, went to a stable where there were twenty-two royal horses, chose one he liked, and gave him the name Pachi. He put a harness and all sorts of decorations on the horse, mounted, and flew up into the sky. After traveling one *yojana*, the horse did not have enough strength, so he came down to the human world to allow the horse to feed and recover his strength. He flew up again, traveled around ten *yojana* to the end of the way, and came down to eat in the Himavanta Forest. Then he flew up again, traveled twenty-two *yojana* to the end of the way, came down in the human world, unharnessed the horse, and went up into the palace. He attended on his father, paid respect, and related what had happened. Then he went to the golden palace of Queen Sandhāmāra, who said, "Beloved son, you are your mother's refuge. Please help me."

The Great Being, who had compassion for his mother and her kin, replied with a verse:

> "*Truth is of great benefit. A bodhisatta has compassion, perseverance, and endurance.*
> *I look after father and mother and have compassion for my kinfolk.*

Truth is of great benefit to the world. Truth is preeminent in the world.
Compassion is of great benefit to the world, the delight of the world."

The Bodhisatta went to his mother, raised clasped hands to take leave, and stood talking above the cave, "Mother, stay here with your kin. I will fetch the medicine from Gajapura."

The mother and sisters wept and wailed until they collapsed from fatigue like a sal forest buffeted by the wind. He paid respect to his mother and went to his father. Then Queen Sandhāmāra prepared a letter and gave it to the Great Being, who tied it on the horse's neck.[6] He went up into the palace and got dressed. Mounting the horse, he flew into the air, traveled one *yojana* to the end of the way, and then flew a further four *yojana*, five *yojana*, six *yojana*, seven *yojana*, eight *yojana*, nine *yojana*, ten *yojana*. As he flew, the ornaments on the horse's hooves sounded like the noise of the clouds. Hearing the sound of the hooves rising up to the Paranimmittava Savatti[7] level, the gods clapped their hands. Lightning flashed and thunder rumbled in the sky. Mount Meru bowed down like rattan shoots singed by fire. Hailstones fell. The ocean was churned into waves. Lord Sakka, king of the gods, applauded. Lord Brahma made salutations. The great earth 240,000 *yojana* thick could not remain still and roared like thunder a thousand times, ten thousand times, a hundred thousand times, echoing fearfully everywhere.

Through the power of the horse Pachi, the Bodhisatta flew ten *yojana* to the end of the way and saw the ashram of a rishi. He descended, unharnessed the horse, fed him grass and food, released him, placed the horse tack near the ashram, and went to sleep.

Inside the ashram, the rishi had heard the sound of the horse and wondered what it was. He came out, saw the horse, and thought to himself, "Whose horse is this?" He approached the horse, stroked its back, and saw the letter tied on its neck. He opened the letter, read it, and thought, "King Rathasiddha is in love with Queen Sandhāmāra. She is sending the king's son to the land of the ogres so that an ogre will eat him. This boy is King Rathasiddha's son called Rathasena. He should be the husband of Kaṅrī,

6. In the folktale, in this letter Sandhāmāra instructs her daughter to kill and eat Rathasena.
7. The sixth and highest level of the heavens, the realm of gods who lord over the creation of others.

Sandhāmāra's daughter and should rule in Gajapura." He wrote, changing the words in the letter,[8] and tied it back on the horse's neck. He approached the Great Being, who was still asleep, lifted his cloth, and looked at his foot. "This is a Great Being who will achieve full enlightenment. I am very fortunate to meet him." He acclaimed the virtue of the Bodhisatta, saying, "This boy is the shoot of a future Buddha. He will become a Buddha." He woke him up.

Rathasena paid respect to the rishi and said, "Good sir, I came from Kutāra City."

The rishi asked, "What is your name? Who are your mother and father?"

"My father is King Rathasiddha. My mother is one of twelve sisters who are the king's queens."

The Great Being then asked for a blessing with a verse:

> "*Good sir, may I have your blessing for success in my aim?*
> *May I enjoy happiness and have power like the gods? Grant me this.*"

To give his blessing, the rishi spoke a verse:

> "*As the Buddha brought happiness and prosperity to all the Sakya people*
> *by victory over the demons by the great bodhi tree, may you have such a victory.*"

The Great Being harnessed the horse, paid farewell to the rishi, and flew up into the air on the horse. He traveled ten *yojana* to the end of the way, and then another twenty *yojana*, thirty *yojana* to the end of the way through the power of the horse. The gods saluted the Bodhisatta with flowers of various kinds. Seeing the flowers, the horse was pleased.

The Great Being saw some demons and their territory.[9] Feeling afraid, he asked the horse, "Pachi, what shall we do?"

"Don't worry. I can defeat these demons."

An army of demons came through the air. Pachi roared loudly, shaking the heavens. Some areas were cloaked in smoke, and others were as bright as flames.

8. In the folktale, the rishi changes the letter to instruct the daughter to marry Rathasena.

9. In the folktale, there is no battle with a demon army, and it is clear at this point that the place they have reached is Gajapura.

The demons and their chief were shocked by this noise. The Great Being saw the demon chief and many troops flying through the air, magically enlarging their bodies from one to ten *yojana* and conjuring them in different forms, some as cows, some as buffalos, some as tigers, some as lions, some as leopards,[10] some as bears, some as rhinoceroses, some as pigs, some as *garuḍa*, some as eagles, some as *kumbhaṇḍa*, some white, some green, some black, some with a thousand arms holding various weapons.

The Great Being thought to himself, "We're in big trouble. What should we do?" As he was scared to death, he gave thought to the virtue of his mother, the virtue of the rishi, and the virtue of all the gods, then uttered a prayer in a verse:

> "*My troops are the true merit of looking after my mother.*
> *O gods, be my refuge, protect me so I may attain enlightenment.*
> *All gods, nāga, gandhabba, and various ogres such as asura, protect me.*
> *May my true merit defeat the demon chief.*"

Pachi took the Great Being toward the demon chief. The Bodhisatta untied the letter from the horse's neck and threw it down on the ground. Seeing the Bodhisatta and the letter, the demon chief had his troops stand down. He invited the Great Being to come down from the sky. He read the letter, placed it on his head, invited the Great Being to sit on a royal throne, paid respect to him, and went to inform Kaṅrī.

When she heard, Kaṅrī blurted out happily, "I shall escape suffering now!" Thirty ladies prepared various delicious sweets. She took them to the Great Being and said, "You have come from so far away. Please eat these sweets that I have prepared, this whole golden tray full." She invited him to eat fruit and then asked, "Of all the fruits, do you like the sweet ones or those of strong taste?"

"O fair of face, fruits with a strong taste are better."

The Bodhisatta's beautiful appearance stirred love in all the women. They invited him to sit on a great dais and gathered around him like stars around the moon. He was surrounded by gods and nonhumans like an emperor surrounded by 108 kings. When the Great Teacher was relating this, he spoke a verse:

10. เสือเหลือง, *suea lueang*, yellow tigers.

All the gods came to surround him and offer their cities, saying,
"We offer you our excellent cities
with many palaces, walls and forts."
All the ladies paid homage and offered their residences to him.
The only greater happiness is attaining nibbāna, the ultimate happiness.
He was like a nāga king, surrounded by lady nāga,
or like a lord of the lions, surrounded by a pride of lions.

The ministers decorated the city like a heavenly city with ornaments all around under guard. The Great Being entered the city, went to the palace, and was anointed to rule the realm as King Rathasena. He presented various articles such as gold, silver, cloths, and ornaments to the generals and soldiers and sent all the retainers home. He ruled in Gajapura for seven full months.

Then the horse said to him, "King Rathasena, you have abandoned your mother. What are you doing in this city?"

"O horse, I abandoned my mother and came to this city where I am surrounded by ladies like Lord Sakka, king of the gods, surrounded by lesser gods and goddesses."

One day, he left the palace on his own, came to find Pachi, saw that Pachi was angry, and thus asked, "What are you angry at me for?" He fed the horse, who ate and then said, "King Rathasena, you may stay in this city, but I'm going to Kutāra City."

"O horse, you have been of great help to me. Is that why you're angry?"

"King Rathasena, what I now tell you is the truth. The ogres will kill you to eat. You will die like a *nāga* eaten by a *garuḍa*, or like a man getting lost listening to the words of his wife and not paying attention to the life of his mother. An evil woman will destroy the life of her husband."

King Rathasena went up to the palace and sought out Kaṅrī. He sat on a bed and feigned having a fever.

Near dawn, the Bodhisatta thought of his mother and could not stifle his sorrow. Through his tears, he pronounced a verse:

"Mother, how are you? How should I go to find you?
I have the feeling that if I am still alive you will see me again."

He went in to sleep in the bedroom. In the morning, ministers went to audience and found he was missing. They enquired from the ladies, heard he was sick, and went home.

The ladies surrounding the Great Being said, "Sire, please find a way to get rid of your illness"

"O fair of face, in this city the illness will not abate. I will go to play in a park, then the illness should abate."

The ladies asked, "King Rathasena, how many *yojana* must you go into a park?"

"Only about ten."

"There is a park where, if you go only twelve *yojana*, it is as delightful as a park in the heavens."

The Great Being was happy to hear this. "My illness will abate." He left the palace, sat on a golden throne in a palanquin surrounded by many troops and people playing music. The ladies ordered the troops, "Tomorrow the king will travel to the park." Courtiers had drums beaten all around Gajapura to summon people to the royal courtyard.

Pachi was happy to show off his strength. He flew up into the air and made noise that echoed ten *yojana* around. All the gods up to Lord Brahma made salutations. The horse returned to the earth, and all the officers acclaimed him: "Our king's horse has great power."

Ladies dressed in white walked along on the right of the Great Being, and those dressed in yellow and carrying whisks walked at the front, while those dressed in various colors walked at the back and all around. The Great Being, surrounded by people like the moon surrounded by stars, traveled to the gate of the park. Seeing him, the thousand ogres who guarded the gates opened only one celestial gate, which required a thousand ogres to open and close.

The female retainers escorted Queen Kaṅrī into the park, which was refreshingly shady with many different trees including *khum*,[11] champaka, ironwood, teak, night jasmine, and coral tree, with beautiful flowers and fruits. Also there were many flowers including cockscomb, silk tree, benzoin, thirty-flower, elephant's tail herb, and sugar. Around the outside were banyan trees with flowers and fruit. The ladies heard the joyful calls of various birds including wild cocks, *hatthaliṅga*, peacocks, *prahit*,[12] sparrows, and cranes, echoing around.

11. กุ่ม, *khum*, *Crateva religiosa*, spider tree, temple plant
12. ประทิต, may be mythical, appears in the Julaphon chapter of Mahachat.

The Great Being asked the ladies, "O fair of face, where are the trees called ironwood and mountain ironwood?"[13]

"Your Majesty King Rathasena, the trees you mention are in the Nandana Park."

The Great Being made a prayer, saluting the Buddha's ironwood and mountain ironwood trees. The tree spirits heard and responded with a great commotion of salutations, saying, "You will achieve full enlightenment!"

The Great Being reached up his arm to pick fruits and was very happy. He had the officers inspect the troops. When they reached the gate, he had the thousand ogres open it for them to leave the park. Queen Kaṅrī followed behind. They returned to the city and entered the palace. Retainers played music, sang, and danced. He went to sit on the jeweled throne surrounded by many people, looking like Lord Sakka, king of the gods. He spoke to Queen Kaṅrī, "Please have the people play entertainments."

She had the courtiers play music, sing, dance, and have entertainments. King Rathasena trickily encouraged Queen Kaṅrī to drink liquor, while he drank none. She became drunk and collapsed down on the throne, saying, "The eyes of the twelve sisters are hanging above the fire-kitchen, sire."

He asked, "Is there medicine to make their eyes bright again?"

She replied, "There is a packet of holy medicine for treating eyes hanging there too. Another packet when emptied out becomes a mountain. Another becomes a forest. Another, the wind. Another, fire. Another, rain. Another, clouds. Another, the ocean."

The Great Being happily thought to himself, "I will see my mother's face again." While Queen Kaṅrī was asleep, he took the packets of medicine, mounted Pachi, and escaped at midnight while she was still asleep.

When Queen Kaṅrī woke and found he was not there, she beat her breast and set out in pursuit. The Great Being emptied a packet of medicine, which turned into a mountain covered with trees. She still kept following him. He scattered another packet, which became a forest. She still followed him. He scattered another packet, which became fire, and another which became wind.[14] She still followed him. He scattered another packet, which became rain. She still followed him. He scattered another packet, which became

13. บุนนาค, *Mesua ferrea*, Lankan ironwood, said to be tree under which four Buddhas (Mangala, Sumana, Revatha, Sobhitha) achieved enlightenment.

14. The Thai translator omitted the wind.

clouds. She still followed him. He scattered another packet, which became an ocean. She halted. She looked at him from afar and could not hold back her tears. While crying, she pronounced a verse of lamentation:

> *"Beloved husband, I weep and lament out of love for you,*
> *but you do not miss me at all.*
> *Without you, I must die. Why live in sorrow and pain?*
> *I have not made merit. While still wandering in the cycle,*
> *may I be with my beloved husband forever, never parted."*

When the Bodhisatta knew that she had composed herself, he replied with compassion, "In truth, you have been very good to me, but my mother and father have been good to me even more by a hundred times, a thousand times, a hundred thousand times." He lamented further in a verse:

> *"Fair Kaṅrī, don't worry. I shall attain enlightenment as a Buddha*
> *and provide release for all beings. I am suffering because of my beloved mother.*
> *I wish to attain full enlightenment. O Kaṅrī,*
> *anyone who does not pine for their mother and kin as their refuge is lost.*
> *Henceforth you must follow me like a mother cow following a calf."*

He rode Pachi up in the air. Kaṅrī stood below, dark with sorrow. Her heart broke into seven pieces, and she died by the shore of the ocean.[15]

The Great Being traveled to Kutāra City. Queen Sandhāmāra saw him coming from afar. She went to the palace, feeling so upset that her heart broke into seven pieces and she died.[16]

The Bodhisatta carried the holy medicine into the cave and put it on the eyes of his mother and sisters. Their eyes became bright again. They could see. The Bodhisatta took them into the city. King Rathasiddha established all twelve as major queens and lived very happily together with them.

Later King Rathasiddha anointed his son Rathasena to succeed as ruler of the realm. He ruled with justice and gave support to the people from then on.

The Great Teacher ended his sermon by saying, "O monks, in the past when I was a bodhisatta, I showed gratitude to my mother

15. In the folktale, Kaṅrī does not die at this point but later goes blind and dies from sorrow. Rathasena comes back to find her and himself dies with her corpse in his arms.
16. In the folktale, Rathasena clubs her to death.

and kinfolk." Then he pronounced the Noble Truths and made the birth connections as a final verse, translated as follows: "Queen Sandhāmāra was reborn as Devadatta; the horse as Kaṇṭhaka;[17] the Thousand-Eyed Lord as Anuruddha; the rishi as Sāriputta; King Rathasiddha as the Buddha's father, King Suddhodana; the mother as Queen Mahāmāyā; other kin as the followers of Buddhism; Kaṅrī as Yasodharā, the mother of Rāhula; King Rathasena as I, refuge of the world, the one of supreme merit and enlightenment, the one who needs no teacher. May you all remember this *jātaka* as related here."

17. A favorite horse of Prince Siddhārtha.

SAMUDDAGHOSA

P1 *Samuddaghosajātaka*

สมุททโฆสชาดก

INTRODUCTION

Samuddaghosa is the leading story in collections of the Fifty Jātaka from Thailand, Burma, Cambodia, Laos, and the Mon country. The origin of the story is unknown. It is referenced in two old Thai poems, *Thawathotsamat* (Twelve Months) and *Nirat hariphunchai*, which probably date to the late fifteenth or early sixteenth century. A version of the story in the *kham chan* genre was begun in the seventeenth century. King Narai commissioned Phra Maharatchakhru, head of the brahman department, to start the work, and continued it himself after the official died, but it was completed only in 1849 by Phra Poramanuchit Chinorot, a son of King Rama I, historian, and litterateur who became Supreme Patriarch.

When the Great Teacher was living at the Jeta Grove and staying in dependence on Sāvatthi City, he spoke of Lady Bimbā Yasodharā as a starting point for a sermon and thus told the life of Samuddaghosa, which the members of the Buddhist Councils[1] called in Pali "Samuddaghosa."

In truth, one day the monks gathered in the teaching hall to talk about the Buddha giving up the realm to have Lady Bimbā Yasodharā. "O friends, our Great Teacher gave up the realm, traveled to another city, demonstrated the sixty-four main arts of knowledge, and thus obtained Lady Bimbā."

1. สังคีติกาจารย์, *sangkhitikajan*, saṅgītikācariya, alluding to the early gatherings that debated the content of the Buddha's teachings.

Hearing the monks' words through his divine power of hearing, the Great Teacher came down from his fragrant quarters to the gathering, sat on a seven-jeweled pulpit, and spoke with a voice like Lord Brahma, asking the monks what they were talking about. The monks told him. The Vanquisher of Māra said, "Not only in this present life did I give up my father, my mother, and the realm to travel to another city for Bimbā; in past lives I did the same." With that he fell silent. The monks, who wished to know a story from the past, asked him to tell the tale.

In the past when King Vindadatta ruled in Brahmapura City with a major queen named Devadhitā, a bodhisatta passed from the Tusita realm down into Queen Devadhitā's womb. At the time of birth, there was a wondrous event, a loud noise throughout the world, and hence they gave the Bodhisatta the name Prince Samuddaghosa [roar of the ocean]. When the Bodhisatta was sixteen years old, his appearance was beautiful. He had studied the arts of knowledge to become expert. His reputation spread throughout the world.

At that time there was another king, called King Sirisīhanaragutta, ruling the city of Rammapura with a queen called Kanakavatī and a daughter called Princess Vindumatī, who was very beautiful and had perfect manners. The princess heard word going around about the handsomeness of the Bodhisatta, and she craved all day and every day to see him.

King Sirisīhanaragutta had built a shrine to the guardian deities as a city pillar at a location in the center of the city. On every eighth, fourteenth, and fifteenth day of the lunar cycle he went to worship there. When the princess went to worship the guardian spirits at the city pillar shrine, she dressed in regalia and went in a golden palanquin, shaded by a short white parasol and surrounded by around twelve thousand maids-in-waiting and musicians. At the guardian shrine, she made three circuits, entered the shrine, paid respect, and prayed with a verse:

> "*Prince Samuddaghosa, whose great power spreads throughout the earth,*
> *whose glory makes even lotuses happy and joyful—*
> *if I can have this prince for a husband as I wish,*
> *I will worship you more than this.*"

Having made this pledge to the gods, she returned home, thinking about the Bodhisatta all the time.

At that time, four brahmans from Rammapura city traveled to the royal capital of Brahmapura. The Bodhisatta was sitting on an elephant under a white umbrella, surrounded by a four-limbed retinue of soldiers and musicians, on his way to the royal park. He looked as beautiful as Lord Amarinda surrounded by deities traveling to the heavenly garden. Seeing the Bodhisatta, the four brahmans went to admire him and offered a blessing in loud voices. Hearing this, the Bodhisatta asked the brahmans in a verse:

"You all look thin and dark. Did you have trouble on the way?
What city do you come from?
And for what purpose have you come to this country?"

The four brahmans spoke a verse in reply:

"Sire, we are all from Rammapura city.
We heard word spreading and hence came to see your appearance."

The Bodhisatta invited the four brahmans into the park. After enjoying the park, he found a place to rest and asked the four brahmans, "What is extraordinary in Rammapura?"

"King Sirisīhanaragutta, who rules Rammapura, his queen called Kanakavatī, and one daughter called Vindumatī, who is so beautiful that no lady of equal beauty exists. Many kings who would like to have her have sent gifts and missives to King Sirisīhanaragutta to ask for her hand, but he has not presented her to anyone. These are the wonders of Rammapura."

Delighted by this news, the Bodhisatta presented five hundred of gold to each of the brahmans. In the evening, he returned home. The next morning, he went to attend on his father and mother, and took leave to go see the princess in a verse:

"Father and mother, may I take leave to depart for a fine city named
Rammapura?
If I have the opportunity, I will go to this city,
where a king named Sirisīhanaragutta rules the realm.
His daughter is peerless, in appearance like a heavenly maiden.
I wish to see her splendor."

His father and mother both embraced the Bodhisatta and sadly lamented while they forbade him to go with a verse:

"Listen, beloved son, we two are your parents.
When we are apart from you, we feel desolate.
How can we live? If you wish to go, delay first.
We will send an envoy to ask for this princess."

The Bodhisatta begged to be allowed to go himself until they agreed. He summoned the four brahmans to eat a meal and presented each of them with another five hundred of gold. At nightfall, he handed his lute (*phin*) to a priest-counselor's son, handed a bundle of regalia to a courtier's son, and invited both of them along with the four brahmans to leave the city and go along the road. Through his power as a bodhisatta, they reached Rammapura City within one night. The Bodhisatta halted to bathe outside the city.

On that day Princess Vindumatī had returned from the guardian deity shrine at the city pillar and gone to attend on her father. When the Bodhisatta had dressed and put on his regalia, he went to the guardian deity shrine. All the people who saw the Bodhisatta were amazed and could not take their eyes off him because he was more beautiful than ordinary people. The Bodhisatta returned from the shrine and entered the palace to attend on King Sirisīhanaragutta. He sat down and played the lute in front of the king. The beautiful sound of the lute captivated everyone who heard it in the city. The king watched the Bodhisatta without blinking, as did the princess.

The king was very pleased. He summoned the four brahmans and asked them, "The young man playing the lute over there, who looks more beautiful than any other man, whose son is he?"

The brahmans replied that he was the son of King Vindadatta, who ruled in Brahmapura, and his name was Prince Samuddaghosa. The king was charmed. He came down from the throne, approached the Bodhisatta, embraced him, kissed his head, and said, "Intent on giving up your realm without regret, you decided to come to this city."

The Bodhisatta replied, "I heard that your accumulated merit is the most excellent in the world. I made the effort to come in the hope of offering myself as a servant beneath the dust of the royal foot."

The king was happy to hear these words. He brought his daughter and the Bodhisatta along with courtiers to the guardian deity shrine and poured water over them from a golden bowl to anoint the couple in unison under a single white umbrella. The Bodhisatta and princess entered a golden palanquin together and returned from the shrine, surrounded by royal retainers. They entered the palace and stayed together in the same residence.

King Sirisīhanaragutta ordered preparation of gifts and a missive informing King Vindadatta that Prince Samuddaghosa had been betrothed and gone to stay in the same residence with the princess, and inviting the king to come for a wedding ceremony in the future. He had an envoy take the missive and gifts to Brahmapura and present them to the king.

King Vindadatta listened to the missive, looked at the gifts, and was pleased. He arranged a four-limbed army and presents, and had the envoy escort him and his queen along the road to Rammapura. King Sirisīhanaragutta and the Bodhisatta came out to greet King Vindadatta and invite him to enter the city. A royal wedding ceremony was arranged. The two kings and queens offered blessings to the Bodhisatta and princess. King Vindadatta addressed King Sirisīhanaragutta in a verse praising the wisdom and power of the couple:

"Our prince and princess come from separate but friendly royal lineages,
separate from times past, but both royal and with friendly relations.
Your realm is like ours; our realm like yours. We are like the same people.
Our hardships are the same. We share the same happiness and hardship.
Henceforth may happiness increase for both of us."

King Sirisīhanaragutta was happy to hear these words. He replied with a verse:

"Excellent king, best of men, your words are good, of benefit for both sides.
We will always be friends. May we act in this way until death."

King Vindadatta and his queen were happy at these words. They stayed in Rammapura for about a month before taking leave from King Sirisīhanaragutta and traveling home. The Bodhisatta stayed in the residence with the princess, and they enjoyed bliss together all the time.

One day, Princess Vindumatī told the Bodhisatta, "I am going to the shrine to worship the guardian spirit in fulfilment of a pledge I made." The Bodhisatta replied, "Fair of face, what was the pledge?" The princess replied with a verse:

"Hearing your reputation, I desired you as husband, thought of you night and day,
so I made a pledge asking the god in the guardian shrine to fulfill my desire."

Hearing this, the Bodhisatta wished to tell her about the past, so he spoke a verse:

"Fair of face, when four brahmans came, I questioned them and heard about you.
I then thought about you constantly until love gripped my heart as if I was mad.
I thus left my father, mother, and the realm without a care for my own life,
thinking only of having you in the future. So I came to Rammapura, your home."

The Bodhisatta took the princess to the guardian shrine to fulfill the pledge with offerings of popped rice, flowers, and floral scents, then returned to the residence.

More than a year later, the Bodhisatta traveled in a golden palanquin with the princess, along with a retinue, to visit the royal park.

At that time, there was a *vijjādhara* staying around the peak of Mount Kelāsa, which shines like silver. He took his wife to gather various flowers to adorn themselves. Holding a sword in one hand and the sheath in the other, he had his wife sit on his lap and flew into the air.

Another *vijjādhara* was staying around the peak of Mount Sudassana, which has an aura like gold. He took his wife to gather magnolia flowers to adorn themselves. Holding a sword, he flew into the air on his own. The two *vijjādhara* met in midair and challenged each other's powers, leading to a fight. The *vijjādhara* carrying his wife was slashed and wounded all over his body. Smothered with blood like a coating of lacquer and at the end of his strength, he fell into the middle of the royal park. The winning *vijjādhara* took the other's wife away.

The Bodhisatta came down from his residence in the royal park and invited the priest-counselor's son and courtier's son to go for a walk in the park. When he saw the *vijjādhara* lying there, he approached and questioned him. The *vijjādhara* told him what had happened. The Bodhisatta was concerned. He had the *vijjādhara* carried to the residence, where a doctor tended to him. After about five days, the *vijjādhara* returned to normal.

Feeling very grateful, he offered his sword to the Bodhisatta, saying, "This sword is powerful. Hold it in your hand and you can fly." Then he took leave of the Bodhisatta.

The Bodhisatta invited the princess to visit the Himavanta Forest. She sat on his lap as he held the sword in his hand and flew up into the air. He turned his face to the north and saw the mountains in the Himavanta Forest—the silver mountain, golden mountain, gem mountain, and seven-gem mountain, five hundred *yojana* high, a hundred tall peaks and 84,000 small peaks, with various precious stones. There were trees of plenty, and groups of *kinnara* and *kinnari* playing music and singing together all the time. There were herds of deer, elephants, lions, rhinoceroses, tigers, and horses. The Bodhisatta flew up onto a mountain. He collected various flowers for the princess and gathered various good-tasting fruit for them to share. They enjoyed bathing in the rivers and streams. They went to stay in a cave through the night.

The royal servants were alarmed by the absence of the Bodhisatta and princess. They looked all around the forest without finding them. In distress, they hurried to attend on King Sirisīhanaragutta and inform him. The king instructed them to make enquiries in Brahmapura, suspecting that the Bodhisatta had gone to visit his father and mother. The courtiers went to inquire in Brahmapura but found no news. They returned and informed King Vindadatta with a verse:

"The prince and the princess went to visit the royal park and have disappeared.
We searched without success. The king sent us here to inform you."

King Vindadatta and his queen were distressed, as if their hearts would break. Unable to eat or sleep, grieving together at their loss, they spoke a verse:

"Alas, alas! Both cities are lost. Alas, alas!
We are lost. The prince and princess have disappeared.
Where have they gone? Why have they abandoned us without thinking?
Why have they abandoned their countries? Why have they disappeared?
Why has no one seen them? As things are, we fear they may not be found.
Separated from our children, how can we live on?"

The courtiers took their leave and returned to inform King Sirisīhanaragutta that they had no news. The kings of both cities sent courtiers out to wait for news in the forest.

The Bodhisatta enjoyed visiting the Himavanta Forest for about two months, then flew up into the sky with the princess to the peak of Mount Kelāsa. Seeing a golden city with groups of *kinnara* dancing beautifully, they came down from the sky to the golden city.

King Duma, the lord of the *kinnara*, saw the Bodhisatta and was amazed because no human had ever come to that country. "This must be someone of exceptional power, and there is only one name famed in the world at this time—Prince Samuddaghosa." King Duma called the Bodhisatta to come and sit near him. The Bodhisatta and princess raised their clasped hands in salute. King Duma embraced and kissed the Bodhisatta and invited him to be his viceroy with a verse:

> "*This happy city is the fruit of accumulated merit.*
> *The walls are made of natural gold. Let me present you with half the realm.*"

The Bodhisatta declined, saying, "Please let us stay in your residence for about a month and then take our leave." King Duma agreed. The Bodhisatta spent about one month in the golden city, took leave of King Duma, and flew through the air to the Anotatta Lake, which had seven gems, one landing for ogres and deities, one landing for rishi and *vijjādhara*, and one landing for Buddhas, Buddhists, and *arahant*. The Bodhisatta enjoyed staying on the bank of the Anotatta Lake for about a month and then flew through the air to Chaddanta Lake, which had an expanse of a hundred *yojana*, completely without water plants, surrounded by six mountains—silver mountain, golden mountain, jewel mountain, jet[2] mountain, orpiment[3] mountain, and crystal mountain. When the Bodhisatta was staying at Chaddanta Lake, he thought back to a previous life and spoke a verse to the princess:

> "*In a past life, at the most beautiful Chaddanta Lake,*
> *I was Chaddanta, king of the elephants,*
> *with a herd of around sixty thousand elephants,*
> *living in this golden cave.*"

2. *anchan*, อัญชัน, añjana.
3. หรดาล, *horadan*, a mineral with red and golden variants, orpiment, realgar. The Pali is jātihiṅgula, vermilion.

The princess could also remember a previous life and so told the Bodhisatta, "In that life I was your consort, with the name Mahā Subhaddā." While the two were talking together in this way, they went down to play gaily in the water of the lake and gathered various flowers to adorn themselves. Both enjoyed themselves in that enchanting place, forgetting to think of their homes. He took the princess flying up to see a seat about one cubit high and seventy cubits long and broad, made of a sheet of gold studded with gems, set amidst the landscape. Looking around this beautiful realm, the Bodhisatta spoke a verse:

> "*Great queen, let us two visit this place of cat's eye and crystal,*
> *stay here for a time, and later return to Rammapura City.*"

They flew down where there were two wells, one full with ordinary water and the other full of scented water.

Here is inserted a question. Why are both these wells full? The answer is that in the past *vijjādhara* brought water for bathing and aromatic materials for scenting their bodies and sat relaxing on this seat.

The Bodhisatta and princess bathed, perfumed themselves with scented water from the well, and went to sleep on the seat.

A *vijjādhara* came flying across the sky, saw the Bodhisatta and princess sleeping on the seat, stole the sword, and flew away. When the Bodhisatta and princess awoke and found the sword missing, they were troubled to the point of despair. The Bodhisatta instructed the princess on the dhamma to allay her sorrow.

She asked him, "How can we go anywhere?"

The Bodhisatta replied, "I think we can cross the water to the other side." He took her down to the shore, saw a floating log, and swam out to drag it to the shore. He asked her to sit on the log and they set off with the aim of reaching the other side. When they reached the middle of the waters, a great storm blew up. Crashing waves broke the log into two pieces and separated them.

In the morning, the princess reached the shore, could not see her husband, and wept sorrowfully with tears streaming, thinking she would die, until she passed out and collapsed down on the ground.

When she recovered, she spread her clothes to dry, bundled up her ornaments, and followed the tracks of an elephant to Maddaraṭṭha City.

On entering the city, she met an aged lady and replied to her questioning that she was going to Rammapura City. The old lady asked, "Why have you come to this place? Do you have any relatives here you wish to visit?" When the princess replied that she had no relatives, the old lady invited the princess to stay with her.

In the morning, she sent the old lady to sell her jeweled ring to a rich man. When the rich man asked the price, the old lady replied, "This ring is priceless, but I need only five cartloads of gold." The rich man took the ring and gave her the gold she asked for. The old lady had people drive the carts home and gave the gold to the princess.

The princess redeemed male and female slaves and had a beautiful house built along with a rest house for ascetics and brahmans. In the rest house, she had pictures drawn telling the tale of her wedding at the guardian spirit shrine, the two of them sleeping on the golden seat, the two sitting on the bombax log in the sea, the fierce wind and waves, the log breaking into two, and the two of them drifting apart. She instructed the guards to watch for any ascetics or brahmans who came to stay in the rest house, to prepare seats for them, and to inform the cooks so they could prepare food in the morning. She also instructed the attendants to observe the behavior of those who stayed there and to tell her if any behaved in an unusual way. She gave the attendants these firm instructions. She still thought of her husband constantly.

The Bodhisatta floated on the waters without reaching the shore.

Here there is inserted a question. What bad deeds caused the Bodhisatta and princess to attempt crossing the sea and become separated?

The answer is that in a past life the Bodhisatta and princess were royals who went to bathe in a river during the hot season. When a novice came paddling a boat along the bank, the two royals beat the water with their hands, stirring up waves that swamped the novice's boat. When the boat sank, the novice swam off, crying out loud. The two helped him up onto land. For just this bad deed to the novice, as a result of high spirits, the Bodhisatta and princess had to swim in an ocean for five hundred lives.

When the Bodhisatta had been on the water for seven days, the goddess Maṇi Mekhalā was returning from a convocation of the gods to inspect the surface of the ocean, as was her duty. She saw the Bodhisatta and went to inform Lord Indra, who chided Maṇi Mekhalā for neglecting her duty and not giving assistance to a worthy individual. He told her to hurry to save him from the sea.

Maṇi Mekhalā told Lord Indra that the Bodhisatta was in this trouble because a *vijjādhara* had stolen the sword from him. Hearing this, Lord Indra raged at the *vijjādhara* and dispatched a jeweled club to fly up high and swing down threateningly over the head of the *vijjādhara*, saying angrily, "Hey, *vijjādhara*, you thief, why did you steal the sword from the Bodhisatta? If you don't return it, I'll split your head into seven pieces with this jeweled club. Don't think you can escape. Return it now."

In fear of Lord Indra, the *vijjādhara* returned the sword to the Bodhisatta in the middle of the ocean. The Bodhisatta gripped the sword, flew up into the air, and landed in Maddaraṭṭha City, intent on having something to eat and searching for his wife. In order to enter the city unknown, he took off all his regalia, put them in a hiding place, and disguised himself as a brahman. When he entered the city, the city folk told him to go and stay in the rest house built by the princess. The Bodhisatta went there and received a warm welcome including food. After eating, he examined the pictures in the rest house and saw they told a story like his separation. He grieved, but then recovered and laughed. The attendant went to tell the princess of this unusual behavior. She rushed there, saw the Bodhisatta, and was overjoyed. She spoke a verse:

> *"I was sad and troubled by separation from my husband.*[4]
> *Now my sorrow is ended, my fear is ended.*
> *Whatever sorrow and fear I had is now ended."*

The Bodhisatta and princess went to the residence she had built. They bathed in fragrant water and dined happily. The Bodhisatta went to fetch the ornaments he had hidden and put them on. After staying there happily for a few days, he had the brahmans come to attend on him and presented them with the rest house and residence along with all the slaves and gold. He took the princess out of that city, flying through the air for a whole night. They reached the royal park at dawn and went to stay in the residence.

On seeing the couple, the keepers of the royal park rushed to inform King Sirisīhanaragutta, who happily went to the park with his queen and their

4. This first line was improvised by the Thai translator.

retinue. He embraced and kissed the Bodhisatta and asked him to relate what had happened from the beginning to their return. After that was done, King Sirisīhanaragutta had the city decked out beautifully, anointed the Bodhisatta, and presented him with the realm, including power over the whole city. The king renounced to become a rishi, practiced meditation until he achieved the treasure of insight, and after death was born in the Brahma world.

When King Vindadatta heard that the Bodhisatta had become ruler of Rammapura, he sent a courtier to present him with the realm. He renounced to become a rishi, practiced meditation until he achieved the treasure of insight, and after death was born in the Brahma world.

The Bodhisatta had almshouses built in both cities for giving alms at all times. The courtiers and people who followed his advice and were established in the five precepts were reborn after death in the heavens.

> After the Master of the Dhamma came to the end of the story of Samuddaghosa, he explained the birth connections: "At that time, Devadatta was the *vijjādhara* who stole the sword; King Suddhodana was King Vindadatta; Queen Mahāmāyā was Devadhitā; Ānanda was the priest-counselor's son; Rāhula was the courtier's son; Sāriputta was King Sirisīhanaragutta; Mahāpajāpati Gotami was Kanakavatī; Moggallāna was King Duma; Anuruddha was Lord Indra; Uppalavanna was Maṇi Mekhalā; Bimbā was Princess Vindumatī; and the Tathāgata was Prince Samuddaghosa."

PRINCE PĀCITTA

P39 *Pācittakumārajātaka*

ปาจิตตกุมารชาดก

INTRODUCTION

Several stories have a close association with a place in Thailand or close by. The archaeologist Manit Wallipodom noticed that several places around the old Khmer town of Phimai in Nakhon Ratchasima (Khorat) Province are related to events in this story.[1] Two verse versions of the tale, one written in 1773 in the Thonburi era and the other in the reign of King Mongkut, also connect the story to Phimai. The first claims that the name of the town was changed to Phimai after an incident in the story where a character calls out *phi ma* ("You have come"). The second, which is only a fragment, incorporates tales about villages in the Phimai region. Both verse versions cite the *jātaka* as their source but are rather different. The *jātaka* tells the same story as the 1773 Thonburi poem, which has the style of a work passed down in oral tradition but omits the section on founding a city and also much of the colorful detail.[2] The story is illustrated in paintings at Wat Bang Yang, Bua Mat, Maha Sarakham, and Wat Thung Si Mueang, Ubon Ratchathani.

This tale is remarkable for its central female character overshadowing the Bodhisatta, defying gender stereotypes, and even temporarily becoming a man, monk, and patriarch.

When the Great Teacher was living in Vesālī City, where he went on almsround, the Refuge of the World spoke of Bimbā, who

1. Tourists are now encouraged to visit 27 places around Phimai supposedly associated with the story, guided by a map available at e-shann.com/?p=6773.
2. *Wannakam samai thonburi lem 2*, esp. (1)–(11), 283–89.

renounced as a nun, and thus gave a sermon as a *jātaka*, beginning with the Pāli "O Blessed One, guardian of the earth" as follows.

One day the monks were seated together talking in the teaching hall, saying, "O friends, when Bimbā became a nun, she had a very beautiful appearance. That should be a wonder."

At that moment, the Great Teacher in his fragrant quarters heard the words of the monks through his celestial hearing. He went to the teaching hall, sat on the pulpit, and asked the monks, "What are you talking about?" They told him.

He said, "O monks, Bimbā did not become a nun only in this life but also in past lives, and she had a very beautiful appearance then too." At that he fell silent. Wishing to hear a story from the past, the monks invited the Buddha to give a sermon as follows.

O monks, one time in the past, there was a king named Mahā Dhammarājā ruling in Brahmabandhu City with a beautiful major queen called Suvaṇṇa Devī.

At that time, the Bodhisatta passed from the world of the gods and was conceived in the womb of this queen. After ten months he was born. The king and other relatives named him Prince Pācitta. When the prince was sixteen years old, King Mahā Dhammarājā wished to have him anointed to rule the realm. A royal missive was sent to the kings of 101 cities to adorn their daughters and send them so a royal lady could be chosen as suitable to anoint as a partner for his son.

The kings of all 101 cities adorned their daughters and sent them to Brahmabandhu City. King Mahā Dhammarājā had them sit in a line in the royal courtyard and commanded his son to choose a partner. The Bodhisatta looked at the 101 princesses and was not taken by any of them. His father asked, "Beloved son, is not one of them to your liking?"

"I don't desire any of them. Sire, if you will allow, I will take leave of your royal foot and go to find a wife that I like."

"Son, I will have the astrologer predict what direction your partner is in so you can search there."[3]

3. The following passage about the astrologer, the prediction, and the umbrella

The astrologer was sent for. "My son is going in search of a partner. Find out which direction she is in, what she looks like, whose daughter she is, and of what lineage."

After examining the manual of lore, the astrologer told the king, "Your Majesty, your son's partner is of excellently meritorious character with the five features of ladyship, but now she is in the womb. Her mother is a poor widow who must plow her fields with her own strength. Through the power of the merit of the daughter in her womb, she is sheltered by an umbrella over her head, but the ordinary people cannot see it. If your son travels eastward, he will find her, sire."

Hearing this, the king could not stop his son. He said, "Beloved son, in this case you must go to find the partner you desire. May you find her as hoped. Go eastward as the astrologer says."

Prince Pācitta, the Bodhisatta, prostrated at the feet of his father and mother to take leave. He left the city and traveled eastward. In one day he covered sixty *yojana*. The next morning he reached Bārāṇasī City. Walking along he came upon a heavily pregnant woman plowing a paddy field with an umbrella sheltering her head, as the astrologer had described. He presumed, "The baby girl in her womb must be my partner."

He approached the woman and asked, "Mother, do you have no husband? Is that why you have to plow like this?"

"Sir, I have no husband, so I have to plow the field."

"Mother, if your child is born a daughter, please give her to me. I will plow in your stead."

"I agree. You plow the field."

From then on, Prince Pācitta plowed the fields. In the evening, he stored the yoke and plow at her house. He did this until her pregnancy reached the tenth month and she gave birth to a daughter who was pristinely beautiful, with the five qualities of ladyship, like an *apsara* in the heavens. No woman in the world was as beautiful. For this reason she was named Arabimba.[4] When she had grown to sixteen years old, she became the wife of Prince Pācitta, who lived happily with her for a long time.

---

over the mother do not appear in the Pali. They appear in the folk version of the story (*Wannakam samai thonburi lem 2*, 284). Perhaps the translator borrowed them from there. In the Pali, the prince takes leave of his father, travels to Bārāṇasī, comes upon the pregnant woman, and asks if she has a husband.

4. Meaning a shape or image, implying beauty. In Thai, she is called Oraphim.

One day, the Bodhisatta thought back to his mother. Tearfully he said, "I do not know how my mother is now. I will go to visit her. If I cannot see my mother, I will not live further."

The next morning, his mother-in-law asked, "Why were you crying last night?"

"Because I was thinking of my mother. I will take leave to visit her. After seeing her face, I will return. Let me entrust my wife, Arabimba, to your care."

Arabimba heard this and cried out, "Let me go with you."

He tried to discourage her. "The way there is very tough. Stay here with your mother."

The mother-in-law could not dissuade him and so tried to console her daughter, "Stay with me. The road there is dangerous. Your husband will return before long. Don't be troubled."

Having taken leave of his mother and consoled his wife, the Bodhisatta left Bārāṇasī and walked along the roads to reach Brahmabandhu safely. He went in to pay respect to his mother and father who were overjoyed to see him return.

"You have been away from us for a long time. Did you find the woman as the astrologer said?"

The Bodhisatta told them the story and said, "I thought of you and thus hastened here. I will return there and bring Arabimba to attend on you later."

One day while the Bodhisatta was away, there was a festival in Bārāṇasī. Everyone got dressed up and went along. Prince Brahmadatta, son of the king of Bārāṇasī, went with his retinue to bathe in the river. Seeing the beautiful Arabimba, he asked her, "Do you have a husband?"

"O prince, I have a husband."

"No you don't!" He dragged her off to his palace.

Thinking of her husband the Bodhisatta, Arabimba wept and lamented in a verse:

> "*In the past I must have parted a mother bird and her chick.*
> *As a result of the karma I am now parted from my husband.*"

At that moment, Prince Brahmadatta entered the palace, lustfully intent on making love. Arabimba reproached him in many ways and spoke a verse:

"You are son of the king of the realm, but I do not wish to see you.
Your body is full of piss and shit. I do not wish to be touched by your foot."

When she spoke this way, the prince was unable to force her. When he approached her, he became so heated he could not bear it and walked off to stay outside the palace.

At that time, the Bodhisatta thought of Arabimba. He quickly paid respect to his parents and traveled to Bārāṇasī. Not finding Arabimba, he asked her mother where she was.

"Prince Brahmadatta took your wife away."

The Bodhisatta went to the royal courtyard. Seeing him arrive, Arabimba said to Prince Brahmadatta, "My elder brother Pācitta has come to find me, sire."

"If that's the case, bring him up to the palace."

"I'm afraid of you. I won't bring him up."

The prince sent a courtier to fetch the Bodhisatta. He came up without knowing the mood of the prince.

Arabimba poured liquor with strong taste and offered it to Prince Brahmadatta, who got drunk and fell asleep. She took his sword and cut his throat, killing him. She quickly told the Bodhisatta, "I have killed Prince Brahmadatta. We must both flee this city at once."

The Bodhisatta was shocked and greatly troubled. He did not know how to flee. He sat with Arabimba in consternation.

At that moment the seat of Lord Sakka, king of the gods, became hot as a result of the meritorious power of the couple. He examined with his celestial eyesight and found the cause. Coming down from the world of the gods, he conjured himself as a horse, hurried to Pācitta the Bodhisatta, and said, "Mount my back, you two, and we'll flee right now."

The Bodhisatta happily obeyed. The horse flew up into the sky and came down in the forest country under a banyan tree. Lord Sakka then flew back to the world of the gods. The Bodhisatta and Arabimba stayed under the tree.

The next morning, the king could not find Prince Brahmadatta, the Bodhisatta, or Arabimba in the palace. He asked his courtiers where they had gone.

"Your Majesty, your son has been killed. None of us has seen Pācitta or Arabimba."

"Why was my son killed?"

"Your Majesty, your son brought this woman in. Perhaps she killed him."

The king fell quiet and said nothing, thinking to himself, "My son did not reside in the true dhamma. He behaved improperly and thus naturally had to die."

At that time, a forest hunter rode a buffalo out from the city into the forest and saw the Bodhisatta and Arabimba under the tree. He thought, "I'll shoot the husband and take his wife." He got down from the buffalo. Taking his crossbow, he walked up and shot the Bodhisatta dead. He put Arabimba on the buffalo's back and rode through the forest country.

Sitting on the buffalo's back, lamenting at the prospect of death, Arabimba thought up a trick. She said to the hunter, "Sitting up front here, I'm terribly scared of the buffalo's horns. Let me sit behind you."

The hunter agreed, and let her sit behind. When the buffalo had gone a little further, she said, "Let me carry your sword. You'll be able to drive the buffalo more easily."

He agreed, and passed her the sword. When the buffalo had gone a little further, she slashed off the hunter's neck with the sword and he toppled off the buffalo. She dismounted and ran back to the body of the Bodhisatta. She embraced his feet, wept, and collapsed. When she revived, she lamented, "O husband, please get up. Why are you lying in a heap of sand like this? If you were ruling a realm, you would bring courtiers and officials to take me. If you had died in the palace, your corpse would be washed with water perfumed with the scent of flowers, and there would be the sound of music. Now you are lying here dead and alone, allowing the worms to suck your pus and blood. It's not befitting."

At that moment the seat of Lord Sakka, king of the gods, appeared unusually hot. Lord Sakka gave it divine thought and knew the cause. He summoned Mātali and said, "A forest hunter has shot the Bodhisatta dead and his wife is weeping pitifully. Transform yourself into a mongoose, and I'll transform myself into a cobra, and we'll approach him." They did so and also conjured up some powerful medicine and put it in a fitting place.

The mongoose and cobra bit each another. The mongoose died first. The cobra fetched a piece of the medicine, chewed it, and spat it over the body of the mongoose. The mongoose got back up and bit the cobra to death, then brought the medicine, chewed it, and spat it over the cobra, which rose up again.

Arabimba saw this. "That is powerful medicine. I shall chew some and spit it over my husband." When she did so, the Bodhisatta came back to life and sat up.

"O fair of face, did I sleep for long?"

"You did not sleep. A hunter shot you dead." She told him about the killing of the hunter and the medicine.

The Bodhisatta praised the virtue of his wife in a verse:

> *"There is nothing that I depend on and think of except you.*
> *This is a wonder without precedent that makes my hair stand on end."*

He asked her, "O fair of face, where is the medicine?"

"I've kept it."

"Make sure you keep it safely so we can rely on it in the future."

She agreed and tied the medicine firmly to the end of her upper cloth. The couple walked until they arrived at the bank of a river. The Bodhisatta said, "O fair of face, there's no boat or raft. How can we cross?" He looked around, this way and that.

At that moment a little novice came paddling along the river in a boat. Seeing him, the Bodhisatta called out, "O young novice, please help us to cross. We are going to that side."

"O disciple, my boat is so small. How can I send you both across? One at a time is possible."

"That's fine. Send us across one at a time." The Bodhisatta got in the boat. The novice paddled him across and returned. When Arabimba got in, the novice did not go across but let the boat drift.

She asked, "Why do you not go across? Where are you taking me?"

"O disciple, I want to seize my brother's wife."

She said nothing. The novice let the current take the boat along the river.

Watching the novice disappear, the Bodhisatta was very dismayed. He looked this way and that without seeing either the novice or his wife. In tears, he spoke a verse:

> *"We two poor people were crossing the river.*
> *Now I don't see my wife. The novice is not bringing her across.*
> *I've looked every which way.*
> *My heart will break apart from sadness.*
> *I am watching the middle of the river but I don't see my wife.*
> *The animals in the water are very fierce—sharks, swordfish,*

crocodiles, and dragons. Have they eaten my wife?
The sun is about to set and the moon is rising in the sky.
Where has the novice taken her? I don't know. Nobody is as troubled as I."

He lamented as if he were mad.

The novice paddled the boat along. Arabimba looked up onto the bank, saw a fig tree covered in fruit, and thought up a trick.

"O novice, I'm terribly hungry. If I can eat some of those figs, I can live longer. Please take the boat over there to pick the fruit—quickly."

The novice steered the boat over, hitched up his lower cloth, got out, and climbed up the fig tree. Arabimba quickly got down from the boat, found thorny branches, and put them all around the tree trunk. She returned to the boat and called out, "O novice, farewell. I'm saying goodbye."

She quickly paddled the boat across to reach the bank at sunset. She left the boat and went up onto the bank, looking for her husband. She walked this way and that without finding him. In tears, she made a prayer of truth: "Now I am suffering as if to death. I don't know which way to go. If my husband has died and become a fish, let me die and become the river where he lives. If he has died and become a tusker elephant, let me die to become the forest. If he has died and become a bee, let me die and become the flower where he takes the pollen. Wherever my husband is reborn, let me die and be reborn there too. If he dies and becomes a king, let me die to become a queen."

She walked along the road to Campāka City, and went to rest in a temple. She paid respect to the Buddha image there and made a prayer of truth in a verse:

"O Blessed One, refuge and good ruler of the beings of the world,
may the two breasts of my body disappear and I become of male appearance."[5]

Through the power of this prayer, her breasts disappeared and she became of male appearance. She changed her name to be Pācitta, the name of her husband, the Bodhisatta. She stayed in Campāka City.

5. เพศชาย, *phet chai*, now the translation of "male gender," but here a translation of the Pali *vesaposo*, of male appearance. At this point in the folk version of the story, she removes her breasts and vagina, and hangs them on a tree, then returns to collect them when reversing the change later in the story.

At that time, the daughter of the king of Campāka City died of an illness. The courtiers arranged to wash her body. Learning about this, Pācitta went into the city, saw the courtiers in turmoil, approached them, and asked, "What are you doing?"

"Our king's daughter died seven days ago. We are preparing the body."

"I am a doctor. I can treat someone who died seven days ago so they come back to life."

The courtiers went to tell the king. Overjoyed to hear this, the king commanded that Pācitta be brought to audience. He asked, "Can you bring my daughter back to life?"

"Your Majesty, I can."

"What do you need for the treatment?"

"Simply surround the body with curtains." The king commanded this be done.

Pācitta paid respect to the king, went inside the curtains, untied the medicine from the end of his upper cloth, chewed it, and spat it over the body. At the first drop, the daughter opened her eyes. At the second drop, she turned over. At the third drop, she sat up. Pācitta came out from the curtains.

The king went into the curtains, saw his daughter alive again, and was overjoyed. He kissed her head, came out from the curtains, and said to Pācitta, "Let me entrust the whole realm, along with my daughter, to you. Please rule the realm in my stead."

Pācitta said, "Your Majesty, your grace is beyond all comparison. Allow me to return your realm and your daughter to you. Please allow me to be ordained, sire."

King Campāka said, "If that is what you want, it is good. I permit you to be ordained." He gave orders to prepare the requirements for a monk. Equipped with these, Pācitta went to find an elder to serve as his preceptor and was ordained as a monk. He studied the scriptures with great diligence and eventually became the patriarch of the city.

One day, Patriarch Pācitta went to find a craftsman to make a beautiful pavilion[6] and an artist to paint pictures telling the tale from the time when the Bodhisatta took Arabimba up on the horse to flee from the palace in

6. This device appears in P1 Samuddaghosa and also in P3 Sudhanu and P45 Varavaṃsa.

Bārāṇasī; to the pair dismounting and staying under the tree; the hunter shooting the Bodhisatta dead; the mongoose and cobra bringing each other back to life with medicine; Arabimba taking the medicine and bringing her husband back to life; the couple walking to the riverbank and meeting the novice in the boat; the Bodhisatta asking to cross the river in the boat; the novice returning to fetch Arabimba; and her tricking him to climb the fig tree then escaping in the boat.

When the paintings were done, the patriarch arranged for people to look after the pavilion and ordered, "If anyone who comes in to this pavilion, whether man or woman, sees these pictures, and bursts into tears, hasten to tell me." He was thinking he could meet the Bodhisatta were he to come to the pavilion.

As for Pācitta the Bodhisatta, after he was separated from Arabimba, he grieved all the time, not knowing where to find her. He forced himself to walk along the road until he reached Campāka City, where he halted to relieve his fatigue. He walked to the patriarch's pavilion, went in, and walked around viewing the pictures from the scene of leaving Bārāṇasī to the scene of meeting the novice paddling the boat at the bank of the river and asking him to send them across. Overwhelmed, he burst into tears.

The caretakers of the pavilion saw this and went to inform the patriarch, who had them fetch the Bodhisatta. The patriarch asked, "Disciple, why are you crying?"

"I was separated from my wife. I saw these pictures, which tell a similar story. That's why I cried."

"If you wish to meet your wife, have yourself ordained. Then you'll meet her for certain."

As he wanted to meet Arabimba, he agreed and was ordained as a monk.

Now that both were ordained, the Bodhisatta and the patriarch were very beautiful, like images of natural gold cast by a skilled craftsman.

From then on, the pair were happy together. The Bodhisatta examined the patriarch and noticed that his appearance was very similar to Arabimba, his wife. He became suspicious but did not know what to think, seeing that the patriarch appeared to be a man.

One day the patriarch said to the Bodhisatta, "O monk, please listen to me. I am Arabimba, your wife. I have been ordained in the city for a long time. We should both disrobe and return home."

"If that is the case, fine. But how did you become a man? I'm still suspicious."

The patriarch walked into the preaching hall, paid respect to the Buddha image, and made a prayer: "Blessed One, lord over beings of the world, let my two breasts reappear as before, and let me be of female appearance."

At the end of the prayer, the two breasts reappeared and the patriarch became a woman, Arabimba. Seeing this, the Bodhisatta was very happy. He disrobed and became a layman immediately. The couple were going to take leave of King Campāka but felt ashamed and could not go. They left Campāka City, hastened to the royal capital of Brahmabandhu, and went to pay respects to his parents and tell them the whole story.

Seeing their son and Arabimba, King Mahā Dhammarājā and his queen were overjoyed. Orders were given for a royal ceremony of anointment to install Arabimba as the major queen, to entrust the realm to the Bodhisatta to rule, and to give blessings for them to rule the realm for a long time in happiness and prosperity.

From then on, Pācitta the Bodhisatta ruled the realm with the Ten Royal Virtues, supported the people with the Four Principles of Harmony, and made merit through good works such as almsgiving. On passing away, he went to be reborn in the celestial realm of the gods.

> When the Great Teacher had given this sermon with a tale from the past, he said, "O monks, Bimbā was beautiful not only when she ordained as a nun at the present time but also in the past when she was ordained as a patriarch, as I have related here." At that, he explained the birth connections: "The little novice at that time was reborn as Lord Ajātasattu;[7] the forest hunter as Devadatta; Lord Sakka, king of the gods, as Anuruddha; Mātali as Channa;[8] King Mahā Dhammarājā as King Suddhodhana, father of the Buddha; his queen as Queen Mahāmāyā, mother of the Buddha; Arabimba as Bimbā the nun; and Prince Pācitta the Bodhisatta as the Tathāgata. Remember this *jātaka* as related here."

7. A prince of Magadha who was recruited by Devadatta to help in his plots against the Buddha, but who later recanted and became a loyal disciple.
8. Gotama's charioteer.

SUBHAMITTA

P9 *Subhamittajātaka*

สุภมิตตชาดก

INTRODUCTION

An inscription from Thawkuthathamuti temple near Pagan dated to 1265/66 CE has a curse that seems to refer to this tale: "In this life may he be separated from his beloved wife and son like King Thombameik [Subhamitta] was separated from his queen and prince." The origin of the tale is unknown. Two passages have been adapted from J547 Vessantara, one from J539 Mahājanaka, and another from the Dhammapada.

Three versions of the tale are known as poems. All follow the *jātaka* closely, with some minor additions. None are dated, but one has a lament very similar to a composition by King Rama II (*Kap nang loi*) and another mentions Samut Prakan, a town founded in that king's reign.

When the Great Teacher was staying at the Jeta Grove, he spoke of Devadatta, the man without gratitude, and for this reason gave this sermon beginning with the words "Sire, you have been careless."

The story of the present is as follows. One day, the monks were gathered in the teaching hall talking about Devadatta, the man without gratitude who did not recognize the virtue of the Great Teacher. The Victorious One came to the gathering and asked, "O monks, what are you talking about?" The monks told him. The Great Teacher said, "O monks, Devadatta showed no gratitude to me in the present life, but that is not all; in the past, he was ungrateful to me also." At that he fell silent. The monks, who wanted to know more, invited him to give a sermon, so he told this tale from the past.

In the past, a king named Subhamitta [good friend] ruled in Campā City. His younger brother named Asubhamitta [bad friend] held the position of viceroy. His queen was called Kesinī. She had two sons, the elder named Jeyyasena [victorious army] and the younger Jeyyadatta [given in victory].

The younger brother Asubhamitta thought, "As long as my elder brother lives in this city, I will not fully own the realm. I should seize power." He presented a great amount of gold, jewels, rings, and cloth to courtiers to win their support for his seizure of the throne. He also readied some troops and waited for an opportune moment. But one courtier who felt gratitude towards King Subhamitta went to inform the king with a verse:

> *"Sire, you have been careless. I have come to warn you.*
> *You must get away quickly. I will tell you what is happening.*
> *Your younger brother is planning a revolt. He will kill you tonight.*
> *Save yourself today by being vigilant."*

King Subhamitta thought, "If we fight, my brother and his troops will face a great disaster. For this reason I will flee from the city tonight." He gave rewards to his loyal courtier and sent him away. He went to the palace, embraced and kissed his two sons, and said to the queen, "Take care. Look after them well. Don't let my younger brother Asubhamitta kill them. He is planning a revolt. He will bring troops to capture and kill me tonight. I know this because a courtier told me." He bade farewell to the queen with a verse:

> *"I beg to take leave to go on my own to the Himavanta Forest,*
> *where there is danger from fierce wild animals.*
> *Do not worry whether I will survive. I will bear the hardship in the forest*
> *among the wild deer, rhinoceros, and tigers who live there all the time.*
> *I am intent on making merit. All you must stay in the slough of sensual pleasure."*

Queen Kesinī could not contain her tears.[1] "Sire, why do you say these things I don't like—that you will go on your own? Allow me to come with you. Though I may fall dead in the forest, that would be better than living separated from you. If I cannot go with you, don't expect me to live. I will light a blazing fire and jump into its midst to die. I do not wish to live.

1. The passage from here until Subhamitta's consent ("If that's so, come along as you wish") is closely modeled on the departure to the forest in the Vessantara Jātaka; see Appleton and Shaw, *Ten Great Birth* Stories, 552, 562–65; Faussböll, *Jātaka*, VI, 506–11.

I will struggle along behind you like a cow elephant following a fine tusker. Please allow me to go with you."

King Subhamitta, the Bodhisatta, forbade her. "O Kesinī, you of beautiful attributes with a body as if anointed with red sandalwood, don't come. Listen to me. How could you tolerate it? The forest is full of mosquitos, midges, and flies that will attack your body. You will lose your color and waste away from hardship. There is an animal called a python, with a huge, shiny, patterned body, that lives in the running streams. If it sees any man or woman, or a deer, it will approach, squeeze that being with its tail, and then eat it. There are also bears that cause terrible hardship; even a man cannot escape by climbing a tree. Wandering around the forest there are many fierce animals such as buffalo and wild gaur, with long, sharp-pointed horns that they use to toss people and break their bones. Don't think of coming with me, Kesinī."

"I realize the road is truly long and very difficult, but I don't fear hardship. I will use my bosom as a machete to cut the *lalang* grass and forest thorns as I follow my husband. I cannot think of being separated from you, fearing I will become a widow. I would rather put up with the danger and difficulty in the Himavanta. The hardship of being separated from a husband like a widow is true hardship. Anyone born as a woman in this world has great difficulty to find a husband. She must know many wiles of speaking well. She worries that her hips are not broad and endeavors to smash them with a wooden hammer like a cow's chin. She fears that her belly will grow big, so she eats only a little rice a day. She fears that her body will get fat and that she will not have a fine complexion. Even when it's cold enough to make teeth chatter, she must bathe at the crack of dawn. Even when it's hot, she must warm herself by a fire, hoping it will make her waist and shoulders shapely, curvy, and charming. Having had a husband, going back to being a widow would be pitiful. If I were old, it wouldn't matter, but for a young woman to be a widow is terrible suffering. Nobody likes leftovers. What would remain for me would be eternal hardship. A widow is looked down on by men. Men are not all the same—some good, some bad. When a man knows someone is a widow he thinks he can tease her to his heart's content, tug on the end of her cloth like crows swarming on a rainbow, and get into her lower cloth[2] without fearing anyone.

2. Literally, make both of them wear the same lower cloth.

"Although I am secure with many relatives, I would not escape gossip, just because of the crime of being a widow. When a river has no water, it's a waste. When a city has no ruling king, it's empty, meaningless. A woman who is a widow without a man as a partner is seen as lonely and pitiful. When a royal carriage appears, there's a flag; where a fire burns, smoke serves as a sign; a woman has rank and status because of the position of her husband—like the flag that makes a carriage look so grand that enemies dare not attack.

"I have heard the old story that when a husband is poor and in difficulty, a wife cannot hide away and escape the situation but must struggle through with him. Such women are considered as models to teach others. Not only humans but also the gods give them their blessings all the time. Even if you hand over to me the throne and all the royal wealth of silver and jewels, I have no desire for such treasure. Whatever country you wish to visit, I will not complain, but beg to follow along with you. Why do I say this? Because my royal husband has been good to me and has supported me to fulfill my every wish, so I beg to go along with you."

These words made the king sad. He sorrowed over his beloved children. He lifted the two princes onto his lap and lamented, "O beloved sons, you are used to eating fine and delicious food, but now you will eat only roots and fruit—sour and poor-tasting, awful. You are used to wearing cloths of fine cotton and silk, but now you must wear tree bark and grass that will irritate your body. You will look pitiful. For your feet there will be nothing. Your feet will swell up in blisters and sores. From now on you will have the shade of a tree as a house; grass, reeds, and leaves to clad your body; and bathing will be miserable. When you were here in the palace, there were servants to fan you all the time. Now you will have only flies, mosquitos, and midges to bother you. You will be sad and out of sorts. How will you be able to stand it? I'm distraught."

Kesinī understood that he was forbidding her to go with him. She said, "Don't talk like this. I don't like it. It makes my heart sink and burn. Let me go with you. Though I may die in the forest, that would be better than living on. Whatever hardship you face, I will follow and suffer the same hardship, towing along the children by the hand."

Unable to discourage her, the Bodhisatta said, "If that's so, come along as you wish."

She packed necessities and food to eat in the forest. Prince Jeyyadatta climbed up to sit on the king's shoulder. The king carried the food on his left shoulder and led Prince Jeyyasena with his right hand. The four royals hurried out of the city at night. They traveled far to a river and stopped under a persimmon tree close to the bank. The parents fed the children. He looked for a place to cross the river and said to Kesinī, "This river is deep and wide. We cannot all four cross at the same time. The princes are still very small. I will take you across first and come back for them."

Queen Kesinī breastfed Jeyyadatta, laid down a cloth as a bed, and waited to see he had gone to sleep. Then she gave food to Jeyyasena, kissed him, and instructed him, "Pay attention. Stay back here and look after your little brother. You two are still very small. We are going to leave you here alone in the night with nobody to look after you. We won't take long. Your father will hurry back to fetch you."

Jeyyasena lamented, "My heart is trembling as if to break."

The king reassured Kesinī, "Crossing the river here is about three *gāvuta* to the other bank." He took her across sitting on a log and told her he was going back for the boys.

That night, two fishermen in a boat were casting nets along the riverbank. The prince heard the two talking and, thinking it was his father, called out to them to come and fetch him. The two hunters came up and found the two boys. As they were very concerned for them, they each picked up one of the boys and took them by boat to their home. King Subhamitta came back across the river to fetch the two boys. When he could not find them, he was distraught, and called out for them through until dawn. Not knowing what to do, his tears streamed down. He collapsed down in sorrow and spoke a verse:

> "*Togetherness and separation are natural for the beings of the world.*
> *When we know this is the usual way, it is even more saddening.*"

He controlled himself and headed back across the river to find the queen.

At that time, the captain of a junk along with five hundred crew was traveling to trade along the banks of the river. The captain moored the ship and went up the bank at the point where the queen was sitting. Seeing such an excellent woman, he approached her and invited her to board his boat. The queen felt as if she would fall dead. Thinking of her husband and children, she expressed her sorrow in a verse:

> "*In the past I must have separated a mother bird and its chick.*
> *As a result of the karma, I am now parted from my dear children and husband.*"

King Subhamitta came up from the river and looked for the queen under the tree. Not finding her there, his heart beat like a fish being pounded. He looked around for her, then fell to grieving, "Now I'm really bereft. I went back across the river but could not find my two sons, and now I come back here and cannot find Kesinī. What a disaster! If matters are like this, it would be better to die rather than stay alive. Why bother to live on alone? On her own, Kesinī will be very lonely in this forest. What to do? Why am I facing such difficulty? O gods who live in the mountains and up in the sky, why do you not grant me some compassion? Release me from this suffering. I will die here. How can I see the face of dear Kesinī? If any human, god, or powerful ogre can help remove my suffering, I will honor and worship him until I die!"

He collapsed down. When he revived, he felt as if he was mad.

Here there is a question. What karma had these four royals made to cause them to be separated? The answer is this. In a past life they were walking along a road and stopped under the shade of a tree. The two sons heard the sound of a parakeet chick calling at the top of the tree. They wanted to play with it so pleaded with their mother, who forced the husband to catch it and give it to the children. When they had finished playing with the chick, they pulled out three of its feathers, and blood flowed from the chick pitifully. Then they let the chick go. As a result of this alone, the four had to be separated from one another for five hundred lives.

King Subhamitta walked along, thinking deeply of his wife and children. Settling his mind, he said,[3] "Being together with someone not loved is suffering. Being separated from someone we love is suffering. We should cut free from these bonds completely. Sorrow arises because of love and wanting, because of desire and pleasure. If we cut free from all this, from love and wanting, from desire and pleasure, then we will have no sorrow, no risk of hopes that are dashed. If we know this clearly, why should we seek the ties of love, want, and pleasure?"

Eventually King Subhamitta reached Takkasilā and went to stay in the royal park. He slept with his head covered on an auspicious stone slab near the foot of a sal tree. The king of Takkasilā had died seven days earlier. The courtiers had carried out the cremation and held a meeting. "The king had

3. This passage is adapted from the beginning of the Dhammapada, ch. 16 (Piyavaggo); www.palikanon.com/pali/khuddaka/dhp/dhp4.html.

no sons. When a territory has no king, we cannot govern it. Now we have no king. Various people are competing to say this person, that person should be king, with no consensus."

A priest-counselor spoke up, "We should release a flower-chariot to find a king.[4] Whoever has merit can become the king."

All the courtiers agreed. They prepared a flower-chariot, loaded it with the five insignia of kingship, and covered it with rabbit thatch.[5] When it was to be released, the priest-counselor said, "The five regalia are a white umbrella, *camari* yak-hair crest, crown, sword, and golden slippers. These are the materials for a royal anointing. Whoever is suitable to be king, give him these five." The carriage was released.

The carriage made a clockwise circuit of the palace compound and then went out through the west gate. Musicians followed behind. The carriage went straight to the royal park, made a clockwise circuit, and stopped ready to be mounted beside the auspicious white stone slab. The priest-counselor saw the Great Being asleep on the slab and instructed the musicians to play. The Great Being woke up, removed the cloth from his eyes, saw the officials, and turned over to go back to sleep. The priest-counselor approached and raised the cloth covering his feet. Seeing the nature of his feet, he announced, "This person is fit to be our refuge, fit to be king of all four continents."

The people raised their hands and invited him to become king in a verse:

"This city is a happy place, with many ramparts and gateways.
We all look after this city well. Now we agree to present it to you.
Here there is a great palace with fine and beautiful spires
and many beautiful ladies. Now we agree to present it to you."

Hearing this, the Great Being slowly raised himself into a sitting position and asked, "Where has your king gone?"

"He has passed away."

"Where have all his sons and daughters gone?"

"He had no son or daughter."

4. This practice appears in J539 Mahājanaka and also in P8 King Canda, P13 Dukamānnika, P36 Siddhisāra, P45 Varavaṃsa, P49 Vanāvana, and P54 Surabha.

5. หญ้ามุงกระต่าย, *ya mung kratai*, which appears in the disciplinary code of the Tipiṭaka, where the Buddha admonishes monks for making footwear from this grass. In the Pali, it is a heap of grass, puñjatiṇavassehi.

"In that case, I accept your invitation."

The ministers and people anointed him as king on the auspicious stone slab, invited him to sit in the royal carriage with the royal regalia, and went in procession into the city to stay in the palace. From then on, the Great Being ruled the realm justly and carried out appropriate good deeds, such as giving alms, according to his wish.

Here will be told about the two princes. The two fishermen fed and looked after them like their own children. When they had grown up, the hunters prepared presents and took the boys to Takkasilā to offer them to the king as royal servants. When the Great Being saw the two boys, he did not recognize them but had some suspicion, so asked, "Whose sons are these two?"

"Your Majesty, they are mine."

"They are good looking. Why are they not like you?"

"Sire, they take after their mother."

The Great Being thought, "They look like my children. If my children are still alive, they would be about the same age as these two."

He loved them from that point on and presented them with various things from compassion.

Here will be told of Queen Kesinī. The junk captain who took her away wanted to make love to her. Through the protective power of her morality and the power of her prayers, the body of the junk captain became hot, and he could not threaten her. He changed his mind and worshiped her as a goddess. He made offerings in worship to various deities, such as the god of the moon. The queen was intent on finding her husband again.

After the queen had been with the junk captain for seven years, the gods induced the captain to take her to Takkasilā to present articles of tribute to the Great Being. They moored the ship at the port for two to three days. When he was taking leave of the Great Being to return home, the captain spoke a verse:

> *"I have been happy staying in this city for several days.*
> *Now I am taking leave to return home with my merchants."*

The Great Being responded in a verse:

> *"Captain, stay and see the music and dancing for one night.*
> *What's wrong with leaving tomorrow morning?"*

"Sire, usually merchants don't like watching such entertainment. If I stay tonight, I fear theft. There's nobody guarding the ship."

"Don't worry about that. Please enjoy the entertainment. I'll send people to guard the ship."

He sent for the two boys and said, "You take some royal servants to guard their junk until the merchants return there." The two took five hundred servants to guard the junk at the coast. The two boys sat on the prow of the junk.

On the previous night, nearing dawn, Queen Kesinī had dreamed that she, her husband, and their sons were sitting together in a throne hall. Two men came and placed a pair of white lotuses on her husband's palm. Her husband presented the flowers to her. She tucked them behind her two ears. The soft pollen of the lotuses fell on her breast. After waking up, she conjectured, "Today I will meet my husband and sons for certain." The sight of them in her dream made her unable to stifle her tears.

That night when all were asleep, Jeyyadatta was groggy and kept nodding off. Jeyyasena kept waking him up. Jeyyadatta had no means to overcome his sleepiness so said to his elder brother, "You know the old tales. Tell me one to overcome my tiredness."

"Jeyyadatta, I don't know any old tales. I only know the tale of our separation."

"But I don't know about that. Tell me."

"I'll tell you how we two got separated from our home."

"Didn't our mother and father live in a fishing village? What story of separation are you going to tell me?"

"Those are not our real mother and father. You and I were born from the same mother's belly."

"If that's the case, tell me about it."

Jeyyasena told the story from the past as follows:

"When we were still little children, our parents ruled as royalty. Our uncle, called Asubhamitta, who held the post of viceroy, planned a revolt. His soldiers were going to capture and kill our father so Asubhamitta would become king. A loyal courtier whispered all this to our father, who could see a big disaster looming so took us and our mother and fled from the city at dusk. We walked to a river where we stopped to rest for a bit. Mother breastfed you, fed me, and told us to wait there. Father took her across to the other side. Two fishermen found us and took us to raise as their own children. This is the truth."

Unable to stifle his sorrow, Jeyyadatta wept. Jeyyasena said, "Brother, don't cry. If our mother and father are still alive, they will search until they find us."

"What was the name of our birthplace?"

"They call it Campā City."

"And what are the names of our parents?"

"I can't say."

Jeyyadatta begged him to tell. Jeyyasena raised his clasped hands above his head, prostrated, and said, "Father's name is Subhamitta and mother's name is Kesinī."

Queen Kesinī, who was sitting in the junk, heard what the two boys were saying and beat her hands on her breast. She pulled back the curtain, saw them, and rushed to embrace the two boys. In fright, the boys shook off her arms and ran away. Distraught, she waved her arms and cried out, "Jeyyasena and Jeyyadatta, I am your mother, Kesinī. Come back here. Where are you running off to? We have been separated for such a long time. I have been so unhappy. Beloved children, please come and greet your mother."

The two were overjoyed to know it was her. They came back and prostrated at her feet. They all wept together in the junk. The merchants heard the uproar and went to tell the captain of the junk. In anger, he went in to attend on the Great Being and complained, "The two men you sent to guard the junk are bothering my wife."

The Great Being was angry. He ordered an executioner to put the two boys to death. The executioner caught them, beat them, put them in the five irons, and took them off to show to the king. The bodies of the two were smothered in blood as if they had been anointed with lacquer. The king ordered, "Take them away and chop off their heads today." The executioner took them to the graveyard used for execution.

A learned priest-counselor met them along the road and thought, "According to ancient royal practice, there must be an investigation to establish the truth before imposing punishment." He called out to the two boys, "What is the story behind this?"

Jeyyasena related the truth from the beginning. The learned priest-counselor told the executioner to wait while he hurried in to attend on the king. He paid respect and said, "Sire, the two boys that you have sent for execution, please examine the case again."

In surprise, the king and Great Being was startled. He said, "If that is so, summon them here for a hearing."

The priest-counselor brought in the two boys and had them sit on the place above, while he sat lower down as he was not the accused. Looking at the boys who faced severe punishment, the king felt terribly sad. He asked, "Why were you two bothering the wife of the junk captain?"

"Sire, we were not doing as you say." Jeyyasena related the truth from the beginning up to their meeting with the queen on the junk.

Still afflicted by doubt, the king questioned them again, "What is the name of the city where you were born?"

"Sire, it is called Campā."

"Who is your father? What is his name?"

"Sire, I don't dare speak my father's name."

"Why is that?"

"Sire, I'm very afraid."

"Don't be afraid. Speak out."

Jeyyasena raised his clasped hands above his head in respect, prostrated down, and said, "Sire, my father's name is King Subhamitta."

"And what is your mother's name?"

"Sire, her name is Queen Kesinī."

The king's heart trembled as if about to break into seven pieces. He quickly came down from the throne and embraced his sons. He let out a loud wail and collapsed, doubled over on the throne. Royal servants including courtiers and palace ladies including queens, along with military officials and other royal staff, could not contain their grief and burst out crying, the sound spreading through the city.

When the king and Great Being recovered, he ordered that the two boys be released from the irons. They were still shaking with fright. To tell them clearly, the king spoke a verse:

> *"O Jeyyasena and Jeyyadatta,*
> *I am King Subhamitta, your father. Please understand this.*
> *Oh, I have been very careless. Why did I not remember well?*
> *You two were here a long time, why did you not tell me but keep quiet?"*

Jeyyasena paid respect and replied in a verse:

"Sire, when the fishermen took us to the fishing village,
I was still young and could not remember my father clearly."

"Then we have been separated for a long time, so I did not recognize you when we met again."

Jeyyasena lowered his face onto his father's feet and described their travails from the beginning. The king asked, "Where is your mother now?"

"Sire, she is in the junk."

The Great Being was overjoyed. Taking the two boys and his courtiers, he went to the place and boarded the junk. The queen was sitting amidships. Seeing the king, she burst into tears and collapsed. The two boys came to embrace her feet. The king wept and spoke a verse:

"Queen Kesinī, please get up. Your husband has come,
along with your beloved children."

Queen Kesinī recovered herself, prostrated at her husband's feet, and spoke a verse:

"My sorrow is now ended! My fears are now ended!
The great sorrow is ended, as if tossed away."

She embraced her two children. The courtiers and palace ladies all gave in to weeping along with the queen.

The four royals grieved together in the ship from morning through until sunset. The courtiers brought golden palanquins. The king and queen sat together in one palanquin and the two sons in another, and they proceeded to the palace. A grand festival was arranged lasting seven days to welcome back the queen and princes. A ceremony was held to install Kesinī as the major queen, Jeyyasena as the viceroy, and Jeyyadatta as a minister. From then on, the four performed good deeds including almsgiving. After passing away, they were reborn in the Tusita Heaven.

The Great Teacher ended the sermon and made the birth connections: "Asubhamitta from that time was reborn as Devadatta; Jeyyadatta as Ānanda; Jeyyasena as Rāhula, the son of the Buddha; Queen Kesinī as Yasodharā; the mother of the Great Being as Queen Mahāmāyā; the father of the Great Being as King Suddhodhana; King Subhamitta as the Tathāgata, the refuge of the world." The words of the Buddha end here.

SIRASĀ

P60 *Sirasājātaka*

สิรสาชาดก

INTRODUCTION

This story is found in the legend of Suwanna Khomkham (the golden lamps), one of several legends about the founding of Tai towns around the middle Mekong, probably between the tenth and twelfth centuries CE.[1] In this legend, chief minister Ayyaka leaves the city of Pothisan Luang to found a new settlement. When his daughter, the queen, has a difficult delivery of her seventh son, he is born through the mouth. After the son shows precocious abilities, the brahman successor as chief minister persuades the king that this son is inauspicious and must be floated away to exile. The queen decides to go with him. The sixth son wants to kill the brahman but is restrained by his siblings. After their exile, the rains fail, the city languishes, and people slip away. Ayyaka returns for a visit and is shocked by the decline. The townsfolk tell him of the exile. Ayyaka returns to his city and performs a great ceremony, calling on all the gods and spirits to help. The gods, spirits, and *nāga* blow and pull the raft bearing the queen and her son to Ayyaka's new city. The city prospers, is renamed as Suwanna Khomkham, and attracts people fleeing Pothisan Luang. The gods arrange for the fragrance of the new city to spread to Pothisan Luang. The sixth son, mounted on a horse born on the same day as his younger sibling, follows the scent to the new city. He returns to escort his father, the King of Pothisan Luang, who apologizes for his earlier fault and is forgiven. Mother and son refuse his invitation to return to Pothisan Luang. After Ayyaka dies, the son succeeds him. At Pothisan Luang, the sixth son succeeds and banishes

1. The story was translated by Camille Notton as "Chronique de Suvaṇṇa K'ôm Khăm" in *Annales de Siam*, Vol. 1. A version in modern Siamese Thai appeared in *Prachum phongsawadan phak thi 72* (1939).

the evil brahman, who travels to Suwanna Khomkham, is forgiven, and is sent off to found another new settlement.

This *jātaka* uses the same names for certain characters (e.g., Ayyaka, Urasi/Surasī) and follows the legend very closely. Parts are almost a direct translation, but elsewhere the *jātaka* adds and changes details. For example, the *jātaka* omits the passages about the evil brahman founding a new town—the core theme of the legend. The *jātaka* gives the hero the supernormal powers of a bodhisatta, and adds an extraordinary ending, in which the hero-Bodhisatta ascends to the heavens but then returns to the earth. Most of the verses are taken from other sources, including five classical *jātaka* and the Dhammapada.

When the Great Teacher was staying at the Bamboo Grove, he thought of Devadatta, who had intentions to kill him, and thus told this Sirasā Jātaka, which begins with the words, "Beloved son."

The theme of this *jātaka* appears in the account of dissension in the sangha,[2] which tells of Devadatta seeking a means to split the sangha, in particular in the account, as presented by the Great Teacher, from when Devadatta ordained into the Buddhist religion up to the time King Bimbisāra died. Please listen as told from here on.

As the book states,[3] when Devadatta incited Prince Ajātasattu to kill King Bimbisāra, he went to attend on the prince and said, "Great one, your wish has been carried out. As for my wish, it will be fulfilled when the Ten-Powered One is killed. I will be a Buddha for certain." Then the prince asked, "What do you wish me to do in this matter? Please tell me."

"Please assemble the bowmen."

The prince ordered them to assemble a hundred families of archers, including a chief hunter, and told them, "You must follow

2. Saṅghabheda Sutta, section 18 of Itivuttika in the Khuddaka Nikāya (suttacentral.net/pi/iti18).

3. Ajātasattu was son and heir of King Bimbisāra of Magadha. Devadatta encouraged Ajātasattu to kill his father to seize the throne, and then asked Ajātasattu to help him kill the Buddha. Several attempts failed. In later life, Ajātasattu attended on the Buddha, repented, and became a follower.

the words of the elder monk." With that alone, he sent them to Devadatta.

Devadatta sent them to try and kill the Tathāgata. When the chief huntsman arrived at the Buddha's place, he was unable to do him harm and instead was converted to Buddhism, was ordained, and became an *arahant*. This matter became known throughout the sangha. Speaking together in the teaching hall, the monks said, "You all know that Devadatta tried to kill the Tathāgata out of envy but was unsuccessful and himself was ruined."

Hearing the words spoken by the monks through his divine hearing, the Great Teacher left his lion seat, went to the teaching hall, sat down, and asked, "What are you monks talking about?" After they told him, he said, "O monks, not only in the present but also in the past Devadatta tried to kill me but failed." With that, he fell silent. As the monks begged him to tell the story, he told a tale from the past as follows.

The story in detail tells that in the past there was a king named Vassavatī ruling in Pupphavatī City. His major queen, named Surasī, who was senior to all the consorts, had seven sons. The first was named Sunakkhatta, the second Canda, the third Suriya, the fourth Sudhana, the fifth Singhadeva, the sixth Kāmadeva, and the seventh was the Bodhisatta.

At the moment when the Bodhisatta was conceived, his mother dreamed that a great man with all the attributes, rank, and power came down from the Tusita Heaven, stood in the sky, and spoke in beautiful words, saying, "Mother, I am no low, ordinary person. I am someone without stain, perfectly radiant, excellent, peerless." After saying this, the great man came down and entered through her navel. She woke up and thought about the dream. She knew that if she had a son, he would have great power and knowledge, comparable to that of an emperor; and if she had a daughter, she would be a gem lady and chief queen of an emperor.

Next morning, she went to attend on the king, her husband, and told him the dream. The king sent for an astrologer and related the dream for him to interpret. The astrologer said, "Your Majesty, the queen will be pregnant. At birth, the son will exit from her mouth. Since in the dream the man stood speaking in the sky, the son will not be an ordinary low person or evil person but a learned man, a teacher of the dhamma, a pure person, a shoot of the Buddha." At the end of this prediction, the astrologer gave a blessing.

Very happy at hearing this prediction, the king ordered that her pregnancy be rigorously looked after. After ten months, when she was about to give birth, a wind stirred in her womb and she felt nauseous. She summoned her maidservants, saying, "Bring some fine linen[4] costing a hundred thousand, and wait to receive what I will throw up."

The maidservants did as bidden. When she retched, a pristine son came out through her mouth, but the queen and the maidservants felt nothing. Hence the maidservants rolled up the cloth and hid it away. When the queen recovered consciousness, she saw her womb had shrunk. Stroking her navel, she asked, "When I gave birth, did you wash the cloth stained with the mucus I threw up? Tell me whether you saw my child." The maidservants unfolded the cloth and saw the prince who had a complexion like gold. They carried him to the queen, saying, "Mistress, your son is born." She was very pleased. She washed her son in water and laid him on a golden throne. All the consorts went to inform the king and father, who thought, "My son has great merit!" He ordered his ministers and courtiers, "Select seven hundred wet nurses for my son."

For feeding the prince, the ministers arranged seven hundred wet-nurses, all with bosoms that did not droop and breastmilk of good taste, excluding any women who were too short. To look after the prince, the king selected seven hundred ladies who were attentive to the task. At the appropriate time for feeding, the wet-nurses offered their breasts, but the prince did not drink the milk. Queen Surasī had to feed him herself. The king arranged for a thousand courtiers' sons to form the prince's retinue.

On the day for naming, the king and others performed a ceremony and gave him the name Prince Sirasā [head] because he was born from the mouth. If a wet-nurse put him to bed on a coarse cloth, the prince would not accept it and cried. His mother thus put him to bed on a fine cloth worth a hundred thousand and he slept happily without crying, still and soundless. The prince happily went to bed by himself but usually studied the precepts before sleeping.

On holy days, the prince ate food and drank milk only once in the day and observed the eight precepts. He checked to make sure he observed the

4. ทุกูล, *thukula*, dukūla, fine cloth made from a plant, perhaps a type of jute.

precepts perfectly, and was very pleased. On a holy day eight months after birth, the Bodhisatta slept through the first watch and woke at the second watch, thinking about his observation of the eight precepts. He pondered, "Do my royal father and mother love me? I will test them out." He looked this way and that and saw a crystal chest close by. He made a prayer, "Through the power of my unblemished observation of the precepts, let my body be hidden in this chest." After this prayer, he was hidden in the chest.

The maids and wet-nurses awoke to find the prince missing. They asked one another, "Where is he?" They split up to search. Not finding him, they ran this way and that in tears and confusion. After searching everywhere without success, they were all greatly troubled. They went together to inform the queen, "Mistress, the prince has disappeared without a trace."

The queen felt so shocked that she lamented greatly and almost collapsed. She gave orders, "Search the whole palace, quickly." All replied, "Your Majesty, we will help." Meanwhile, the queen lamented in a verse:

"Mother's beloved, your mother's heart will break for certain.
If I do not find you, I will die of sorrow.
I have raised you for only nine months. Where have you gone?
Has someone killed you, or have you run away in anger at me?
Why do you not appear, Sirasā? Has an ogre or demon abducted you,
or has Sakka, king of the gods, taken you off?"

After lamenting, she went to attend on her husband and said, "Your Majesty, have you gone to your son's residence and hidden him away somewhere?"

The king asked, "Why are you saying this?"

"My child has disappeared, sire."

The king was shocked and totally stupefied. He had people search all night without result.

Then the queen saw the crystal chest and said, "Open this closed chest and take a look." A maidservant said, "Mistress, we cannot open it." The queen had them carry the chest to the king and said, "Your Majesty, our child may have got into this chest. Please open it and see."

The king sent for courtiers of the treasury and said, "Open this chest." The courtiers brought a key to open the chest, saw the prince sleeping inside, and felt very relieved. They lifted the chest for the king to see. The queen looked, saw the prince, and could not contain herself. She rushed to pick him up in her arms, hugged him, kissed his head, and suckled him. Then she said, "Beloved child, why did you make me so upset by hiding in this chest?" Hugging the child, she returned to her residence and said to the maids, "Do not ever be careless again!"

From then on, the maids and wet nurses never failed to take turns at watching him from all four directions, like stars surrounding the moon, or cow elephants surrounding Lord Chaddanta.

At that time there was an evil-minded brahman called Majjahāyaka who had been appointed as a minister to teach the dhamma to the king. He bothered the people in many ways including threats. When judging cases, he accepted bribes, and in the courtroom he introduced false witnesses causing those who should win the case to lose. The people were very angry. The king's appointment of this brahman as a judge amounted to destroying the general people's welfare. The people became angry that there were always false witnesses.

This brahman thought, "Prince Sirasā has great merit. He was born from the mouth. At nine months, he hid away from his mother and father in a crystal chest. Amazing! When he grows up, the people will make accusations against me, and I will be removed from this position. I must kill him quickly."

The next morning, the brahman bathed and went to attend on the king. When he had an opportunity, he said, "Your Majesty, your son Prince Sirasā is an inauspicious person. You will have trouble for certain. According to the nature of the world, all beings, including red ants, white ants, and termites, give birth through the lower portal. However, Prince Sirasā was born from the upper portal. While he was still young, he hid himself in a crystal chest locked with a key. Perhaps this child is an ogre, a water spirit, or a demon that can make itself small. Usually humans cannot do this. For this reason, I beg to inform you that this prince is an inauspicious person who will cause trouble and danger. If Your Majesty still considers him your own son, there will be danger of three kinds: first, deaths will occur among the people; second, the king or the country will collapse; and third, the queen or royal kin will face danger of death."

Hearing this made the king apprehensive. He asked, "Minister, what should I do?"

"Put this prince in a boat and toss it onto the ocean."

The king said, "You kill him yourself."

"Your Majesty, wherever the blood of this prince drops, a fire will occur."

"In that case, go to attend on the queen and tell her about this matter."

The minister paid respect to the queen and said, "Your son is an inauspicious person. The king gave orders to put him in a boat and toss it onto the ocean today."

Hearing this made the queen as upset and sorrowful as if her heart would break into seven pieces. Her heart trembled like someone who had fallen from a high peak. Unable to stifle her sorrow, she wept as she cradled her son to her bosom, saying, "Dear child, why does your father want to put you in a boat and toss it onto the ocean?"

She went to attend on her husband and asked, "Your Majesty, why do you wish to expel the prince?"

"The minister said our son is an inauspicious person."

"Your Majesty, my son has great merit. At birth he came out through the mouth. Why does the minister say he is inauspicious? Please do not believe the words of this minister, who is motivated by envy. Once he has killed my son, he will kill you and seize the throne."

"The minister speaks only the truth. This son of ours is an inauspicious person. For this reason, do not be upset. You and I will die because of this son."

The queen spoke further in a verse:[5]

> "*Please do not kill the prince. Present him to Majjahāyaka*
> *to be used as a slave or servant, to look after his elephants and horses.*
> *Please do not kill the prince. Chain him by the neck*
> *and make him work as a slave, clearing elephant dung.*
> *Please do not kill the prince. Chain him by the neck*
> *and present him to the minister, who can force him to go begging.*
> *Please do not kill the prince. Chain him by the neck*
> *and make him collect the droppings of elephants and horses.*
> *Please do not kill the prince. Present him to Majjahāyaka.*
> *Do not expel him. Please make him work like a slave.*"

5. This verse uses a format, and several lines and phrases, found in J544 Prince Canda (Appleton and Shaw, *Ten Great Birth Stories*, 409; Faussböll, *Jātaka*, VI, 138). The second couplet is missing from the translation in the Thai original and has here been added.

The queen writhed around in lamentation. Hearing her pleas, the king felt as if his heart would break. With eyes flooded with tears, he went to his bedroom.

After hearing the king weeping in this way, all the inner consorts could not contain themselves. They wept and writhed like a sal forest battered by a howling storm wind.

The queen hugged the prince, kissed his head, went down from the residence, and said to the brahman Majjahāyaka, "You evil fellow, why don't you throw your own daughter in the water?" She lamented on and on.

Hearing about this upset, all the royal servants including maidservants, consorts, and slave-girls wept and writhed in distress.

Minister Majjahāyaka prepared a boat with a canopy for the prince-Bodhisatta. He ordered seven brahmans, "Go to the queen's residence and tell her that I have ordered you to bring the prince." The seven brahmans did as bidden.

The queen shouted at the brahmans and refused to hand over the prince. The brahmans returned to tell the minister, who ordered them, "Don't listen to the queen's words. Go and fetch the prince." The brahmans went back to address the queen again. She still refused. The brahmans requested three times but she still refused. Majjahāyaka thus gave them an ultimatum, "Seize him. Don't be afraid."

They went to the queen and said, "Minister Majjahāyaka is very angry. He ordered us to seize the prince." They stretched out their hands to take the prince. Through the power of the merit of the prince, the hands of the brahmans flew off in front of their eyes. The brahmans went back to Majjahāyaka with their hands awash in blood and told him what happened. The minister ordered other people to go. They went back and forth asking for the prince seven times. The queen said, "All my sons do not know what is going on. I must tell them everything." She sent maidservants to inform all her sons. The maidservants went to the residence of each prince and said, "The queen invites you to attend on her."

Before the other princes arrived, Prince Kāmadeva went to their mother and heard what had happened. He went to attend on the king, paid respect, sat in an appropriate place, and asked, "Your Majesty, are you really expelling my younger brother?"

"Yes, really, because your younger brother Prince Sirasā is an inauspicious person. Do not fall for him."

Weeping tears of lament at this answer, Prince Kāmadeva spoke a verse:[6]

> *"Please spare the life of my younger brother. Look at me who has grown up.*
> *You have seen me practice with elephants and horses on the parade ground.*
> *If there is trouble at borders of the realm you may use me in your place.*
> *You wish to exile my brother without need, kill your beloved son without cause.*
> *Birds who love their chicks know how to make a nest for them.*
> *You intend to kill your beloved child.*
> *Do not believe the words of Majjahāyaka.*
> *He is not a loyal man. His heart is filled with envy.*
> *Please do not kill my younger brother. Present me to Majjahāyaka as a slave.*
> *To save his life, I will collect the droppings of elephants and horses like a pauper."*

Hearing this plea, the king felt his heart would break. His eyes flooded with tears. He embraced his son and consoled him, "Most beloved of sons, do not be sad. Your younger brother is an inauspicious person. When he grows up, he will kill you, me, and your mother—all of us. For this reason, I must expel him from the capital."

The prince had no other way to plead further and thus took leave and went to attend on the queen. All six princes wept and lamented in despair.

The brahmans who had taken orders from Majjahāyaka had just arrived and were opening the door to the residence. Seeing them, Prince Kāmadeva grew angry. He drew his sword and rushed over intending to kill these scoundrels. Seeing him, the brahmans fled, saying, "Sire, do not kill us brahmans, because you will be punished!"

The six princes went to attend on their father. After paying respect and relaying their grievance, they begged for their younger brother's life in a verse:[7]

> *"Sire, please kill us first. Do not rush to kill our most beloved,*
> *your own son, who is still very young and is of beautiful appearance.*
> *Please do not do away with him. The hearts of all of us will break.*
> *If we heard of such happening, we would wish it happened*

6. As in the prior verse, this is adapted from J544 Prince Canda (Appleton and Shaw, *Ten Great Birth Stories*, 410–11; Faussböll, *Jātaka*, VI, 139–40).

7. Again adapted from J544 Prince Canda (Appleton and Shaw, *Ten Great Birth Stories*, 418; Faussböll, *Jātaka*, VI, 152).

in a family of chariot mechanics, hired workers, or tradesmen,
not in a royal lineage, and would not be so troubled as this."

Without achieving their wish, the six princes returned to attend on their mother, summoned the brahmans to audience, and said, "We six, his elder brothers, wish to see the body of our brother which looks as if filled with gold. Do not take him away. Hand him over to us."

The brahmans refused. The princes implored them, "We will give you seven hundred thousand and seven hundred of gold, along with elephants, horses, chariots, cows, bulls, slaves, and slave girls."

The brahmans refused to accept these. The princes said, "We will give each of you seven hundred thousand of gold."

The brahmans declined. The princes swore, "If our younger brother grows up to become an inauspicious person and intends to harm our father, you may cut off our hands, feet, and mouths." After the princes swore this oath, the brahmans sat quiet.

The queen said to her six sons, "Do not be so troubled and so angry. It's normal that a mother does not love her children equally. Your younger brother Sirasā is still at the breast, so his mother must be with him. Kāmadeva here is still small. Please enter the service of your father. Conduct yourselves well. Know what is right and what is wrong." She embraced Kāmadeva, kissed his forehead and the crown of his head, while she grieved.

Hearing their mother's command, the six princes led by Prince Sunakkhatta all prostrated at her feet, wept, and wailed, writhing around in lamentation, not in their senses. He then said, "We must have made some sin in past lives which causes us to part from our mother and our beloved little brother. Now we face disaster!"

Not one of the royal staff throughout the palace, including nursemaids, wet nurses, serving girls, and servants, both male and female, could contain their sorrow. All grieved and lamented beyond description.

The queen ordered the nursemaids to bring a pair of valuable jewels, a pair of cloths worth a hundred thousand, and the prince's toys, such as toy elephants and horses, and placed them in a chest with gold and silver. She had the serving girls carry the chest along behind, while she cradled her son. She went down from the palace and gave a blessing and advice to all the royal retinue including the consorts, saying, "Do not quarrel as a result of the four wrong courses,[8] namely love, hate, stupidity, and fear. Do not abuse one another. Be without sorrow, and have only happiness. I take leave of you to follow my fate."

After delivering this lesson, she went to attend on her husband, paid respect, and said, "Sire, you of excellent virtue, please live happily. I take my leave to embrace sorrow and reach the end of my life today. I beg to take leave of you for the last time, and wish you every happiness. I who have fallen into difficulty take my leave now." Cradling her son, she left the audience and turned her face to leave the palace.

The people of the palace and the city, including courtiers and soldiers, followed behind her, beating their chests with their hands. She walked along until she saw the princes and people in lamentation, then said, "Please weep no further. Do not be upset. Whatever karma I have made, I must accept its fruit."

Hearing this, the people wept and wailed and spoke in a verse:[9]

> "*Living in the palace, you ate fine and pure rice*
> *and well-cooked meat with good flavoring.*
> *With only fruit, how can you manage now?*
> *Without receptacles of gold and silver,*
> *and using tree leaves in place of a bed,*
> *how can you live, O queen? Used to sleeping in a superb residence*
> *with no drafts,*[10] *how can you sleep where nothing blocks the sun and wind?*
> *Where once you slept on a covered bed*
> *laid with soft and fine wool cloth, how can you manage, O queen?*
> *Used to cushions, couches, wool covers, and colored rugs,*
> *now lying on a plank of wood, how can you sleep, O queen?*
> *Once bathed in eaglewood, sandal, and perfumes,*
> *now bathed in itchy sweat and grime,*[11] *how will you manage, O queen?*
> *Used to resting happily, being fanned with peacock fans,*
> *now bitten and stung by bugs and mosquitos, how will you manage, O queen?*"

8. อคติ, *akhati*, agati, a conventional set of four forces leading to bad judgment.

9. This verse is adapted from J547 Vessantara, the chapter on generosity, where Vessantara laments over his children's condition in the forest (Appleton and Shaw, *Ten Great Birth Stories*, 565; Faussböll, *Jātaka*, VI, 510).

10. In the Pali, this is "in a good roofed house with fastened doors."

11. In the Pali, this is "wearing dirty old rags."

The wicked brahmans invited the queen and her son to board the great boat, took the boat out three *gāvuta* to the ocean, and set it loose. The brahmans returned. The boat floated on the ocean, but there was someone to take care of it, namely Maṇi Mekhalā, who has the duty to watch over the ocean.

The city people followed her as far as they could to the edge of the ocean and stood lamenting there. Birds that heard the sound of their lamentation flew up into the sky in alarm. Seeing the birds, the people called out in a verse:

> *"O birds, if you want meat, fly to the middle of the ocean,*
> *for the queen and the king's son will die there for sure.*
> *O birds, if you want meat, fly to the middle of the ocean,*
> *for the queen and the king's son will die there for sure."*

After this, the people wept and grieved until all collapsed, without one person left able to bring water to revive them.

At that moment, the realm of Lord Sakka, king of the gods, felt hot through the power of the compassion that the people felt for the Bodhisatta. This made Lord Sakka think, "What caused this?" When he knew that the people who had compassion for the Bodhisatta were overcome with sorrow to the point of losing their senses, he thought, "I should make rain fall on them like rain falling on a lotus." He immediately did so.

When the people's bodies were soaked by the rain, everybody revived and joyfully called out their praises of the Bodhisatta, turning their faces back toward him in blessing.

From that time on, all the people of the capital, without a single exception, refrained from indulging in entertainment. Before this time, they had all had fun enjoying themselves every day and night. The city at that time was never peaceful because of ten kinds of noise. Now it was stone quiet, with no sound of enjoyment, like a graveyard. All sorts of people in the city set their faces to do good works, such as distributing alms, and sent the merit to the Bodhisatta and his mother with the words, "May this merit go to the two royals. May all the gods accept this merit and protect the two royals."

The gods and heavenly maidens came down from the world of the gods to take care of the two royals and to caress away their sorrow with the sound of celestial soft music and chanting by the gods. The sound was heard throughout the city. The people who heard it were happy every night.

For four months without a break, the Bodhisatta sat in the boat floating on the ocean, watched over by a retinue of gods.

At that time there was a brahman called Ayyaka who had held the post of minister for King Mahāprathama, the father of Prince Vassavatī. When King Mahāprathama had died, minister Ayyaka presented the realm to Prince Vassavatī and presented the post of minister to the brahman Majjahāyaka. He himself resigned, saying, "I am old. Let me go to reside outside the city." King Vassavatī gave his consent. Minister Ayyaka left the city, traveled for three *yojana* to a certain great village, and founded a city there. Every year without fail he went to attend on King Vassavatī.

Thus when Minister Ayyaka came to attend as usual, he arrived at the capital and found it was dead quiet, unlike before. He thought, "In the past the city folk used to go around eating, dancing, singing, and enjoying themselves noisily to the sound of drums and gongs. Why is it all dead quiet now?" He went into audience and sat in an appropriate place.

Since the time when the queen and prince left the capital in a boat, which floated down to the great ocean, King Vassavatī had thought, "My son and queen who have gone to the ocean cannot return, as they will face dangers for sure." This made him very upset, but tears had never filled his eyes even once in the four months past even though his heart felt dried up, his eyes were clouded, and his face was darker than usual. Seeing the brahman Ayyaka, he stayed quiet and did not speak with him. Ayyaka thought, "Before when the king saw me he would converse with me. Today he seems to be in a bad mood." To find out why, he addressed the king in a verse:

> *"In the past when Your Majesty saw me, your face would light up,*
> *but now it is like a living lotus flower that has been picked*
> *and crushed in someone's hands, when you see me."*

Ayyaka thought, "The king is probably angry at someone among those at court or someone outside the palace." He addressed him again in a verse:

> *"Has someone made Your Majesty angry, or caused you some pain,*
> *so that your face does not bloom when you see me arrive?"*

The king replied in a verse:

"I am separated. For a month now, I have not come down from the residence.
I am not happy by night or by day.
My queen gave birth through the mouth. Nine months later,
the son hid in a crystal chest. So the minister said he was inauspicious,
and I had both mother and son put on a boat and released on the ocean,
to float on the current. Since then I have been unhappy.
People of the cities, towns, and villages
are all very sad and upset.
Hence my city is quiet in this way."

Minister Ayyaka thought, "Prince Sirasā is not an inauspicious person but someone of merit. Animals and humans in tens and hundreds of thousands are not born from the mouth. Besides, there is no other person who has hidden himself away alone in a chest at the age of nine months. Hence Prince Sirasā must be someone of great merit."

With these thoughts, he addressed the king, "Minister Majjahāyaka is a trickster. He always decides cases by planting false witnesses. He knows that the prince has great accumulated merit and hence fears that in the future, when the prince has grown up and has great merit and knowledge, he will dismiss Majjahāyaka from his post of minister. That's why he said the prince is inauspicious."

Ayyaka asked for minister Majjahāyaka and other courtiers to be summoned. When they had all assembled, Ayyaka instructed them in verse:[12]

"A royal servant of the court does not achieve fame while unknown
or if a coward, idiot, or heedless person,
but when the king knows his virtue, wisdom, and purity,
he will have confidence to share even secret matters without concern.
A royal servant, when called upon, must not waver,
and like a weigh-scale in balance or stick always level,
must bear everything to act properly
as a wise man in the service of the king.
When called upon, whether by day or by night, he must not waver

12. This passage is adapted from J546 Vidhura (Appleton and Shaw, *Ten Great Birth Stories*, 482–84; Faussböll, *Jātaka*, VI, 292–98). The Thai translation adds words for clarification and emphasis throughout, but the only major changes, reflected in this translation, are as follows: added phrase "and lower than the king"; added line "He should not be loud . . ."; "harm the king's deer in the forest" changed to "kill animals that the king has allowed to live"; added line "He must look after his father . . ."; added phrase "discarded in graveyards."

but act wisely in the service of the king. Even if so instructed,
he should not travel on a road well made and prepared for the king
or enjoy the same pleasures of the king at any time,
but always keep himself to the rear of the king and lower than the king
and have no clothes, garlands, or scents equal to the king.
He should not carry himself or speak in ways similar to the king,
but ensure his appearance and manner are different.
He should be modest, steady, prudent,
keeping his senses under control, and being mentally resolute.
He should not sport with the king's consorts or talk privately with them.
He should not be loud and assertive in action and speech, but show self-control.
He should not take wealth from the treasury, not think much of sleep,
not drink liquor for intoxication, and not kill animals that the king has allowed to live.
He should not think himself worthy to mount the king's seat, elephant, or chariot.
Attentive, he should be neither too far from the king nor too close,
and stand in his presence to see the king and hear him speak.
The king is not a friend and the king is not an associate.
Kings anger quickly, like an eye touched by a husk of grain.
A wise and intelligent man does not act like a sage,
imagining he is honored and speaking coarsely or overconfidently.
If the king favors his own son or his brother
with villages, towns, kingdoms, or countries,
he should not speak good or ill but should remain indifferent and silent.
If elephant riders, cavalry, chariot soldiers, or foot soldiers
are given higher wages by the king
in recognition of their exploits, he should not interfere.
Wisely, he should be empty-stomached like a bow and bend like bamboo.
He should not go against the grain, but be tongueless like a fish,
with an empty stomach like a bow, eating little, prudent and courageous.
Wisely, he should not visit women too often, at risk to his reputation,
and foolishly suffer from coughing, breathing problems, and weakness.
He should not talk too much or be silent all the time.
When it is time, he should speak words that are precise and measured,
not angry or provoking anger, truthful, mild, not slanderous,
and not frivolous, making himself appear unreliable.
He should study knowledge and be restrained, accomplished,
steadfast yet mild, honest, straightforward, and hardworking.

He must look after his father, mother, and senior kinfolk.
He should be humble, deferential, respectful, and polite to his elders.
He should keep his distance from people who have been sent away
and from envoys of foreign countries on secret missions,
merely giving support to those who are responsible for the matter.
He should look out for his patron and not for another king.
He should respectfully attend on ascetics and brahmans,
develop himself by learning about sin and merit, good and bad,
continue to give alms to ascetics and brahmans as before,
and not refuse anything of mendicants when it is the time for almsgiving.
Virtuous and intelligent, he should understand the rites and provisions,
knowing the proper times and occasions, and being energetic,
diligent, and attentive regarding his duties so matters go smoothly.
He should go often to the threshing floor, hall, cattle, or field
and keep account of the paddy stored and amounts withdrawn for cooking.
Children, siblings, and kin who are not firm in virtue
should not be given authority, only food and clothing to survive,
for limbless fools are like the dead, discarded in graveyards.
Slaves, servants, and menials that are well established in virtue,
skillful, and industrious, he should place in powerful positions.
Virtuous, unwavering, and devoted, he must be loyal
both to the king's face and behind his back. He must know the king's will,
acting according to his wishes and not to the contrary.
He should bow his head, wash the king's feet, rub him with perfumes,
and even if punished, he must not be angry."

After the brahman Ayyaka had taught the royal servants in this way, he spoke another verse to put pressure on them:[13]

"Those who do harm to people who have no fault and are harmless
will immediately be punished by falling into one of ten states:
sorrow, loss, bodily harm,
severe pain, or derangement.
If the wrong was done to the king, they will be severely criticized,
deprived of relatives, deprived of wealth,
have their house consumed by flame and fire,
and be reborn in hell after death."

13. This verse is from the Dhammapada, chapter 10, Daṇḍavaggo, about the stick (punishment).

After this, brahman Ayyaka paid respect to take leave, saying, "Your Majesty, I am taking leave to return to my home city. If Prince Sirasā is someone of merit, he will return through the power of my prayer. If he is an inauspicious person he will die on the ocean." He left the audience, and gave teaching to the city people: "Do not be sorrowful. Do not weep. Prince Sirasā is someone of merit. He is still alive. He will return through the power of my prayer."

Ayyaka then returned to his own city. After eating a meal, he went out to sit among the courtiers and said, "King Vassavatī is already aged. He has one son, who was born from the mouth. After nine months he went to uphold the precepts in a crystal chest that was locked with a key. For this reason, the brahman Majjahāyaka told the king that his son was an inauspicious person. The king believed it. He had the son placed on a boat and floated away on the ocean. We are ready to worship the Triple Gem with offerings of candles and incense, and to dedicate the merit to the prince, to implore the gods to protect him and bring him to our home city."

He gave orders to have a drum beaten to announce to the people of the capital, "Please help to decorate the city like a city of the gods, decked with flags and so on. Build a residence on the bank of the river, erect flags, plant banana trees and sugar cane, and set up water pots on both sides from the residence to the riverbank. Decorate the route along which he will come with garlands of flowers, scents, candles, and incense on both sides of the road to look as beautiful as the road on which the gods go to a park."

All the city people worshiped the Triple Gem and made prayers every day, saying, "Through the power of this merit, may the gods help protect the prince and bring him to this city."

The Bodhisatta, who was now protected by the gods and by the virtue of the Triple Gem, faced no obstacles and dangers. He was joyful all the time. The boat floated on the ocean safely for five months.

Brahman Ayyaka erected seven hundred flagpoles hung with garlands and bells as worship to the gods. He raised his arms to pay respect to the Triple Gem and the gods, including the protective deities of the ocean, and praised the Triple Gem, saying, "Allow me to bow before the Blessed One, the *arahant*, the fully enlightened Buddha. Allow me to bow before the dhamma that the Blessed One spoke. Allow me to bow before the sangha, the followers of the Buddha, those who practice well." As a prayer, he said, "If Sirasā is a person of merit, the shoot of a future Buddha, let him come to my city along with his mother. If he is not a person of merit but a bad person, let him die on the ocean." From this time on, he made worship every day.

Gods, ogres, *nāga*, *garuḍa*, and *kinnari* surrounded and protected the boat of Prince Sirasā floating in the ocean. They serenaded him with the five types of music for four months. Through the power of brahman Ayyaka's prayers, the boat floated against the current to the entrance of the bay and then to the city of his royal father. But, through the power of the gods, nobody saw the boat. The boat floated to Ayyaka's city in eight days and berthed at the port during the night.

That night, Ayyaka had a dream. A man brought a tree in which the trunk was wisdom and the branches were the five precepts. The tree was placed in the center of the city, surrounded by many elephants and horses. People came from the four directions to bow down and worship this tree together.

When Ayyaka woke up, he pondered on the nature of the dream. He understood, "This great tree must be Prince Sirasā. Deities have brought this prince of great merit to this city. Today I will see him." He sat on his seat, listening to the celestial music. He knew it was music played by the gods and that Prince Sirasā would arrive before long.

When the people heard the celestial music, they went down to the port and saw the boat decked brightly with gold and gems and with a canopy amidships. They thought, "This is wondrous! This has never happened before. It must be the prince's boat." They went to inform the courtiers.

The courtiers were very pleased. They went to inform Ayyaka, who had all the consorts and palace women carry flowers of gold, silver, and crystal down to welcome the prince at the port. They saw Prince Sirasā and his mother sitting under the canopy. The courtiers, royal servants, and city folk paid their respect and crowded around in audience.

Brahman Ayyaka raised both his arms to pay respect and said, "Royal mistress, I have heard your story and it makes me very sad. Along with the city people, I have made worship to the Triple Gem, dedicated the merit to you, and begged for this merit to help bring you to this city. Royal mistress, now that you have both arrived here, please rule the realm in this capital. I will shelter under your accumulated merit. Please consent to be the refuge of the people."

The queen replied, "Ayyaka, I thought I would die on the ocean and never see your face again. Now we have survived through the power of your merit." With these words, she accepted his invitation.

The city people, including courtiers and brahmans, made offerings of incense, candles, flowers, scents, and various unguents to the prince and his mother. Ayyaka carried the prince up from the boat and invited the queen to board a golden palanquin under a white umbrella. The people started up music immediately.

Ayyaka sent for goldsmiths and commanded them to make a golden tray weighing 100 *rājikā*,[14] set with seven gems and decorated with a thousand patterns, to be finished in seven days. The golden tray was placed on a throne under a white umbrella, and the Bodhisatta was invited to sit on the tray. Ayyaka made a prayer, "If you are someone of miraculous wisdom, the shoot of a future Buddha, and will be a Buddha in the future, may celestial water fall from the sky to wash your head at this moment. In addition, may this celestial water spread to your father's city and may your father and the city people realize two things—namely, that you have come to this city and that you are the shoot of a future Buddha."

After the prayer, Ayyaka got up from the seat, grasped the flower garlands hanging in all directions, made worship, and gave a blessing: "May you be happy, without disease, with no enemies as thorns, and may you not go elsewhere, but rule the realm in this capital."

The gods who resided in the palaces of the sky poured celestial water to wash the heads of the prince and the people there as well. For those people who had morality, wisdom, and devotion, this celestial water falling on their heads was scented. For those who were sinful and had wrong thinking, their whole bodies grew hot and they had to run off to hide in houses.

Then Lord Sakka, king of the gods, made celestial rain fall like rain on a lotus leaf. People of merit who felt such rain were refreshed in the heart; if they wished to be wet, they were wet; if they did not wish to be wet, they stayed dry. Those without merit who were hit by the rain felt unbearably hot and had to hide away in houses. That is why it is called lotus-leaf rain. In addition, all the trees hit by this rain, including sugar palms, immediately

14. A weight measure used for gold, based on a corn seed.

sprouted leaves, flowers, and fruit. Domestic animals such as buffaloes, cows, sheep, and goats that were hit by this rain felt refreshed and happy.

This rain spread throughout the country, right to the city of the royal father. The people of Pupphavatī City smelled this celestial water and talked among themselves, "Whose smell is this?"

King Vassavatī asked, "Who does this fragrant smell come from? From where? From what place?" He ordered the courtiers, "Investigate in all four directions to find from which direction the fragrance comes."

The courtiers spread out to investigate in all four directions but could not find which direction the scent came from. At that time there was a certain Sindh horse that was strong, fleet of foot, and fierce-looking. Nobody except Prince Kāmadeva was able to ride him. The king summoned Prince Kāmadeva to audience and said, "Nobody except you can find the source of this water. Please ride out on your horse that is strong and fleet of foot to investigate where the water comes from."

Prince Kāmadeva acknowledged the royal order and went to the horse stables. He stroked the back of the horse, saddled him up, mounted, and left the city with other courtiers following. The gods induced him to turn his face to the north. In one day he traveled thirty *yojana* to the city of brahman Ayyaka. After entering the city, he saw the people going to a festival. Smelling the scent of the celestial water and seeing the articles of worship including the lantern posts, he thought, "What is this festival?" From asking the people, he heard that Prince Sirasā and his mother had come to live in this city. He was very pleased. He quickly went into the palace and up to the residence. He paid respect to his mother, embraced Prince Sirasā, and wept. She said, "I thought I would never see you again, but Ayyaka and the city people made merit and dedicated the fruit, so I survived. Why did you come to this city?"

Prince Kāmadeva told her about his father's orders. Brahman Ayyaka told Prince Kāmadeva about all the things that had been done since the making of the golden tray and said, "Please return to tell your father that Prince Sirasā will be anointed king seven days from now. If the king wishes to admire the accumulated merit of the queen and his son, let him come to attend. If that is not his wish, let him not come."

Prince Kāmadeva returned and related what he had seen and heard to his royal father, who was overjoyed. He ordered a quick preparation of the four-limbed army. The six princes were all very pleased. In the morning on the seventh day, the king and his six sons each mounted a royal elephant and left the city surrounded by troops. Arriving at Ayyaka's city, they billeted the troops in the city and took articles of worship, including scents, up into the residence to make worship to Prince Sirasā. The king embraced his son, who was sitting on the golden tray. He bathed his son with celestial water and gave a blessing: "May you be without disease, be happy and free of all sorrows." Then the courtiers, royal generals, and great teachers all bathed the prince and gave their blessings.

The seven hundred evil brahmans, including Majjahāyaka, came with bowls of water to bathe the prince, but their various receptacles including conches and *khontho* ewers broke and shattered over these brahmans, who were not able to bathe the prince. Ayyaka gave orders to his courtiers, "Seize, beat, and kill these evil brahmans! Drive them out of our city!" In fright, the brahmans broke and fled. The gods in the Tāvatiṁsa and Yāmā heavens, and the four guardian kings, bathed the prince and gave their blessings. Humans heard the sound of these gods and were so amazed that their hair stood on end. Everybody raised their arms to pay respect.

From the day of his birth, Prince Sirasā had not spoken. On this day he spoke with his father and mother. When he gave teaching to brahman Ayyaka, he spoke in a verse:

> "*Ayyaka, please listen to my words. I am a shoot of the Buddha,*
> *not a low person. I was born here,*
> *and I was abandoned to the ocean because of old karma. In a past life as a king,*
> *I built a flower garden and collected the flowers*
> *in seven hundred boats along with torches and lanterns,*
> *which were floated on the water every day in worship of the Triple Gem.*
> *I shared the merit with the gods, nāga,*
> *garuḍa, and all the beings in hell.*
> *At that time I made a prayer: 'With this merit,*
> *may I be the son of a king and rule the realm in this place.'* "

To offer another example, the Bodhisatta said, "At that time there was a bird that flew into the garden and pecked various flowers. I caught the bird, put it on a raft of banana trees, and floated it on the water. For this karma, the brahman Majjahāyaka had me floated away on the ocean. All of you, do not underestimate the effect of karma, large or small."

Having heard this teaching, the king, people and even the gods, *nāga* and *garuḍa* were happy and sang their praises. As further teaching, the Bodhisatta spoke in verse:[15]

"People should not follow bad teaching, should not consort with bad people
but only with good persons, people of high moral sense.
Those who consort with low people will cause themselves trouble,
and will not flourish but find disaster.
Those who consort with good people will flourish
both in wisdom and in merit.
Good people with gratitude will be of benefit to others.
After death they will be born in the heavens.
Bad people without gratitude will be of no benefit to themselves or others.
After death, they will be born in hell.
Bad people who think only evil, speak only evil,
do only evil things—are on the way to hell.
Wise people who think only good, speak only good,
do only good things—can avoid the way to hell.
Wise people who know right from wrong
will gain benefit in the present and the future.
Wise people act for the benefit of themselves and others.
Bad people are of no benefit in two ways, namely,
they do only things of no benefit, and lead both themselves
and others who follow their words toward hell."

In giving advice to the king, he spoke a verse:[16]

"Your Majesty, those who consort with others,
whether with good people or bad, fall under those people's power.
Those who make friends with people of certain types will be like them,
because being together causes them to be the same.
If a good student consorts with a bad teacher,
he will be like an arrow that is treated with poison and will get stuck.
A wise person fears being tarnished and does not consort with bad people.
If someone wraps a rotten fish in a leaf, the leaf will stink.

15. The first two lines come from the Dhammapada, 6 Paṇḍita Vaggo. The eighth couplet (*diṭṭhe dhamme . . .*) is close to the ending of the 43 Iṭṭhasutta in Aṅguttara Nikāya 5.

16. This verse appears in J503 Sattigumba (Cowell, *Jataka*, IV, 270–71). It is also similar to a passage from J545 Narada (Appleton and Shaw, *Ten Great Birth Stories*, 440–41; Faussböll, *Jātaka*, VI, 235–36).

Consorting with bad persons also has a stink, namely the stink of bad deeds.
If someone wraps eaglewood in a leaf, the leaf will be fragrant.
Consorting with wise persons is the same.
Hence when we know the change in a leaf wrapping rotten fish,
and the change of ourselves, a wise person
will not consort with bad persons, only good ones.
Bad people go to hell. Good people go to heaven.
Hence, avoid bad friends and consort only with good friends."

After giving this teaching, the Great Being got up from his seat and went straight to see his mother, paid respect, and ate a meal. At that time, the courtiers, royal servants, and people all sang their praises, and the gods including Lord Amarinda made salutations, scattered celestial flowers, and made worship in wonder. In addition, two angels came down from the Tusita Heaven in a *vimāna*. They halted in the sky, appeared half-shown at a window in the *vimāna* with hands raised in salute, and called out to the prince, "Excellent prince, please leave your human body and assume a celestial body. Please leave the human world and come to the heavens. Please leave the sorrows of humanity and enjoy celestial happiness. Please leave a house of grass and come to this celestial *vimāna*."

Hearing this, the prince took leave of his mother, raising his hand in salute, and spoke a verse:

"*This celestial vimāna, shining with the seven jewels,*
resounding with the sound of various music coming from the Tusita level,
has come to receive me. Allow me to take leave of you, mother,
and go to be born in the heavens at this time."

Hearing this, his mother's heart trembled. She asked the prince, "O son, beloved as my own eyes, if you are going to the heavens, take me too."

The Bodhisatta said, "Mother, there is also a *vimāna* made of gold, embellished with seven gems, resounding with celestial music, and gay with thousands of heavenly maidens. This is for you, mother. It is a sign that arose from merit."

She said, "Please take me to the heavenly city."

"Mother, at the moment, you cannot go. A person cannot travel on a long journey of a thousand *yojana* within one day. You cannot go to the heavenly city today, mother. Please give alms, follow the precepts, and make prayers throughout your life—then you can go."

The king, queens, consorts, courtiers, priest-counselors, and people all prostrated to pay respect to Prince Sirasā. He invited his mother, father, and brahman Ayyaka to sit in order and pay respect, then he disappeared in a flash in front of their eyes. He was born in the *vimāna* that came from Tusita, and went to Tusita with the angels.

After he disappeared, everyone including his mother cried out and writhed around as if they had lost their hands and feet. His mother spoke a verse:

> *"O little son, most beloved of your mother,*
> *why did you leave me and go to the heavens alone?*
> *How can I follow in order to see your face? I must be parted from you,*
> *my beloved, forever. How can I follow after you?*
> *Someone has plucked out my heart. No pain is worse than being parted from you."*

After a time, her lamentations fell quiet and she lost her senses. Everyone was distraught. His royal father could not contain himself and collapsed down on the spot. Ayyaka and others were filled with sadness, and all collapsed down senseless in rows.

Seeing everyone collapsed, the gods felt sympathy. They went up to the Bodhisatta and said, "Great man, because you disappeared, your mother has fainted. If you do not go there, her heart will break, and she will die without recovering her senses. All of those who have collapsed will die because they are thinking of you, and they must fall into hell since they die without recovering their senses. Please return for the sake of your father, mother, and the people."

Hearing these words of the gods, the Bodhisatta felt compassion for his mother. He went into the *vimāna*, sat on the bed, and set his mind to think, "May I be like a young child who goes to sit on the lap of his mother." As a result of setting his mind in this way, he reappeared on the lap of his mother. Seeing that she had lost her senses, he stroked her bosom with his palm and called out to her, "Mother wake up, please wake up. I am Prince Sirasā, your beloved child. I have come back to wipe away your tears."

She revived and immediately embraced and kissed her son, feeling overjoyed. The father and everyone else also revived and were happy when they saw the Bodhisatta.

A hundred thousand heavenly *apsara* maidens who were the retinue of the Bodhisatta brought the *vimāna* down from the world of the gods to stand in the sky, surrounded by a hundred thousand chariots. The aura of the deities, celestial maidens, and the jeweled *vimāna* illuminated an area of around a hundred thousand *yojana*. They say that the lord of the lions and lord of the elephants surrounded by their lady lions and lady elephants look as beautiful as a royal lotus and white lotus surrounded by their petals. The jeweled *vimāna* of the Bodhisatta, surrounded by thousands of chariots, looked just as beautiful.

The two angels called Nandasiri and Sittā stood on either side of the Bodhisatta's throne. These two were senior to the hundred thousand other angels. They came down to carry the Bodhisatta up to the throne in the jeweled *vimāna* and then stood around him.

When the Bodhisatta came down from the world of the gods to his mother's lap in the form of an infant, the angels saw he was a divine youngster with a complexion like gold or the light of the sun at sunrise. He looked grand with a hundred thousand *apsara* maidens. The Bodhisatta amid the *apsara* maidens looked as beautiful as five hundred jewels shining bright and beautiful on a mountain peak. Everyone, including the king, courtiers, and brahman Ayyaka, offered articles of worship and sang the praises of the Bodhisatta in a great uproar. The angels on the right-hand side were decked with yellow decorations, all made of gold. Those on the left were decked with white decorations, all made of silver. Brahman Ayyaka asked the Bodhisatta, "The decorations of the two sets of angels are not the same. What karma did they make when they were human?"

The Bodhisatta replied, "Those in yellow had worshiped the Triple Gem with yellow flowers, and those in white had worshiped the Triple Gem with white flowers. They have beautiful figures and complexions because they upheld the precepts in past lives."

The gods and humans made worship and played music for the king. The courtiers, royal servants, and people of the city stood with hands raised to salute the Bodhisatta. The king and queen looked at the Bodhisatta's *vimāna* floating in the sky. They raised their hands in salute, saying, "Son, why are you leaving your mother and father to be lonely? Please come back."

Hearing this, the Bodhisatta thought, "When I was born in the human world, I had not given alms or accumulated merit from renunciation. I must do good works to accumulate merit." With this thought, he immediately went down and was reborn spontaneously[17] with a body of someone aged twenty years. The angels on the left and right went down and were born in the same way.

At that time a gem wheel came up out of the sea to support the Bodhisatta, and a pair of shining jeweled slippers floated from Mount Vipula to fit on the Bodhisatta's feet. A gem elephant from the Chaddanta lineage and a gem horse from the Valāhaka lineage came to be in the elephant stable and the horse stable. The two angels who had been reborn without parents became gem women. A gem treasurer appeared who had celestial eyes that could see one *yojana* into the earth and who knew whether any wealth had an owner or not. A gem soldier appeared with celestial ears that could hear sounds a hundred *yojana* away, so he knew of anyone who praised or criticized the king in any way and knew if anyone had bad intentions toward the king.

The Bodhisatta became an emperor with the name King Sirasā. He ruled with justice, instructed the people righteously, and did not punish with beating or death. The people followed his advice, did good works such as almsgiving, and after death went to be born in the world of the gods.

His royal father and mother went back to the capital, had the seven hundred evil brahmans including Majjahāyaka arrested, placed them on a raft, and floated it on the water, as they had done to the Bodhisatta. After it had been floating for a short time, the raft broke due to the power of the wind and waves. The brahmans died and were reborn in hell.

There is a comparison here. The moon on the day it is full looks more beautiful than all the stars. The lord of the lions is four times grander than all the animals. The lord of the swans named Dhatarattha[18] is finer than all the swans. The lord of the *garuḍa* is grander than all other birds. An ocean is larger than any river. Mount Meru is more special then all seven of the Satta Paribhaṇḍa ranges. Lord Amarinda is more excellent than all the gods. Mahābrahma is greater than all the Brahma. The following comparison is like these other comparisons: the jeweled *vimāna* of King Sirasā the emperor established in Ayyaka City was more excellent than all residences. King Sirasā the emperor was the highest of the eighty-four

17. อุปปาติ, *upapati*, upapātika, spontaneous rebirth, for instance, without parents.
18. Name of the Bodhisatta when he is born as king of the *haṁsa* in J502 Haṁsa.

thousand kings. His body was like a jewel. When he wished to assume the body of a deity or the body of a human, the wish was realized.

From the time he ruled as emperor he had almshouses built in ten places—one to store gold, one to store silver, one to store jewels, one to store copper, one to store white gold, one to store tin, one to store various cloth and costumes, one to store wood, one to store vehicles, and one to store food. Whenever someone wanted something, he could have what was wished.

The Bodhisatta gave alms, followed the precepts, and made prayers all the time. When he grew old, he saw the wrong in being a householder and saw the beneficial result of renunciation. Hence he entrusted the realm to his son and went out as a rishi. He accumulated merit until he achieved the *jhāna* meditative states. After passing away, he was born in the Brahma realms.

When the Teacher ended this story from the past, he said, "O monks, Devadatta did not have bad intentions toward me only at the present but also in the past in the same way." He then gave the Four Noble Truths and explained the birth connections: "Brahman Majjahāyaka at that time is Devadatta; his followers are the followers of Devadatta; the minister Ayyaka is Sāriputta; of the six princes, the first, Prince Sunakkhatta, became Upāli; the second, Prince Canda, became Nanda; the third, Prince Suriya, became Bhagu Thera; the fourth, Prince Sudhana, became Bhaddiya Thera; the fifth, Prince Singhadeva, became Kapila Thera;[19] the sixth, Prince Kāmadeva, became Ānanda Thera; Nandasiri became Janapada Kalyānī; Sitta became Bimba Yasodharā; the royal father and mother became the great royal family; the followers of King Sirasā are the followers of Buddhism; King Sirasā is I, the Tathāgata, at this time. May all remember this *jātaka*."

19. Upāli was a barber and prominent early disciple; Nanda was a half-brother of the Buddha; Bhagu and Bhaddiya were Sakyan relatives and also early converts; Kapila was a prominent and renegade monk during the time of the Kassapa Buddha (probably included here mistakenly for another early follower).

SELF-SACRIFICE

RATANAPAJJOTA: THE SHINING GEM

P4 *Ratanapajjotajātaka*

รัตนปโชตชาดก

Nothing is known on the origin of this tale, which is also found in Cambodia, Laos, and Burma. The same theme—of a son who is prepared to sacrifice his life through gratitude to his mother but is saved by a prayer of truth and the intervention of Sakka—is found in P25 Narajiva, P27 Mahāpaduma, and P29 Bahalāgāvi. A slight variant, where the son sacrifices his life for his father, is found in P5 Sirivipulakitti and in two classical *jātaka*, J398 Sutano and J513 Jayaddisa.

When the Great Teacher was staying in the Jeta Grove, he thought about a monk who was supporting his mother, and hence gave this sermon beginning with the words "I am distraught" as follows.

The background of this story is this. Since this monk was ordained, he had gone on almsround to support his mother. All the other monks criticized him on grounds that it was not fitting for a monk to support a layperson. The full story is similar to the Suvaṇṇasāma Jātaka in the Ten Jātakas collection.[1] Here is an abridged version.

The Great Teacher said, "O monks, don't criticize this monk for supporting his mother. Wise men in the past have supported their mothers while in the monkhood in the same way." He then fell quiet. Wanting to know the story, the monks begged him to give

1. The story of the past in J540 Suvaṇṇasāma is completely different, but the story of the present is a similar but longer version of the tale here, about a monk who goes on almsround in order to support his parents and is criticized by other monks until the Buddha intervenes (Appleton and Shaw, *Ten Great Birth Stories*, 122–26).

them a sermon. The Great Teacher thus told a tale from the past as follows.

O monks, in the past there was a king called Mahāratha ruling in the city called Meghavatī with a queen named Siriratanabha. At that time, the Bodhisatta passed from the Tusita level of heaven and came down to be conceived in the queen's womb. After she had given birth, the queen had a desire to visit the royal park, and informed her husband as such. The king sent for the park keeper and had him clean up and decorate the park to look fine. The park keeper hastened to organize matters as the king wished. On the appointed day, the king, queen, and their courtiers and retinue journeyed to the royal park, and she was happy at what she saw. From morning to evening, the king and queen did not return to the city and so spent the night in the park.

That night the king and queen slept on the same bed. Near dawn, the queen had an ominous dream. A man with dark skin and red hair, dressed in red upper and lower cloths and carrying a sword, came running from the west into her bedroom. He grabbed hold of her hair, dragged her down, gouged out both her eyes, and cut off her right arm with the sword. He collected the blood, and to cap it all, sliced open her breast and took out her heart, then turned and left toward the west.

The queen, scared to death, started awake, trembling. She thought about the dream and feared that there would be some danger as a result. She told her husband. After listening, King Mahāratha ordered an astrologer who interpreted dreams to examine this one. The seer said, "Sire, this is a strange omen, meaning that you and the queen will be parted for certain."

"What will be the cause of this separation?"

"Sire, this evening, great clouds will gather, heavy rain will fall, and floods will rise, first only to foot level, then to the knee, waist, breast, throat, head, and will increase further to the depth of seven sugar-palm trees."

"What should we do?"

"Sire, the only refuge is a boat."

The king sent for the head carpenters and ordered them to build a boat and inform him as soon as it was finished. The carpenters worked together to finish a boat, and informed him.

That evening great clouds gathered in every direction, rain fell without pause, floods rose first to the level of a foot, and then to the shin, waist, and to seven sugar-palm trees deep. Seeing the flood rising, people were frightened to death and sought somewhere to stay. Waves swept them away to disaster. The king and queen boarded the boat. Great waves swept the boat along on the current. The queen was heavily pregnant and not courageous. She felt she would not survive. Tears streamed down her face as she pronounced a verse:

> "*O king, I am distraught. This hardship is immense and strange.*
> *On the great ocean, where there is nowhere to stay, how can I survive?*
> *Alas, I shall be like an orphan with no patron in this great expanse of water.*
> *Now I am adrift on the waters, with nobody to help,*
> *how can I reach some island shore? I will die and not see you again.*"

King Mahāratha comforted her, "Beloved, don't fear. Why grieve? What is the use? The way I see it is this. We have enjoyed wealth and now comes misfortune. First there is the prime of life, and then old age. First there is good health, and then there is pain and fever. After life, there is death." He gave this advice, and spoke a verse:

> "*Do not grieve deeply. The world is always like this.*
> *All bodies are impermanent.*[2] *All Buddhas have said so.*
> *One good deed that you can do for me*
> *is to set your mind to look on the bright side of things.*"

When the king had advised and comforted her in this way, a great wave swept over them. The boat broke in two. The queen greatly feared death, seeing no way she could survive. She wept and cried out to her husband for help, with a verse:

> "*Oh, please help me to escape this hardship.*
> *Parted from my husband, I cannot survive. Do not abandon me, sire.*"

King Mahāratha heard her plaintive cry about being separated, and was so distressed he took off his shoulder cloth to tie her firmly to him. But then the cloth slipped from them, as if showing some karma made in the past. The king and queen each floated away alone on the waves.

2. See note 3 in P47 Rathasena above.

There is a question. What karma had the king and queen made that caused them to be separated? The answer is this. In a previous life the king and queen went swimming in a river. A seven-year-old novice was paddling a boat to the bank close by. The pair teased the novice by rocking his boat. The novice, fearing it would capsize, cried out loud. As fruit of the karma made with this novice, the king and queen had to be separated.[3]

For this reason, the Blessed One taught, "Do not carelessly believe that something small will not affect your karma. Don't be careless about the fruit of good and bad deeds like this. Good and bad deeds, however small, have consequences. Though the king and queen only bothered the novice a little, it contributed to their separation."

Separated from her husband, the queen was driven by the waves to the foot of Mount Canda. She landed but saw no one there. She spread half her cloth to dry while covering herself with the other half. Once all was dried out, she sat under a tree and felt pitifully lonely, without friend or patron. Tears streamed down her face as she spoke a verse:

> "*In the past, I must have parted a mother bird and its chick.*
> *As a result of the karma I am now parted from my husband.*[4]
> *The king has power to rule the earth. What can I do to see the face of him alone?*
> *Now I am lost in a great forest with no one to rely on. I will probably die today.*"

The power of merit of the being in the queen's womb immediately caused the heaven of the Thousand-Eyed Lord to become hot. He reflected and knew what had taken place. He sent for Vissukamma and ordered him, "Go to Mount Canda and conjure up a lake together with five lotuses, and a leaf hut along with all the equipment an ascetic needs. Make the place elegant, shady, and cheerful."

Vissukamma came down and conjured up a lake and a leaf hut with a sign on the door saying, "Whoever wishes to renounce, please stay in this hut and use the equipment." Vissukamma returned to his abode and informed the Thousand-Eyed Lord.

3. This vignette appears also in P1 Samuddhagosa, P3 Sudhanu, P41 Sanghapatta, and P61 Candagadha.
4. This couplet appears also in P9 Subhamitta and P39 Prince Pācitta.

Here will be told of King Mahāratha. When the wind and waves floated him away, King Mahāratha experienced great hardship drifting for about seven days before arriving back at his own city.

The queen was suffering at Mount Canda, grieving heavily over the king. One day she set off along a road, saw the leaf hut, read the sign, and knew it was built by the Thousand-Eyed Lord. She went in and took up the life of a female rishi there.

One day at midnight, the queen gave birth to a son as beautiful as gold. At dawn, she bathed and suckled him. She named the Bodhisatta from an omen. On the night of his birth, there was a crystal bright light throughout the Himavanta Forest, and so she named him Ratanapajjota, the shining gem. In the morning she left him in the hut, went into the forest, and brought back roots and fruit. She carried on like this until the Bodhisatta was five years old.

One day he asked, "Mother, who is my father? Where is he? Why are you here alone?"

"O mother's darling, your father is a king and I am a queen." She told him the story. Unable to stifle the power of his gratitude, he said, "From today, let mother stay in the hut. I will go to find fruit for you to eat."

"Darling child, you're not going into the forest. While I am alive, understand that I will attend to it. You know why? Because you are still a small child, you cannot go into the forest."

Seeing no opportunity, the Bodhisatta kept quiet.

Every morning when the queen went into the forest to find fruit, the Great Being left the leaf hut and followed her footprints until he could remember the paths and directions. One morning when she had collected a full bag of fruit, she sat and rested under a banyan tree before returning. When her tiredness had gone and she was thinking of setting out, an ogre called Balāhaka who dwelled at that banyan seized her arm. Seeing the ogre, the queen was scared to death and worried about the Great Being, so she spoke a verse:

"Now my beloved son is alone in the hut with nobody to help
and no fruit to eat, so he will come out to look for me in the forest.
I don't see him. Perhaps he has died.
My beloved son will search and call out
until late at night, until midnight,
until his voice disappears, like water in a river that dries out."

The Bodhisatta sat waiting for his mother in the leaf hut. From morning to evening she did not return. He thought, "It's almost dusk. Why is she later than other days? Something must have happened."

He left the leaf hut and walked along the mountain paths, winding this way and that through the forest and hills, calling out to her, missing her pitifully, like the son of a golden swan who strays away from his mother and is distraught at not seeing her. Eventually he reached the banyan where the ogre was holding his mother.

Knowing the Great Being had come after her, she called out, "I'm here." He approached and saw her sitting beside the ogre. He felt as happy as if he would achieve enlightenment as a Buddha the next morning. He sat hidden close to the ogre and pleaded, "Ogre, sir, please eat my blood, flesh, and heart. Please release my mother quickly." He spoke a verse:

> *"Great ogre, let me give my life instead of my mother. Eat my blood, heart, and flesh.*
>
> *Just eat only me, whole. Please release my mother. Please allow her to survive."*

The ogre replied, "If you speak the truth, slice open your breast and give me your heart to eat right now."

The Great Being thought, "Where can I find a knife?" He composed his mind, thought of his merit, raised his eyes to look at the sky, and spoke a verse:

> *"I wish to be a Buddha in future through the power of my gratitude and sincerity.*
>
> *Please give me a sharp weapon. Please make it drop down in front of me now."*

Before he could complete the prayer, a sharp weapon floated down from the sky in front of him. He said, "If I am to be a Buddha in future, let me pay respect to my mother before she dies, and let me give my own life for hers." He sliced open his chest with the knife, took out his heart, held it in his left hand, raised both arms above his head and pronounced a verse:

> *"Through the power of my gratitude, may I be a Buddha in the future.*
>
> *O ogre, please eat my heart, but allow me not to die just yet."*

He wished to present his heart to the ogre with respect, so he raised his arms in salute and placed it on the ogre's palms, announcing, "Great ogre, here is my heart for you. I have no desire for the treasure of this world or the treasure of the gods or of a Pacceka Buddha. As a fruit of my giving this heart, may I be a fully enlightened Buddha in the future, raise people to fill the boats of truth, and lead them out of the cycle of birth to the shore of *nibbāna*, of bliss." The Great Being then told the ogre to eat his heart as he wished. The ogre happily handed back his mother.

He took his mother to sit under a tree, prostrated before her, and said, "Mother, from my conception until today, whatever wrong I have done or said, please give me your forgiveness." With these words, his eyes closed, and he collapsed in front of her.

She started up in alarm, hugged him to her breast with both hands, and grieved as if her heart would break in two, saying a verse:

> *"O child, you have gone, like the sun or moon that has set.*
> *Beloved child, get up. Why are you lying gloomy and lifeless.*
> *If you have died, I will die to follow you. Why should I live on alone?*
> *Mother's utmost beloved son, I'm now desolate,*
> *with no one to depend on, like a mother parted from an infant child.*
> *Where shall I go in this forest? I will die here.*
> *O gods of the mountains, streams, forests, woods, earth, and sky,*
> *all the deities who have the power to look after the world and the waters,*
> *including Indra and Brahma, allow me to pay my respect*
> *and beg you to spare my son from death at this time."*

She embraced her son and grieved.

At that time, the world of the Thousand-Eyed Lord seemed unusually hot because of the power of the Great Being's gratitude. The Thousand-Eyed Lord reflected, understood the cause, and hastened down from the heavens to stand in the air in front of the ogre. He shouted menacingly, "Ogre Balāhaka, you are making some dreadful karma! If this fellow does not rise up alive right now, I will split your head into seven pieces with my thunderbolt weapon."

The ogre shivered in fear. He raised the Great Being upright and bathed him with heavenly medicine. In an instant, the Great Being revived.

The queen thought, "I shall make another oath." She spoke a verse:

> *"My son is resolute in gratitude. He will be a Buddha in the future.*
> *With the power of my sincerity, may my son return to life right now."*

After the first line of this prayer, the Great Being's complexion turned as bright as gold. After the second, he breathed easily, turned over and back, left and right. After the third, he recovered, sat up, and paid respect to his mother.

When relating these events, the Great Teacher spoke a verse:

The Great Being recovered, sat up, and paid respect to his mother.
He sat thinking about the merit of his own befitting goodness.
While he was thus, the earth roared,
Mount Meru swayed, and the oceans frothed up in great waves.
The gods from the Catumahārājikā, Tāvatiṁsā, Yamika,
Tusita, Nimmānarati, and Paranimmitavasavattī levels of heaven,
up to the deities of the Brahma levels,
looked on with gladness, strewing divine magnolia flowers,
Pārichattaka flowers, and lotuses to carpet everywhere in all directions.
Crowds everywhere scattered grains of sand and various flowers,
such as champaka, to cover everywhere in the sky in all directions.
And all the gods, including the spirits of the earth,
gathered together to pay respect to the Great Being of noble[5] *lineage*
and offer up their praises. "O Great Being of great merit and bravery,
you repaid the merit of your mother. May your wish be fulfilled as you hope.
Before long, you will surely be a Buddha in this world."

Then the ogre paid respect and begged the forgiveness of the Great Being. The gods, with Lord Sakka, king of the gods, presiding, conjured up a golden palanquin, invited the queen and Great Being to sit there, and sent them to Meghavatī City in one night, to sit on a jeweled throne in a seven-storied palace. The gods paid respect and returned to their abode.

King Mahāratha saw the Great Being and recognized him. He happily anointed the Great Being to rule the realm from then on. After the ceremony, the Great Being experienced the five sensual pleasures[6] as appropriate and gave alms for a month. He returned the realm to his father, making his father and mother very happy. He paid respect to beg forgiveness and ask permission to go forth. The people of the city all wept as they sent him off.

5. นรุตตม, *naruttama*, nara-uttama, "best of men," name of ancient kings and an epithet of the Buddha.

6. เบญจกามคุณ, *benja kamakhun*, pañcakāmaguṇa: form, sound, smell, taste, touch.

He went on his own, setting his face toward the Himavanta Forest like a young swan journeying to the peak of a mountain.

When explaining this tale for the first time, the Well-Farer and Teacher spoke a verse:

> *When the Great Being ruled the realm, he gave alms for about a month, entrusted the realm to his father, paid respect, and left for the Himavanta Forest.*

He renounced as a rishi, practiced the five states of knowledge and eight achievements of meditation in full, acquired insight that would not decline or end, and was reborn in the Brahma world.

King Mahāratha, Queen Siriratanabha, and the people of Meghavatī City followed the teaching of the shoot of the Victorious One, including making merit by almsgiving, and after death were reborn in the heavens.

After the Great Teacher gave this sermon, he pronounced the Four Noble Truths once again, and the monk Mātuposaka[7] achieved the fruit of stream entry as a noble person in the religion. The Great Teacher then made the birth connections: "The mother of the Bodhisatta at that time returned as Mahāmāyā; his father as King Suddhodhana; Lord Sakka, king of the gods, as Anuruddha; ogre Balāhaka as Angulimāla; and Ratanapajjota as the refuge of the world. May all of you remember this *jātaka*."

7. The subject of a *jātaka* (J455) and a sutta on the same theme of a monk supporting his parents.

BAHALĀGĀVĪ

P29 *Bahalāgāvījātaka*

พหลาคาวีชาดก

INTRODUCTION

This story of self-sacrifice for a mother is distinctive because the two are a cow and calf. There is some echo of J359 Suvaṇṇamiga, the golden deer, in which a stag is snared and the doe offers herself instead to the huntsman, who is so impressed by this selflessness that he releases both of them,[1] but there is no known origin of the story.

When the Great Teacher was staying at the Jeta Grove, he spoke of his gratitude to his mother and thus gave this sermon beginning with the words "No merit is equal to truth" as follows.

One day the monks were sitting together in the teaching hall, praising the gratitude of the Blessed One. The Great Teacher arrived there and asked, "What are you talking about?"

"We are praising your gratitude."

"O monks, it is not only in this time that I have shown gratitude but also in past times." At that, he fell silent. Wishing to know the story, the monks begged him to explain. The Buddha thus told this story from the past in a sermon as follows.

One time in the past, there was a man in Kosala who was looking after a mother cow called Bahalā [stout] that had one calf.

One day Bahalā and the calf left the house to look for grass along with the herd. Bahalā went into the forest on her own while the calf stayed with the herd. A tiger in the forest saw the cow eating grass and approached

1. Cowell, *Jātaka*, III, 120–23.

with the thought of catching her to eat. The cow raised her head, saw the tiger, and said, "O great tiger, what have you come here for?"

"To catch you to eat."

"Please wait a while. I have a young calf. I will go and feed her with milk, then come back for you to eat me."

"If you're speaking the truth, I'll wait for you."

Bahalā went to her calf and said, "Beloved child, you must hurry to drink your mother's milk. I will go to be eaten by a tiger."

"Why do you speak to me like this?"

Bahalā cried from love of her calf. The calf spoke with loyalty and gratitude, "Don't go to be eaten by the tiger. Let me go instead."

"I have already promised the tiger I would let him eat me. I am true to my word. It's normal that sincerity is a condition for gaining the treasures. It is praised by gods and humans. Speaking untruth is vile and dirty. For this reason, even though my body will be destroyed, I will not break my word."

Bahalā went and stood close to the tiger. The calf followed her, crying out, and stood behind the mother, saying, "O great tiger, please eat me and spare my mother's life."

The Great Teacher gave a sermon: "It is normal that gratitude is a condition for gaining the treasures. It is praised by gods and humans. For this reason, the tiger should know that the calf has gratitude and should refrain from doing harm. Such forbearance would be a good deed more excellent than any other form of merit, and a condition of gaining the treasures. Gods and humans will give their praise."

Hearing the calf's words, the tiger said, "I will do no harm. I won't eat either of you."

Through the power of this truth, forbearance, gratitude, and appreciation of the good done by others on the part of all three animals, the realm of Lord Sakka, king of the gods, became hotter. Lord Sakka reflected and knew the cause. He came down from the heavens, approached the three animals, and spoke a verse:

"Of all the fine and beautiful good deeds of merit,
none is equal to sincerity, forbearance, gratitude,
and appreciation of the virtuous deeds done to us by others.
These three—sincerity, forbearance, and appreciation of others—
are the most splendid and excellent good deeds of merit.
The fully enlightened Buddha taught that anyone who does all good deeds

but does not show sincerity, forbearance, gratitude, and appreciation of others
will not prosper, will not benefit from the fruit of his own good deeds."

Lord Sakka took the three animals to the world of the gods and gave each of them a celestial palace full of a thousand *apsara* divine maidens and celestial goods, enlivened by dancing, singing, recitation, and the five kinds of music, decked with many flags and pennants, complete with all the sensual pleasures of the heavens. The three animals lost their own identity, became deities in Lord Sakka's abode, and enjoyed celestial happiness in the heavens. For this reason, the Great Teacher gave teaching in a verse:

Truth is the great master of the world.
Where there is truth, all good deeds will prosper,
as in the case of the cow Bahalā who, by keeping her word,
was born into the heavens through the power of that truth.
Forbearance is the great master of the world.
Where there is forbearance, all good deeds will prosper,
as in the case of the lord tiger who showed forbearance toward the cow
and thus was born into the heavens through the power of that forbearance.
Gratitude is the root of the goodness that is master of the world.
Anyone who shows gratitude, their good deeds will prosper,
as in the case of the calf who showed gratitude to the mother
and was born in the heavens through the power of that gratitude.
For these reasons, all good and devout persons who wish for the treasures
should have the wisdom and discretion to show sincerity, forbearance, gratitude, and appreciation of the good done to them by others at all times.
Anyone who approaches their father, mother, or teacher
must endeavor to display gratitude, speak the truth, and show forbearance.
Such persons will enjoy great happiness in the human world and divine world.
They will not suffer from any kind of ailment or affliction
such as dumbness, diseases that require organs to be covered,[2] *deafness, disability, blindness,*
epilepsy, leprosy, skin rashes, ringworm, asthma, meloidosis, or the yellow-thin disease.
Avoiding these diseases is the fruit of truth.
They will escape all suffering and have all forms of well-being.

2. Perhaps any deformity that can be disguised, like a withered hand.

They will have fingers, fingernails, teeth, eyes, nose, and mouth, all bright, clean, fine, and attractive,
complete with all organs great and small, not swelling and not shrinking.
They will be born in a family that has quick wisdom, having organs and body perfect, and all beautiful.
They will not be at odds with anyone but have sharp wisdom, not cold toward anyone,
with fluent speech. All these good qualities are the fruit of forbearance.
Longevity, a bright color and appearance, bodily strength,
happiness when standing, sitting, or lying, and not causing death—
all these good qualities are the fruit of showing gratitude.
It's natural that those who behave well will have happiness.
Behaving well brings happiness to them.
That is the beneficial result of behaving well.
Such persons will not be born in the realms of woe.

When the Great Teacher came to the end of the sermon, he explained the birth connections in a verse:

Sakka at that time was reborn as Anuruddha, superior to all monks with divine insight;
the great tiger from the forest as King Suddhodana, father of the Buddha;
the cow Bahalā as Mahāmāyā, mother of the Buddha;
the calf as the great refuge of the world. All of you, remember this jātaka.

SUVAṆṆA KACCHAPA: THE GOLDEN TURTLE

P43 *Suvaṇṇakacchapajātaka*

สุวรรณกัจฉปชาดก

INTRODUCTION

This tale is a unique variation on the theme of sacrificing the body to help others. This story is an old one, found in several collections of *jātaka* in Sanskrit, Chinese, Khotanese, and Tibetan. The closest is found in *Avadānakalpalatā*, an eleventh-century collection by the Kashmiri poet Kshemendra. In that version, the shipwrecked merchants are intent on killing the turtle, but the turtle sacrifices itself first.

When the Great Teacher was staying at the Jeta Grove, he spoke about the giving of flesh and thus told this *jātaka* in a sermon beginning with the words "I have learned what is to be learned" as follows.

One day the monks gathered to sit and talk in the teaching hall, saying, "O friends, we praise our Great Teacher for never tiring of the acquisition of merit, both minor merit and major. He is primarily intent on giving."

Hearing these words with his divine power of hearing, the Great Teacher came to the teaching hall and asked, "What are you sitting here talking about?" They told him.

He said, "O monks, it is not only in this life that I have not tired of the acquisition of merit. In past lives, I was the same. I gave alms of flesh to acquire further merit." With that he fell silent. Wishing to know the story, the monks invited him to tell a tale from the past in a sermon, as follows.

In the past there was a king named Brahmadatta ruling in Bārāṇasī City. At that time the Bodhisatta was born as a turtle living in the ocean. He had a color of natural gold and a body twenty fathoms long and twenty fathoms wide. His name was Suvaṇṇa Kacchapa [golden turtle] on account of the fact that he was a beautiful color like pure gold all over. He searched for food in the ocean and lived at the foot of a mountain on a large island.

Some five hundred merchants left Bārāṇasī on a single junk and had sailed across the ocean for three days when their junk was hit by a fierce wind and great waves. Unable to withstand the buffeting and the power of the waves, the timbers of the junk split apart. The junk was about to sink in mid-ocean. The merchants shouted, wept, and prayed loudly to the guardian gods to help rescue them from danger.

Hearing the sound of human cries, the turtle-Bodhisatta came up to the surface of the ocean, saw the merchants shouting, and felt compassion. He went toward them and said, "Get up on my back, all of you. I'll take you to safety." The merchants did so. The turtle carried them across the ocean to his island home. The merchants got down from the turtle's back but were too weak to go up to the island because they had not eaten for seven days. They slept from exhaustion on the beach.

The Bodhisatta thought, "These merchants have nobody to turn to and will probably die. This should not be! I'll give them my own flesh as alms so they may live longer."

He said to them, "Please grill my flesh to eat and recover your strength, then use my shell as a boat and my breast shell for other purposes, and keep some leftover meat for supplies on the way."

The merchants all raised their clasped hands to salute the turtle-Bodhisatta, saying, "O great golden turtle, your generosity is great. What you have done for us already is virtue beyond estimation. We cannot possibly kill you."

The Bodhisatta thought, "They don't want to kill me because they are full of gratitude and recognize my generosity. This should not be! I'll go up to the peak of the mountain by myself and fall back down so the shell of my breast breaks and my flesh will be alms for these merchants. Once they have eaten my flesh, they will survive. It will be the same as if I were the cause of beings being born. The five aggregates of me have no solid substance, in the same way that a banana plant has no solid trunk. There are the words of the noble lord: even if I am determined to live for a long time, still I will die. I am not content to live. I will die on this day and will give my flesh as alms. This will give substance to the five aggregates of myself and will be a support for my advance toward full enlightenment in the future. That is more excellent! The fruit of this action will achieve my desire."

He climbed up the mountain, paused on the peak, and announced to the gods his wish to be a fully enlightened Buddha in a verse:

"O gods who reside here,
please come to rejoice in the gift of my flesh as alms.
I will give my life as alms
with the desire to become a Buddha in the future."

Hearing the words of the turtle-Bodhisatta, all the gods residing there gathered together at the mountain peak and spoke their praise in a verse:

"It is good, it is good, great striver. Through the good karma that you make
in giving yourself, you will be in the lineage of a Buddha in the future."

The Bodhisatta stated his wish: "If I am to become a Buddha, when I fall down from the mountain, may my breast shell break open, may my flesh and blood break into pieces, big and small, but may my shell not break so that it may serve as a boat to enable the five hundred merchants to escape death." After this prayer, he launched himself off the mountaintop, landing at the foot with a great crash. His breast shell broke open. His flesh and blood broke into big and little pieces, but his back shell did not break, as was his wish. On his death, the turtle-Bodhisatta was reborn in the Tusita Realm.

The merchants were startled by the loud crash and saw the turtle dead at the foot of the mountain. All of them wept, beat their own breasts, and paid respect to his virtue. After they had recovered, the leader of the merchants said, "This turtle has donated us his flesh as alms. We did not wish to kill him, so he sacrificed his own life. Let us spark a fire alight and roast the turtle's flesh to eat now, keeping some leftover for supplies on our journey to Bārāṇasī City."

The merchants followed their leader's words. After eating their fill, they made the shell into a boat and fashioned various things from the breast shell. They boarded the shell-boat and paddled their way towards Bārāṇasī. Wherever they stopped on the way, they ate the leftover turtle meat. In one month, they reached Bārāṇasī and sang the praises of the virtue of the turtle-Bodhisatta to the people, who in turn sang the praises of the virtue of the turtle-Bodhisatta throughout the city.

When King Brahmadatta saw the shell of the turtle, colored like gold, he was filled with joy. After hearing about the virtue of the golden turtle, he said, "This animal must be none another than the sprout of a future Buddha, without a doubt." He commanded that the turtle shell be set up at a suitable place in the south of the city, where it remained forever like a golden mountain.

> When the Great Teacher ended this tale from the past, he followed with a verse:[1]
>
> *I have learned what is to be learned, developed what is to be developed,*
> *abandoned what is to be abandoned, therefore I am a Buddha, O monks.*
> *The way is long and hard. One blind from birth, with no one to lead the way,*
> *will sometimes go by the right way, sometimes by the wrong way.*
> *Sometimes I can show the right way to both gods and humans,*
> *can lead all beings in the cycle of rebirth to achieve the greatest happiness.*
>
> At the end of the sermon, many beings achieved a fruit such as stream-entry. The Ten-Powered One then explained the birth connections: "King Brahmadatta from that time was reborn as the monk named Sāriputta; the leading merchant as the monk named Moggallāna; the remaining merchants as the five disciples;[2] and the golden turtle as the Tathāgata, the great refuge of the world."

1. The first couplet is found in the Sela chapter of the Theragathā (Verses of the Elders) section of the Khuddaka Nikāya (suttacentral.net/pi/thag16.6), poems by early members of the sangha.

2. ปัญจวัคคีย์, *panjawakkhi*, pañcavaggiya, the five brahmans who were present at the first sermon and accompanied the Buddha when he became an ascetic.

SIRI CUḌĀMAṆI

P7 *Siricuḍāmaṇijātaka*

สิริจุฑามณิชาดก

INTRODUCTION

Six stories in the collection are about a king giving "internal alms," meaning not something external like wealth or food but something internal to his life, such as his wife, his child, his realm, his own flesh and blood, or his life. The Buddha discouraged self-sacrifice along with other forms of killing. In these stories, however, self-sacrifice is presented as an ultimate form of generosity and a renunciation of selfhood, and thus a positive step for the Bodhisatta in pursuit of enlightenment.[1] The model is Vessantara. Most of the stories of this type borrow verses from J547 Vessantara.

This theme is found in J499 Sivi: after the king resolves to give internal alms, Sakka appears as a blind brahman; the king donates his eyes, then abandons his realm and goes into the forest; Sakka appears and induces the king to make a prayer of truth; his eyes are restored as divine eyes with exceptional sight; on return to the city, the king exhorts the people to give generously. The opening here closely follows the sequence in the Sivi story, and the sawing matches Sivi's gruesomeness, but the wording is different, as are the verses.

The similar stories in the Fifty Jātaka are P6 King Vipula, P12 Āditta, P14 Mahasurasena, P25 Narajīva, and P46 Arindama, which combines this theme with sacrifice for parents. In addition, P30 Seta Paṇḍita has a similar theme, with a mouse as the Bodhisatta, echoing J316 Sasa,[2] in which a rabbit tries to sacrifice himself as alms by throwing himself into a fire.

1. Arthid, "Self-sacrifice."
2. Cowell, *Jātaka*, IV, 34–37.

When the Great Teacher was staying at the Jeta Grove, he thought of his own accumulated merit and thus gave this sermon, beginning with the words "I give and I do not waver."

The story of the present is as follows. One day the monks were gathered to talk at the teaching hall. "Our Great Teacher is not sated with giving. When he was still a bodhisatta, he gave his life as a great almsgiving. Then when he achieved enlightenment as the Buddha, through compassion he gave the noble path and the noble fruits to all the disciples." The Great Teacher arrived and asked, "Monks, what are you gathered to talk about?" They told him. "Not only in this life have I happily given alms. In the past when I was a bodhisatta, I once sliced away half of my body as alms for those who came to ask." He then told the tale from the past, as follows.

In the past, there was a king called Siri Cuḍāmaṇī [splendid crest jewel] ruling in Bārāṇasī. His major queen was called Padumāvatī and he had a son named Canda. The king ruled justly. He had alms halls built at six places and gave alms of six hundred thousand every day. In the mornings, he gave advice to the people, including courtiers, to give alms and follow the precepts. After bathing and dressing, he mounted his royal elephant named Puṇḍarika and, surrounded by his retinue of courtiers, went to the alms halls and distributed alms to mendicants with his own hands, as befitting. Any alms left over he always gave to his courtiers to distribute further.

One day, King Siri Cuḍāmaṇī awoke in the morning and sat pondering, "I would like to give internal alms.[3] If anyone comes to beg for my eyes, head, heart, flesh, blood, half my body, or the whole thing, I will slice that off to give to that beggar, to be a support in gaining full enlightenment."

At that point, wonders arose. The earth 240,000 *yojana* thick groaned like the sound of an elephant trumpeting. The peak of Mount Meru bowed down beside Bārāṇasī like tips of rattan when singed by fire. Oceans were stirred into waves. The gods gathered to give salutations. The uproar echoed from the earth up to the Brahma worlds.

At that point, the world of Lord Sakka, king of the gods, immediately felt warmer. The Thousand-Eyed Lord pondered, "Is this a god or a human, someone who behaves properly with his father and mother, or someone

3. อัชฌัตติกทาน, *atchattika than*, ajjhattika dāna.

living a chaste life,[4] who is shaking me off my seat like this?" Once he knew, his mind was clear: "King Siri Cuḍāmaṇī, a shoot of a future Buddha, wishes to give internal alms to gain enlightenment as a Buddha in future. I should immediately go and help increase his accumulated merit." The Thousand-Eyed Lord descended to Bārāṇasī and transformed himself into a brahman with half a body. He placed himself at the royal courtyard, raised his clasped hands, and called out a blessing: "O Your Majesty, may you have victories!"

Hearing this, King Siri Cuḍāmaṇī came out on an elephant to the front of the palace. Seeing the brahman with half a body, he dismounted close by, unable to hold back his tears. He questioned the brahman with a verse:

> *"Allow me to ask: for what reason and what purpose did you come to my city?*
> *Please tell me the background and the reason, right now."*

The Thousand-Eyed Lord in the guise of a brahman made his body tremble, raised his hands in homage, and replied in a verse:[5]

> *"You are just as the river that flows at all times and never dries up.*
> *So I have come to make a request: give me one half of your body."*

King Siri Cuḍāmaṇī was as overjoyed as if he would attain full enlightenment on the following morning, or as if he were a poor beggar who put out a hand to beg and someone placed a thousand of silver there straight away. When the king spread the news to the city folk, he spoke a verse:

> *"O brahman, I give what you ask from me and I do not waver,*
> *I do not hold back. My mind delights in giving."*

He added, "Brahman, please wait here a while." He went up to the palace and had the people, including courtiers, gather together. He invited Queen Padumāvatī and Prince Canda to attend, embraced and kissed his son, and said, "My beloved son, please take care to follow the precepts. Today I will give internal alms." He invited his son to sit up on the jeweled throne,

4. พรหมจรรย์, *phrommajan*, brahmacariya, Brahma-faring, a chaste, ascetic, or religious life.

5. This verse and the next are slightly adapted from the scene in J547 Vessantara where Sakka, disguised as a brahman, asks for Vessantara's wife (Appleton and Shaw, *Ten Great Birth Stories*, 618; Faussböll, *Jātaka*, VI, 569).

poured water from a golden bowl to anoint him as ruler, and entrusted the realm to his son.

The Bodhisatta then returned to the brahman, looked up into the sky, and announced, "O gods, please come to hear my words. Now I will offer my life as alms with the sole wish to attain full enlightenment." He made a prayer of truth: "Following the custom of Great Beings in the past, may I advance toward full enlightenment through the five great offerings. Through this prayer of truth, may a saw drop down at once."

At that point, through the power of the Bodhisatta's prayer and accumulated merit, two ugly ogres with long green fangs, red teeth, red eyes, and red eyebrows and moustaches, holding a sharp saw, came up through a breach in the earth and stood in front of the throne. All the people there shuddered and fled away in fright. King Siri Cuḍāmaṇī looked at the ogres and said, "Good, great ogres. Please rejoice in my internal almsgiving. I wish to give one half of my body to this old brahman. Please help. Please saw my body from head to foot into two parts. I will give one part to the brahman. The rest, you can eat."

The two ogres saluted this order, and went to stand close to the Great Being, who felt the saw to check, looked up into the sky, and announced to the gods, "I am offering my body as alms. I do not desire the treasure of human life, the treasure of the gods or of an emperor, or the treasure of a Buddhist disciple or follower. May this help me advance to full enlightenment so I may then help worldly beings to escape from the cycle of suffering."

At that point, the gods raised an uproar. The people including courtiers, who had gathered together in a mass, beat their breasts with their hands, let down their hair, and shouted and shrieked as if their hearts would break. The ogres cut the Great Being's head with the saw—a painful sight.

Queen Padumāvatī and Prince Canda sorrowfully embraced his feet, wept, and lamented. When the sharp saw reached his forehead, the blood flowed out shockingly. The gathering of gods waved flags, and their cheers echoed around. Flowers rained down all around. Lightning flashed back and forth across the sky. The gods made worship with offerings of lamps, incense, and flowers.

When the sharp saw passed from forehead to mouth, the Great Being still instructed the people, "Do not be sad." When the saw reached the neck, his suffering was intense, but he suppressed it and praised the virtue of the fully enlightened Buddha. When the saw approached the heart, he said to the ogres, "Make sure you cut well." The ogres diverged to avoid the heart, and went down past the belly and below, making two halves, two parts. Astonishingly, he was not dead.

Queen Padumāvatī, her son, the courtiers, royal servants, and people collapsed down on the ground. The king presented one half of himself to the brahman who took it and joined it to his own body. The gods all made salutations once again, as described above.

Then Lord Sakka, king of the gods, made the two pieces of the Great Being's body join together as they were before. The Great Being got up to a sitting position. His flesh was as beautiful as an image cast in gold. Lord Sakka knew that the Great Being had a pure and clear mind and thus praised him, "Sire, you have given alms this time with three intentions—that is, when offering to give, when giving, and after having given, with a pure and clear mind. May you be sated with giving only this!" The king of the gods made salutations, and took leave to return to the Vejayanta Palace. Then the neighboring lords and people, including householders, recovered their normal selves, and all made salutations in an uproar.

When the Ten-Powered One who gave alms in this way reached old age, he went out to be a rishi in the forest, developing insight that did not decay. On passing away, he went to the Brahma worlds.

> After giving this sermon, the Great Teacher said, "Monks, I do not delight in giving only at the present, but also in the past I gave internal alms in such a way." He then made the birth connections. "Queen Padumāvatī at that time was reborn as Bimbā Yasodharā; the prince as Phra Rāhula; the people as the followers of Buddhism; King Siri Cuḍāmaṇī as the refuge of the world, the Tathāgata." The words of the Buddha end here.

DULAKA PAṆḌITA

P11 *Dulakapaṇḍitajātaka*

ทุลกบัณฑิตชาดก

INTRODUCTION

In several stories in this collection, the Bodhisatta sacrifices himself for the sake of the religion. In this tale, he saves thirty-three monks from execution. In the Dhammapada-Aṭṭhakathā,[1] there is a story of a novice Saṅkissa who offers himself to thieves to gain the release of thirty brahmans, but this story is different and apparently unique. Three other stories on the same theme are P17 Viriya Paṇḍita, P18 Dhammasoṇḍaka, and P26 Surūpa.

> When the Great Teacher was staying at the Jeta Grove, he spoke of the perfection of giving and hence gave this sermon, beginning with the words "Beings have karma, inherit karma."[2]

As has been heard, in Cina City in the past, seven days after the refuge of the world called Kassapa had achieved *nibbāna*, there was a king called Cina Rāja and a brahman holding the post of the king's priest-counselor. One day, thirty-three monks came walking along the road through the city, looking beautifully composed. The brahman saw them and thought, "These are disciples of the Buddha. If I allow them to come to this city, our king will become a devotee of these monks. The offerings we used to receive will disappear. How can I induce the king to execute these monks?"

1. Vol II, 48, see Jaini, *Paññāsa Jātaka*, 2:xiii.
2. A famous statement found, for instance, in the Majjhima Nikāya, the Middle Length Discourses of the Buddha, no. 135. The Thai translator, presumably judging this too brief, added a story of the present in the standard form, here omitted.

He went to attend on King Cina. When the opportunity arose, he addressed the king, "Your Majesty, some robbers have disguised themselves as monks and come to plunder this city."

The king was deceived into believing the words of this brahman and bad companion. He asked, "What should we do?"

"Sire, don't delay. Arrest them immediately, tie them up, cane them, and have them impaled on stakes."

The king agreed with the priest-counselor. He summoned the executioners and commanded them, "Arrest these robbers, tie them up, cane them, take them to the graveyard, and impale them alive on stakes."

The executioners had no compassion and no knowledge of the virtue of the Buddha, the Dhamma, and the Sangha. They went straight to where the monks were staying, broke their almsbowls, ripped their robes, slapped their heads and mouths, and beat them until blood flowed from their ears, noses, and mouths. The monks cried out in protest.

An elder[3] consoled the monks with a dhamma saying: "Friends, don't think anything and don't cry heavily. The Blessed One told us that when we are punished like this, it is because of karma we have made in the past."

The elder taught with a verse:

> "*Beings have karma, inherit karma, own karma of various kinds.*
> *Whatever karma is made, so the fruit will be experienced.*
> *All beings own karma, inherit the fruit of karma, and have karma as their refuge.*
> *Karma that is suffering will give a fruit of suffering.*"

The city people spoke among themselves, "These thirty-three monks are going to be impaled alive!"

At that time, there was a bodhisatta, called Dulaka Paṇḍita, who had been born in a rich family. He heard about this matter, rushed to the residence of the elder, Nāgadīpa,[4] paid respect, and asked, "Master, what is the crime for which you are to be impaled in this way?"

"O disciple, we have not committed any crime in this birth, but we don't know about crimes in some past life."

3. In the Pali original, this is Nāgadīpa, who appears below.

4. "Light of the *nāga*," name of an island and temple to the west of Jaffna in Sri Lanka, said in the *Mahāvaṁsa* chronicle to have been visited by the Buddha after he subdued the *nāga* kings.

The Bodhisatta removed their manacles and begged the executioner, "Please have the mercy to spare these people from execution for a short time. I will go to attend on the king."

He rushed to the palace, paid respect, and said, "Your Majesty, I will offer money to redeem the thirty-three monks. Please have compassion for me, sire."

"Will you truly give this, Dulaka Paṇḍita?"

"Truly, sire."

"In that case, you must give the weight in gold of each person you redeem."

Dulaka Paṇḍita was delighted. He paid respect to take leave, returned home, and begged his mother, "How much gold do you have? Please give it to me."

"Son, what will you do with this gold?"

"Mother, I will redeem the thirty-three monks condemned to execution."

She stroked her own breast and said, "O, I have a son who seeks merit in this way! That is very good. Please take all the wealth."

The Bodhisatta was overjoyed, bright like the moon floating in the sky on full-moon day. After dressing himself in expensive upper and lower cloths, he had people carry the gold and pile it up at the royal courtyard. He went in and addressed the king, "Your Majesty, please accept this gold."

"You must divide up the gold according to the weight of each of the thieves."

Dulaka Paṇḍita went to the elder Nāgadīpa, paid respect, and said, "Please sit on the scale so I can measure your weight. I will take only your weight in gold."

When he wished to gain the release of the thirty-three monks with gold equal to their weight, he spoke a verse:

> *"O gods, please come and gather to hear my words.*
> *I will redeem the monks to escape death, solely to attain enlightenment."*

He redeemed each of the monks by presenting their weight in gold. But when the gold was all finished, three monks were still remaining.

King Cina asked, "Dulaka Paṇḍita, do you have any more gold?"

"Sire, I do not."

"In that case, what will you do?"

"Sire, please delay the execution a while."

The Bodhisatta paid respect to take leave and went home. He told his wife, "I have offered the gold to the king to redeem the thirty-three monks from execution but the gold is all used up and three monks remain. I will sell myself and use the money to buy gold. I can still complete our merit to the full. How do you feel?"

"O husband, don't sell yourself. Better to sell me and the children. When you have the money, use it however you like."

The Bodhisatta happily responded, "That is good."

He led his wife and child by the hand and mortgaged them with a rich man of property. With the money, he bought gold and took it to weigh against the monks. It was enough for only two of them. After the gold was all used up, one young novice still remained.

This young novice was in great fear of death. He sat crying until his head drooped. He said to the executioner, "Please stab me dead with a stake."

Listening to the helpless novice, the executioners felt pity for him. They released him from the manacles. The novice took the opportunity to go to where the elder Nāgadīpa was staying. He paid respect and said, "O elder, allow me to take leave and die today. Since the day I was ordained until now, if I have committed any offence by body, word, or thought with any of you, please have mercy to forgive that offence as I pay my respect now for this one last time. In addition, if my mother and father come to ask after me, please give them this girdle and robes. It will help them to overcome their sorrow." The grieving young novice embraced Nāgadīpa and wept.

Hearing the novice's lamentation, Nāgadīpa felt very sad. He consoled him, "Novice, don't think so much and be so sad. We will not let you alone die." He taught him dhamma with a verse:[5]

> "*All dhamma is impermanent. Things grow and decline as a matter of course.*
> *Having arisen, they pass away. Happy is the peace when they cease forever.*"

Hearing this teaching, Dulaka Paṇḍita reproached himself, "Look here, do I love myself or do I love the Buddha, the Dhamma, and the Sangha more than my own life?"

He went to attend on King Cina, paid respect, and said, "Sire, I volunteer to die in the place of the novice."

"Truly, Dulaka Paṇḍita?"

5. See note 3 in P47 Rathasena above.

"Sire, truly, I will die in his stead."

"In that case, give your life for his."

Dulaka Paṇḍita went to the novice, removed his manacles, and spoke a verse:

> *"O gods, please come and gather to hear my words.*
> *I will die in the place of the novice solely to attain enlightenment."*

He continued, "Gods of great power who live in the sky, hills, and forests, hear my words. What I said just now is all true. Whoever wants my heart, head, eyes, mouth, flesh, or blood, please slice them away at will. I shed my life now as alms for merit. Through the power of giving life as alms, may I be enlightened as a Buddha in the future to carry beings sunk in the cycle of birth and death across to the other side, namely to *nibbāna.*"

He paid respect to the novice and said, "Novice, set your mind to follow the precepts, chant prayers, and have a mind of compassion. If I have made mistakes in my body, words, or thoughts, please give me your forgiveness." He said to the executioners, "Manacle me and cane me in the prescribed fashion." The executioners laid hands on Dulaka Paṇḍita, put him in the five irons, beat him with a rattan cane, and took him to the graveyard of fresh corpses.

At that time, the city people were in uproar talking about the matter of Dulaka Paṇḍita giving up his life for the novice. His mother heard the word going around. Shaking and in shock, she beat her breast with both hands, let down her hair, and writhed around in tears. She ran to the graveyard of fresh corpses and saw her son, who had done no wrong, clapped in the five irons. Her heart felt it would break into seven pieces. With tears flooding down, she spoke a verse:

> *"Son, beloved like my heart, don't do this. You will die before your mother.*
> *I will have no refuge and will die following you.*
> *You still have a great deal of wealth.*
> *You and I do not suffer from want of food and water. Please come home, son."*

She lamented on, "I'll die today or tomorrow for certain. I will hand over all my wealth to you. Please have consideration for your mother."

The Bodhisatta replied, "Don't grieve like this, mother. I will sacrifice my life now for the sake of the Buddha, the Dhamma, and the Sangha. Please don't forbid me, mother. The reason I say this is because the Buddha, the

Dhamma, and the Sangha are the lamps that shed light for the beings in this world to know about merit and demerit, right and wrong. Like the light of the sun that illuminates every place on this earth, the Buddha, the Dhamma, and the Sangha are the refuge for anyone. With them, people have no fear of danger. They will find the way to happiness and joy. For this reason, don't stop me, mother."

Unable to prevent him, she walked after him to the place of execution. The Bodhisatta stroked the stake with his hand, and said, "O wood, there are other pieces of wood that are used to make teaching halls, Buddha images, places for meditation, monasteries. Why did you take on this impure job?"

The gods heard the words of the Bodhisatta and caused the stake to shatter into dust. The city people came in excitement to look and talk about this wonder.

The brahman Sujāta, father of the Bodhisatta, who had been to trade at Pātalīputta, returned that day with a boat full of gold. When he arrived at Cina City, people told him, "Didn't you know? Your son Dulaka Paṇḍita is sacrificing his life as an offering to the Buddha, the Dhamma, and the Sangha. Right now the executioners are about to lift him onto the point of the stake." Sujāta was shocked. He rushed to the graveyard and begged the executioners, "Don't kill my son. Let me redeem him."

He rushed to attend on the king, paid respect, and said, "Your Majesty, have mercy. Let me redeem Dulaka Paṇḍita."

"Brahman, you must give his weight in gold."

Sujāta rushed to the hold of his ship, brought out gold, and measured out the weight of his son. After he was redeemed, the two returned home.

The elder Nāgadīpa gave a teaching to the monks: "O friends, let me warn you. We have all escaped suffering because Dulaka Paṇḍita redeemed us with our weight in gold. We should praise his virtue and devotion and recognize his support. We should endeavor to meditate more deeply."

The elder and monks committed themselves to practice meditation, and in a short time became *arahant* with analytic insight.[6] The elder spoke with the thirty-three monks, "We must together help Dulaka Paṇḍita." All were happy to do so. They put on their robes, took up their almsbowls, and flew up into the sky, looking as beautiful as the king of the swans. Some of

6. ปฏิสัมภิทาญาณ, *patisamphithayan*, paṭisambhidāñaṇa, discrimination, analytic insight, usually a set of four.

them sat, some of them walked in meditation, some lay down, some stood above the peaks of mountains and stroked the sun and the moon—making miracles to be seen as wonders.

King Cina witnessed these miracles never seen before. He was shocked and his hair stood on end. He commanded his courtiers, "Look, these robbers are flying in the air! They intend to kill us. What can we do?"

"Your Majesty, please send for Dulaka Paṇḍita and ask him what would be best."

Courtiers were sent to fetch Dulaka Paṇḍita to audience. The king asked him, "These thirty-three robbers that you redeemed are now flying in the air with intent to kill us. Please help us to overcome this danger."

The Bodhisatta was overjoyed to hear this request. His face bloomed like the moon on full-moon day. He paid respect and said reassuringly, "Sire, don't be concerned. I will ask them to come down today."

He had people prepare a fine pulpit. King Cina stood waiting, holding articles of worship, including flowers and scents. Dulaka Paṇḍita raised his clasped hands in salute, looked up into the sky, and said, "Monks and servants of the Buddha, please come down from the sky. I, Dulaka Paṇḍita, invite you. Please accept this invitation."

The thirty-three monks recognized Dulaka Paṇḍita's voice. They came down and sat together in front of the pulpit in the palace compound. King Cina made a five-point prostration and gave worshipful offerings to the monks. Nāgadīpa spoke a lesson to the king in verse:[7]

Your Majesty, consorting with good persons,
not often but only once, benefits those who do so.
You should consort with and love good persons.
The benefit is excellent, with no unpleasantness.

"Your Majesty, both a fine royal carriage with gold and silver decoration and a handsome human body will age and deteriorate day by day. The dhamma of a good person will never age and decay. Good persons know the dhamma of other good persons. Good persons and bad persons are distinct and far apart, like the sky and the earth or the opposite sides of a great ocean.

7. This verse is adapted from J537 Mahāsutasoma, in which the Bodhisatta teaches the dhamma to a man-eating king who had been an ogre in his previous life, and thus saves the lives of several kings (Faussböll, *Jātaka*, V, 494; Cowell, *Jātaka*, V, 264).

"For householders who enjoy a sensual life, being lazy is not good. For those who renounce, not being composed is improper. For a king, failing to examine cases properly is not just. For a teacher, getting angry quickly is not good. For someone who is lost, asking the way from another who is also lost will result in getting even more lost and unhappy. People without wisdom have too many wants.

"Your Majesty, someone who wants to walk straight but who gets lost among the hills will not be happy but will fall into crevasses and gorges. Someone who befriends evil people will have the same experience. Leaves that are used to wrap eaglewood or *kalambaka*[8] become suffused with the fragrance. If you befriend wise persons, those wise persons will lead you to good things.

"Anyone who befriends and loves an evil person will come to accept the thinking of that evil person, and his suffering will multiply like the sprouts from a planted seed. Anyone who does bad or does good will get the fruit of that goodness or badness. An evil person will experience suffering in hell. A sage will enjoy the happiness of *nibbāna*.

"An evil person does not listen to the teaching of parents or teachers. A sage does listen to the teaching of parents and teachers. Those who constantly create sin and karma will go to hell, which is a place to be avoided. Those who make merit and avoid sin will go to heaven and enjoy its true treasure."

When the teaching was over, King Cina had a mind full of devotion. He offered himself as a disciple of the Triple Gem. He ordered officials to beat a drum to inform the people everywhere that all in his realm should honor the Triple Gem without fail. From that time on, all the people of Cina City who were wrong believers changed to be right believers. The king said to Nāgadīpa, "Master, I have committed major wrongs in word and deed both in the past and present because I consorted with evil people. Please pardon me." He spoke a verse:[9]

> *"Master, the moon in its waning phase becomes less bright day by day.*
> *To consort with a bad person is to be like the moon in that phase.*
> *Consorting with the brahman priest-counselor led me into darkness.*

8. กะลำพัก, *kalamphak*, *Euphorbia antiquorum*, Malayan spurge, a tree with a fragrant core.

9. This verse is also adapted from J537 Mahāsutasoma (Faussböll, *Jātaka*, V, 507; Cowell, *Jātaka*, V, 277).

I entered the state of woe because of committing great sins.
The moon in its waxing phase shines brighter by the day.
To consort with a good person is to be like the moon in that phase.
Consorting with you has revealed the truth to me.
Understand that I will seek heaven through doing every good work that I can."

King Cina sent off the thirty-three monks with a blessing. He appointed Dulaka Paṇḍita as minister and drove the brahman priest-counselor out of the city. The people all made merit, including giving alms and supporting monks with the four articles,[10] and were born in the heavens after passing away. King Cina and Dulaka Paṇḍita made merit including almsgiving and were born in the land of the gods after passing away.

When the Great Teacher finished the sermon, he made the birth connections: "The wrong-thinking brahman at that time was reborn as Devadatta; King Cina, who wronged the monks, as Ānanda; the mother of Dulaka Paṇḍita as Queen Mahāmāyā; the father of Dulaka Paṇḍita as King Suddhodhana; the wife of Dulaka Paṇḍita as Bimbā Yasodharā; the son of Dulaka Paṇḍita as Rāhula; the people as the followers of Buddhism; and Dulaka Paṇḍita as the refuge of the world."

10. ปัจจัยทั้งสี่, *patjai thang si*, jatupaccaya; clothing, food, lodging, medicine.

DHAMMASOṆḌAKA

P18 *Dhammasoṇḍakajātaka*

ธรรมโสณฑกชาดก

INTRODUCTION

This deceptively simple story is old and widely known across Buddhist Asia. It appears in the Nirvana Sutra, a text originating in India in the early Common Era and widely known throughout the Mahayana Buddhist world, especially China and Japan.[1] It also appeared as the first of 103 moral tales about people achieving happiness or misfortune as a result of their deeds, collected in *Rasavāhinī* ("stream of delights"), compiled in Sri Lanka by Elder Vedeha in the thirteenth century, based on an earlier compilation by Elder Raṭṭhapāla in Anuradhupura. There are visual representations in Taiwan and Japan, notably on the small seventh-century Tamamushi shrine at Horyuji in Nara. The *jātaka* follows the *Rasavāhinī* story, omitting poetic flourishes in the early stages to speed the flow, "possibly to enhance the *jātaka*'s function in the oral teaching of lay villagers."[2]

This translation has benefited from the earlier unpublished translation by Dorothy Fickle ("Historical and Structural Study," 168–80).

The tale of King Dhammasoṇḍaka [one who thirsts for the dhamma] is known by the sages as follows. Not long after the disappearance of the teaching of the Buddha Kassapa of ten powers, a son of the king of Bārāṇasī named Prince Dhammasoṇḍaka succeeded to the throne at the death of his father. He wished to listen to the dhamma as taught by the Buddha Kassapa of ten powers, but he had no opportunity. After he had been ruling only about a month, he possessed great power like a world-emperor, and his

1. Yamamoto, *Mahayana Mahaparinirvana-Sutra*, 1:349–56.
2. Fickle, "Historical and Structural Study," 192.

capital, Bārāṇasī, was filled with wealth and royal possessions like a city of the gods.

King Dhammasoṇḍaka pondered, "My kingdom has glory and power, but without the dhamma there is no beauty—like the sky without the sun, like the night without the light of the moon, like a *nāga* king without his brilliant jeweled fangs, like an ocean without salty water, like well-polished utensils that no eyes see and admire, or like a Pārichattaka tree that has blooming flowers but no fragrance. When my glorious kingdom is not beautiful because it lacks the teaching of the noble dhamma, how can the cities and towns, large and small, and the frontier regions be beautiful?"

The king commanded that a bag with one thousand coins be placed in an urn on the head of a royal elephant and that a drummer go around every street, large and small, within the capital city of Bārāṇasī proclaiming, "If anyone knows the dhamma of the fully enlightened Buddha, even one line of a verse, or two lines, or three, or ten, that person can take this bag with a thousand in the urn on the head of this elephant. The king will also honor and worship the one who knows the dhamma."

Royal retainers sent out drummers to make the announcement throughout the city of Bārāṇasī, but there was no one who knew the dhamma, not a single person. No one could be located who knew even one line. They returned to inform the king.

When King Dhammasoṇḍaka had received this report, he ordered that the sum of money be increased to two thousand, three thousand, four thousand, ten thousand, one hundred thousand, a hundred million, a billion, a trillion. But still he could find no one who could teach the dhamma. He offered to give over a district with villages and towns; he offered to hand over his white umbrella and even himself because he wanted to worship one who knew the dhamma, but no one could be found. He became despondent and miserable, saying, "Of what use to me is the kingdom without the true dhamma?" He handed over the kingdom to the viceroy and went into the forest to seek someone who knew the true dhamma.

At that moment, the throne of Lord Sakka, king of the gods, became unusually hot. While Sakka was wondering why, he spoke a verse:

> "*Any person who cares for his mother and father and teaches by the dhamma,*
> *gives alms, or leads a chaste life, causes me to move from my throne.*"

The Thousand-Eyed One examined the human world with his divine sight and saw King Dhammasoṇḍaka wandering in the forest seeking someone who could teach the dhamma. He thought, "I shall transform myself into someone else and demonstrate the evil of the bodily faculties—that there is only the eternal affliction of birth, old age, disease, and death. I shall demonstrate to King Dhammasoṇḍaka the impermanence of things first and then teach him the dhamma afterwards."

He transformed himself into an ogre and stood in front of King Dhammasoṇḍaka. The king was not startled or fearful but instead thought, "Perhaps an ogre such as this knows the true dhamma well." He approached the ogre and said, "O you of great power of merit, is there anyone in this forest who knows the true dhamma?"

"Your Majesty, I know the true dhamma."

"If so, please teach me now."

"I shall do so, but what will you offer me as your teacher?"

"If you first teach me the dhamma, I will then let you eat the flesh of my body."

"But I am very hungry and thirsty now. I want to eat your flesh first, and then I shall teach you the dhamma. If I cannot eat flesh first, then I cannot teach the dhamma because of my hunger and thirst."

"But, great ogre, if you eat me first, who will listen to the dhamma?"

"I have been without food. I am extremely hungry and thirsty. I cannot teach you the dhamma first. You must let me eat you first."

"Understand that listening to the dhamma is my desire, and eating my flesh is your desire. Don't spoil both benefits. The dhamma is food for me, and my flesh is food for you. Find a way to benefit us both."

Lord Sakka, disguised as the ogre, replied, "Your words are well spoken. There is a way to benefit both sides." He conjured up a large mountain about three *gāvuta* high close by and said, "If you climb to the top of this mountain, jump into the air, and let yourself fall directly into my mouth, I will teach you the dhamma while you are falling through the air. That way we shall both attain our desires, the dhamma for you and your flesh for me."

King Dhammasoṇḍaka pondered, "In the cycle of birth, which has no beginning or end, if there is no dhamma, no readiness for the dhamma, then there is no dhamma in the world, and beings have no desire to listen to the dhamma. They just destroy life, steal, commit adultery, tell falsehoods, drink liquor, and so on. Some people will do only evil deeds, such as killing pigs, goats, sheep, deer, or birds. Like village children who do not know the difference between right and wrong, they do not know that animals are living beings, since these people have never listened to the true dhamma. Moreover, the tears shed by beings in the cycle of birth who cry out for love—such as sons and daughters who cry out to their parents, and parents who cry out sadly for their children—are more than the water in the four oceans. When people with compassion realize that the true dhamma can lead to great fruit and reward, they should give away wealth as alms in order to protect their own bodies, or give away their own bodies to protect their own lives, or give away their lives to protect the true dhamma, or give away their wealth, bodies, and lives in order to listen to the dhamma, which produces great fruit and rewards. Thus I should sacrifice my life and body to serve as food for the ogre in order to listen to the true dhamma, as I wish."

King Dhammasoṇḍaka said, "Great and powerful ogre, I shall gladly do as you suggest to be of benefit to both of us."

He climbed the mountain, stood on the peak, and proclaimed, "Let all the gods hear my words and remember them as divine witnesses. I shall sacrifice my body together with my life to serve as food for the great ogre so that now I might hear the dhamma. I do not desire the treasure of the human world, the treasure of the heavens, the treasure of a Brahma, the treasure of a disciple, the treasure of a Pacceka Buddha, of the four guardians of the world, of an emperor, of the six realms of desire, or the treasure of the sixteen levels of the Brahma world. I sacrifice my body and my life as alms to the great ogre because of my desire to listen now to the true dhamma, with the wish that I might become a fully enlightened Buddha so that I can release myself and others from the four-flood cycle[3] of birth and death in the future. May the gods be my divine witnesses."

Lord Kosiya transformed said, "Your Majesty, now you must jump into the air and let yourself fall directly into my mouth."

King Dhammasoṇḍaka said, "Great ogre, I give you my life together with my kingdom in order to listen to your dhamma. Therefore hurry to teach

3. จตุรโอฆสงสาร, *jatura okha songsan*, catura ogha saṁsāra, the four cravings that lead beings to disaster.

the dhamma at once." His heart became filled with joy, and he leapt from the mountain into the air.

At that point, Lord Sakka could not continue in the form of an ogre. He returned to the form of the thousand-eyed god, rose up into the air, and caught King Dhammasoṇḍaka in his arms. With his divine touch he cradled the king close to his breast and flew up to the Tāvatiṁsa Heaven. There he placed the king upon the Paṇḍukambala throne at the foot of the Pārichattaka tree and paid him homage with offerings including heavenly garlands and scents. To teach the dhamma to King Dhammasoṇḍaka, he spoke a verse:[4]

> "*Impermanent indeed are bodies. By nature they arise and pass.*
> *Having arisen, they pass away. Happy is the peace when they cease forever.*
> *All bodies are impermanent. People who understand this*
> *grow weary of suffering and turn onto the path toward purity.*"

Lord Sakka explained to the king the treasures of the heavens and finally said, "Your Majesty, your desire to hear the dhamma has been fulfilled. I have just explained the dhamma to you. Be mindful and remember it well."

To exalt King Dhammasoṇḍaka still further, he said, "You will be enlightened as a Buddha in the world under the name of Gotama, in accordance with your desire. You will lead beings to escape from the flood-cycle of birth and will attain the immortality of *nibbāna.* But now, without delay, you must return to the human world and rule your kingdom according to the Ten Royal Virtues. In the future, you will be enlightened as an all-knowing Buddha in this world."

The wielder of the thunderbolt carried King Dhammasoṇḍaka down from the heavens to rule in Bārāṇasī. He offered him a blessing for good fortune and a long life in a verse:

> "*As long as the sun and moon shine brilliantly,*
> *so long may you govern your kingdom and protect your territory.*"

After instructing King Dhammasoṇḍaka to uphold the dhamma, Lord Sakka returned to the heavens and entered the Vejayanta Palace. King Dhammasoṇḍaka accumulated merit, including through almsgiving. When he passed away, he was reborn in the Tusita Heaven.

4. See note 3 in Rathasena.

After the Great Teacher had told this story from the past in his sermon, he pronounced the Noble Truths. Many gods and humans attained an understanding of the dhamma, such as stream-entry. The Ten-Powered Lord then explained the birth connections: "The royal mother of that time was reborn as Mahāmāyā, the mother of the Buddha; the royal father as King Suddhodana, the father of the Buddha; Lord Sakka as Anuruddha; the chief queen as Bimbā Yasodharā; royal retainers as the disciples of the Buddha; and King Dhammasoṇḍaka as the Tathāgata. Remember this *jātaka* as taught by me today."

GOOD WORKS
FOR THE RELIGION

KING KANAKAVAṆṆA

P16 *Kanakarājajātaka*

กนกวรรณราชชาดก

INTRODUCTION

The core story of a famine and the king giving away his last cup of rice is found in the Divyāvadanā, a Sanskrit collection possibly from the second century CE that also has P2 Sudhana. It also appears in several other Sanskrit collections as well as Tibetan and Khotanese versions. In these Sanskrit versions, the early part of the story differs in several details but is clearly the same as this tale found in the Thai and Cambodian collections of the Fifty Jātaka.

Pacceka Buddhas are beings who have achieved Buddhahood but remain in the world incognito. In several of the classical *jātaka*, a Pacceka Buddha appears as the worthy recipient of gifts that confer great merit on the giver. In J415 Kummāsapiṇḍa, for example, a poor man gives a portion of gruel to each of four itinerant Pacceka Buddhas, and as a result is reborn to become a king.[1]

This translation has benefited from the earlier unpublished translation by Dorothy Fickle ("Historical and Structural Study," 106–19).

One day, the monks were sitting together in the teaching hall, praising the power and virtue of the Great Teacher in the matter of giving food as alms. At that moment, the Great Teacher entered the teaching hall and said, "O monks, there was giving of food as alms in the past, when King Kanakavaṇṇa [golden color] was ruling in the city of Kanakavadī. His chief queen, the daughter of a king, was named Kanakadevī. King Kanakavaṇṇa was a primary king

1. Cowell, *Jātaka*, IV, 244–48; Appleton, "*Jātaka* Stories and Paccekabuddhas."

with great power in the Jambu Continent. His priest-counselor was well versed in all the arts and disciplines."

One day King Kanakavaṇṇa sent for the priest-counselor and asked, "Tell me, teacher, will there be great happiness this year or will there be great hardship? What do the stars reveal? Examine them and find out what is to happen both in the present and in the future."

The brahman examined the planetary bodies in accordance with the manuals of lore and learned both the bad and the good that would occur in that year. He then addressed the king, saying, "Sire, I have calculated according to the ancient texts of lore and see that this year there will be great happiness. As in a year of the Krita Yuga,[2] there will be little sorrow. The people will be happy and contented. Grain will be abundant in the kingdom. However, ten years from now, there will be a famine. Rice will be expensive. There will be a drought for twelve years; not one drop of water will fall on your kingdom, sire."

King Kanakavaṇṇa felt his heart had been shot by a poisoned arrow. He was filled with dismay. He thought, "How pitiable! Many people will perish. The Jambu Continent will be deserted—only a few will remain. What shall we do about this famine and drought?"

In low spirits, he ordered his courtiers to gather in the royal courtyard and told them about the priest-counselor's prophecy. "Good people, go everywhere throughout the Jambu Continent and inform them that after ten years there will be a famine as a result of a twelve-year drought. Tell the people to prepare the upland fields, plow the paddy fields, and plant rice seedlings in both the low-lying land and the uplands. When the rice has ripened, store it in granaries in every village and house."

The courtiers went off to different parts of the Jambu Continent to deliver the message. Once told, the people tilled both upland and paddy fields and stored the unhusked rice in granaries in every village and house. When King Kanakavaṇṇa was informed that the people of the Jambu Continent had finished storing unhusked rice in their granaries, he instructed his courtiers to go about and inspect how much unhusked rice the people had in the small villages and large cities, in frontier settlements, and in royal

2. กฤตยุค, *kritayuk*, also known as Satya Yuga, the first and most benign of the four ages.

capitals. The courtiers returned to inform the king of the total amount. King Kanakavaṇṇa used royal treasure to buy and store the rice for distributing after the famine began.

When the ten years had passed and the eleventh year was just beginning, no rain fell on the Jambu Continent, not even one drop. The people were in difficulty for lack of food, and many began to die—on some days one hundred people, sometimes one thousand, sometimes ten thousand, and sometimes a hundred thousand on a single day. All over the Jambu Continent hung the stench of human corpses, just as in a cemetery or graveyard. It was strange and horrible.

Seated on the terrace of his palace, King Kanakavaṇṇa said to his courtiers, "Here in the Jambu Continent vultures, crows, and dogs are feeding on corpses. The stench hangs everywhere. Noble daughters have concealed themselves in their houses and never see the moon and sun. You should all go together to dwell at the edge of the forest. Soon you will die. Or else go wherever you wish, taking your wives and children with you."

The courtiers replied, "Your Majesty, we beg to dwell under your royal protection in this city along with our wives and children. Even if death should come, we beg to die close to the soles of your feet."

King Kanakavaṇṇa gave no answer. Every day he distributed royal rice to the courtiers and to the people, also to their infants. After about four months, the supply of royal rice was exhausted. What remained was only enough for the king, queen, and royal children. After another month, all that rice was gone, leaving only one coconut-shell measure, enough for one last meal for the king and the prince. The chief queen, Kanakadevī, took the measure of rice, steamed it, and put it aside to give to her royal husband and the prince.

At that moment there was a Pacceka Buddha dwelling on top of Mount Gandhamādana. He possessed great power because of the omniscience of a Pacceka Buddha. For seven days he sat meditating. On the eighth day he came out from his meditation and began to examine the world with his pure, divine sight, which had passed beyond the sight of a human and resembled that of a god. He saw the situation that existed throughout the Jambu Continent, and thought, "How pitiable! Beings in the world are so heedless. They do not practice giving or observe the virtues. They are not compassionate, nor do they practice meditation. They do not honor the Buddha, the Dhamma, and the Sangha. They do not care for their parents or respect the elders of their families, such as their parents and other senior members. Because beings in the world have become so heedless, great sickness and danger have appeared everywhere in the Jambu Continent."

The Pacceka Buddha thought further, "Whom should I help first?" With his divine sight, he saw that King Kanakavaṇṇa was a nascent Buddha, destined to become a Buddha in the future. "We should assist King Kanakavaṇṇa to perform an act of giving that will be praised by all the people of the Jambu Continent."

The Pacceka Buddha rose up into the air and floated directly to the palace of King Kanakavaṇṇa. When the courtiers and the royal servants saw him coming through the air, they exclaimed to King Kanakavaṇṇa, "Sire, an ogre is flying down to eat us!"

The king looked up and saw the Pacceka Buddha. He said, "Courtiers, the figure coming through the air is not an ogre but a Pacceka Buddha." He admired the Pacceka Buddha, who moved with great beauty. He rose up from his royal seat and folded his hands in obeisance to the Pacceka Buddha, and then showed him honor with objects of worship including scents and flowers.

The Pacceka Buddha descended from the air and stood directly in front of King Kanakavaṇṇa. The latter noticed that the Pacceka Buddha was carrying an empty begging bowl, and realized that he wanted food. He thought, "Now we are so poverty-stricken because rice is so dear. I cannot offer alms of food." He addressed the Pacceka Buddha: "Noble sir, I have many things—silver and gold, jewels, pearls, upper and lower cloths. But in my house there is not even one coconut-shell measure of rice, unhusked or husked. I am troubled and dismayed that I cannot present food alms to you at this time." The Pacceka Buddha remained standing, without answering.

When King Kanakavaṇṇa saw his manner, he thought, "This is a person who is worthy of receiving alms, but it's truly difficult to give him anything. I'm at a loss. I can't think what to do." He asked his retainers, "Does anyone have some food?"

The queen replied, "Sire, there is one coconut-shell measure of rice which I have steamed as a meal for you and the prince."

King Kanakavaṇṇa commanded that the food be brought. He took hold of his own portion, thinking to himself, "If I eat this food, my life will not last long anyway. It is finer to give it to the Pacceka Buddha. I shall then receive great rewards in the future. Furthermore, the Buddha has taught that the body is not long-lasting. It will be destroyed in the future. Of what use is the body? If I present this food to the Buddha, my body will have more meaning." He spoke a verse:

> "*Noble ones, the body has no permanence, like lightning that flashes and disappears in an instant.*
> *Wise men understand this and thus have given their bodies and possessions more substance*
> *by distributing alms, paying respect to those who follow the precepts, and looking after their parents.*
> *They believe that this will be useful and meaningful for them in the future.*"

King Kanakavaṇṇa's face lit up. He took the golden dish filled with food and, with his body suffused with joy, approached the Pacceka Buddha, paid respect at his feet, and entreated him, "Your honor, this gift of food, however little or much, whether sullied or fine, I present with a devout heart. Please accept these alms to be of benefit and happiness for me long into the future." He placed the food in the almsbowl, saying, "With the power of the merit of my gift of food, into whatever life I am born, into whatever world, may there be no misery, sorrow, or danger for me. Furthermore, in the future may I become an enlightened Buddha. As long as I am still wandering in the cycle of birth, may I never experience another famine like this one until reaching *nibbāna*."

To express his gratitude for receiving this food, the Pacceka Buddha spoke a verse:[3]

> "*May your wishes quickly be granted*
> *and all your purposes fulfilled, like the full moon on the fifteenth day.*
> *Though as small as a sesame seed, a good deed done, with knowledge,*
> *purposefully, produces fruit the size of Meru or a spreading banyan tree.*
> *From seeds that are sown, there is always growth.*
> *In giving to worthy ones, there is no danger.*
> *Whatever is coarse or fine, when given with a joyful heart*
> *and faith, that gift is worthy of praise.*
> *Alms given with faith will bear great fruit.*
> *Alms unaccompanied by faith will not yield great fruit.*"

3. The opening couplet is a standard blessing, given for instance by monks in return for alms. It appears also in P10 Siridhara.

The Pacceka Buddha then rose up into the air. When he reached the top of Mount Gandhamādana, he ate the food. As soon as he had finished, through the power of the fruit of the alms presented by the king to the Pacceka Buddha, a great cloud appeared in the sky. When the people of the city saw it, they shouted loudly, "A great cloud has appeared! Come see! What a great miracle!"

Hearing the uproar, the courtiers said to the king, "Sire, a great cloud has appeared in the sky through the power of the merit resulting from your gift of food. The cloud will rain down today on all of the Jambu Continent."

King Kanakavaṇṇa thought, "This great cloud has appeared due to the virtue and power of the Pacceka Buddha. It is indeed a great miracle!"

Immediately, the great cloud released a shower of rain, which cleansed the surface of the earth, purified it, and washed the carrion away into the sea. Next there fell a shower of heavenly blossoms, which smothered the odor of feces and carrion, leaving a fragrant perfume throughout the earth. The great cloud next released a shower of rain mixed with edible sweets onto the earth. People who had been starving gathered the edible sweets, ate some, and stored the remainder in their houses. Next, a downpour of milled rice fell for seven days, then a downpour of lower cloths, of upper cloths, and of ornaments, then a downpour of silver and gold, and finally a downpour of the seven kinds of jewels, each downpour lasting for seven days. The capital city, Kanakavatī, became wealthy, like the abode of the gods in the heavens.

When the Great Teacher wished to explain about the fruit of giving, he spoke a verse:

Alms should be given with devotion. Anyone who does a good deed,
if he has firm faith and devotion during all three times—devotion before giving,
happiness at the moment of giving, joy after the gift is completed—
he will naturally achieve three kinds of happiness: happiness in the human world,
happiness in heaven, and the ultimate happiness of nibbāna.

After the Great Teacher had told this story from the past as a teaching, he pronounced the Four Noble Truths and explained the birth connections: "The prince of that time was reborn as Rāhula, the son of the Buddha; the courtier as Sāriputta; the priest as Moggallāna; Queen Kanakadevī as Bimbā Sundarā; and King Kanakavaṇṇa as the Tathāgata. Remember this *jātaka* as told by me."

KING VAṬṬAṄGULĪ

P20 *Vaṭṭaṅgulīrājajātaka*

วัฏฏังคุลีราชชาดก

INTRODUCTION

This *jātaka* is really two stories, with the first being an unusual form of the story of the present. This story of King Pasenadi of Kosala and the creation of the first Buddha image appears in *Kosala-bimba-vaṇṇanā*, "Laudatory acount of the Kosalan image," a Pali text that circulated in Sri Lanka and Southeast Asia. A similar story was recounted by the Chinese pilgrim-monk Faxian in his fifth-century account of his visit to Sāvatthi and by another pilgrim-monk, Xuanzang, two centuries later, and is widely reproduced in Chinese and Japanese sources.[1] The account in this *jātaka* is similar in general terms to that in *Kosala-bimba-vaṇṇanā*, including some details such as the comparison of the Buddha's outstretched arm to the trunk of the Erāvana elephant, but in many details is quite different, and the Pali of the two accounts has little similarity. These are two tellings of a similar story, not a reproduction of the same text.

The second story—of repairing the finger of a Buddha image—is also old. In the *Chiang Mai Chronicle* for 1288/89 a monk called Mahākassapa tells King Mangrai "that King Vaṭṭhakuli had [repaired] the broken-off finger of an image of the Lord Buddha of great power, which allowed him to defeat the 101 kings as if he had constructed the Buddha image himself." Thus inspired, Mangrai has a carpenter make five Buddha images, the largest equal to his own height, vows to build a *vihara* for them if he is victorious over the Mon, and fulfills the vow after a successful expedition.[2]

1. Gombrich, "Kosala-Bimba-Vaṇṇanā"; Beal, *Si-yu-ki*, xliv, 235-6; Bizot, "La consécration des statues," 102–3; Jaini, *Paññāsa Jātaka*, 2:xxxii–xxxiii.

2. Wyatt and Aroonrut, *Chiang Mai Chronicle*, 35–36.

This is one of eleven stories in the collection that describe the benefits of performing various services in support of Buddhism and the monkhood. The others are P10 Siridhara (giving alms to a Pacceka Buddha); P17 Viriyapaṇḍita (affixing gold leaf on a Buddha image); P19 Sudassana (supporting an ascetic); P21 King of old Kapila (reproducing the teachings); P22 King Dhammika Paṇḍita (various); P23 Cāgadāna (giving cloth); P31 Puppha (bathing a monk); P37 Narajīva's *kaṭhina* (offering robes); P38 King Atideva (offering robes); and P42 Candasena (repairing a Buddha image).

The words at the head of this *jātaka* are those of Ānanda saying, "I heard this teaching in front of the Blessed One as told here." When Ānanda pledged to escape from self-existence[3] like this, he told the tale as follows.

At one time, the Blessed One went to stay at the Jeta Grove, a monastery built by Anāthapiṇḍika, a stream-enterer, for the Blessed One to stay at Sāvatthi City where he went on almsround.

When King Pasenadi of Kosala ascended the throne in Sāvatthi, he practiced the Ten Royal Virtues, ruled the people without imposing royal punishments and executions, and cared for the people of the city with the Four Principles of Harmony. In the evenings, the king had a courtier bring worshipful offerings including garlands, flowers, and scents and went to the teaching hall of the Jeta Grove to hear a sermon. He behaved in this way all the time without fail.

One day at the present time, when the Refuge of the World was studying the living beings of the world with his Buddha-insight, he saw a Buddhist disciple who needed to be constrained to achieve the paths and fruits. In the morning, the Ten-Powered One came from his fragrant abode, did his bodily functions according to custom, put on robes, picked up an almsbowl, and walked gracefully out on his own. He gave a sermon to that disciple, who achieved the fruit of stream-entry. The Buddha had not yet returned to the teaching hall.

3. สยัมภูวิสัย, *sayamphuwisai*, sayaṃbhuvisaya. Meaning unclear. The Pali begins, "Evam me sutaṃ," the standard beginning of a text claimed to have been remembered from the words of the Buddha. The Thai translator has elaborated this into a paragraph.

That evening, King Pasenadi Kosala had a courtier bring offerings and went with his retinue to the Jeta Grove, as the king wanted to hear a sermon. On arrival, he was upset at not seeing the Great Teacher and thought, "It's a pity that this Jeta Grove is here but the Omniscient One is not. My wishes on coming here at this time have been disappointed. It is not as I had hoped."

He felt irritated. He worshiped the pulpit with offerings including the lamps, candles, flowers, and scents that he had brought with him, and returned to Sāvatthi City. That night in his bedroom, the king thought of the Teacher with emotion and did not sleep all night. In the morning he summoned courtiers, brahmans, and householders to audience and said, "It is well known that all the Buddhas have been persons of great compassion. They do not stay in one place, because they will go wherever there are disciples who need their teaching to achieve the fruits of the way and will give them the teaching so the disciples may achieve the fruits of the way according to their accumulated merit. The Buddha, who is the Great Teacher of all of us, has the same great compassion. However, we wish to be close to the Triple Gem all the time. If the Buddha goes to give teaching to disciples elsewhere, our observance goes forfeit for the sake of others. For this reason, when our Great Teacher returns, I will attend on him and ask permission to make a Buddha image in his likeness to take his place so that at times when he goes to teach disciples elsewhere we can still worship him constantly as we wish."

The courtiers all felt uplifted by these words. They paid respect and said, "Sire, we agree. If the Buddha consents, let us make the image as wished. It will be of benefit to all beings forever. We will be able to worship to the best of our ability, as fitting. May Your Majesty please go to attend on the Refuge of the Three Worlds and ask permission as you stated."

When the king heard that the Great Teacher had returned to stay in the Jeta Grove, on the evening of the following day he had a royal courtier bring offerings, including garlands and scents, and went to the Jeta Grove with courtiers and royal retainers. They made worship to the Teacher with lamps, candles, and incense and sat at a fitting place in front. The king paid respect and said, "Blessed One, yesterday I and the people of Sāvatthi came to attend on you, but on arrival at the Jeta Grove we found you had gone elsewhere. We felt disappointed that you were not present at the Jeta Grove and so made worship to the empty temple and returned home. For this reason I wish to make a Buddha image to place in the teaching hall in your stead, so all the faithful can come to worship when Your Honor is not residing in the Jeta Grove. Please give me permission to make this image as wished."

The Great Teacher said, "Sire, that is good. I give my full permission."

The king was very happy to hear this. He listened to a sermon, paid respect, and returned to the palace. On the following evening, he had craftsmen summoned and gave them priceless red sandalwood to sculpt into a Buddha image. When finished, it was painted with beautiful colors in various suitable places, such as the eyebrows, mouth, and hair. Good-quality bright cloth was used to make robes to clothe the sandalwood Buddha. The image looked beautiful and wonderfully like the Buddha.

The king had already built a *maṇḍapa* pavilion adorned with the seven jewels and an elaborate, jeweled baldachin. He invited the image to reside in the baldachin in the center of the *maṇḍapa* and worshiped it with a great many offerings. Then he went to attend on the Blessed One at the Jeta Grove along with courtiers and retainers. He paid respect and said, "O Blessed One, I have created the image. It is very beautiful. I have invited it to reside in a jeweled baldachin. Please come to see it."

The next morning, accompanied by monks, the Great Teacher went to the palace and viewed the image in the beautiful jeweled baldachin.

Seeing the Great Teacher, the image reacted as if thinking, "While the Enlightened Buddha is still alive, it is not fitting for the Great Teacher to come to see me, just an image in his likeness, sitting on a high throne like this," and wanted to slide down from the jeweled baldachin.

The Great Teacher saw this reaction. He stretched out his right arm, as beautiful as the trunk of the Erāvana elephant, raised it aloft, and said, "Do not come down. Please stay there in the baldachin. Before long, I will attain *nibbāna*. You must stay to look after the religion and my teachings to be of benefit to all the beings of the world for five thousand years." The image reacted as if it had heard these words and thus remained sitting in the baldachin as usual.

Seeing this marvel, the subjects of the king offered their own bodies and lives to the religion. About a hundred thousand people raised sheets of cloth and waved them above their heads like flags. The king paid respect to the Blessed One and asked, "O Blessed One, for any man or woman who creates a Buddha image in your likeness, what will be the beneficial result received?"

The Great Teacher opened his mouth, colored red like wool[4] and fragrant like the scent of lotus, and said, "Sire, any man or women who devotedly has a Buddha image made from clay, stone, metal, copper, wood, or tin, or with jewels, silver, or gold will have countless beneficial results. O king, when a Buddha image is established in any world, that world is thought not to be without a Buddha. This Buddha image means that Buddhism is firm and permanent. In addition, anyone who has a Buddha image made will enjoy only happiness in the future. Anything he desires he will gain. Creating or restoring a Buddha image is a custom of all the Buddhas who are still wandering in the cycle of rebirth. When I was living as a bodhisatta and accumulating merit in the past, I saw a Buddha image made of clay with a finger missing on one hand. I found some clay and molded it to repair the image, then made offerings with a few garlands and scents. Later I passed away and ascended to enjoy the treasures of heaven. Then, through the power of the beneficial result from restoring the finger of the Buddha image and making offerings, when I passed from the heavens I was born as a great king, the sole ruler of the Jambu Continent for a long time. Later, when my accumulated merit was complete, I sat at the bodhi tree, overcame the king of the demons, and achieved enlightenment, the final release."

After this sermon, the Buddha fell quiet. King Pasenadi Kosala, wishing to know about the past, invited the Buddha to tell a tale from the past, as follows.

4. In ancient India, wool was commonly dyed red, and hence the Pali word for wool, kambala, is sometimes used to mean "red."

In the past there was a merchant called Kulabhadda Kumāra [son of a lofty clan] living in Amaravatī. One day he invited all the merchants, around a thousand of them, to leave home and go to trade elsewhere. On the way he saw a Buddha image made of clay in a temple in the thick forest. One finger of the image was broken off by the rain. He found some clay, mixed it with sugarcane juice, molded a finger, and repaired the image to have the full five fingers. He worshiped the image with offerings, including lamps, garlands, and scents, and presented a female slave with eight *kahāpaṇa* of his own money to look after the image and to pay for lamps, incense, candles, and scents for worshiping the image.

Then he made a wish: "O image, through the power of the beneficial result from restoring the finger of this image, may I have no enemies in the time ahead of me, and may I achieve enlightenment as a Buddha in the future."

As wished, from that time on Kulabhadda Kumāra had no enemies and no dangers at all, such as snakes, centipedes, and cockroaches intruding into where he was staying. When he died from the human world, he ascended to enjoy the treasures of the heavens; the *asura* there did not approach him but fled from the world of the gods and never returned to the heavens. When Kulabhadda Kumāra passed from the heavens, he came down to be conceived in the womb of the major queen of the king of Bārāṇasī. The thousand heavenly beings who formed his retinue also passed and came down to be conceived in the wombs of the wives of courtiers. When the major queen reached the tenth month, she gave birth to a son, a bodhisatta, with all the excellent attributes. The thousand courtiers' wives gave birth on the same day as the queen. When the Bodhisatta had grown up, the thousand born on the same day formed his retinue.

At that time, it was difficult to prevent the mahouts and riders mistreating animals used for transport, such as elephants and horses. But when they saw the prince-Bodhisatta lift a finger and point, those mistreating these transport animals would fall off and stagger around. The royal clan, including his father and mother, gave the Bodhisatta the name Prince Vaṭṭaṅgulī.[5] When he was eleven years old, his father, the king of Bārāṇasī, died. All the courtiers, brahmans, and householders anointed the Bodhisatta to ascend the throne in succession and rule the realm, as was the custom.

5. Meaning a rounded (well-formed) finger.

He ruled by avoiding royal punishments, beatings, and executions and looked after the people through the Four Principles of Harmony. He was a just king who upheld the Ten Royal Virtues and had a heart of devotion. He ordered the construction of alms pavilions at six locations—at the four gates of the city, the center of the city, and the gate of the palace—and distributed six hundred thousand of royal property at these pavilions every day without fail.

King Vaṭṭaṅgulī showed compassion and mercy. He did not spill the blood of even a fly that drinks the blood of other animals, and, needless to say, would not torment or kill other animals. He had no wish to take the property of others, not even a mite of trash; did not look upon the wives of others with lust and envy; did not tell even a single lie; and did not drink liquor, not even a single drop. He practiced the precepts, the five abstinences, with dedication.

When the 101 rulers in the Jambu Continent heard of the reputation of the Bodhisatta King Vaṭṭaṅgulī, they assembled together and said, "We should all together go to seize the realm of King Vaṭṭaṅgulī, which is like a lotus flower ripe for plucking. As King Vaṭṭaṅgulī has compassion and mercy and does not kill any animal before its time to die, if we take our troops to besiege his city, we should take the realm as wished."

Each of the 101 rulers then prepared eighteen *akkhohiṇī* of troops and officers of the four divisions and marched to Bārāṇasī. On the way, they wrote a missive demanding King Vaṭṭaṅgulī hand over his city to them or else prepare troops to come out and fight, and had an envoy take the missive to the king before they arrived at the city. The envoy hurried to the city and stood waiting at the royal courtyard. A courtier saw him, made inquires, and once knowing he was an envoy with a missive, conducted him to see the king.

When King Vaṭṭaṅgulī read the missive, he showed no surprise or alarm but appeared as a young lord of the lions. He smiled and asked the envoy, "How many officers and men are there in this army that has come?"

The envoy replied, "There are 101 rulers and around eighteen *akkhohiṇī*, sire."

The king said, "I alone will make these 101 rulers and eighteen *akkhohiṇī* flee away through the power of a single finger. I do not wish to use weapons to kill the troops or the 101 rulers."

The courtiers present paid their respects and said, "Sire, we have powerful abilities and skills. We do not shrink from war. Allow us to volunteer to capture these 101 rulers and crush their entire army without flinching—like an elephant tusk which never shrinks as that is not the common nature of a tusk."

The king replied, "Courtiers, do not go out to fight. The 101 rulers and their troops will kill you all. No use. When all of you are dead and not a single person is left, who will go and tell your wives and children what happened? I think I can get them to flee through virtue, without causing any trouble or danger to life and limb, so you all go back home now. Tomorrow morning, after bathing and eating, get arrayed in your finery and come to accompany me as usual. I will ride my principal elephant out to meet these 101 rulers and their troops and make them flee away using only one of my fingers, without a single person dying."

The courtiers paid respect and returned home. Next morning all hurried to eat, array themselves in their finery, and await the king at the courtyard.

At dawn, King Vaṭṭaṅgulī left his bedroom, bathed, washed his face, ate a delicious meal, donned his royal decorations, and went to sit at the courtyard, where the courtiers and retainers were gathered in audience. He mounted an elephant that was arrayed in the decorations of a royal mount and well trained by elephant masters to destroy other soldiers.

The mass of courtiers and troops surrounded the king along with royal consorts of beautiful appearance, decked in splendid ornaments, like celestial maidens in the heavens. Some held fans and fly whisks of gold with elegant jeweled handles. Some held white umbrellas decorated with gold and gems. Some carried flags and pennants, or various musical instruments. They surrounded King Vaṭṭaṅgulī, who looked as beautiful as the thunderbolt-wielding god surrounded by deities.

The king left the city by the west gate and saw the troops of the enemy drawn up in front of him. He questioned his courtiers in a verse:

> *"O generals, these elephants, horses, chariots, and foot soldiers—the four divisions—*
> *drawn up in units looking as fine as the sun, whose army are these?*
> *There seem to be a great many officers and men, beyond estimation,*
> *massed to left and right, front and rear, like waves in the ocean."*

The courtiers replied, "Sire, the armies of all the 101 lords of the Jambu Continent have come to make war against you with the aim of seizing the realm. The four divisions massed there in numbers beyond estimation, like waves on the ocean, are the troops of these 101 rulers."

The king said, "You are to go and tell these 101 rulers that if they wish to make war against me, let all their elephant troops mount their steeds, their cavalry mount their horses, their chariot troops mount their vehicles, their foot soldiers grasp their weapons, and all bravely do their duties in warfare."

The courtiers conveyed this message. The 101 lords clapped their hands and laughed loud enough to make the world collapse, then prepared all their troops in units and brigades with weapons, shields, swords, spears, javelins, pikes, and lances. The elephants trumpeted, the cavalry cheered, the chariot troops and infantry made a racket like the storm wind that blows Mount Meru down at the close of an era. The 101 lords mounted their principal elephants and headed straight for King Vaṭṭaṅgulī in order to make war according to royal tradition.

King Vaṭṭaṅgulī, the Bodhisatta, raised a finger and pointed straight at the troops. Immediately the 101 lords fell off their elephants. All the elephant troops fell off the necks of their mounts. The horsemen fell from their saddles, and the charioteers from their seats. The foot soldiers collapsed all over the place. Then all of them fled away, many abandoning their weapons, running into caves and forest and undergrowth, some to the shore of the ocean, some with their clothes slipping from their bodies, from fear of the Bodhisatta pointing his finger, which had power as the beneficial result of restoring the finger on a Buddha image in a past life.

Seeing them all flee away in such confusion, King Vaṭṭaṅgulī felt compassionate and so said, "Get up all of you. Don't be afraid of me. I will not endanger your lives."

The troops led by the 101 lords came up, saluted him, and sat down there, scared to death. The 101 lords offered their realms and their daughters to the king.

After this victory, the Bodhisatta gave advice to the 101 lords to uphold the Ten Royal Virtues, and sent them back home to rule their realms. Along with his troops and retinue, he returned to the city and presented incalculable wealth as alms to the poor and destitute. He ruled the territory with the Ten Royal Virtues. The 101 lords sent tribute to King Vaṭṭaṅgulī every year without fail.

Later, it was heard that the world of Lord Sakka, king of the gods, became warm through the power of the compassion of King Vaṭṭaṅgulī. The god examined with his divine eye and learned everything about the matter, and so came down from the heavens to the residence of the king. His aura lit the place brilliantly, like the soft rays of an early-dawn sun rising over Mount Yugandhara. The god asked the king in a verse:

> *"I'd like to ask, sire, what merit made in a past life*
> *lets you defeat enemies with a single finger? Please explain."*

The king blossomed with joy at this question. Able to recall his previous lives, he replied in a verse:

> *"Lord Sakka, in a past life I was born as a merchant named Kulabhadda.*
> *On a trading trip with fellow merchants,*
> *I saw a Buddha image with a single broken finger.*
> *Out of a feeling of devotion, I could not resist*
> *mixing clay with sugarcane juice to mold a finger to restore the image.*
> *As a result, in this life I overcome enemies by pointing a finger.*
> *Should even a fierce lion king or a thousand elephants in musth*
> *or troops of all the four divisions come with intent to do me harm,*
> *I just lift a single finger and point, and that protects me from all threats.*
> *Enemies, including the lion king, fall over and flee away.*
> *Moreover, Lord Sakka the thousand-eyed, through the merit earned by restoring the finger,*
> *in the future I shall achieve enlightenment and help beings escape from the eternal cycle of death and rebirth.*
> *Good people, understand this, all of you—*
> *even a small act of worshipping a Buddha has a great beneficial effect.*
> *Remember this."*

Moved by devotion and admiration for the king, Lord Sakka, wielder of the thunderbolt, king of the gods, said, "I, Lord Sakka, greatest of all deities, have come to your palace today. In the future you will sit at the bodhi tree, win victory over the army of the demons, eradicate the demon of craving and all the race of evil demons so none are left, and achieve full enlightenment as a Buddha. You will preach the dhamma to teach beings to achieve heaven and *nibbāna*." After he had praised the Great Being in this way, Lord Maghava returned to his residence in the heavens.

The Ten-Powered One, having related this story from the past about the beneficial result of restoring a Buddha image, pronounced a verse:

> "*Anyone who creates a Buddha image will become Indra, king of the gods, in seven lives,*
> *will become an emperor in eighty or a hundred lives,*
> *and will become a king in countless lives.*
> *Anyone who devoutly restores an imperfect Buddha image using only clay,*
> *without thinking whether this is a great matter or small, the beneficial result is enormous:*
> *he will be reborn in the heavens every time for eternity.*
> *Whether the repair is done with clay or by drawing, whatever is fitting,*
> *that person will have great power like the bright and immaculate rays of the sun;*
> *when reaching the end of life as a human, he will not be reborn in hell,*
> *the netherworlds, the realms of loss and woe, nor as a beast with a body, big or small.*
> *Whether the Buddha image made is big or small, whatever material is used,*
> *the beneficial result is the same, neither more nor less.*
> *Three other groups of people—those who plant a bodhi tree, those who renounce,*
> *and those who create a Buddha image—will become true Buddhas.*
> *Whoever creates a Buddha image with ivory, animal horn, stone, brick, or plaster,*
> *in the future will be born in the world to meet Phra Ariya Metteyya*
> *and will experience the end of suffering; or else, if they wish to achieve enlightenment,*
> *they will be reborn as a Buddha at a later time, according to their wish.*"

When the Great Teacher finished this sermon, many deities and humans achieved the paths and fruits, starting with stream-entry. The Ten-Powered One thus explained the birth connections: "The troops in that time were reborn as the followers of Buddhism in this life, and King Vaṭṭaṅgulī as the Tathāgata, *arahant*, and enlightened Buddha in this era."

MORAL TALES

DUKAMMĀNIKA

P13 *Dukammānikajātaka*

ทุกัมมานิกชาดก

INTRODUCTION

A handful of tales have a simple plot that single-mindedly illustrates a particular moral lesson. In the case of this story, the lesson is about good judgment. A poetic version appeared in the early Bangkok era with different names for the Bodhisatta (Suthikan) and some other characters, suggesting it drew the tale from oral tradition rather than directly from this *jātaka*.

Similar tales include P32 The King of Bārāṇasī (the next story in this collection), on friendship; P8 King Canda, on kindness to animals; P55 Suvaṇṇakacchapa: The Golden Turtle (not the one translated above, but a second tale with the same title), on the importance of associating with good people; and P33 King Brahmaghosa, on adhering to the precepts.

When the Great Teacher was staying at the Jeta Grove, he spoke about his own suffering and for this reason gave a sermon beginning with the words "Anyone who does wrong to another."

As was heard, the monks were sitting gathered in the teaching hall, saying, "O friends, it is most praiseworthy that the Great Teacher of ours bore such great bodily suffering and mental suffering before he achieved full enlightenment." The Great Teacher came from his fragrant quarters, sat on the great pulpit, and asked, "Monks, what were you talking about?" They told him. He said, "Monks, I tolerated great suffering not only at the present but also in the past. When I was born into a merchant family, thinking of escaping from suffering, I shrewdly had myself condemned to execution by an unrighteous king." At that, he fell silent. As the monks wanted to know further, they paid respect and invited him to tell a tale from the past. He told the tale as follows.

In the past there was a king called Brahmadatta ruling in Bārāṇasī City. When he passed away, his son called Dhudhara succeeded him. After King Dhudhara passed away, his son succeeded him.

At that time a bodhisatta was born to a merchant family in the countryside. His name was Dukammānika. When his father was close to death, he advised Dukammānika, "If a woman has had three husbands, do not take her as wife. If a man has been ordained and disrobed three times, do not take him as a friend. If a king acts carelessly without studying matters, do not associate with him[1] at all costs." After giving this advice, he departed for the next world. The Bodhisatta pondered, "Were these words of advice from my father true or not?"

Sometime after, a woman who had had three husbands got to know the Bodhisatta. He thought, "I will test whether father's words were true or not." He took this woman as his wife. Later he befriended a man who had disrobed three times. He looked for a means to test the wife.

At that time, the king of Bārāṇasī had a golden swan that flew along the river landings looking for food. One day, when the Bodhisatta's wife had not yet returned from shopping in the market, the Bodhisatta managed to catch the golden swan. He dug a wide hole, put the swan there, gave it enough popped rice and honey to eat, and closed the hole with a tile, leaving a passage for the swan to breathe. Then he returned home, caught another swan, killed it, made a curry, and put it aside for his wife. When she returned home from the market, the Bodhisatta told her untruthfully, "I caught and killed the king's golden swan to make this curry."

She cried out, "Don't you understand that catching a swan that was not given to you will bring heavy karma!"

Local people passed on the news that the king's golden swan had disappeared. Officials went around searching everywhere and announced, "Anyone knowing who stole the golden swan can come and collect a thousand *kahāpaṇa* of gold."

1. The Thai version has "do not take him as a friend," same as in the previous sentence, but that is a slip that undermines the logic of the story, and thus the translation here follows the Pali.

The Bodhisatta's wife wanted to live with someone else and had the idea of getting the thousand *kahāpaṇa* of gold too. She told a courtier, "I know who stole the golden swan. Give me the gold."

"Who caught the golden swan?"

"My husband."

"Really?"

"Really."

The courtiers took the matter to the king, who said, "If that's the case, arrest him and bring him here."

The courtiers arrested Dukammānika, clapped him in the five irons, beat him with rattan canes, and took him to the king. The Bodhisatta's friend who had disrobed three times met the Bodhisatta on the way and showed no compassion. Instead he begged the Bodhisatta to give him his lower cloth, saying, "Friend, you're going to die for certain. Give me your lower cloth."

The Bodhisatta took off both his upper and lower cloths and gave them to the man.

When the king of Bārāṇasī saw the Bodhisatta coming into the audience hall, he commanded, "Take him off for execution outside the city today."

The Bodhisatta spoke up: "If I am to die, that golden swan will also die. If I do not die, same with the swan."

A courtier responded, "You killed the swan to make curry already. There's no other golden swan." Nearing evening on that day, the courtiers took the Bodhisatta to the east gate of the palace. The gatekeepers had closed the palace gates in all directions.

The courtiers called out to the gatekeeper, "This man is condemned to death. Open the gate. We are under king's orders to execute him today."

The gatekeeper said, "In the past when anyone was arrested for wrongdoing, the king would try the case to discover the truth before passing sentence. I've closed the gate and will not open it for three days. This sloppy action by the king, not investigating the truth and simply ordering a man executed, will result in trouble in the future."

The courtiers asked further, "Gatekeeper, if not trying the case will create trouble in the future, please give us an example." The gatekeeper related the story as follows:[2]

2. This story appears in "The Brahman and his weasel," no. 13 in the "Peace"

"As was heard, there was a couple with a single son. The couple kept a female mongoose and loved her like their own child. One day they went off to farm, leaving the son and mongoose at home. A snake bit the son, who died. The mongoose attacked the snake and bit it to death. The mongoose went off to find the couple. When the couple saw blood on the body of the mongoose, they angrily accused her, "She bit our son to death." They beat her head with sticks until she died. They then returned home and saw their dead son and the dead snake on top of one another beside the house wall. They realized that the mongoose had not bitten their son to death. They wept for love of their son and the mongoose. See, courtiers. If our king has been sloppy in not studying the case, there will be trouble just like in the story I have told."

The courtiers took the Bodhisatta to the southern gate of the palace and called out to the gatekeeper, "This man is condemned to death. Open the gate. We are under the king's orders to execute him today."

The gatekeeper said, "In the past when anyone was arrested for wrongdoing, the king would try the case to discover the truth before passing sentence. I've closed the gate and will not open it for three days. The fact that the king has not tried the case and rushed to have this man executed will create trouble in the future."

The courtier asked, "Gatekeeper, if not trying the case will create trouble in the future, please give us an example." The gatekeeper related the story as follows:

"As was heard, there was a hunter of birds who kept a hawk. One day he went to the forest to shoot birds. The hawk flew along behind him. The hunter went to drink water from a stream. A snake was coiled up out of sight. The hunter bent down to drink the water without seeing the snake, which could bite his eye. The hawk saw the snake waiting to bite the hunter and thought, 'My master has not seen that snake. I should warn him.' The hawk used his wings to splash the water. In anger the hunter beat the hawk on the head with a bamboo cylinder containing honey. When the hawk

---

section of the *Hitopadesha*, a collection of Sanskrit tales, translated in 1830 by Lakshmi Narayan Nyalankar (but not in the translation by Edwin Arnold; see Nyalankar, *The Hitopadesha*). It also appears in the *Pancatantra* collection and elsewhere. In this *jātaka* in the Burmese collection (Dukammarājajātaka), this same story appears, but the other three gatekeepers' stories are different (Horner and Jaini, *Apocryphal Birth Stories*, 2:222–26.)

was dead, the hunter drank the water. The snake took the opportunity to bite his eyes. The hunter realized, 'The hawk had seen the danger and was warning me.' He wept in the forest. Neither of his eyes could see anything. Courtiers, if our king has been sloppy in not studying the case, there will be trouble just like in the story I have told."

The courtiers took the Bodhisatta to the western gate of the palace and called out to the gatekeeper, "This man is condemned to death. Open the gate. We are under the king's orders to execute him today."

The gatekeeper said, "In the past when anyone was arrested for wrongdoing, the king would try the case to discover the truth before passing sentence. I've closed the gate and will not open it for three days. The fact that the king has not tried the case and rushed to have this man executed will create trouble in the future."

The courtier asked further, "Gatekeeper, if not trying the case will create trouble in the future, please give us an example." The gatekeeper related the story as follows:

"As was heard, there was a king called Brahmadatta ruling in Bārāṇasī. He had a daughter called Sundarā, who used to play in the water at a lotus pond every day, always taking a pet dog with her. One day when Princess Sundarā went to play in the pond with her dog, she was wearing a necklace. A man who had a grudge against the princess followed her and stabbed her with a spear. She died on the bank of the pond. Nobody saw. The dog had foreseen the incident and had tried to prevent her setting out that day but had been ignored. The dog picked up the necklace in its teeth and placed it in front of the king's throne. When the king saw it, he thought the dog had killed his daughter and taken her jewelry. In anger, he had the dog killed. Later he found his daughter's corpse with the mark of the spear stabbing her body, and knew the dog had not killed her. He wept. Courtiers, the fact that the king did not try the case will create trouble as in this tale I have told."

The courtiers took the Bodhisatta to the northern gate and called out to the gatekeeper, "This man is condemned to death. Open the gate. We are under the king's orders to execute him today."

The gatekeeper said, "In the past when anyone was arrested for wrongdoing, the king would try the case to discover the truth before passing sentence. I've closed the gate and will not open it for three days. The fact that the king has not tried the case and rushed to have this man executed will create trouble in the future."

The courtier asked further, "Gatekeeper, if not trying the case will create trouble in the future, please give us an example." The gatekeeper related the story as follows:

"As was heard, there were two men who were close friends. One lived in a house to the east, and the other to the west. One day, the man in the house to the west went to visit his friend in the house to the east and stayed there overnight. When he took leave to return home, the friend in the house to the east gave him a dog. The friends in the house to the west said, 'I thank you for giving me this dog. May you be happy and free of illness.' He hugged the dog and returned home.

"Sometime later, the friend to the west made an ornament for the dog's neck and sent it to the house of the friend to the east. The dog was happy, thinking, 'My master loves me. He has made an ornament for my neck. I will go to tell my old master.' He went to tell his old master in the house to the east. When the old master saw the dog wearing the neck ornament, he thought, 'Perhaps the dog has stolen the ornament from my friend.' He cut off the dog's head. Two or three days later, the man to the west went to visit his friend to the east and said, 'I sent the ornament back to you. Have you seen it?'

'Yes I have, but I wrongly thought the dog had stolen the ornament from you, so I killed it.' The two friends wept in distress.

"Courtiers, the fact that the king did not try the case will create trouble as in this tale I have told."

Dawn had arrived. The courtiers took the Bodhisatta back to the king, who said, "I sent you to execute Dukammānika. Why have you brought him back again?"

"Your Majesty, the gatekeepers in all four directions would not open the gates." They related the stories to the king.

The king of Bārāṇasī asked the Bodhisatta, "Dukammānika, what is your story? Tell me."

"Sire, when my father was nearing death, he gave me three points of advice. First, do not take a woman who has had three husbands as wife; second, do not befriend a man who has disrobed three times; third, do not at all costs associate with a king who acts carelessly without studying matters.

"Sire, I have been testing whether my father's words are true or false. I married a woman who had had three husbands, befriended a man who had disrobed three times, and I caught Your Majesty's golden swan, hid it away where nobody could see, caught another swan to make a curry, and misinformed my wife that I had killed the king's swan. My wife wanted to go off with another man and was also greedy for the reward, and so she had the courtiers arrest me. Your Majesty did not investigate the case but ordered my execution. When the courtiers were taking me off for execution, the friend who had disrobed three times ran into me and begged me to give him my lower cloth, which I did. This lower cloth was of good quality but was covered in blood. Sire, the swan is in a hole that I dug over there."

The king of Bārāṇasī commanded, "Go and fetch the golden swan." The Bodhisatta brought the swan and placed it at the royal courtyard. The king was pleased. He presented the Bodhisatta with half the royal realm, saying, "Great man, You must take the post of viceroy."

The Bodhisatta said, "Your Majesty, my father advised me that I should not stay in the court of any king who acts carelessly without studying matters. Your Majesty did not examine whether I should be executed or not but ordered the execution with no trial. I should not remain in Your Majesty's territory." He spoke a verse:[3]

> "*Anyone who does wrong to another should not be taken as a friend. Such friends will only lead one to hardship.*
> *Even though they bring happiness, they may even kill their friends and cause suffering forever.*
> *A woman who has had three husbands already should not be taken as a wife. It will only lead to suffering.*
> *Even though she brings some happiness, she will cause disaster in the future. There will be hardship forever.*
> *Anyone who transgresses against the dhamma through the four wrong courses of love, hatred, fear, and ignorance will lose his status and reputation, like the moon that fades in the waning phase.*

3. Parts of this verse, after the first four lines, are found with slight changes in J537 Mahāsutasoma, in which the Bodhisatta teaches the dhamma to a man-eating king who had been an ogre in his previous life and thus saves the lives of several kings (Faussböll, *Jātaka*, V, 507; Cowell, *Jātaka*, V, 277–78). P11 Dulaka Paṇḍita has some of the same verses.

Anyone who does not transgress through the same four wrong courses will have high status and reputation, like the moon in its waxing phase.
Your Majesty, the moon in its waning phase becomes less bright by the day. To consort with a bad person is to be like the moon in that phase.
The moon in its waxing phase shines brighter by the day. To consort with a good person is to be like the moon in that phase.
By nature, fish like to be in deep water, not on land. In the same way, befriending a bad person is like being a lotus that does not rise above the surface and bloom at all.
Sire, fish can live underwater for a long time; in the same way befriending good people will have benefit for a long time.
Consorting with good people is the highest virtue, is an advantage, like water in a great lake, which is bothered by nothing. Consorting with bad people has only disastrous results. For this reason, the dhamma of good people differs from bad people.
Any king who fights with someone that he should not defeat is said to destroy his own power.
A friend who exploits and takes advantage of a friend is not considered a friend.
A wife that has a sinful, obstinate mind should not be counted as a wife.
A child who does not support his own parents, whom he must support, is not counted as a child.
People who do not have a peaceful, self-controlled mind are not counted as good people.
People who speak non-dhamma are considered bad persons.
Good persons should avoid non-dhamma—namely, lust, anger, and ignorance—and must be able to teach other people.
Good people know how to speak only words of morality and wisdom, how to show the way to nibbāna."

The king of Bārāṇasī said, "Great Being, from now on I will follow your advice. Please stay in this city."

"Sire, I must follow my father's teaching."

"Great Being, please become king and rule justly. Don't go elsewhere."

"Sire, any king who acts carelessly without studying matters, I should not live in his realm at all costs. I cannot remain in that king's city." The Bodhisatta asked for the king's forgiveness, and took leave to go to Takkasilā. There he went to sleep on an auspicious stone slab in the royal park.[4]

4. This scene with the flower-chariot is found in J539 Mahājanaka, several other

The king of Takkasilā had passed away seven days earlier. The city folk including courtiers gathered for the cremation, ending on the seventh day. The courtiers discussed, "Our city now has no ruler. Who should become king?"

One wise courtier responded, "We should release a flower-chariot. Whatever house the chariot goes to, that person will become our king." They agreed.

They harnessed a chariot with four Sindh horses and released it at random, saying, "Go now to the house of our king."

The flower-chariot made a clockwise circuit of the palace compound without going to any house, then left the city and went straight to the royal park. The courtiers followed along behind, carrying musical instruments. The carriage made a clockwise circuit of the auspicious slab and stopped as a mounting platform for the Bodhisatta. A brahman priest-counselor raised the Bodhisatta's foot, saw its characteristics, and said, "This wise man can rule any realm in the four continents." The brahman nudged the Bodhisatta awake and said, "O sage, a realm has come to you. Please come to rule the realm."

The Bodhisatta asked, "Priest, did your king have no son or younger brother?"

"None."

"Are you all in agreement?"

"We are all in agreement."

"In that case, it is good."

The brahman priest-counselor was pleased. They anointed the Bodhisatta there and then and invited him to board the flower-chariot to travel into the city. The people including the courtiers, some with musical instruments, went in procession in front and behind all the way to the palace. From then onward, the Bodhisatta ruled the realm according to justice and tradition. He had alms halls built in six places and gave alms of six hundred thousand every day.

His former wife and former friend became husband and wife. This couple never made merit in any way but committed many sins. One day, the husband said to his wife, "I have heard that the king of Takkasilā gives

classical *jātaka*, and also in six other stories in this collection.

alms on a grand scale. We should go and ask for alms to support ourselves in Takkasilā."

They went to Takkasilā and found one of the king's alms halls. The Bodhisatta saw them and remembered that they were his former friend and former wife. He asked the couple, "Are you husband and wife?"

"We are, Your Majesty."

The king ordered officials to arrest them, tie them up, and throw them out of the city. The officials carried out these orders. The Great Being continued to give alms on a grand scale.

Relating this story for the first time, the Well-Farer spoke a verse:

Then onwards, the King of Takkasilā, elevated by merit and karma,
had a gem body, great power, enormous merit,
great wisdom, many relatives, and high status.
He had great power and royal authority.
He accumulated excellent merit. He announced, "I have ruled justly
and accumulated great merit. The fruit will support me
to have the highest happiness, resplendent in every place."

The Great Teacher ended the sermon and pronounced the Noble Truths. Many people achieved a fruit of the way such as stream-entry. The Ten-Powered One then made the birth connections: "The mother of the Bodhisatta at that time was reborn as Queen Mahāmāyā; the father as King Suddhodhana; the man who did wrong to his friend as Devadatta; the immoral wife as Ciñcā Māṇavikā; the four palace gatekeepers as *dhutaṅga* monks; the people as the followers of Buddhism; Dukammānika as the refuge of the world, the Tathāgata." The words of the Buddha end here.

THE KING OF BĀRĀṆASĪ

P32 *Bārāṇasīrājajātaka*

พาราณสิราชชาดก

INTRODUCTION

This moral tale emphasizes the importance of friendship. It may be related to a tale in the Dhammapada Aṭṭhakathā (III, 412) of two monks, attached to one another like brothers from the same womb, who become estranged when a third party tells each of them false tales about the other.[1] The *jātaka* does not have the standard opening, but the latter part places the story within the history of the Buddha in an interesting way.

Once upon a time, it is said, in the time of the Kassapa Buddha during this era, there was a woman who loved her husband greatly and was utterly devoted to him. One day, while she was giving offerings and alms to the troop of monks headed by the Buddha, she made a wish: "In whatever world I am born, may I escape from being a woman and may my husband be my elder brother, loving and intimate with me. Also, if we two are born as animals, may we have the same body but with two heads." The Great Teacher gave a blessing and returned to the temple with his retinue of monks.

This woman and her husband came to the end of their appointed time in the human world. As a result of merit, they were born once in the family of a rich man, once in the family of a leading brahman, and once in the family of a great noble. Each time, the two were born one after another as twins. The first born was the elder and the other the younger sibling. They loved each other very much.

The two then passed from human form and were born as golden swans living at a lotus lake in the Himavanta Country. The swans each had a head,

1. Jaini, *Paññāsa Jātaka*, 2:xxvii.

but their bodies were joined together. The two heads were in complete harmony, of one mind. If they were going to eat somewhere, they agreed on the place. They never argued.

One day, a hunter came to where they were living. He saw the golden swan with two heads and was amazed. He went back to attend on the king of Bārāṇasī and tell him about it. At that time, a bodhisatta had been born as the king of Bārāṇasī. He presented money and food to the hunter and said, "If you bring this swan here, I will give you even more money than this."

The hunter paid respect to take leave. He left the city carrying a ram's horn bow[2] and entered the Himavanta Country. He captured the two-headed swan using a trick and took it to present to the king, who happily presented the hunter with money and a fine village. The king took the swan in his hand and gave it to his major queen to hold. The two heads of the swan emitted rays like gold and called out in a way that was beautiful and captivating. The queen was delighted. She gave orders to put the swans in a golden cage and feed them every day with popped rice and honey on a golden tray.

The queen attended on the king and said, "About this swan with two heads and joined bodies, if we can divide the bodies into two, we can keep one in the palace and the other in the animal park for people to view."

The king agreed. He summoned his courtiers together and asked, "Who can divide this two-headed swan into two? I will give gifts to such a person."

One courtier who had a means to do the separation paid respect to the king and volunteered to do it. The king rewarded him with money and handed over the swans to him. The courtier took the swans to look after at his home.

One day this courtier leaned over so his throat was close to one of the swan's heads, made clucking sounds as if whispering a secret, and then drew away. The head on the other side was curious so asked the other one, "What secret was the courtier whispering to you just now? Tell me."

"Partner, I heard him talking but it wasn't clear."

"Partner, I don't believe you. I saw this with my own eyes. You're being condescending. We've been partners for a long time. You're acting as

2. เมณฑสิงคธนุ, *mentasing thanu*, meṇḍusiṅgadhanu, a bow made from the horns of a ram.

if you're waiting for me to go to sleep so you can reveal your heart to someone else. I can see it all. Your heart is crooked, not honest with me. When I know you truly love and trust me, I will give you my deepest love."

The one head could not make the other believe him. After the two had fallen out, the courtier did not visit them for two or three days. Then he came and whispered to the head on the other side in the same way as before, and the other partner questioned in the same way. The two did not believe each other and got into a huge argument, each saying, "For ages, we may have made mistakes and blamed each other, but we never did anything bad to each other. Now you are using the words of someone we have known for just a short time to throw away the longtime goodness between us. From now on, don't talk to me."

Their quarrel got much worse. They blamed each other. They raised their beaks and pecked at each other in rage. The bodies split into two.

The courtier took the two swans to the king, who happily presented the courtier with money and a fine village. He had one swan looked after inside the palace and sent the other to the animal park. The king asked the courtier, "What means did you use to separate them into two?" The courtier told him what he had done from start to finish.

Feeling sadness and pity, the king said, "I'm devastated. These swans with two heads and joined bodies were loving partners up to now. Now you fooled them into separating by getting them to find fault and get angry at each other, breaking their longtime mutual love, to the point that they split apart. What else can I say? If people find fault with each other and don't examine what the cause is, they can become estranged in the same way.

"In truth, there are many ways in which people become estranged. Some are estranged because of some harm done to one another. Some lose their tempers. Some split because of worshiping possessions, or because of love for their master, or through making use of the words of their master. Some fall out because of bravery in royal service.[3] Some split up over a vehicle and because of their lack of common sense. Some fight over a house, land, or some building, over a lamp, elephant, horse, or male or female slave. Some fall out because they forget the goodwill they have accumulated for a long time. Some blow a tiny matter up into a mountain and make the great

3. Perhaps meaning that people fall out through competing to show off in service to the king.

virtue they once had shrink and disappear. Those who are good at cutting words make only a little out of something at first, but then more and more each time, like someone who releases water by first digging a channel for only a little to flow, but then the water itself makes the channel wider and deeper until it becomes a great gush.

"People in the habit of deceiving others with sweet words can reduce someone's mind to rubbish. As soon as they see that person is vulnerable, they gradually pile it on a little at a time until disaster and ruin occur, like a river or pond that overflows and destroys the plant life on its banks. People who regularly create division lead both themselves and others to disaster. Those who respond to people's inciting words without thinking convert something external into something inside their mind, and find themselves in great trouble."

The king also spoke this verse:

"A gem mine may be truly deep, but a wind may still shake it.
A king governs the realm, but the courtiers may rise against him.
Mountains and oceans are not as permanent as thought.
People destroy their friends. Being destroyed by someone close is the worst.
Earth, ocean, and mountain disappear at the end of an age
of a hundred thousand eras. People cause injury without seeing the sin.
They whisper in ears and may bring the family to ruin,
like water that beats on a rock as big as a paddy basket until it shatters."

After that the king had the courtier who set the swans against each other arrested and driven out of the country, but pardoned him too. To teach people, he spoke a verse:

"Even if life is separated from body, people should not make accusations
and row with one another but should be restrained in their words and deeds,
find out the truth before taking action, and study wise men before taking action.
Without such preparation, they should not act.
People who act without studying and investigating will run into trouble,
like the swans with two heads and one body, lured by the courtier to split apart.
Each of them listened to the courtier's luring words and so ended up estranged,
one in the palace and the other outside, separated from each other's sight."

From then on the king ruled with an even hand. The people of the city lived in harmony. People in the state were levelheaded and constrained in their speech. The king accumulated his merit for the future until he passed away and went to the heavens. In his last life he took the form of Vessantara, performed the seven hundred great almsgivings, and went to reside in the Tusita Realm. As a result of his full stock of merit, the gods in ten thousand worlds implored him to be reborn. He made the five great examinations,[4] then descended from the Tusita Heaven and was conceived in the womb of Queen Mahāmāyā. After birth he lived for twenty-nine years and then had a son. One night, he had the desire to renounce. With the gods of ten thousand universes and Channa[5] as his companion, he undertook the Great Renunciation.[6] He practiced the great exertions[7] in the forest for six years. After that he ate honeyed rice[8] brought to him by Sujāta and went to sit under the bodhi tree, facing to the east, and concentrated his mind. He overcame the lord of the demons and his troops, and attained full enlightenment. From then on, he gave teachings to gods and humans. He could remember his birth in Bārāṇasī and hence told this story and then gave a sermon with this verse:

All of you who love your friends, do not consort with enemies.
Act according to the white dhamma. Do not indulge in the black dhamma.

"When a good person consorts with a bad person he becomes the same. Whatever kind of seed one sows, one reaps that kind of fruit. Those who do good will have good result. Those who do evil will have evil result. Do not consort with low people. Consort only with friends and good people. A person becomes more and more like those taken as friends and intimates. Don't befriend low people for fear you will become similar. If rotten fish is wrapped in *lalang* grass, the grass will smell rotten too. Consorting with evil people is the same. If eaglewood is wrapped in leaves, the leaves will take on the smell.[9] When breathed in, the scent is very strong. Dishonest

4. ปัญจมหาวิโลก(นะ), *panjamahawilok*(*ana*), pañca mahā vilokāni: the time, continent, country, royal lineage, and mother for his birth.
5. His charioteer.
6. มหาภิเนกษกรมณ์(usuallyมหาภิเนษกรมณ์),*mahaphineksakrom*,mahābhinikkhamana.
7. มหาปธานวิริยะ, *mahapathanavirya*, mahāpadhānaviriya.
8. มธุปายาส, *mathupayat*, madhupāyāsa.
9. These similes with rotten fish and eaglewood appear in P60 Sirasā with minor differences in the Pali.

persons will go to hell and honest persons to heaven. Those who find fault with others destroy many people. A hunter uses a mule's head to lure a deer toward himself and then slashes it dead, as desired.

"Humans lure others with rice, water, and sweet words, then find fault for just one thing, creating suffering and destroying all goodness completely. Dogs, foxes, and birds can understand one another and live together happily. But human living with human is difficult. They have difficulty in understanding one another. People change their minds according to circumstance. People should avoid finding fault. They should not induce people to become estranged and antagonistic because of cutting words. Anyone who starts off using cutting words will go to hell to be burned and be repeatedly broken apart for one hundred thousand eras. When released from hell as a human, he will be poor, weak-bodied, and bereft, with a body like a suffering ghost, ugly and hateful, starved of food and drink. All this is the result of fomenting division. Those using cutting words in past eras will have only worms to eat. Wise and learned men understand this fault and carefully avoid this wrongdoing. Doing good results in good; doing evil results in evil—of this there is no doubt."

After explaining the result of friendship, the Great Teacher spoke a verse:

Anyone who values merit, friendship, and sympathy
will achieve the treasure of heaven, and later nibbāna, the state of bliss.

"When traveling in the circle of birth, be in harmony with many kinfolk, like a plant that puts down many roots in the forest. Harmony is unity, is a defense and guard against threats and dangers. A great herd of pigs that acts in unison may even capture a tiger that can harm or kill them. Hence, those of you who delight in the great dhamma should maintain a good attitude, constrain your body, speech, and door of action,[10] and avoid cutting words, argument, and dispute. Those who appreciate harmony will achieve happiness in every activity and will enjoy the eleven beneficial results."[11]

10. มโนทวาร, *manothawan*, manodvāra, the gate of the mind, the medium by which an action is manifested.

11. ekādasānisaṃsakāti, probably the eleven beneficial results of loving-kindness (metta) described in the *Visuddhi-magga* (the path of purification): "A man sleeps in comfort, wakes in comfort, and dreams no evil dreams . . ."

The Great Teacher ended his sermon and explained the birth connections: "The hunter at that time was reborn as Channa; the swans as Ānanda and Kāludāyi;[12] the smart courtier as Sāriputta; the people as the followers of Buddhism; and the king of Bārāṇasī as the Tathāgata." The words of the Buddha end here.

12. A childhood friend of the Buddha and early convert.

SISORA

P44 *Sisorajātaka*
สิโสรชาดก

INTRODUCTION

This longer moral tale focuses on the significance of karma made in past lives. The distinctive story is not found in any other collections of the Fifty Jātaka and has no known origin. There are at least two Thai literary versions, both of which change the name of the leading character to Si Sao. The *kham kap* version follows the *jātaka* but with additions of both entertainment and moral messages. The *klon an* version is probably from the late nineteenth century.

When the Great Teacher was staying at the Jeta Grove and going on almsround in Sāvatthi City, he spoke of his own karma and thus gave a sermon with this *jātaka*, which members of the Buddhist Councils define through the first line of verse, "Oh, I face trouble."

At the time when the Great Teacher had gained enlightenment, the monks were sitting talking together, saying, "O monks, do you see—only the Great Teacher of ours is the most excellent and superb of all the gods and humans, yet bad deeds from the past still catch up with him. At the time when he was drinking in the Kakuṭṭhā River, water that was clear and clean changed into water that was cloudy. So it's a waste of time talking about ordinary humans!"

The story of clear and clean water in the Kakuṭṭhā River becoming cloudy as if from mud is related in the text of the Buddha Vipāka.[1]

1. พุทธวิบาก, buddha vipāka, the effect, ripening, or maturation of karma. This paragraph and the last sentence of the prior paragraph were inserted by the Thai translator who seems to have muddled this story. On the way to Kusinārā, where he will enter *parinibbāna*, the Buddha asks Ānanda to fetch him water, but the stream has been

At that time, the Great Teacher heard the monks talking over his old karma and so said, "O monks, it is not only in this life that the consequence of bad karma from the past has caught up with me, but also in past lives. When I was still accumulating merit as a bodhisatta, I experienced great suffering due to the consequences of bad karma." At that, he fell silent. Wishing to know the tale from the past, the monks invited him to give a sermon with a tale from the past, as follows.

In the past, a bodhisatta was born as a king called Sisora ruling in Ananta City, anointed together with a major queen named Ananta Devī, the seniormost of all the 66,000 consorts. Her perfectly beautiful appearance inspired the king's love.

King Sisora had an army with the full four divisions. His great and meritorious power spread throughout the Jambu Continent like an emperor of great and splendid power. All the kings in the Jambu Continent feared his meritorious power and could not continue on as normal. They flocked to attend on King Sisora, bearing sprays of gold and silver flowers, in such countless numbers that the jewels decorating the crowns and breast chains of these kings rubbed and scraped against one other and were dislodged, dropping all over the place. After these kings had left, the caretakers who swept the palace collected about seven coconut-shell measures[2] of the fallen jewels a day. They took them to present to King Sisora, who did not accept them but gave them back to the caretakers to use at will.

The king had two perfect horses with very nimble hooves that he loved greatly. The first, called Tipaka, was a fleet royal mount. The king mounted on his back to go down to visit the realm of the *nāga*, up to wash and drink in the Anottata Lake, and back to the palace within the same day. The other horse was named Mahālada. When the king wished to visit the heavens, he mounted this horse, which flew through the air to visit the divine treasure and jeweled palaces in the world of the gods, then returned to Ananta City within the same day. The king's power spread throughout the Jambu Continent. No other king was his equal, as here described.

---

muddied by carts. Ānanda urges the Buddha to go further to the Kakuṭṭhā River, which is clear. When the Buddha insists, the stream water miraculously clears. See the Digha Nikaya, sections 24–25.

2. ทะนาน, *thanan*, a measure made with a coconut shell.

King Sisora ruled by the tradition of the Ten Royal Virtues. He made merit, gave alms, and upheld the five precepts—and the eight and fifteen holy-day precepts on the appropriate days—without fail.

One day, when King Sisora the Bodhisatta went to sleep at night on the royal bed, he dreamed he saw the pinnacle of his own palace break off, tumble down to the ground, and shatter into large and small pieces. He started awake in apprehension and remained sitting on the royal bed until dawn. He thought, "The pinnacle of my palace is fine. Why should I dream it falls to the ground?"

At that point, the king experienced the five abnormalities: his mind was sad, his sweat streamed, his body felt dark, his head shook, and his eyes clouded. At dawn, he sent for all the brahmans, led by the priest-counselor, and related his dream. "Does this strange dream mean that something will happen to me?"

The brahmans studied the manuals of astrology and predicted, "Your Majesty, some misfortune will afflict you. Seven days after this dream, Saturn will enter the same house as the king's ascendant. This will cause Your Majesty to be shaken and blown away as if by a powerful wind originating within the earth. Do not ignore this. Your Majesty has great power. Please prepare offerings and articles of worship to welcome the god Saturn, who will come seven days from now. If the king gives offerings to welcome him, he will be generous toward you, and you will remain happy forever, sire."

King Sisora was fiercely angry, like a lord *nāga* when someone beats down on the base of his tail. He thundered at the brahmans, "O evil brahmans, why do you come to beg me to make offerings to Lord Saturn? He is a deity. I am a god complete with the four military divisions. When Lord Saturn comes, I will go out to fight him with my troops, and whoever has the greater power will triumph. I will never make offerings to this Lord Saturn."

The brahmans said, "Your Majesty, when Lord Saturn comes, he will not show his body to you—only his shadow or shade will cover your ascendant. Please do not act haughtily toward Lord Saturn. Please welcome him with worshipful offerings as we suggest, and your happiness and well-being will continue into the future, sire."

King Sisora refused to follow their advice, drove them out of the audience, and sent for his military chiefs. "Chiefs, from this day forward for seven days, have a thousand soldiers stationed at each of the gates in the four directions, and a hundred soldiers on each story of the seven-storied palace. Give them orders that, should they see Lord Saturn approaching, they must slash and stab him dead or else capture him, place him in chains, and bring him to me."

The military officers carried out these orders. The king was careful to carry the five weapons at all times for his own protection up to the seventh day, when Lord Saturn was predicted to appear. He was very troubled, and his body shook as if he were mad. When he saw the guards in the palace, he lost his temper and drove them away, slashing with his royal sword, killing some of them and severely injuring others. Those remaining kept their distance from him. Some backed off but remained there. King Sisora slashed with his royal sword at the soldiers on guard on all seven stories of the palace in this way. Then he went down from the palace to the ground, mounted a horse, and galloped out of the city. The soldiers on guard at the gate could not stop him. They hurried after him but not one was able to keep up because the king's horse was so fleet of foot.

In truth, as bad fortune had appeared in this way, the horse that the king usually rode up into the sky was unable to fly but took him fast along the road, covering almost thirty *yojana* in one day. In the evening, they reached a large banyan tree in the great forest. The horse was tired out, unable to go any further. King Sisora was uncomfortable because of the sun and wind and racked by pangs of hunger from not eating. He dismounted and embraced the neck of the horse. He thought back to the city and realm and lamented in a verse:

> "*Oh, I face trouble. I am separated from the city and must suffer in the forest.*
> *I brought this on myself by not believing the priest-counselor.*
> *I used to live happily in the city.*
> *When I ate, I ate from golden plates. When I slept,*
> *I slept in a bedroom on a bed lain with fine cloth, soft to the touch.*
> *When I sat, I sat on a splendid throne surrounded by officials and royal retainers.*
> *Now I have nothing to eat and must suffer hunger.*
> *I must sleep on leaves laid on the earth.*
> *I must sit under this banyan tree.*
> *I came alone with just the horse as comrade,*

the shining moon as a lamp, the cries of birds instead of music.
Oh, my hardship now is great! What to eat and where to sleep?
Tomorrow morning, I don't know where to go.
There is no friend to point the way. I feel sorry for Ananta Devī,
alone, worried, and lamenting sadly. She will not bathe or eat all night long
and will drink only her own tears until she sees her husband again."

The next morning both King Sisora and the horse were weak because neither had eaten anything. Their bodies shivered. He steeled himself to lead the horse by the rein into the forest until they reached a wheat field just beyond the forest rim. The peasant who looked after this wheat field had food in a little basket that he had placed on a field bund to be eaten on his return. While he was chasing away birds eating the wheat, a dog sneaked up at the end of the field and took away the basket in its mouth. Just as King Sisora led the horse there, the peasant came back and saw the basket was missing. He spotted the crown on King Sisora's head and thought it was the basket. He approached, punched the king, and stabbed him with a goad, saying in coarse language, "O villain, why did you filch my food and put my basket on your head?"

King Sisora replied, "O good sir, I'm not a thief stealing anything of yours. This is my crown, not your basket. Why do you say my crown is your basket?"

The peasant became more enraged, and said threateningly, "Hey, you villain, I can clearly see my basket on your head with my own eyes. Do you want an argument? Where did you get a 'crown'? Why are you picking a fight with me?" He hit the Bodhisatta in the mouth with his goad again.

Blood flowed down King Sisora's body. In great pain, he asked, "Sir, it really is my crown. If you think it's your basket, then take it. Just spare my life. Have mercy."

The peasant calmed down and lifted the crown off the king's head. "From now on, don't you ever come here again. If you do, you die." With that, he drove the king away.

Bruised and bloodied, the king thought to himself, "I'm having a bad time, suffering almost to death because I haughtily refused to believe the prediction of the priest-counselor." He led the horse away from there to another field.

The owner of this field was an idle fellow. For two or three days, he had not checked on the rice in the field. Each day robbers had come and stolen some grain. That day, he took a pike and went to inspect the field. He saw the king-Bodhisatta leading a horse, and noticed his regal sword, which looked like a scythe. He ran up, hit the Bodhisatta with his pike handle, and asked accusingly, "You villain, so you've been cutting and stealing my grain every day? Today I've caught you!"

King Sisora was shocked. Not knowing the cause, he asked, "Sir, I'm not a robber stealing anything of yours. Why do you hit me and accuse me of stealing?"

"You stubborn villain, the scythe in your hand is evidence you're a thief, but you still have the nerve to lie. If you did not come to steal my crop, why are you holding a scythe?" He hit the Bodhisatta again, bruising his body and bathing him in blood.

The king thought mournfully to himself, "Why does this fellow think the sword in my hand is a scythe. Perhaps it's because of some karma I made."

He begged the landowner, "Sire, truly this is my sword. If you think it's a scythe, take it. Just spare my life. Please don't beat me to death."

The landowner calmed down. He picked the "scythe" out of the king's hand and ordered, "Don't ever come here again. If you do, you die." With that, he drove the Bodhisatta away.

King Sisora managed to tolerate these harsh words and bear the pain of being badly beaten. Tears streamed down his face. He led the horse away from that man's field to another field.

In the next field, the owner had tethered one cow from a herd to crop the grass and gone off to have his own meal. The cow broke his tether and ran back to the herd. The owner returned and could not see the cow where it had been tethered. He looked across and thought the horse led by the Bodhisatta was his cow. He ran over and shouted, "You treacherous thief, why are you leading my cow away?"

"Sir, let me tell you, this horse I'm leading is my horse. Why do you think I've taken your cow? What does your cow look like? I don't see why you are accusing me this way."

The cow's owner came over and hit the Bodhisatta with both hand and foot. "You stubborn villain, you're leading the cow you stole from me. I can see it with my own eyes, but you have the nerve to say it's your horse. Since when have a horse and a cow looked the same? Don't you know?"

He seized the horse from the Bodhisatta's hand. As a result of some karma from the Bodhisatta's past, the horse had turned into a cow.

For this reason, the Great Teacher gave a sermon: "All beings have karma or merit, and sometimes they must receive the inheritance of what they have done, that is, the fruit of the merit and demerit they have made. Demerit or unwholesome karma will have a fruit of great hardship and will create trouble and danger. Wholesome or meritorious karma will have fruit that brings well-being and happiness. In truth, all beings that wander in the cycle of rebirth will experience both happiness and hardship as a matter of course. Any wholesome action will be repaid with happiness at that time. Any unwholesome action will be repaid with hardship at that time. Beings of this world will have both happiness and hardship as a result of the fruit of karma. If the fruit of wholesome and meritorious action catches up with them, it brings good fortune, rank, happiness, and great power. They are loved and admired by both gods and men. Whichever country they visit, they are respected and worshiped by everyone there. They shine like the moon's aura on a full-moon day. If the fruit of unwholesome action catches up with them, their fortune diminishes, their rank declines, and their happiness disappears. They lose their great power. They are not loved and admired by relatives, friends, or the general people. Whatever country they visit, they are not respected and worshiped by the people there. They do not shine, like a firefly when the sun rises at dawn."

When King Sisora had been relieved of his crown, sword, and horse, there remained only the king himself and his lower and upper cloths. He felt bereft because he had loved the horse very much and had no idea what to do. He had to pull himself together to walk along, alone and in tears. By evening he was very hungry because he had eaten nothing. He sat down to rest under the shade of a tree at the edge of the forest. When his hunger eased, he made the effort to get up and continue walking. He arrived at a temple and thought, "I haven't eaten for two or three days. Never mind. I'll go into this temple and beg for the leftover food in the almsbowls of the monks and novices."

He went in, saw a young novice, and was overcome with love for him. "O novice, I haven't eaten for several days and I'm famished. If you don't mind, I'd like to stay here and eat for two or three days to ease my suffering, and then I'll depart."

The novice looked at the king-Bodhisatta and was overcome with compassion as a result of familiarity from helping each other in a previous life. He took the king to a fitting place. King Sisora was weak from lack of food. His body shivered and was smudged with blood, some wet and some dry, all over. Unable to contain himself, he collapsed down unconscious. The novice was shocked. He rushed to tell the monks, "A layman who came begging to stay here has collapsed down unmoving, and I don't know whether he will live or die."

The monks rushed to look. They asked the supine Bodhisatta, "O layman, why is your body bruised all over?"

King Sisora raised his hands to greet the monks and said, "I am a king separated from my city. I made a mistake. The peasants who saw me coming treated me to harsh words, saying I was a villain and thief. They beat and kicked me, and took away my crown, sword, and horse. I stumbled here and asked to stay in the temple. Please have sympathy for me."

Hearing this, the monks were moved to concern through their hearts of compassion. They boiled water to bathe his wounds and washed his body totally clean. Each brought oil and medicine to treat his wounds and food for him to eat. Some two or three days after this treatment, King Sisora was free of any sickness and felt physically comfortable and mentally happy as a result of the monks' care.

There is a question. Why did the monks care for King Sisora? The answer is this. In a past life, when King Sisora was born as a teacher, he gave his life as alms to the monks. For this reason, when the monks saw he had suffered hardship, they were intent on treating him so that he recovered happily.

After his recovery, King Sisora went to pay respects to the monks and begged them, "I wish to be ordained in this temple. Please allow me to do so."

"O layman, for you to be ordained in the Buddhist religion is a good thing! We have all the monk's requisites ready. We're missing only a *cīvara* robe, which is something hard to find."

"O monks, I have my existing lower and upper cloths. Please arrange things for me." He took off his upper cloth and handed it to the monks.

The monks took it and worked together to cut and sew it into a *cīvara* robe, then returned it to him, saying, "O layman you must wash this *cīvara* clean and then chop some wood from the core of a jackfruit tree trunk and boil it to dye the cloth the correct color."

He took the *cīvara*, washed it and spread it to dry, chopped the wood, and put it in a pot. He thought, "If I boil it here near the monks' quarters, the smoke will bother the monks. Better to go and dye the cloth outside the temple." He took the robe and pot of jackfruit dye and went outside the temple. He spread the robe to dry, lit a fire under the dye pot, and sat down there.

At that time, a cow had gone missing and its five owners were searching for it. They arrived near the temple, saw smoke from the fire outside, and approached to look. At that moment, the robe which had been spread to dry turned into a cow skin, the sash turned into a cow's intestine, the jackfruit wood in the pot turned into lumps of cow meat and offal, and the water in the pot turned into cow's blood—all through the power of bad karma catching up from the past.

The five owners saw this. They came up and punched and kicked King Sisora, shouting, "You villainous thief! Why did you steal, kill, and boil our cow?"

King Sisora was knocked down by the blows. He got up and said, "Sirs, I'm not a thief. I haven't stolen anything. I was sitting here stirring some boiling jackfruit dye. Why did you beat me up and say I stole your cow?"

"You evil and stubborn thief. We can see the cow's skin and intestines with our own eyes, yet you have the nerve to say you were stirring jackfruit dye and deny stealing the cow. Just look at all the evidence."

"Truly I haven't stolen your cow. I'm stirring jackfruit wood to dye a *cīvara* because I'm being ordained in this temple. If you don't believe me, ask the monks."

The five owners tied King Sisora by the neck, dragged him to the quarters of the monks, and asked them, "This fellow claims he was stirring jackfruit wood to dye a *cīvara* robe. Do you know anything about this?"

"O laypersons, we'll tell you the truth, so please listen. This fellow is a king who has become separated from his city. He came here because he had some difficulty. Some peasants took away his crown, sword, and horse, and so he came running to us and begged to be ordained in this temple. We told him a *cīvara* was hard to find, so he took off his upper cloth, then we cut and sewed it as a *cīvara* and sent him off to dye it. He cut some jackfruit wood, and took the pot of wood to boil outside the temple. That's the truth. This fellow is probably not the thief who stole your cow."

This angered the five owners. "You forest monks are looking after a thief so he can steal cows and cook them as curry for you to eat. That's why you make these assertions." They abused the monks with many harsh words and dragged King Sisora away with them. When the little novice saw this, his heart leapt as if to break into seven pieces, and his tears spattered down. He begged them, "O laymen, please let us keep this fellow. Should he ever escape, you may come and arrest us."

The five owners were softened by the novice's plea. They released the king and said to the monks, "Don't mix with thieves in the future. If you do, you'll suffer." With that, they left.

The monks and little novice tended to King Sisora, giving him food and treating him with hot water and medicines. After some two or three days, his bruises disappeared and he cheered up. The monks said, "O layman, you should not stay in this temple any longer because the villagers around here are a rough and tough lot. If they want to beat you up, we cannot prevent it. For this reason, you should seek happiness elsewhere."

King Sisora paid respect to take leave of the monks and the little novice, saying, "May you live here happily." He walked out of the temple.

The eyes of the little novice were flooded with tears. He walked out of the temple to see the king off and watched until he disappeared from sight. Overcome with pity, he walked back to his quarters in tears. King Sisora was in distress thinking with affection of the little novice. He did not want to leave there. In tears, he lamented in a verse:

> "*Oh, what karma did I make in a past life that I'm alone, bereft?*
> *Something I did wrong has caught up with me.*
> *I feel pity for myself. People treat me with contempt for no reason.*
> *I must sleep where I should not sleep, eat what I should not eat,*
> *wander where I have never been, lost, with nobody to take pity on me,*
> *to become my relative or friend, to know that I am a king,*
> *deserving of fear and respect. I face danger everywhere and must suffer.*
> *Where can I find a place to stay? There's no one who will help me,*
> *who can offer food, without which I shall die for certain.*
> *I have reached a fitting time to die because I have no food to eat.*
> *If I still have merit, then I shall find food, or else die of starvation.*
> *Who caused my suffering? I alone. Each person is his own refuge.*

Beings of this world should not ignore the merit and demerit they have made,
belittle and ignore the karma created, and believe it will not catch up with them.
Karma that has been made, however small, will have full consequences.
I am suffering now as a result of karma catching up with me."

After calming his sorrow, he walked on and at dusk came to an upland village. He saw a house with an aged couple and thought he would ask to stay there. He approached the old lady and said, "I have traveled from afar. It's too late to go further. If you are not troubled, may I sleep in this house for one night."

The old lady was angry. "Where were you during the day? Now you come asking to stay at dusk. How do I know you're not a bad sort?"

Hearing this, her old husband called out, "He's traveled a long way. As he's asked to stay, be generous." King Sisora went to stay in the house.

During the night, the couple could not sleep and so got up and talked together. He said, "We have seeds for various gourds. We should plant them, then water and tend them so they sprout and bear fruit that we can sell to make lots of money. Then we can get some beautiful female slaves to sit and fan both of us on the left and the right."

His wife laughed and said, "Before you see the water, you're think of cutting a container.[3] Before you see the squirrel, you bend the bow. If things don't turn out as you wish, you'll feel ashamed."

The next morning they got up and went to find the seeds, but they were missing. She said, "I wrapped up the seeds and stored them nicely. They've never gone missing until that fellow came to stay in this house, and now they've all disappeared."

Hearing this, King Sisora said, "Grandma, what would I take your seeds for? I'm very grateful that you let me stay here. Don't have suspicions about me."

The couple examined King Sisora, saw a knot in his lower cloth, and untied it. At that moment, through the power of some sinful deed done by the Bodhisatta, the jewels wrapped in the knot changed into seeds. Seeing

3. ตัดกระบอก, *tat krabok*, cutting a length of hollow bamboo to use as a water container.

them, the couple shouted, "You evil thief, why did you steal our seeds and knot them in your cloth?"

"I have not stolen anything of yours. These are my jewels. Why do you say they are your seeds?"

"You villain, you still have the nerve to argue. Those are our seeds, aren't they? Where would you have got jewels? I can see the seeds with my own eyes. Why do you claim they are jewels?" She took the jewels-turned-into-seeds, punched him, and drove him out of the house.

King Sisora did not know where to go. He wandered off in this direction and that until he reached Acala City. The next morning, he saw mendicants going to beg. Not wishing to join them, he stood around waiting until the mendicants had left. Then he disguised himself as a mendicant, begged for some food, and went to eat it by a sweetshop. After finishing the food, he said to the sweet seller, "I'd really like to eat your sweets." At the sight of the Bodhisatta, the sweet-seller's mind was filled with love. She passed some sweets to him. He ate the sweets and stayed in the shop all day and all night for two or three days.

The king ruling in Acala City was called Kinnuvatta, and his major queen was Suddhivatī. Their daughter named Sudatta Devī was very beautiful, her skin and face like the *apsara* maidens in the heavens. She was greatly loved by her father and was a well-behaved young lady in every way.

One night, King Kinnuvatta was sleeping on the royal bed. Near dawn he awoke and said to his daughter, "Now, my daughter, you have come of age. When will you have a husband?"

That morning he summoned the priest-counselor to audience, gave him her horoscope to study, and asked, "Priest-counselor, now that my daughter has come of age, when will she have a husband?"

The priest-counselor took the horoscope, made calculations according to the manuals of astrology, and said, "Your Majesty, before very long she will have a husband. He has arrived in this city already."

"What lineage is he from? Does he come from near or far? Whose son is he? A rich man or a pauper?"

"Your Majesty, do not be angry, but this husband of your daughter is a poor man. He goes begging for his livelihood every day. In the future, he will be of high rank."

Hearing this prediction, King Kinnuvatta felt more troubled. He thought, "I have only one beloved daughter. I have made efforts to bring her up with the intention of dividing the kingdom with her. Now this bad fortune has befallen me. If I keep her in this city, there will be shame." In anger, he ordered that Princess Sudatta Devī be driven out of the city.

Queen Suddhivatī heard of this. In tears she rushed to attend on the king, lowered her face onto his feet, and begged him, "Your Majesty, you and I have but one daughter and no other son or daughter. You mistakenly believe the words of this jealous priest-counselor and want to have her driven out of the city. I think the priest-counselor's prediction is wrong. Don't believe him. Even if it turns out as he says, treat it lightly. It's normal for one born a woman to have a husband that is good and a life that is fortunate. If she has merit, she will have a husband that is good; if demerit, a husband who is bad. It depends on the karma made. Please have mercy on me. Do not drive our daughter far away from this city. Have a house built for her just outside the city, according to her fate."

Hearing her pleas, King Kinnuvatta felt remorseful. He ordered that his daughter be driven out of the palace only.

Queen Suddhivatī paid respect to take leave. Wiping away her tears, she walked to her daughter's residence, embraced her daughter, and lamented in a verse:

> "*You are always my most beloved daughter, in your mother's one-eyed view,*
> *the beloved of both my arms, like my own heart.*
> *You were born in my womb, and I carried you for ten months.*
> *Anything too hot or too cold I refrained from eating, despite the difficulty.*
> *Walking, standing, or sitting, I suffered. Once you were delivered, I looked after you day and night—*
> *bathing, feeding, putting to sleep in a golden cradle, guarding against insects, until you came of age.*
> *Your figure and skin are beautiful, beloved by all. Your face is like the full moon.*
> *Your cheeks swell like a maprang fruit. Your breasts are like cups.*[4]
> *Your arms are pliant as an elephant's trunk. Your ten fingers are even, round, and straight.*
> *Your body shines, with a perfect figure, neither too thin nor too plump,*
> *neither too dark nor too fair. Everything is beautiful.*

4. ผอบ, *phob*, a cup or container, usually round with a peaked lid. The Pali compares them to conch shells.

O daughter, you used to sleep on a golden bed, now you must sleep on the ground—so pitiful.
You used to eat food of heavenly taste all the time, now you will eat whatever fruit and roots there are.
You used to live in a palace surrounded by a retinue of female slaves, now you will be alone,
with nobody as a companion, nobody to invite you to eat.
O child, you made some karma in the past and so must be separated from your mother.
Wherever you went in the past you went in a golden palanquin, now you must walk on foot.
Now you are separated from me, why should I live to suffer? Dying is better than living on."

As the queen lamented, tears bathed the face of her daughter. She prostrated to her mother's feet, saying, "Because of karma I have made, I must be separated far from you. You raised me from childhood until I have grown this far. Do not be sad. Think that you have made merit from raising me. Whether I will repay you or not, only time will tell. Let me say farewell, bow my face, and go according to karma." She lowered her face onto her mother's feet. They both collapsed down in grief. When they recovered, Queen Suddhivatī gave orders for building a house outside the city and arranged for slaves and workers, along with gold, silver, cloth, and ornaments for her daughter.

When Princess Sudatta Devī went to stay in the house outside the city, her mind felt bright. She gave alms and did good works, giving food and drink to mendicants, including monks, constantly without fail.

The mendicants talked together: "I've heard that the princess named Sudatta Devī has been driven out of the palace by her father. She has a house outside the city and gives alms that are clean and good. Let's all go to eat there." They went there and paid respect by prostrating themselves down on the ground.

King Sisora wrapped himself with one end of his lower cloth and put the other end over his head. He walked to where the alms were being given and stood examining the princess, not prostrating like the other mendicants. She was surprised to see him standing with his head covered, not prostrating like the others, and her gaze kept returning to him, while he looked at her constantly. Their eyes met. Through the power of predestination, through having been married in a previous life, she expressed a saying in a verse:[5]

> *"Through being together in the past, or bringing benefit in the present,*
> *this love springs up like a water lily that grows in water for two reasons—*
> *because of the water and because of its roots in the mud."*

The princess summoned her female slaves and said, "A strange mendicant has come, unlike the others. He's the only one standing with a cloth on his head. Go and tell him to take the cloth off his head. When I can see his face, I will give him alms depending on his appearance."

The female slaves went over, paid respect to King Sisora, and said, "Good sir, you came to beg for food. Why do you cover your head with a cloth so your face cannot be seen? Do you think she'll give you alms when you're like this? Take the cloth off and she'll give you alms."

He replied, "The sun is very hot. I'm sweating. That's why I'm covering my head. If she gives me alms quickly, I'll take them. If not, I'll go to beg elsewhere."

The slave girls relayed this reply to the princess who felt even stronger love. She thought, "That fellow is not a real mendicant." She asked her slave girls, "Did you see who he is? Is he someone of high or low birth and lineage? Are his speech and manners uncouth? Might he be a drinker or a gambler? How can I find out what sort of man he is when I cannot see his face?"

One of the slave girls, who was sharp, clever, and knowledgeable about the manners of men, replied, "Mistress, it's known that all young men, even those who are poor or in some kind of trouble, when they catch a glance of a young lady, they want a better look. Hence mistress should dress up well in finery and walk back and forth so he can see you. He'll take the cloth of his head to look and you'll be able to examine him as you wish."

"That's a good idea. I'll get to see his face that way."

She bathed, dressed up in her finery, and went to walk up and down where he could see her. King Sisora the Bodhisatta saw her walking and took the cloth off his head to look. She saw him. The pair looked at each

5. This is the second verse of the two-verse J237 Sāketa Jātaka (Faussböll, *Jātaka*, II, 235; Cowell, *Jātaka*, II, 162–63), also in the Dhammapada and much requoted. The Thai translator has embroidered the third line with the two reasons; the original says only ". . . springs up like a blue lotus as long as there is water."

other. The princess ordered her slave girls, "Bring that man to my fire-kitchen." Two of the girls went to tell King Sisora.

He said, "Does she not have the devotion to give me alms? Never mind. Why are you two taking me off? I don't know what you'll do with me." He asked three times. The slave girls took him to the fire-kitchen. He thought, "I think I shall escape hardship and enjoy happiness now." He thought this way because he was knowledgeable on the behavior of women.

The princess prepared various delicious foods and ordered the two slave girls, "Take this food for the fellow to eat and watch his manners while eating. When he's finished, don't let anything happen to the leftovers. Bring them to me." The slave girls took the food to King Sisora.

He was angry. "My body is in bad shape, covered with sweat and scurf. How can I eat like this?" The slave girls relayed these words to the princess. She had water and fragrant lotions sent to him. He bathed, applied scent, and ate the food in the manner of a king, as the princess could see. She examined the leftover food and was very happy, thinking, "He eats like my father the king. He is no ordinary fellow but a king for sure."

She had the fire-kitchen swept clean and laid with mats and had a bed prepared for King Sisora. At dusk she had all the seats taken away, leaving only one bamboo mat. During the night, she sent her slave girls to comfort him. He shouted at them in various words. In the morning, she sent some common food to him.

He looked at the miserable food and said, "I can't eat this. It doesn't suit me. Take your own stuff away."

The slave girls relayed this to the princess. She ordered them, "Go and flirt with him, using all your womanly wiles." But they could not please him and returned to tell the princess, "Mistress, you must go yourself. Once he sees you, his anger will disappear and he'll answer you."

She went to his room with the slave girls, greeted him with respect, and sat in a suitable place.

Seeing the princess was happy, King Sisora said, "You did something good for me before, then later you have done me wrong shamefully. Even so, I still think the good you did for me, at a time I'd fallen into difficulty, was great. I should do something good for you in return, but as I have no wife, child, or blood relatives, you must be my refuge. Later I will repay you, through to the end of my life."

Princess Sudatta Devī replied consolingly, "O king, do not be angry with me. I have prepared everything, including food, sent to you. There was nothing you did not have."

They talked together and showed their royal manners to each other in this way.

She said, "You must come up to stay comfortably in the house." He went there and ate various delicious food. He made love with the princess. Eventually she became pregnant.

Princess Sudatta Devī's mother heard about this and was greatly upset. She went to see her daughter in tears, saying, "You are my most beloved daughter. I made the effort to bring you up to this point, wishing to have you married to a husband of equal lineage. I have given you slaves, workers, gold, and silver so you do not feel ashamed in front of everyone. But you have made a quick decision to find a husband by yourself with no deference to your father and mother. You've fallen for a mendicant of low lineage from another country. It shames me in front of slaves, workers, ministers, and people in general." The queen returned to the palace.

Princess Sudatta Devī's pregnancy reached the tenth month. She gave birth to a son with all the qualities of merit, very like his royal grandfather.

King Kinnuvatta heard about this and became angry, like a *nāga* king beaten on the base of the tail. He thought, "This slave daughter has shamed me. That fellow insults us. I shall kill him." One day after, he thought, "What's this newborn son like? I'd like to see him." He commanded a group of consorts to bring the child to audience.

The consorts went to tell the princess. She gave her consent and took him to audience. King Kinnuvatta looked at his grandson and was greatly moved by love, as if his own skin were cut open and the love penetrated his bones. He embraced the child, kissed his head, and had him sleep on his lap. "Grandson, I want you to bring your mother here, but I detest that father of yours. Don't disappoint your grandfather." He had ornaments made for the child and a golden tub for bathing, then gave the child to the consorts and wet nurses and instructed them, "I want you to find fault with this fellow. If there's an opportunity, have him killed. Then I'll bring my daughter back here."

From then on the wet nurses tried to find some fault or wrongdoing by King Sisora. When there was nothing, they consulted together, "It's been a long time and we've found nothing. Let's do this. We'll get into a shouting match. When he sees us, he'll be angry. Then we'll abuse one another, following the king's idea, saying, 'You son of a slave from a family of outcastes. You wandered here from a far-off city. Nobody knows your clan. You're on your own with no friends or relatives. We're not scared of you. You're like a layabout who lives off figs. You just eat and sleep, sleep and rise to eat. You don't *do* anything. Aren't you ashamed?'"

When King Sisora the Bodhisatta heard the wet nurses shouting abuse at one another, he felt sad. His eyes filled with tears. He pretended he had not heard them, and sneaked away, thinking, "Whatever suffering I have faced in the past is nothing compared to this abuse from these slave women." He told Princess Sudatta Devī about it, saying, "I suffered as a homeless pauper until I found happiness with you, but this hardship is worse than what I bore in the past. We must be parted. I cannot stay with you. Please remain here and be happy. Bring up our son. Do not miss me. Find another husband. I will go where my fate takes me."

Princess Sudatta Devī felt as if her heart were breaking into seven pieces. Her tears spattered down with no break in the stream. She collapsed down at her husband's feet and implored him, "O husband, don't bother about the words of the slave women. Have a care for me, and have mercy on our child. Don't go."

King Sisora the Bodhisatta felt love and concern for the child. He swallowed his hurt over the abuse and remained there.

As the wet nurses had not found the fault they hoped for, they discussed another trick. One day they did not feed the child with any milk or sweets, left him near a pathway, and went off to hide in a secret place. The child was very hungry. He cried out and thrashed about.

King Sisora found the child and was very concerned. He hugged the child and washed him in the golden tub. The bathing made the child very cheerful. He hit the water in the tub, which splashed all over the Bodhisatta, drenching him. Seeing this, the wet nurses went to tell the king. "That fellow has the nerve to bathe himself in the golden tub with the child, your grandson."

King Kinnuvatta was angry at this presumption. He summoned executioners and commanded them, "Go and arrest that outcaste, put him in chains, and throw him in jail." The executioners quickly carried out the order.

When the executioners were tying up her husband, Sudatta Devī asked them, "What has my husband done wrong? Why are you arresting and jailing him?"

"We're following the king's orders."

She balanced her son on her waist and went to attend on her father. "Father, sire, what did my husband do wrong? When you hated me and gave orders to drive me out of the territory, I bore the hardship because of some karma I had made. In the course of fate, I acquired a husband. Why are you ashamed? Do you think my husband had fallen on hard times? Will you execute my husband and present me with another fine man as husband? Father, if my husband dies, both I and our son will die too, all three of us together. I was born in a royal lineage. It is not proper for me to have two or three husbands. I will fall down at your feet, say farewell, and be born again in a better life."

Hearing this, her mother, Queen Suddhivatī, was concerned. Tears filled her eyes. She implored her husband, "Your Majesty, do not make this karma. You felt ashamed about having your daughter in the palace and drove her out of the territory. Why did you feel ashamed? If you have any thought for your daughter, please have mercy on the grandson."

King Kinnuvatta's anger eased a little. He summoned his officials and ordered, "Bring the offender here. I'll question him a little."

King Sisora was brought from the jail to the front of the throne hall. He did not pay respect to the king but sat down normally. King Kinnuvatta saw this. In anger he asked, "You evil criminal, your life is already bad enough. Why then do you not pay respect to me? Why do you insult me?"

"Your Majesty, I am condemned to death. I should pay respect to you, but even if I do, it will not bring you any blessing. You are one of supreme reverence. My show of respect will be worthless because I am a criminal. You are the supreme king. It is fitting for you to receive respect from all free people, such as your officials and ministers. Also you should receive respect from the 101 kings ruling in the dependent states. That will bring you blessings."

King Kinnuvatta thought, "This fellow is clever with words, and his words are memorable. He's no mendicant. His figure and skin are very fine, and he has a beautiful blooming face. He was probably born into a rich family of high rank. My beloved daughter Sudatta Devī had the wisdom to understand this and so seized on him as her husband."

He asked, "Sir, whose son are you to act so arrogantly, to bathe with my grandson in the golden tub? Tell me the truth."

"Your Majesty, I'll tell you the truth. One day, the wet nurses left the child lying by the pathway and did not feed him with food or milk, so he was screaming and thrashing around in hunger for milk. The wet nurses paid no attention to him. I saw he was uncomfortable and took pity on him. I carried him to bathe in the golden tub. He enjoyed it and beat the water in play, and I got drenched. I know I am a poor man. Why would I bathe with the royal grandson? From the time you took to your grandson until now, I have been careful and very fearful of royal authority. All my words here are true."

King Kinnuvatta said, "Whether it's true or not we'll get to later. Whose son are you? What is your name and clan? You came to my territory and had no fear of me. On top, you became the lover of my daughter. So why don't you pay respect to me, your father-in-law?"

"You ask after my clan and name. I'll tell only the name, not the clan. Your Majesty, my name is King Sisora, ruler of Ananta City."

Hearing the name, King Kinnuvatta was shocked and fearful. His face fell and his hair stood on end. He came down from the throne and collapsed down at the feet of King Sisora, saying, "Your Majesty, I did not know you. Please forgive me." He invited King Sisora to sit up on the throne, while he sat on a low seat, and asked, "Your Majesty, you are a supreme king. Why did you leave your city and travel alone in this way?"

"One night, I saw a bad omen. I told the priest-counselor and he told me to worship Lord Saturn. I have a stubborn nature and did not follow his advice. For this reason, I had to leave my city. Peasants took my crown, sword, and horse, and treated me very badly. I suffered a lot for around one year and six months until today." He described it to King Kinnuvatta in full detail.

King Kinnuvatta was saddened by this. He anointed King Sisora to rule the realm with his daughter and held a wedding over seven days. He commanded his ministers, "You must send out people to find the royal possessions that the peasants took, and bring them here quickly."

The ministers sent out groups of officers in all directions. Once King Sisora's bad karma diminished, the things that the peasants had taken returned to normal—the crown as a crown, the sword a sword, the horse a horse. The peasants who had seized these things became worried. They thought such royal articles should not be in their houses and wanted to take them to present to the king. They left their homes and met together on the same road. The officials out searching saw the royal articles in their hands. "Whom did you get these from? Where are you going?"

"We are taking these royal articles to present to the king."

The officials tied them by the neck and took them and the royal articles to the king.

King Kinnuvatta was angry when he saw the peasants and the royal articles. He ordered his officials, "Punish these thieves one thousand."

King Sisora opposed this punishment. "Your Majesty, I suffered because of my own karma. Please release these peasants." The king did so. He sent for the monks and the little novice from the temple where King Sisora had stayed. He gave them a feeding with delicious food and presented each of them with triple robes and monk's articles. He gave orders for renovating their temple, gave patronage to the monks, and had the little novice disrobe and be appointed to an official post. In the future, he supported him lovingly like a son of his own. Later he sent a royal missive to his major queen in Ananta City. She was overjoyed at this missive. She summoned a minister and said, "At present our king is staying in Acala City. We will take the four divisions of troops to invite him to return. Please arrange this quickly."

The ministers went to announce, "Elephant troops, horse troops, chariot troops, and foot troops are to assemble. Brahman priests and rich merchants, please follow us."

Around sixty thousand elephants were assembled, all decked in finery and brave in battle, with bodies looking beautiful in their decorations, each with a rider mounted on the neck. Next, around sixty thousand cavalrymen were assembled, all decked in finery, wearing golden helmets and leather armor, each mounted on the back of a horse. Next, around sixty thousand chariot troops were assembled, each clad in rhinoceros skin, tiger skin, or leopard skin, with flags and pennants on each car, and an officer on each driving seat. Next, foot troops were assembled, all brave and expert in war, with beautiful accoutrements and each with weapon in hand. After seven days, the ministers informed the queen that the massive force of around ten *akkhohiṇī* was ready. She instructed them to proceed rapidly to Acala City. She traveled out with her great ministers to send them off, then returned to the palace to await news of her husband.

The two cities were very far apart, requiring a march of three months. On arrival they camped outside the city and sent a message to inform the king.

King Sisora summoned ministers and high courtiers to audience and enquired about the queen and the city. They replied, "Your Majesty, after you left, the queen was very sad and ate only tears all the time. She ordered us to search for you through various cities, but not this one. We did not come here—not because of enmity, but because we thought it a small city. Why did you come here?"

King Sisora replied, "Because I did not believe the astrologer, I had to leave the capital and suffer hardship. I did not eat for many days. Peasants stole my crown, sword, and horse and beat me so badly I almost died and never saw your faces again."

The courtiers could not contain their sorrow. Wiping away their tears, they said, "Your Majesty, please return to your city."

King Sisora informed King Kinnuvatta, "Your Majesty, allow me to take leave and go to my home. I return the realm for you to rule."

King Kinnuvatta arranged a group of consorts to accompany his daughter, appointed four military officers to take charge, and then asked King Sisora on what day he would leave.

"Your Majesty, tomorrow is a very auspicious day. May I leave then. May Your Majesty rule the realm happily in accordance with the Ten Royal Virtues."

That night King Kinnuvatta summoned his daughter and gave her instruction on the proper behavior of a daughter-in-law. "Beloved child, you go to stay with your royal husband's family. Do you know the proper behavior of a daughter-in-law?"

"Father, I do."

"Then tell me what it is."

"It's known that a woman going to stay in her husband's family must study ten pieces of advice: (1) do not take outside fire that is inside; (2) do not bring inside fire that is outside; (3) give to those who give; (4) do not give to those who do not give; (5) give to those who give and to those who do not give; (6) sit properly; (7) eat properly; (8) sleep properly; (9) tend the fire; and (10) worship the gods."

"Beloved daughter, 'do not take outside fire that is inside,' how do you explain that?"

"Father, if a daughter-in-law staying in her husband's family sees her husband or his mother or father do something wrong, she should not tell anyone outside the house."

"And 'do not bring inside fire that is outside,' how do you explain that?"

"Father, if a daughter-in-law staying in her husband's family hears the neighbors criticizing her husband or his mother and father, she should not report those words to them, not say that this person or that has gossiped, or criticized, or found fault in some way."

"And 'give to those who give,' how do you explain that?"

"Father, if someone who has borrowed something and returned it after use comes to ask to borrow again, the daughter-in-law should give it."

"And 'do not give to those who do not give,' how do you explain that?"

"Father, if someone who has borrowed something and not returned it after use comes to ask to borrow again, the daughter-in-law should not give it."

"And 'give to those who give and to those who do not give,' how do you explain that?"

"Father, if friends or relatives who are poor come to borrow something, whether or not they return it after use, if that poor person comes to borrow something again, the daughter-in-law should give it."

"And 'sit properly,' how do you explain that?"

"Father, a daughter-in-law living in her husband's family should not sit in a place where she has seen her husband or parents-in-law sitting. That is called 'sitting improperly.' She must get up from such a place. She should sit elsewhere, where she does not need to get up. That is 'sitting properly'."

"And 'eat properly,' how do you explain that?"

"Father, a daughter-in-law living in her husband's family should not eat before her husband or her parents-in-law, but should look after them first, and only eat herself afterwards."

"And 'sleep properly,' how do you explain that?"

"Father, a daughter-in-law living in her husband's family should not sleep before her husband or her parents-in-law but should do whatever she can to look after them first, and only sleep herself afterwards."

"And 'tend the fire,' how do you explain that?"

"Father, a daughter-in-law living in her husband's family should tend to her husband and her parents-in-law, as if they were the fire that a rishi or monk tends."

"And 'worship the gods,' how do you explain that?"

"Father, a daughter-in-law living in her husband's family should pay respect to her husband and her parents-in-law as if they were the gods that are honored and worshiped."

When the sun rose at dawn, King Sisora the Bodhisatta rose from his jeweled bed, bathed, and dressed in royal attire. He took leave of King Kinnuvatta and Queen Suddhivatī and mounted the neck of an elephant along with Princess Sudatta Devī. Surrounded by masses of troops, they left Acala City and traveled through the forest country for around three months to reach Ananta City. He took Princess Sudatta Devī into the palace.

Queen Ananta Devī came to lower her face onto her husband's feet, lamenting through her tears, "O husband, since the day you left, I have eaten only tears. I sent officers to search for you in different directions through the countryside and the cities without success. I thought you had passed away. But because you and I still have merit, we have met each other again today. O king and husband, may you live more than ten thousand years without aging or sickness, ruling the populace properly and joyfully!"

King Sisora told Queen Ananta Devī his story of leaving the city and suffering various hardships until he wed Sudatta Devī, had a son, and recovered his crown, sword, and horse. Then he said, "Sudatta Devī gave me great assistance, as I have described. Please have no hatred or prejudice towards her. Please love each other as kinfolk." He anointed Ananta Devī as his major queen of the right and Sudatta Devī as queen of the left. He had now been anointed three times. The wedding celebration lasted seven days.

The people of the city were very pleased. They made worship to the Bodhisatta with a great many worshipful offerings and gave him blessings for a life longer than ten thousand years.

King Sisora had an alms hall built for giving alms to mendicants, including ascetics and brahmans. He upheld the Ten Royal Virtues and helped the city folk through the Four Principles of Harmony. He followed the five precepts, gave alms himself, and encouraged others to follow suit. On holy days he gave sermons to teach the people. The city folk were all very joyful. The realm was free of robbers and villains and was not threatened by enemies. The realm was happy and prosperous like the era when the Buddha was born.

King Sisora the Bodhisatta made merit till the end of his life and was reborn in the heavens. Later he achieved the thirty perfections, attained full enlightenment, and defeated the lord of the demons and his troops at the bodhi tree.

> After the Great Teacher had told this story from the past as a sermon, he explained the birth connections: "King Kinnuvatta at that time was reborn as Devadatta; the five who did wrong to the Bodhisatta went after death to burn in the realms of woe; Suddhivatī, the mother-in-law of the Bodhisatta, was reborn as Visākhā, the special laywoman;[6] Ananta Devī, the major queen of the Bodhisatta, as Paṭiccharā the nun; Sudatta Devī, the queen of the Bodhisatta, as Bimbā Yasodharā, the mother of Rāhula; the son of the Bodhisatta as Rāhula, the Buddha's son; the people and officials as the followers of Buddhism; and King Sisora the Bodhisatta as I, the Tathāgata, the fully enlightened Buddha. Remember this *jātaka*, all of you, as I have told here."

6. Chief of the Buddha's female lay disciples.

TEACHING BY STORIES AND RIDDLES

BHAṆḌĀGĀRA: THE TREASURER

P28 *Bhaṇḍāgārajātaka*

ภัณฑาคารชาดก

INTRODUCTION

Four stories use the device of riddles or questions to portray the Bodhisatta as a person of exceptional knowledge while simultaneously delivering some teaching. In this and P35 Salabha, the riddles are the main theme of the story. In P54 Surabha, P55 Suvaṇṇakacchapa, the golden turtle (2), P48 Suvaṇṇasirasā: The Golden Head, and P49 Vanāvana, the riddles are a subsidiary theme. The same device is found in the classical J257 Gāmaṇi Caṇḍa[1] and J542 Mahosadha. However, apart from the riddle device, each of these stories is quite unique.

In the version of this tale from Burma, titled Prince Suvaṇṇakumara (The golden prince), the central character is not a treasurer but an executioner.[2] In fact, the Thai version is told that way, but in the Pali the man is called a bhaṇḍakār(ik)a, treasurer, not ghaṭika, executioner. Was this a slip or sensitivity over associating the Bodhisatta so closely with a professional taker of lives?

While the Great Teacher was staying at the Jeta Grove, he spoke about the power of his wisdom and gave a sermon beginning with the words "Listen, O great king" as follows.

One day the monks were talking together in the teaching hall. "It's amazing that the Great Teacher has such great wisdom—so solid, quick, stimulating, always apposite, and sharp. He should be venerated by both gods and humans. He makes both gods and

1. Cowell, *Jātaka*, III, 207–15
2. Horner and Jaini, *Apocryphal Birth Stories*, 1:181–89.

humans live under the three refuges and the five precepts, on the way of the stream-enterer, once-returner, and *arahant*."

Hearing the monks through his divine power of hearing, the Great Teacher came down from his fragrant quarters to the teaching hall with his incomparably elegant stride, sat on the pulpit, and asked the monks, "What are you talking about?" The monks said, "The whole assembly was praising your wisdom as great, solid, quick, and stimulating."

The Buddha said, "Monks, as a teacher I have had such wisdom not only in this era but in the past. I solved problems with my wisdom, causing Lord Sakka and all of humanity to venerate me in a grand way." He then fell quiet. As the monks begged him to explain, the Buddha told a tale from the past as follows.

In the past there was a great king called Korabya in Mithilā City in the state of Videha, with a queen named Sumanā Devī. The king upheld the teaching and practiced the precepts constantly.

At that time the Bodhisatta passed from the Tāvatiṁsa heaven and was conceived in the womb of the queen. A thousand deities passed from Tāvatiṁsa heaven and were conceived in the lineages of nobles and rich men. After the Bodhisatta was conceived, the king and queen were not sick. One night at ten months, Lord Sakka, king of the gods, appeared in the sky under a white umbrella and posed questions to King Korabya in a verse:

"O king, listen to my questions. What is one but not two?
What is two but not three? Tell me.
What is three but not four? What is four but not five?
What is five but not six? What is six but not seven?
What is seven but not eight? Tell me.
What is eight but not nine? Tell me.
What is nine but not ten? Tell me.
What is ten but not eleven? Tell me.
Answer within seven years, seven months,
and seven days. Answer the questions quickly."

He spoke further, "If you know the answers, speak out. If not, a divine punishment will be visited on you. You will die." Lord Sakka returned to his heaven.

After this, King Korabya was unsettled all night through to dawn, when he sat up and thought, "I cannot answer these questions." In the morning, he sent for his courtiers and asked them, but they did not know the answers. So he asked the keeper of the treasury and the palace gatekeepers, but none knew. The king began to worry, "I'll die for sure." He summoned the queen and asked her. "O fair-of-face, the god asked these questions, but I don't know the answers. Please give some thought to this matter."

The queen said, "On questions that need answers, I know nothing. How can a mere human answer the questions of a god?"

These words made the king more worried and fearful. He felt angry enough to execute the queen. He sent for the treasurer[3] to take her away for execution. The queen told the treasurer what had happened. After hearing the queen's words, the treasurer turned to the king and said, "Now is a time I should help look after the queen, sire. She should not be troubled or disheartened. However angry you are, sire, I know you are a man of compassion." He happily took the queen, thinking to himself, "Somebody should know the god's answers. We should not execute the queen now." He said to the queen, "May you preserve your life."

At that time the queen's pregnancy had reached the tenth month. At dawn on the following day, which was the day the moon entered the Uttarā Āsāḷha constellation,[4] she gave birth to a son. The treasurer looked after her. After leaving her womb, the son had a body like gold. Seeing his golden body, the treasurer was happy to support the queen and her son. The royal son and the thousand sons of gods who passed down from the world of the gods and were born from the womb all grew up. The queen raised her son. Because the treasurer had helped her, she named the son after him.

On the night when the son was seven years, seven months, and seven days old, Lord Sakka came down from the heavens under a white umbrella and said to the king, "You haven't answered my ten questions. If you cannot, I will split your head into eight pieces with my club."

3. ภัณฑาคาริกอำมาตย์, *phanthakharika amat*, bhaṇḍāgārika amacca, keeper of the royal treasury. This character should be the executioner, as is clear in this sentence, and as is the case in the version of the story from Burma.

4. อุตตาสาธนักขัต (usually อุตราษาฒนักษัตร), *uttasat nakkhat*, uttarāsānakkhatta, the eleventh constellation, five stars in the shape of a *garuḍa* or cow elephant, called the curved horn of the lion-king's wife; June–July by the modern calendar.

The king was startled by these words. He came down from his bedroom and sat thinking, "Lord Sakka asked these questions and I've been thinking for seven years, seven months, and seven days already, but I don't know the answers." So he said, "Lord Sakka, after you asked the questions, I consulted all my learned courtiers but they don't know. I'll ask them again this morning."

That dawn, after the king had washed his hair, put on clean clothes, and eaten breakfast, he sat clad in his regalia in the throne hall. All his courtiers paid respect and sat in the big courtyard.

The king first asked the treasurer with a verse:

"I depend on you because you know all the very clever people.
If there is a clever person in our fine city,
I will give him silver, gold,
pearls, cat's eye, diamonds, beautiful ladies in fine clothes,
a hundred elephants, hundred horses, hundred carriages, hundred cows,
hundred thousand of gold, and half the realm."

The courtier paid respect and replied with a verse.

"There is one lady's son who has a beautiful body.
I have seen him from the beginning.
He was a clever child from the time of his birth on an auspicious day.
I saw he was a learned fellow with all the organs and a fine appearance.
He is in my house."

Happy to hear these words, the king said, "Go and ask this son of yours whether he can answer the god's questions or not. And if the answer is yes, tell me."

The treasurer paid respect, hastened home, and asked the boy with this verse:

"The king has been greatly troubled
because Sakka posed several questions that he cannot answer.
He sent me to ask you, son, if you know the answers.
If you do, tell me."

The Bodhisatta was happy at these words. After studying the questions that Sakka asked, he could answer them confidently and completely and so said, "Father, I can answer these questions confidently and completely."

The treasurer happily said, "It is good."

The mother said, "Beloved son, you're only a child. What do you know? If you cannot answer, the king will be angry and you'll be in danger."

The Bodhisatta replied, "Mother, I can answer them."

She said, "If so, that is good."

The Bodhisatta said, "Father, go to tell the king that your son can answer Lord Sakka's questions."

When King Korabya heard the treasurer's words, he said, "It is good that your son can answer. Go and have your son bathe, dress in clean clothes and ornaments, and eat, then bring him here."

The father returned home and reported that the king had summoned the boy. The Bodhisatta said, "Father, ask the king to prepare a pulpit in the palace and decorate it beautifully with flowers, scents, unguents, candles, incense, and beautiful offerings; make a roof above; place white umbrellas and golden water pots; have the area around cleaned; cover a bench with colored cloth in red, white, and green; have the city folk gather, including the courtiers; arrange for music; and when everyone has gathered for the ceremony, place good cloth and ornaments on the back of a royal elephant with a white umbrella and send it here surrounded by people. Then I will go."

The treasurer relayed all this to the king, who commanded his courtiers to do as the son had asked. An elephant was decked with a golden breast-strap, white umbrella, fine cloth, and ornaments and sent to fetch the son accompanied by a crowd of people, all finely dressed. At the house, they paid respect with clasped hands and invited the Bodhisatta to go.

The Bodhisatta bathed in scented water, dressed, ornamented himself, went down from the house surrounded by courtiers, people, the four brigades of infantry, cavalry, elephant troops, and chariot troops, and mounted the elephant.

When the Great Teacher explained this passage, he spoke in verse:

Then the Bodhisatta left the house,
mounted an elephant, looking like a golden Buddha image
on a royal elephant, surrounded by many courtiers
and people of all kinds who had heard it said
that a boy of seven years was clever enough to answer the questions.
A thousand people, all dressed in finery,
flocked to see him in procession on the royal road,
riding elephants, horses, or carriages, or going by foot;
flocked to see him, splendid on the royal road,

with shields, helmets, armor,
going in full procession, splendid on the royal road.
The treasurer, dressed in finery, walked along scattering popped rice.
They passed through the fort guarding the city.
They were fed with rice and water.
They danced, sang, and waved cloth in the air in salute.

King Korabya sat waiting like a drinker who has no liquor and can think only of his next drink. When he heard the uproar and saw how beautiful the boy was, he pronounced a verse in praise:

"His face looks bright like gold heated with fire by a goldsmith,
shining like the molten gold poured from the mouth of a crucible.
Sitting on an elephant, he looks as fine as a Buddha image."

Arriving at the gate of the palace, the Bodhisatta dismounted while music played and people made a racket.

When the Great Teacher explained this passage, he spoke this verse:

Watching the boy arrive,
King Korabya and all his courtiers welcomed him with hands clasped in respect
and invited him to enter the palace.
The king led the boy by the hand into the palace,
sat with him on one throne,
and said in a teacher-like way,
"I hope you are not a drunkard, that you are not fond of liquor,
and I hope you think of and delight in the dhamma, truth, and giving."[5]

The Great Being addressed the king in a verse:

"Father, I am not a drunkard, and I am not fond of liquor,
and I think of and delight in the dhamma, truth, and giving."

The king said, "Lord Sakka came and posed ten questions. He ordered me to answer them or else I would be in great difficulty. The god said he would split my head into seven pieces with his club. Seven years, seven months, and seven days have now passed, so please answer the questions quickly."

5. The last two lines, and the response, are part of a conventional exchange, found in fuller form in P59 Varanujja; see note 16 in that tale below.

The Bodhisatta replied, "Sire, even if the god's questions range from the depths of the Avīci hell up to the Akaniṭṭha level of the Brahma worlds,[6] I can solve them." He then demonstrated his insight in various ways, comparable to scattering gold dust from the peak of Mount Meru, or the full moon in the sky. Gods, humans, palace ladies, and the faithful in King Korabya's palace were all amazed.

When announcing his powers of insight, the Great Being spoke a verse:

"O gods and people, listen to my words.
The god posed some questions.
The gods and people have gathered here
to enjoy hearing me answer these questions.
King Korabya, courtiers, and people will then salute me."

He then asked King Korabya, "What were the questions that Lord Sakka asked?"

The king replied, "The god's first question was 'What is one but not two?'"

The Great Being said, "Sire, listen to my words. In this world, there is nothing the same as Mount Meru. So the answer to the question 'What is one but not two?' is Mount Meru."

Hearing this answer, Lord Sakka felt wonderfully happy. He took off cloth and ornaments to offer in worship. He grasped a jeweled flask of scented water and poured it down. King Korabya and all the people gathered there were happy to see this wonder. They took off cloths and ornaments to make offerings to the Great Being. They exclaimed, "He's still just a child, only seven, but so clever!"

The Great Being asked the king, "What is the next question, sire?"

The king replied, "What is two but not three?"

"Sire, listen to my words. There is nothing in the world the same as the sun and the moon, so the answer to the question is the sun and the moon."

Hearing this, Lord Sakka pushed aside his gold umbrella to reveal his body, and said, "You answered my question correctly!" The god venerated him with a beautiful voice and then disappeared.

Everybody raised their clasped hands in salute and offered praise. Music sounded through King Korabya's palace.

6. อวิจี, *awiji*, the lowest of the hells, and อกนิฏฐ, *akanittha*, the sixteenth and highest of the material Brahma worlds in the cosmogony of the Three Worlds.

The Great Being asked, "What is the god's next question?"

The king replied, "What is three but not four?"

"Sire, listen to my answer. The threesome is the Buddha, the Dhamma, and the Sangha. There is nothing the same as the Buddha, the Dhamma, and the Sangha, so that is the answer."

Hearing this, Lord Sakka made offerings to the Great Being of flowers, scents, candles, and incense and then disappeared.

The king saw this wonder and was so happy he presented the Great Being with gold, silver, and jewels, such as diamonds and pearls. The courtiers, ministers, ladies, and everyone else made worship to him. People began playing music loudly.

The Great Being asked King Korabya, "Sire, what is the god's next question?"

"What is four but not five?"

"The four continents are Jambu, Pubbavideha, Aparagoyāna, and Uttarakuru. There is nothing the same as these. So that is the answer."

Lord Sakka was so happy that he caused rain of seven gems to fall in worship of the Great Being. All the gods saluted and venerated him too. The king saw this wonder and raised his hands in worship.

On this event, the Ancient Teacher pronounced a verse:[7]

This was an awe-inspiring thing, enough to make hair stand on end.
The king saluted him and said in praise,
"You have boundless wisdom to answer the god's questions so easily!"

He added, "Son, though still a small child, you are so clever! I will give you a hundred cattle, hundred horses, hundred elephants, and a thousand bars of gold."

The Great Being asked, "What is the god's next question?"

"What is five but not six?"

The Great Being wished to reply to this question at length. "Sire, the answer is the five precepts. There is nothing in the world that can be compared to upholding these five precepts. Through their power, one can be reborn from this world into the Tāvatiṁsa Heaven of the gods. So the answer to the god's question is the five precepts."

7. In the Mahāparinibbāna Sutta, Ānanda speaks this line after the Buddha passes away (suttacentral.net/pi/dn16, section 36), and it is repeated in many texts.

Lord Sakka scattered scents and ornaments down in worship of the Great Being. Seeing this wonder, the king was so happy that he presented a hundred female slaves and a hundred male slaves along with a thousand gold bars. Music resounded.

"What is the god's next question?"

"What is six but not seven?"

"The answer is the six levels of heaven, Catummahārājikā, Tāvatiṁsa, Yāmā, Tusitā, Nimmānaratī, and Paranimmita Vasavatti."

Lord Sakka was so happy he grasped a jeweled flask filled with the seven gems and scattered them down in worship at the Great Being's feet. King Korabya presented jewels worth a hundred thousand.

"What is the god's next question?"

"What is seven but not eight?"

"The seven hills around Mount Meru. There is nothing like them, so the answer is the Satta Paribhaṇḍa, the seven ranges encircling Mount Meru."

Lord Sakka scattered seven thousands garlands of gold down in front of the Great Being. The gods, King Korabya, courtiers, officials, royal ladies, and people in the palace made worship to the Great Being. Music played.

"What is the god's next question?"

"What is eight but not nine?"

"There is nothing like the eight precepts, so that is the answer."

Lord Sakka sent down a hail of holy flowers in worship. The king was so happy to see this wonder that he offered a huge amount of gold, silver, and ornaments. Others brought more gold and silver and jewels. The king invited people to play drums and fiddles and all kinds of instruments. People made loud salutations.

"What is the god's next question?"

"What is nine but not ten?"

"In this world there is nothing like the nine supermundane ways[8] that the fully enlightened Buddha revealed. So that is the answer."

Lord Sakka caused a rain of seven gems to fall in worship. The king saw this wonder and was so happy he presented half his realm. People took off their jewelry and offered it in worship.

"What is the god's next question?"

"What is ten but not eleven?"

8. Lokuttara dhamma, made up of the four paths, four fruitions, and *nibbāna*.

"Sire, listen to my words. The ten precepts. Nothing in the world is the same, so that is the answer."

Lord Sakka sent down a rain of seven gems like a great cloud. All the gods, including the spirits of the earth, trees, and sky and gods born in the universe, offered worship in unison in beautiful voices. The king was so amazed he offered all of his realm. Other royals presented their own daughters. Others gave gold, silver, jewels, and cloth. All raised hands in worship, waved cloth, and cheered as drums and music played. The people gave flowers and sang their praises and blessings so loudly that it seemed the earth would overturn.

Each time the Great Being answered a question, the Thousand-Eyed Lord gave salutations but did not reveal himself.

The Great Being asked Lord Sakka in a verse:

> *"Are you a god, gandhabba, or Lord Sakka the fort-breaker?*[9]
> *I have answered all ten questions, and each time I heard veneration."*

Lord Sakka replied with a verse:

> *"I am Lord Sakka, king of the gods. I came to your abode.*
> *I asked these questions that King Korabya could not answer.*
> *As you have answered them, I offer my veneration.*
> *Be praised, be praised! Your wishes will be fulfilled.*
> *Before long you will become a Buddha in this world.*
> *Son, I offer to grant you four wishes."*

While Lord Sakka spoke, standing in the sky, because of his divinity a bright glow shone forth like the soft and bright aura of the sun. The son of the treasurer accepted the blessings with a verse:[10]

> *"O Lord Sakka, greater than all beings, you have granted me a wish.*
> *May my father take delight in having me return to my own home,*
> *and may he call me to sit upon my seat. This is my first wish.*
> *May I not consent to the execution of any man, even if he has committed a terrible crime,*
> *and may I free the condemned from death. That is my second wish.*

9. Purindada, an epithet of Indra.

10. The first eight and a half lines and last couplet come from J547 Vessantara, 2299 (Faussböll, *Jātaka*, VI, 572; Appleton and Shaw, *Ten Great Birth Stories*, 621–22). In the Vessantara version there are eight wishes.

May all the people, with no distinction between young, old, and those between,
live close to me and find support in their lives from me. This is my third wish.
May I not go with another man's wife; may I be true to my wife alone.
May I not use force on women; may I do no wrongs that trouble other beings;
may I be a king into old age; may I win victories over all lands through the dhamma;
may I inspire those who are dishonest and stray from dhamma to uphold the dhamma;
may my generosity never be exhausted. May I never regret any gift.
May my heart become tranquil through giving. This is my fourth wish."

Lord Sakka said, "Not long from now, your father will anoint you king." He granted the wishes to the boy and returned to the world of the gods.

King Korabya gave orders for the boy to be bathed, fed, and dressed in various ornaments, then sat him on his lap to talk further.

When the Great Teacher explained this passage, he pronounced a verse:

King Korabya did not yet know the boy was his own son
until he asked the treasurer, who told him.
The king kissed the boy's head and, seeing the likeness,
wept with tears running,
splashing onto the boy's head, clothes, and ornaments.
He embraced him on his lap and asked,
"Son, I did not know you were my son.
Where is your mother? Please tell me."

"My mother is in the treasurer's house. He looked after me for seven years, seven months, and seven days. Father is the lord of all knowledge but did not know I was his son, though I did know you the king were my father."

King Korabya instructed servants to summon military officers to bring the four brigades of elephant, horse, foot, and carriage troops into the palace and to find a thousand palace ladies and dress them up well to welcome the queen into the palace.

All was done. Officials went to the treasurer's house, paid respect to the queen, and said, "Mistress, the king knows the boy is his son, and they have spoken together lovingly. The king wishes to see your face and thus has sent us to fetch you."

Queen Sumanā Devī thought to herself, "I will see the king's face." She washed her hair, dressed in a fine cloth and ornaments, and went on an elephant surrounded by royal ladies.

King Korabya waited, watching the way she would come. On seeing her, he felt happy that he would touch and feel the body of the queen. He came down from the throne to welcome her as she dismounted from the royal elephant. He took hold of her with his right hand and led her in.

When the Great Teacher explained this passage, he pronounced a verse:

The king took the queen to sit together on the same throne.
"In anger I ordered the treasurer to punish you with death, though innocent.
Now you still survive alive and are my great love.
The treasurer saved your life. You survived in his house.
Please live with me henceforth.
You have a son, our son, who has great merit.
Lord Sakka and the gods venerated him with holy woolen cloth
and worshiped him with holy flowers.
Lord Sakka granted him four wishes, including that he would become a Buddha."

King Korabya had Queen Sumanā Devī bathe her body and wash her hair in scented water, be adorned with many decorations, and eat fine food. He established her as his queen as before.

The son was anointed king. When the Great Teacher explained this passage, he pronounced this verse:

When the son had washed his hair
and put on fine clothes and ornaments,
he sat on a jeweled throne under a white umbrella
for the anointing. People gathered to call out good wishes.
"Hurrah! May you win every victory.
May you rule the realm happily without growing old or dying.
May you be the sole ruler, upholding the Ten Royal Virtues."
The sound of the people cheering, along with music,
drums, singing, and dancing merged into one uproar.
The people of the city and the countryside throughout the realm
gathered to offer their veneration. Both men and women
swarmed to enjoy watching the singing and dancing.

After his anointment as king, the Bodhisatta gave a great amount of wealth to the treasurer.

The Bodhisatta upheld the Ten Royal Virtues and ruled justly. Other kings offered him their realms, dressed up their daughters well, and brought them to present to him, raising their hands in homage. The Bodhisatta advised all these kings, "Take care to uphold the five precepts and to make merit through charity. Do not torment living things, do not take the property of others, do not tell lies, do not take others' wives, and do not drink liquor. May you live long."

After hearing the Bodhisatta's advice, these kings returned home. The Bodhisatta gave alms. All the people on reaching death were reborn into the divine world and enjoyed bliss.

On passing away, the Bodhisatta was reborn in the divine world and enjoyed bliss.

When the Great Teacher finished this sermon, he said, "Monks, I have had great wisdom not only in this life but in times past too." He pronounced the Four Noble Truths and then explained the birth connections in a verse:

Sumanā Devī, so troubled, returned as Mahāmāyā;
Korabya as Suddhodana, the Buddha's father;
Sakka as Anuruddha, with the most divine vision;
the treasurer, who looked after the Bodhisatta's mother, as Ānanda;
the courtiers and royal servants as the Buddhist laity;
the Bodhisatta of such merit as the refuge of the three worlds.
Remember this jātaka, all of you.

STORY CYCLE

SABBASIDDHI

P40 *Sabbasiddhijātaka*

สรรพสิทธิชาดก

INTRODUCTION

A few tales in the collection have a main story that acts as a frame for other stories.

This tale seems to have roots in at least two stories about a legendary Indian king named Vikrama that are known in many collections in different Indian languages. In one story, the king wins a silent princess by persuading her to talk. In another, the king is able to transfer his heart into other bodies, including an elephant and a parrot. As the parrot, he is adopted by a princess. Both stories involve riddles.

These two stories are found combined in a single tale in *Kathā-ratnākara*, a seventeenth-century collection by the Jain poet Hemavijaya. The combination in the *jātaka* is rather similar, and perhaps the two have a common (unknown) source.

The same two stories are found combined in other ways. In Thailand, there is a children's version, *Nok krajap* (The weaverbirds), used as a school reader, in which the central couple had been a pair of weaverbirds in a previous life. The core of the story is similar to this *jātaka*, but the ending has a complex tale of swapping hearts between bodies, which resembles the tale of Vikrama as a parrot.[1]

A verse version of the story, closely following the *jātaka*, was composed by Phra Poramanuchit Chinorot in the early nineteenth century.

The device of nesting stories within the main story is also found in P13 Dukammānika (above) and in P54 Surabbha, where around twenty tales are chained together by a series of framing devices.

1. Skilling, "Romance and Riddle," 178–80.

When the Great Teacher was staying at the Jeta Grove, he spoke of his special qualities[2] and thus gave the sermon as follows beginning with the words "Suvaṇṇa Sobhā."

At that time, the monks were gathered together in the teaching hall talking of the unusual virtue of the Buddha, saying, "O friends, the Buddha, our great teacher, has so many activities, methods, and thoughts, so much art and cleverness. He already has attained complete virtue as a result."

Hearing the monks' words, the Great Teacher left his fragrant quarters like a lord of the lions leaving his jeweled cave, came to the teaching hall, sat on the pulpit, and asked, "O monks, what are you gathered to talk about now?" They told him.

"I have many activities, but not only at this time. Even before, when I was born as a bodhisatta searching for the completion of my perfections, I had great arts, expertise, and wisdom in the same way, all admirable things. The kings in the Jambu Continent who had already mastered the Three Vedas, and had mastered all kinds of arts were not equal to me, as I was a royal son more excellent than those kings. Now that I have achieved full enlightenment and known the full dhamma, I am more excellent than all beings. No greater insight can be found."

At that he fell silent. The monks, who wished to hear more, invited him to give a sermon, and thus he told a tale from the past as follows.

A long time in the past, there was a king named Usabha [bull, strong man] ruling in Giribhaja City, with a daughter named Suvaṇṇa Sobhā [golden beauty] sired with a queen named Kusuma [blossom]. When the daughter was sixteen years old, she had a very beautiful appearance with the five womanly qualities. No woman was her equal.

There is a query inserted here. Why was she more beautiful than any other woman?

The answer is as follows: In a past life, she had followed the precepts, done many good works, been cheerful and sympathetic toward all beings without discrimination, been devoted to the virtue of the Triple Gem,

2. คุณวิเศษ, *khunnawiset*, guṇa visesa.

and conducted herself humbly toward her elders and betters. When she listened to sermons, she had made offerings of alms and followed the holy-day precepts. For these reasons, in this life she was born into a family with great rank and wealth and was more beautiful than any other woman. Her fame was known throughout the Jambu Continent.

When they heard of this princess, all the kings of the Jambu Continent fell in love with her. They had royal officials prepare articles of tribute, adorned their elephants and horses, and mounted these elephants and horses to leave their cities, go to the seat of King Usabha, and present the tribute. When they conversed with King Usabha, they spoke a verse:

> "*Your Excellent Majesty, your humble servant has come from afar*
> *to ask for the hand of your daughter. Please present your daughter to me.*"

Happy to hear these words, King Usabha replied, "I invite each of you to talk with my daughter for each of the four watches within one night—as the sages have defined as the first, middle, and last watches.[3] When one of you talks with my daughter for one night and she talks also, I will give her to that person."

The kings were pleased and made salutations to accept King Usabha's words. They gathered at a suitable place and reached an agreement on who should go in which order. One king then took leave of King Usabha and went up into the princess's palace at the first watch, sat down outside, and spoke words of love to Princess Suvaṇṇa Sobha. Although he spoke in this mood throughout the night, the princess did not say a single word. At dawn he came down from the palace, paid respect to King Usabha, and told him what had happened.

King Usabha said, "Leave this matter for now, until all of you have spoken with my daughter in order."

From then on, each night one king went up to the princess's palace, sat outside, and spoke sweet words to her through to dawn, but she did not speak a word. Each came down from the palace and went to tell King Usabha, who responded in the same way. The princes all went up to the princess's palace again in order and spoke words of love all through the night until

3. ยาม, *yam*, four-hour periods starting at six o'clock p.m. The "four watches" means the beginning of each watch, and the ending of the final one: 18:00, 22:00, 02:00, 06:00.

dawn, but she did not say anything to any of the princes. Eventually they all went to King Usabha and each told him, "Your Majesty, your daughter did not say one thing to me, hence I pay my respect to take leave now."

King Usabha had his officials return the articles of tribute to each of them and gave them the blessing "May you travel happily." Each returned home.

At that time in Alika City there was another king called Vijaya [victory], who followed the Ten Royal Virtues and had a major queen named Uppala [lotus].

A bodhisatta passed from the divine world, was conceived in the womb of this queen, and ten months later was born. King Vijaya commanded all the brahmans to come and predict his son's nature. They studied his qualities and gave their prediction: "Your Majesty, this son of yours will be thoughtful, skilled in the arts of knowledge, and equipped with wisdom, expertise, and ingenuity." The king was very pleased to hear this prediction.

After he grew up, this son had a perfect appearance, which was attractive and invited devotion. He was an object of love and delight for King Vijaya. Wanting his son to study the arts, King Vijaya presented him with a thousand bars of gold and said, "Beloved son, please go to study the arts at the court of a famous teacher in Takkasilā City." The Bodhisatta took the gold bars and did as was bidden. He went to the teacher, paid his respect, and said, "Allow me to study the arts of knowledge at your institution."

The teacher asked, "Which art do you wish to study?"

"The art of breaking open a chest, taking out the heart, and then placing it back as before. Please teach me this ability."

The teacher agreed. The Bodhisatta was pleased. He completed the study within one month, gave the teacher a thousand bars of gold for recompense, and returned home. He paid respect to his royal father and mother and told them everything.

The day after his return, King Vijaya commanded royal officials to beat a drum all around the city and announce that the king's son had completed his study and for this reason had been given the name Prince Sabbasiddhi [all the accomplishments].

Prince Sabbasiddhi heard about Princess Suvaṇṇa Sobha and fell in love. He boarded a royal chariot, accompanied by the four divisions of troops, left Alika City, and traveled twenty-five *yojana* along the road to reach

Giribhaja City. He went in to offer gifts to King Usabha and asked for the hand of the princess, saying, "Your Excellent Majesty, I am a person of more excellence than all humans. I have come here to ask for your daughter's hand. Please present her to me."

King Usabha asked, "You're called Prince Sabbasiddhi, are you?"

"Yes, sire."

"Please go and talk to my daughter. If she replies, I will give her to you."

"Good. I will do as you say." He took leave of the king.

At the first watch of the night, he took one courtier with him, went up to her palace, sat outside the room and talked with the courtier. After night fell, he split open the chest of the courtier and, using his arts of knowledge, took out his heart and placed it in a dish that was there. He returned to his seat and addressed the courtier's heart, asking, "Courtier, let me ask you a question."

The heart replied, "Sire, please ask at will."

The Bodhisatta said, "There were four sea merchants who were friends. Each of them slept near the mooring rope to guard their boat. In the night, they all went to sleep. One woke up and saw a sandalwood log float down on the current and hit the boat. He knew it was the core of a sandal tree, so he collected it and carved it into the shape of a woman with a beautiful figure, suitable for love. Later, one of the other men saw the figure and dressed it in fine clothes and ornaments, making it very attractive. Yet another of the men saw the figure all dressed up, fell in love with it, and placed the figure in front of his seat. Then yet another man saw the figure and sat talking with it as if it were his own. The four men were all in love with this figure of a woman, and all wanted it. They sat arguing over it without reaching any agreement. Of these four men, who should have the figure?"

The courtier's heart replied, "The man who carved the sandalwood into the image of a woman with a beautiful figure suitable for love. He should have it."

Hearing this, the princess said, "O courtier, that's not right. The man who carved the figure from sandalwood should be the father. The man who sat talking with the figure should be the elder brother. The one who fell in love with the figure and placed it in front of his seat should be the mother. The man who dressed the figure finely should be the husband."

Hearing the princess speak, the king's officials played loud music. This was the first time.

At the second watch, the Bodhisatta brought the courtier's heart to the foot of the princess's bed and went back to sit as before. He asked the heart, "There were four princes who went to Takkasilā City to study the arts of knowledge with a renowned teacher. One studied archery, another studied how to bring dead beings back to life, another studied how to stay underwater for a long time, and the other studied astrology. At the end of their study, they took leave of the teacher and returned home. Arriving at a certain city, they went to sit under the shade of a banyan near the ocean shore and discussed, 'When will we have good fortune?'

"Three of them asked the prince who had studied astrology, 'When will we have good fortune according to astrology?' He made calculations and predicted, 'Friends, a *hatthaliṅga* bird will bring a woman flying through the air.' He said to the prince who was skilled in archery, 'Be ready to shoot an arrow.'

"At that moment, a *hatthaliṅga* bird swooped down and seized the major queen of the king of that city. She was wearing a fine red cloth that the bird mistook for meat. One prince saw them in the air and said to the expert in archery, 'Friend, shoot now!'

"He shot an arrow. In alarm, the *hatthaliṅga* bird dropped the queen and flew away. The queen fell into the ocean. The prince who was skilled in staying underwater dived down into the ocean and brought her up. The prince skilled at bringing beings back to life chanted a formula to revive her. The four princes all wanted to have the queen. They discussed who it should be." The Bodhisatta asked the courtier's heart, "Who should have her?"

"Sire, the prince who shot the arrow and made the *hatthaliṅga* bird drop the queen. He should have her."

Hearing this, the princess said, "O courtier, you're wrong. The prince who dived down into the ocean should have her because of the effort he made."

Hearing the princess speak, the king's officials played loud music. This was the second time.

At the last watch, the Bodhisatta placed the courtier's heart close to the bed and went back to sit as before. He asked the courtier's heart, "There were four men, and four women who were their lovers. They went to sit under a tree. The four men talked together intimately. Each asked his lover, 'Where is your house located?'

"The first woman stroked her head with her hand and said, 'My house is here.'

"The second woman stroked her breast and said, 'My house is here.'

"The third woman stroked her cheek and said, 'My house is here.'

"The fourth woman stroked her eyebrow and said, 'My house is here.'

"The four women then left to return home. Not knowing where they lived, the four men discussed together but could not say where the houses of each of their lovers was located.

"At that time, there was a robber who had been impaled alive on a stake and was lying rolling on the ground not far from the four men. Hearing the four in discussion, the robber called out, 'What are you talking about?'

"One replied, 'About the location of our lovers' houses.'

" 'Don't you know?'

" 'No, we don't'

" 'Well, I do.'

" 'If so, then tell us.'

" 'Bring me some water to drink first, then I'll tell you.'

"They brought him water to drink. The robber then asked, 'What did your lover tell you?'

"The first man replied, 'My lover stroked her head and said her house was there.'

"The robber said, 'In that case, go east from here for around five *usubha*, and you'll find a banyan tree. Your lover's house is there.'

"He asked the second man, 'What did your lover tell you?'

" 'She stroked her breast and said her house was there.'

" 'In that case, go west from here for around eight *usubha* and you'll find a jackfruit tree. Your lover's house is there.'

"He asked the third man, 'What did your lover tell you?'

" 'She stroked her cheek and said her house was there.'

" 'In that case, go south from here for around half a *yojana* and you'll find a potter's kiln. Your lover's house is there.'

"He asked the fourth man, 'What did your lover tell you?'

" 'She stroked her eyebrow and said her house was there.'

" 'In that case, go north from here for around one *yojana* and you'll find a pond with weeds. Your lover's house is there.'

"The four were very pleased. They took leave of the robber, and each went to find his lover's house. One went east, one west, one south, and one north. Each found their lover's house and was very pleased. Their lovers each asked, 'How did you know where my house is?' The men told them. The women said, 'Chasing after me because of lust is improper.' Each of them drove the men away, saying, 'From now on, don't come here again. Get out!'

"The women went to release the robber from the stake and gave him food and water. From then on, one woman brought him food, another brought him water to wash his face, another brought him hot water, and another took away his urine and feces. With this treatment, the robber was rid of disease. Which of these women should have this robber as a husband?"

The courtier's heart replied, "The one who takes away his urine and feces. She should have the robber as her husband."

Hearing this, the princess said, "O courtier, you're wrong. The woman who brought food should have the robber as her husband."

Hearing the princess speak, the king's officials played loud music. This was the third time.

In the dark before dawn, the Bodhisatta brought the courtier's heart, placed it near her pillow, and went back to sit as before. He asked the courtier's heart, "O courtier, there once was a beautiful woman with a slender figure and very fine hair. She was very attractive. Everybody liked her. Now, which feels softer—kapok or a woman?"

The courtier's heart replied, "Kapok feels softer than a woman, sire."

Hearing this, the princess said, "O courtier, you're wrong. A husband who has a soft heart without any hardness feels softer than either kapok or a woman."

Hearing the princess speak, the king's officials played loud music. This was the fourth time.

The Bodhisatta took the heart, put it back in the courtier's chest, and went back to sit as before. When the sun rose, he went down from the palace. Surrounded by his retinue of courtiers, he went to sit on a seat, beautifully prepared, in front of the throne hall of King Usabha. He told the king what had happened.

King Usabha discussed with Queen Kusumba, "O fair of face, this Prince Sabbasiddhi is more powerful, more excellent than all the kings in the Jambu Continent. He is right to marry our daughter. How do you feel?"

The queen agreed with no objection. The king had brahmans fetched and said, "Calculate a good day for a marriage." They made the calculations and told him.

King Usabha went to his daughter's palace and told her what had taken place. She happily agreed. The Bodhisatta went to the throne hall and sat on the beautifully prepared seat, and the king praised him in a verse:

"You are an excellent prince, more excellent than all other men.
You are thoughtful. You uphold the dhamma.
You have special power, wisdom, thoughtfulness, and great skill.
You are more excellent and intelligent than other princes.
You are versed in the dhamma with more wisdom and better thinking.
Your words are loveable and pleasing. Hence, I give my daughter to you."

The Bodhisatta responded in a verse:

"I have more thoughtfulness than other kings
because I have studied the arts of knowledge.
Besides, in past lives I followed the precepts, made merit, and showed devotion.
I now enjoy the fruit of this karma. Hence, I now enjoy the supreme fruit,
more than all other humans."

King Usabha was happy at these words. He summoned his ministers to audience and commanded, "Have the craftsmen build and decorate a beautiful palace along with a throne, accoutrements in gold, and a canopy above. Come and tell me when they are finished."

When the work was done, King Usabha escorted the Bodhisatta with a large retinue to the new palace and installed him on the golden throne. Princess Suvaṇṇa Sobha was seated on a golden throne on the left side of the Bodhisatta, like Princess Sujāta seated with Lord Sakka, king of the gods.

Palace ladies sat all around—to left and right, front and back—and spoke their praises in auspicious words. Queen Kusumba gave a blessing in a verse:

"Through the power of some fruit of merit made by me or her father,
may you both know neither old age nor death."

In the evening after the ceremony, the Bodhisatta went to the bedroom and lay with Queen Suvaṇṇa Sobha. After that, the royal couple went to pay respect to the king and queen with various worshipful offerings, such as flowers and scents, and said, "Your Majesties, allow us to take our leave to go to Alika City. May you be free of any illness, and may you enjoy every happiness in every activity."

The Bodhisatta took her to his city and went to stay in the great palace with a large retinue. In the evening he took her to bed. In the morning, they went to attend on his father and mother and sat in an appropriate place. The people came to pay respect to the Bodhisatta with various worshipful offerings.

The king of Alika City had the Bodhisatta anointed with Suvaṇṇa Sobha as his major queen and presented him with the five insignia of kingship, namely the white umbrella, *camara* yak-tail shade, golden slippers, golden palanquin, and jeweled crown. He also handed over all the royal property and had them rule the realm and continue the royal line. Yet at that time, the Bodhisatta did not rule the realm because his father was still alive. After his father passed away, he ruled in Alika City. He did many royal good works including following the precepts and giving alms. When he passed away, he was born in the Tusita Heaven. When he passed from there and was reborn in the human world, he still wandered in the cycle of birth for four *asaṅkheyya* and a hundred thousand eras before he achieved enlightenment.

When the Great Teacher had given this sermon, he explained the birth connections: "King Usabha at that time was reborn as King Suppabuddha at this time; Queen Kusumba as his queen; King Vijaya as King Suddhodana, the Buddha's father; King Vijaya's queen Uppala Devī as Queen Mahāmāyā, the Buddha's mother; Suvaṇṇa Sobha as Bimbā Yasodāra, the mother of Rāhula; Prince Sabbasiddhi the Bodhisatta as the Tathāgata, the enlightened Buddha, the refuge of all beings in the world. Remember this *jātaka* as I have told it here."

COMPLEX QUEST

VARANUJJA

P59 *Varanujjajātaka*

วรนุชชาดก

INTRODUCTION

In the latter part of the collection are a dozen longer quest-type stories with complex plots that borrow scenes and plot elements from the famous quest stories in this collection and from the classical *jātaka*. These plots often include an exile and separation engineered by an evil brahman or jealous queen; magical items such as shoes, sticks, rings, and swords; dreams predicting the near future; threats from demons, ogres, water spirits, *vijjadhara*, and enemy kings; benign supporting roles for *nāga*, *kinnari*, and *apsara*; interventions by Sakka; a horse or other animal as the Bodhisatta's comrade; visits to the Himavanta Forest; the Bodhisatta repeatedly thinking of his mother and acquiring many wives; successors for dead kings found by a flower chariot; dramatic battles won by supernatural devices; and scenes of reunion and reconciliation at the end. The action flows between the human world, the Himavanta, and the *nāga* realms, and there is close interaction and marriage between beings of different kinds. The main teaching delivered is on the inescapability of karma. The model for these stories is perhaps P3 Sudhanu. In that story, the Bodhisatta acquires several wives. This tale avoids that indelicacy by having twins, one being the Bodhisatta and the other acquiring several wives. Other tales in this genre split the roles in a similar way.

This tale exhibits all of these elements and is arguably the most accomplished of this subgenre. The frame story in which a jealous queen disposes of the favorite queen's twins at birth is similar to the Padumāvati story in the *Mahavastu* collection, though other details, such as the block of wood, are different.[1] The woman born in a large lotus, discovered by

1. Jones, *Mahāvastu*, III, 148–67. In the *Mahāvastu* story, both twins are floated

an ascetic, and presented to a king is found in J380 Āsaṅka Jātaka, though again other details are different.[2] The major plot arc revolving around the two brothers and the creation of an ideal city seems to be unique. Curiously, the *jātaka* is named after Varanujja, though his brother is the Bodhisatta.

There is a *kham kap* version from the first to third reign and a fragmentary *kham chan* from the fourth to fifth reign; both follow the *jātaka* closely and are clearly derived from it. There is another *kham chan* and a drama version, both probably from the fifth reign, that are very different in the plot details and most likely come from the story as told in oral tradition. All of these include both brothers' names in the title (*Woranetworanut*).

Other tales of this type include P41 Saṅghāpatta, P45 Varavaṃsa, P48 Suvaṅṅasirasā, P49 Vanāvana, P50 Bākula, P51 Sonanda, P56 Devandha, P57 Supina, P58 Suvaṅṅavaṁsa, and P61 Candagādha. None of these is found in collections outside Thailand

When the Great Teacher was staying at the Jeta Grove, the temple that the householder Anāthapiṇḍika built for him, he thought of his gratitude, and this was the reason he gave this teaching, beginning with the words "Where have you come from, miss?"

The story of the present goes as follows. One day the monks were seated together at the teaching hall speaking of the gratitude of the Blessed One, saying, "See, the Tathāgata is truly steeped in gratitude. He made the effort to travel to the Tāvatiṁsa Heaven to preach the Abhidhamma for a full three months for the benefit of his mother. He gave otherworldly treasure to his mother to repay her goodness. His perseverance arose from his gratitude. Such a virtue is difficult for others to emulate. Such great devotion!"

Hearing this with his divine hearing, the Great Teacher came to the teaching hall, sat on the pulpit, and asked what the monks were talking about. After they told him, he said, "O monks, I have been steeped in gratitude not only in this life but also in past lives, when still a bodhisatta. I have assisted my mother out of gratitude

---

away; courtiers shelter the wronged queen Padumāvati while telling the king she has been killed; the twins are found by chance; though the king wishes to reinstate her, she renounces and goes to the forest, but the king eventually brings her back.

2. Cowell, *Jātaka*, III, 161–64.

in the same way." The monks begged him to tell the story, and so he told the tale from the past as follows.

Long ago in the past, there was a king of the *kinnara* called Udumbarā ruling in Upala City, near Mount Kelāsa. His queen named Sundarī was senior to one hundred thousand consorts.

A younger sister of the king named Subhaddā, who had not found a husband, was stirred by feelings of lust. One day she took leave of her elder brother and asked permission to visit the Himavanta Forest. When King Udumbarā consented, she put on her wings and tail, flew up into the air, and traveled by stages to a certain great lake. Seeing a large and shady tree with flowers in bloom on the bank, she flew down, took off her ornaments beside the lake, and went to gather flowers to decorate her body. She sang and danced in the style of a *kinnari* while bathing in the lotus lake.

At that time, a forest hunter who was hunting deer in the forest arrived at the lake. Seeing him, the *kinnari* trembled in fear and went to hide in a bush where the hunter could not see her. The hunter came looking along the edge of the lake and saw the ornaments that the *kinnari* had left there. He thought, "These wings, tail, and decorations must have been left here by a *kinnari*." He picked them up and went looking for their owner, but did not find her. He went down to bathe and then went off with the *kinnari*'s things.

After he had left, Subhaddā came up from the lake, climbed up to sit on the fork of a tree, and wept in lament, saying, "Where can I go? Who will inform my elder brother? Who will help me? In whose house will I end up?" She lamented from the first watch until dawn came up.

At that time a wood spirit thought, "This Princess Subhaddā is beautiful and has great merit and high rank. She is fit to be the queen of a meritorious king. Hence I must help her overcome her current situation."

At that time in Videha City in Cetaraṭṭha, there was a king of great merit called Cetarāja, greater than the 108 kings. His queen called Khemā was the senior of sixteen thousand consorts and the favorite of King Cetarāja. He upheld the Ten Royal Virtues, observed the five precepts, followed the true dhamma, and was compassionate toward the people in every way.

For this reason, the wood spirit thought, "This Princess Subhaddā is a fitting match for King Cetarāja." He went to attend on King Cetarāja and whispered in his ear, "Your Majesty, if you awake from sleep and go off to the forest, you will find a gem woman." The king awoke and heard what the spirit said. He quickly went out to the hall of judgment, summoned his ministers, and said, "Tomorrow morning I will visit the forest. Have the four divisions of troops ready in the royal courtyard." The ministers hastened to carry out the order.

At dawn, King Cetarāja along with his troops and ministers left the city and entered the great forest. They halted to stay at a place called Ramma. The wood spirit transformed himself into a golden deer and ran to disport himself in front of the king. The king was delighted by the sight. He rode his horse in chase of the golden deer up to a great lotus lake. Not seeing the deer, only his tracks, he walked ahead until he reached a big tree and was even more delighted to see the gem woman in a fork of the tree. He thought, "The words spoken by the spirit last night have come true!" He approached and inquired in a verse:

> "*Where have you come from, miss? What brings you to this tree alone?*
> *Where is your birthplace and home? Whose daughter are you?*"

Princess Subhaddā explained in a verse:

> "*I am a younger sister of King Udumbarā.*
> *I came wishing to visit the forest, hills, and rivers.*"

She told him everything from the beginning. The king said, "Fair lady, do not be sad. I will take you to my city and make you a major queen, senior to sixteen thousand consorts." He had the *kinnari* come down from the tree, lifted her onto his horse's back, and took her to the army's camp. They returned to the city. He carried out a ceremony to anoint Princess Subhaddā as his major queen. She became his favorite, and he gave no thought to any of the other consorts.

The other consorts, including Queen Khemā, talked together: "This Queen Subhaddā has taken away our royal husband. She has him under her power. Why does he love her so much? It's suspicious. She is not beautiful at all. She was all alone in the forest with no relatives. Why does the king love her so much? We must think up a means to ruin and break the relationship."

Queen Khemā summoned a brahman astrologer, gave him a thousand of money, and said, "Uncle, if you can successfully deliver what I desire, I will reward you even more than this."

"What do you wish me to do, mistress?"

"Don't you see? My husband is besotted with Queen Subhaddā alone. What can I do to make the king love me too? If you can make him love me so much he abandons Queen Subhaddā, I will reward you with many times what I have given you now."

The brahman astrologer said, "I will think up a means for you." He took the money and left. At home, when he related the matter to his wife, she said, "I have already thought up one method. When Queen Subhaddā becomes pregnant, I'll carve a log of wood into the shape of a baby and place it underneath her when she gives birth. I'll snatch the child and throw it away in the forest, bring some blood to smear on the wood, and take it for the king to see. In anger he will drive Queen Subhaddā away."

The brahman astrologer went to tell his wife's idea to Queen Khemā, who was very pleased. She summoned slave girls, presented them with money, and said, "Now, girls, when you know Queen Subhaddā is pregnant, come to tell me." The slave girls saluted to take the order, and kept on the lookout from that day onward.

Some twelve years later, Queen Subhaddā became pregnant. When the slave girls knew, they informed Queen Khemā, who ordered a close aide to carve wood into the shape of a baby and hide it away. She commanded, "When you see the *kammajavāta* wind is blowing for Queen Subhaddā, hurry to inform me."

After Queen Subhaddā's pregnancy reached the tenth month,[3] the *kammajavāta* wind blew for the birth. The slave girl went to inform Queen Khemā. At that time, King Cetarāja had gone to visit the gardens and had not yet returned.

Queen Khemā had a good opportunity. She went to Queen Subhaddā and stroked her to allay her suspicions. Queen Subhaddā was in great pain. She gave birth to twins, and lost consciousness. Queen Khemā put one of the infants in a chest and ordered a slave girl to dispose of it in the forest. She put the other infant in a pot and ordered a slave girl to float it away on the river. The two slave girls went off in separate ways to carry out these orders.

Queen Khemā smeared blood on the wood, placed it on a golden cot, and said, "Queen Subhaddā has given birth to a baby that is a block of

3. The Thai translator converted this to "twelfth."

wood!" When Queen Subhaddā came round, Queen Khemā said, "Mistress Subhaddā, look at your child." Shocked when she saw the child, Queen Subhaddā asked, "How did this happen?" In tears, she said, "O mother's beloved child, when you were in my womb, you could move around. How can you have become a block of wood? This is the result of my karma."

In the evening, King Cetarāja and his retinue returned from the royal park. He went up into the palace and sat on the throne. Queen Khemā brought the block of wood on the golden cot for him to see, saying, "Your Majesty, this is your beautiful child!"

He asked, "What is this?"

"Your Majesty, Queen Subhaddā has given birth to this block of wood."

"How can a human give birth to a block of wood?"

"Your Majesty, you must consult an astrologer."

The king summoned an astrologer and asked, "If a human woman gives birth to a block of wood, will something perilous occur?"

"Your Majesty, if a human gives birth to a block of wood or a wild animal, that woman is inauspicious. If a woman gives birth to a dog, elephant, or pig in any house, that house will experience something bad."

"What should we do about Queen Subhaddā giving birth to a block of wood then?"

"Your Majesty, you must float her away on a raft."

The king believed the astrologer. He had courtiers make a raft, load it with food, place Queen Subhaddā on the raft, and float it away as the astrologer suggested. Queen Subhaddā begged to attend on the king first, but the courtiers gave her no opportunity. She was lifted onto the raft and the raft was pushed off into the river.

Queen Subhaddā floated away on the current down to the great ocean. She reached an island in mid-ocean and went ashore to stay there. The guardian spirit of the island saw her and took pity on her. He conjured up a retreat for her to stay in and various fruits for her to eat. She knew all of this was provided by the spirit. She lived as a hermit in the retreat on the island from then on.

As for the two sons of Queen Subhaddā, one slave girl took the elder son in the chest, buried it by the trunk of a large tree in the forest, and returned home. The guardian spirit resident in the tree saw this and thought, "What is in that chest that the slave girl buried here?" He came down, burrowed into the earth, opened the chest, and saw a child as beautiful as gold. Examining with his divine sight, he knew that this was Queen Subhaddā's child and that the envious Queen Khemā had substituted a block of wood and told the slave girl to bury the child. The spirit lifted the child out, took him up to his abode, and brought him up with loving-kindness. He fed the infant with milk that flowed from his own finger. When the child grew up, he was the delight of the spirit, who loved him as much as his own eyes. For this reason, the spirit gave him the name Varanetta [noble eyes].

The younger son, whom Queen Khemā put in a pot for a slave girl to float away on the river, was carried by the current to the landing at the retreat of a rishi, Agginetta [fire eyes]. When he returned from the forest and went down to bathe at the landing, he saw the floating pot, opened it, and found the child. He took the child to raise as his own, fed on milk that flowed from his finger. The rishi examined the matter and knew what had happened from the beginning, and hence gave the child the name Varanujja [noble younger brother].

At that time there was a rishi named Kassapa who built a retreat on the bank of a lake in the Himavanta Country. A divine lady passed from the Tāvatiṁsa realm and was conceived in a lotus flower in that lake. One day when Kassapa went to bathe in the lake, he saw a large lotus flower and thought, "Why is this lotus flower bigger than all the others?" He picked the flower and took it up to his retreat. He was delighted when he saw the child in the flower, and raised her by feeding milk from his finger into her mouth. When she had grown to sixteen years old, she was as beautiful as a divine *apsara*. The rishi thus gave her the name Puṣapā [flower, blossom].

After some time, a pregnant mare came from Valāhaka, gave birth at the retreat of the rishi Kassapa, and returned home. The rishi raised the foal to play with Puṣapā. She rode the foal to gather flowers and fruits in the forest and returned to bathe and fetch water for the rishi to bathe.

When Prince Varanetta had grown to sixteen[4] years, he asked the spirit raising him, "Father, where is my mother? I have never seen her. In addition, you are a spirit but I am a human. How did that happen?"

4. Some editions of the Thai translation have twenty-six here, but the Pali is sixteen.

The spirit told him the truth, "Your father is King Cetarāja and your mother is Queen Subhaddā, who used to reign in Videha City. When you were born, Queen Khemā put you in a chest, made a block of wood in your place, and told the king that the block of wood was Queen Subhaddā's son. A slave girl came to bury you here. The king was very angry. He had your mother placed on a raft and floated away. The current took her to an island in the middle of the ocean. She is living as a hermit there."

Prince Varanetta was saddened by this news. As he wished to see his mother, he asked, "O spirit, what can I do to see my mother?"

"You must take this bow and go to the north. You will find the rishi Kassapa in the Himavanta Forest. He knows about this matter. He will give you his daughter. You must ask to study the arts with him. Once you are accomplished, then you may go to find your mother."

The spirit gave his ornaments and divine sword to Prince Varanetta. He summoned a lord swan, a comrade of his who lived close by, and said, "Comrade lord swan, please help this son of mine. Please let him ride on your back, and take him to the home of the rishi Kassapa." He returned to his abode and passed to be born in the Tāvatiṁsa realm.

The lord swan invited Prince Varanetta to mount on his back, flew through the air for three days, and came down to land close to the retreat of the rishi Kassapa. Prince Varanetta went in to find the rishi and related the matter from the beginning. The lord swan saluted the rishi to take leave and returned home.

When Prince Varanetta arrived there, Puṣapā and the horse had gone to the Himavanta Forest and not yet returned. Kassapa said happily, "I will give you my daughter. You must take her in the human way as you wish."

In the evening, Puṣapā gathered various fruits, mounted the horse, and returned to the retreat. When she saw Prince Varanetta, she fell in love. She brought the fruits from the back of the horse, took a pot to go down and bathe with the horse, then came up to greet the rishi, give him fruits, and do the chores. She looked at Prince Varanetta with longing. He avoided her gaze and did not look at her out of respect for the rishi. She finished her chores for the rishi and went to her own retreat.

That night, the rishi Kassapa made a prayer of truth: "O all you spirits including Lord Sakka, king of the gods, please gather together here through the power of my prayer."

Lord Sakka and the gods of the four directions arrived at the retreat. The rishi said, "Lord gods, I will hold a marriage ceremony for Varanetta and Puṣapā. Please lend me a hand."

The gods saluted in agreement. They left the retreat and conjured up a ritual pavilion hung with flower garlands and laid with coverings. They made a heap of gems along with crystal lamps and lamps on handles, and arranged various decorations.

All the divine maidens, headed by Sujātā, arrived at Kassapa's retreat. They helped to deck Puṣapā with various ornaments, making her as beautiful as an *apsara* maiden. They led her by the hand into the pavilion and had her sit on the heap of gems. Lord Sakka decked Prince Varanetta with various decorations, making him as beautiful as a young god, took him into the pavilion, and had him sit on the heap of gems.

At an auspicious time, Prince Varanetta took Puṣapā's hand and lowered it into a tray of sacred water. All the gods gave a blessing to the couple: "May you both be happy and content, free of illness. May you not be afflicted by disease or old age." The gods returned home.

Prince Varanetta lived and loved together with Puṣapā in the retreat, enjoying great happiness. He studied the arts with the rishi Kassapa for seven years, and then thought of his mother and became sad and tearful. Puṣapā asked her husband, "Why are you sadly weeping?"

Prince Varanetta told her that he was thinking of his mother, and said, "Beloved, I am thinking that my mother will be suffering, and I do not know where she is. For this reason I wish to take leave and search for her."

"Husband, I beg to go along with you."

The next morning, Prince Varanetta and Puṣapā went to do chores for the rishi and then said, "We beg to take leave to follow after my mother. Please tell us the directions to find her." Kassapa summoned the horse and ordered, "Take this couple, go to the north, and be always on guard. May you be happy and content."

Prince Varanetta and Puṣapā made a clockwise circuit of the rishi as a mark of respect. Taking the celestial bow and sword, Varanetta mounted the horse with his wife. The horse turned toward the north and flew up into the air. Reaching the Himavanta Mountains, he came down to land on a peak. Prince Varanetta and Puṣapā dismounted and released the horse, who said to them, "If you come upon any danger, think of me." He took his leave and went off to where there was grass and water. Prince Varanetta and

Puṣapā gathered various flowers on the mountain and happily decorated themselves.

In truth, the Himavanta Mountains are very extensive and very high, with eighty-four thousand peaks, five beautiful rivers flowing around them, and seven great lakes including Lake Anotatta, which is surrounded by five hills, namely Sudassana, Citta, Kāla, Gandhamādana, and Kelāsa.[5] Mount Sudassana is all gold. The peak has an overhang curved like a crow's beak that shelters Lake Anotatta. Mount Citta is decorated with the seven jewels and shaped like Mount Sudassana. Mount Kāla is strewn with sapphires and gems the color of *anchan* flowers. Mount Gandhamādana is all patterned gems. At the front of the mountains there is a forest suffused with the ten types of fragrance, namely the fragrance of roots such as spurge,[6] the fragrance of wood core such as sandalwood, the fragrance of wood sap such as pine or *masang*, the fragrance of bark such as cinnamon, the fragrance of wood oil such as wood-apple, the fragrance of resin such as benzoin, the fragrance of leaves such as betel, the fragrance of flowers such as ironwood,[7] the fragrance of fruit such as nutmeg, and the fragrance of trees that are wholly fragrant. In addition the forests are strewn with various medicinal trees. At night in this forest, there is a glowing light like the light of the sun or light of a charcoal fire. Mount Gandhamādana has three caves—a golden cave, silver cave, and jewel cave. It is the home of all the Pacceka Buddhas. Mount Kelāsa is strewn with silver. These seven hills such as Sudassana which surround Lake Anotatta are full of the power of the gods and the power of the *nāga*. In addition the rivers that flow into Lake Anotatta have clean and shady landings, with jeweled stairways at two places, as if made by people. One is a landing for Pacceka Buddhas, disciples, and *arahant* of great power to bathe, and the other for beings of power such as gods, ogres, and *kinnara*.

After they had gathered flowers to adorn themselves, Prince Varanetta and Puṣapā wished to go to another mountain and so thought of the horse, which appeared, invited them to mount, and took them to another mountain. Later they visited various mountains until they arrived at Lake Chaddanta.

5. There is a similar description of Himavanta in P58 Suvaṇṇavaṁsa.
6. กะลำภัก (usually กะลำพัก), *kalamphak*, *Euphorbia antiquorum*
7. บุนนาค, *bunnak*, *Mesua ferrea*, Ceylon ironwood.

In truth, Lake Chaddanta is surrounded by ten forests and seven mountains, first Mount Culakāla, second Mount Mahākāla. third Mount Udaka, fourth Mount Candapassa, fifth Mount Suriyapassa, sixth Mount Maṇipassa, and seventh Mount Suvaṇṇapassa. Mount Culakāla, which lies outside the others, is five *yojana* tall and fifteen *yojana* wide. The ten forests there are the small lima-bean[8] forest, cucumber-vine forest, bottle-gourd and pumpkin forest, sugarcane-plant-as-big-as-areca-palm forest, banana-as-big-as-elephant-tusk forest, jackfruit-as-big-as-a-water-jar forest, mango forest, tamarind-pod-as-big-as-cartwheel forest, wood-apple-as-big-as-pot forest, and the mixed forest. These ten forests are in circles one *yojana* apart. Forests appearing in the water are of ten types: green lotus forest, white lotus forest, red *uppala* lily forest, white *uppala* lily forest, red *paduma* forest, white *paduma* forest, red *kumuda* forest, white *kumuda* forest,[9] water morning glory forest, and mixed forest. All ten are in circles around.

Prince Varanetta and Puṣapā roamed around enjoying the rivers and lakes, so carried away they forgot about his mother completely. One evening after they had been in the Himavanta Forest for seven days, they went into the golden cave and slept there on a golden throne.

On that night the hermit Subhaddā, mother of the Bodhisatta,[10] had a dream. She saw an evil ogress cut open her breast, pluck out her intestines, and go away for a long time. When the ogress came back, she replaced the intestine through her breast into her womb, and the wound completely disappeared, back to normal as before. Subhaddā started awake and was worried that something was about to happen, but had nobody to ask.

On that same night, Prince Varanetta and his wife were asleep in the golden cave. A forest spirit examined them with his divine eyesight and thought, "Prince Varanetta here was intent on finding his mother, but now he has turned to enjoying himself and does not think of his mother. He will never meet her this way. I must help him to find her." He stealthily lifted up Prince Varanetta and Puṣapā, flew through the air to the retreat of the Bodhisatta's mother, put them down there by the trunk of a tree, and then returned home.

8. ถั่วราชมาส, *thua rachamat*, *Phaseolus lunatus*.

9. *Paduma*, *kumuda*, and *uppala* are three types of lotus or water lily. *Uppala* is usually blue, *kumuda* white, and *paduma* either red or white.

10. The first mention of the Bodhisatta and an indication that it is Varanetta, not Varanujja.

Since waking up, Subhaddā had eaten and was now sitting thinking of her dream, perplexed that she did not know what would happen, making her very unsettled and upset. She went out of the retreat and saw the two people asleep. She slowly approached them and saw the bow and sword. She picked them up and hid them away in a bush, then went back to the retreat and watched what the couple would do.

In the light of dawn, Prince Varanetta woke up and looked around in every direction in surprise. He thought, "How did I get here?" He roused Puṣapā and said, "Beloved, please wake up. We went to sleep in a golden cave so how did we come to be here?" The couple embraced and sadly said, "Which way should we go?" Finding that the bow and sword were missing, they became more troubled.

After watching the couple's behavior, Queen Subhaddā took pity on them. She approached them and asked, "Where did you two come from, and where will you go from here?"

"We came from the retreat of the hermit Kassapa and will go to find my mother."

"Where is your mother?"

"We do not know."

"What is her name?"

"Subhaddā."

"And your father's name?"

"Cetarāja."

"How did you come to be separated from your mother and father? Tell me."

Prince Varanetta told her the story from beginning to end, as the spirit had told him.

Queen Subhaddā was amazed. She drew Prince Varanetta into an embrace, kissed his head, and said, "I am your mother." Then she sadly related in a verse:

"O mother's most beloved son, some karma has drawn us apart.
In my womb, you could move. At birth, I heard you cry.
How could you be a block of wood? I had my doubts
but I did not dare to ask others. I just wept on my own.
Now my bad karma is exhausted. My merit has arrived,
and so I have found my beloved son,
just as I dreamt. Today my sorrow has disappeared.
I thought you had died for certain.

Your father angrily punished me for giving birth to a block of wood,
by floating me away on a raft on the river.
Through my merit, a spirit helped me to come here.
Sadly, I have been here rather than raising my son from birth.
May you not know sickness, old age, and death. May you live long,
and may we not be separated from each other."

Prince Varanetta told her what had happened in the past. "Mother, when I had grown up, a spirit told me that a slave girl had buried me by a tree trunk. The spirit raised me as his son. He told me that my father floated my mother away on a raft down the river and that she had become a hermit living on an island in the middle of the ocean. Knowing this, I wished to find her. The spirit told me to go and study the arts with the hermit Kassapa first and then follow after my mother. He kindly gave me his divine ornaments and weapons, and he asked a lord golden swan to take me on his back to the rishi's home. The rishi Kassapa was kind enough to marry me to his daughter, Puṣapā. After I acquired expertise from studying the arts, I thought of my mother and wished to find her. When I told this to the hermit, he gave me a horse to ride and told me the direction. My wife and I mounted the horse and flew through the air to the Himavanta Mountains. We stayed there to enjoy the hills and forests for seven days. Yesterday we visited Lake Chaddanta, bathed in the lake, and went to sleep there. When I woke up, I was here! I do not understand. Mother, the divine bow is missing. The horse will not know how to find me. He will weep and his heart may break apart. How can I find the divine bow, mother?"

"Your bow is still here. I hid it in a bush." She got up and fetched the bow for him. He strung an arrow, and made a wish, "May a great city like the Tāvatiṁsa realm appear in this forest." With this prayer, he shot the arrow.

Through the power of his wish, a great city appeared. In the city were three residences: one for his mother, one for Puṣapā, and one for Prince Varanetta. Queen Subhaddā ceased to be a hermit and went to stay in the residence that her son gave her.

After this, people coming from the four directions saw this beautiful and pleasant city and thus brought their wives and children and invited their friends and relatives to come and live there. For this reason, the learned teacher spoke these verses:

This city called Sākala
has beautiful parks and gardens, rivers, and hills,
four streets, and pleasant houses,
with fine lakes in the gardens, all bringing happiness.
The city is surrounded by walls, with forts,
gates, and towers that are tall, beautiful, grand, and dazzling.
The city has fine shops and markets,
with lanes and alleys in every locality.
There are many nobles
with wealth in thousands,
and throngs of beautiful young ladies
who sing and play sweet, captivating music.
Inside, the palace is splendid
with elephants, horses,
carriages, and other vehicles.
There are crowds of monks walking back and forth.
It is the home of various merchants and householders
and has storehouses full of various goods—
such as the storehouse of silk, Kāsika cloth,[11]
fig cloth, and wool of various colors—
and storehouses of silver, gold, and jewels,
as well as food and drink of every kind.
It is a place of joy and comfort, like the Uttarakuru Continent
and the city of the gods called Alakamanda.[12]

Prince Varanetta had already been anointed king with the name King Varanetta and had established Puṣapā as his major queen. He established his mother like a divinity and made worship every day. He appointed the people who came from the four directions as courtiers and brahman priest-counselors. As people came from every direction, King Varanetta changed the city to have a new name: Sākala [whole, universal] City.

The great King Varanetta ruled in Sākala City, supporting the people with the Four Principles of Harmony and upholding the Ten Royal Virtues. He had many ladies as retainers in his golden palace, like Lord Sakka, king of the gods, in the Vejayanta Palace. Queen Puṣapā was senior to eighty-four

11. From Kāsi, Bārāṇasī.
12. The residence of Kubera.

thousand consorts of good morality who serviced their royal husband and his royal mother every day. The two royals lived in great comfort and joy.

King Varanetta thought of the horse. He had a stable built as beautiful as a heavenly mansion with a roof like a superb night sky with moon and stars, screened by elegant curtains with fine coverings on the floor and with a great resting place placed under a white umbrella for the horse to live.

At that time, the horse came back from his wanderings to Lake Chaddanta and was disappointed not to see Prince Varanetta and Puṣapā. He looked around for them everywhere. However much he cried out, not one squeak came in return. He lamented in a verse:

"O great son and Puṣapā, where have you gone?
What did I do that angered you enough to abandon me and disappear?
Or are you teasing and fooling me? Don't be angry at me.
How can I know where you are? Are you still alive, or have you died?
In the past, wherever you went, I could follow
and find you every time, but now I do not see you.
O gods, please help me to find where the prince has gone."

The horse thought, "I should go back and ask Kassapa the hermit." He flew to the retreat of the hermit who saw the horse and asked, "Why have you abandoned your master and come here?"

"I took the couple to Lake Chaddanta. They traveled around and enjoyed themselves in the golden cave. I went off to find grass to eat for seven days. When I returned, they were gone. I searched for them in the forest and hills for seven days without success, and thus came to find you, sir."

After listening to the horse, Kassapa examined with his divine sight and saw the two royals had met with his royal mother in the great city. He said, "O horse, a forest spirit carried the two royals to his mother's abode. She has met with them. They have created a great city with residences. If you wish to go there, you must halt outside the city first. When people see you, they will tell the royal couple, who will come out to find you."

The horse took leave of the rishi, flew in the direction he indicated, and came down to land outside the city. Seeing him, people happily spoke together, saying, "We have not yet found a mount for our lord. Let's catch this horse and present it to him." They tried to catch the horse, which reacted fiercely by biting and kicking them. Unable to catch the horse, they went to inform Prince Varanetta.

Prince Varanetta came out with the people to where the horse was staying. The horse pranced around in delight at seeing him, then approached and prostrated down at his feet. Seeing this, people backed off. Prince Varanetta said, "O horse, I have been thinking of you and crying every day. My merit is great! I have found you." The horse related where he had been, how he had grieved, and how he had asked the rishi Kassapa.

Prince Varanetta invited the horse into the city, placed him in the fine stable, and went to tell Queen Puṣapā, who came out, asked the horse about this and that, and then returned. Prince Varanetta anointed the horse as lord of the horses and presented him with people to cut grass for him every day. At night, the horse flew off and made announcements in all the towns and villages throughout the realm, saying, "Good people, if you are not happy where you are, let me tell you there is a celestial city in this direction with a king named Varanetta who rules justly. Please go to live there. You will be happy."

People who heard this thought, "Tonight a god has come to announce that we should take our families to settle in this Sākala City, which has every facility and where people are all secure with wealth and property." Those who heard took their dependents to live in Sākala City.

King Varanetta supported the people with the Four Principles of Harmony and gave teachings, saying, "Please be heedful. Give alms to the monks and teachers. Observe the precepts." For this reason, Sākala was a pleasant city, full of people and beloved things, like a heavenly city.

The story of King Varanetta ends here.

Here will be told of his younger brother, Prince Varanujja. The rishi Agginetta raised him for a year. The rishi had a friend who was a lord ogre called Aggisikha [flame] with a wife called Rājaputtī, a daughter of an *asura* lord.

One day the ogre Aggisikha thought of the rishi and thus took his wife to visit him. After they paid respect, they noticed Prince Varanujja and asked the rishi, "Where did you get this child?"

"He was floated away in a pot, and beached at the landing in front of my ashram. I took him in to raise."

Queen Rājaputtī begged the rishi, "I have no son or daughter. Please let me raise him as my own child." The rishi Agginetta gave his consent. She took him to raise as her adopted child.

When Prince Varanujja was sixteen years old, he was as handsome and beautiful as a child of the gods. He always ate celestial food and was the delight of his adoptive mother and father. Lord Aggisikha the ogre king provided over a thousand consorts to look after him, presented him with much finery, and raised him in the correct way. While he was living in the ogre city, the child did not know it was an ogre city, because the ogre king had announced that the ogres should not let the prince see them as ogres. As a result he thought it was a city of the gods, not a city of ogres.

One day Prince Varanujja went to find his foster mother and asked, "You are a goddess and my father is a god, so how come I am a human?"

"You are the son of Agginetta the rishi. I asked to raise you. That's why you are a human."

Prince Varanujja heard this without comment. One day he said to his foster mother, "I wish to visit the rishi."

"Do not go at the moment. At an auspicious time, your father and I will take you there."

Later Prince Varanujja thought, "Who is really my mother and father?" Through the power of the prince's gratitude, the realm of Lord Maghavā seemed hotter. The lord examined and knew clearly that Prince Varanujja was moved by gratitude, wished to know his father and mother, and was wondering who could tell him. The Thousand-Eyed Lord went to the human world, transformed himself into a mynah bird, perched at the window of Prince Varanujja's residence, and said, "O Varanujja, I can tell you who your mother and father are. Do you wish to know or not?"

"I wish to know very much. Please tell me right now."

In his guise as a mynah, Lord Sakka told him the story from the beginning, "Queen Subhaddā is your mother and King Cetarāja is your father. He has two wives, first Queen Khemā and second Queen Subhaddā, your mother. On the day you were born, the king had gone to the park. Your elder brother was born first. Queen Khemā had a slave girl bury him in the forest. When you were born, Queen Khemā put you in a pot and had a slave girl float it away. Your elder brother, Varanetta, was raised by a spirit, and you were raised by a rishi. Lord Aggisikha, king of the ogres, asked to raise you as a foster-child. When your father King Cetarāja came back from the park, Queen Khemā showed him a block of wood smeared with blood and told him, 'Queen Subhaddā gave birth to a block of wood.' In anger, the king had Queen Subhaddā floated away on a raft. Now she is living alone and lonely as a hermit on an island in the middle of the ocean. If you find her and ask her to raise you, you will gain great merit." After saying this, Lord Sakka disappeared.

In distress, Prince Varanujja thought, "How can I find out where my mother is?" He felt agitated and was not playful as before. His nursemaids saw he was troubled and went to tell Lord Aggisikha, who ordered them, "Look after him well. If he runs away, your lives will be over."

Through the power of Prince Varanujja's gratitude, the realm of Lord Maghavā seemed hotter. The lord examined and knew that Prince Varanujja was thinking of his mother badly. "I should help him find his mother." He told Vissukamma to transform himself into a great peacock and take Prince Varanujja to the home of Lord Agginetta the rishi.

That night, Vissukamma transformed himself into a golden peacock and went to Prince Varanujja. He told him to mount on his back to be taken to the rishi. Prince Varanujja was happy. While his foster mother was asleep, he mounted on the golden peacock's back and said, "Nursemaids, may you be happy and content. Allow me to take leave to find my mother. Once that is done, I will return here." The golden peacock carried him up into the air. After one night they reached the retreat of Agginetta the rishi. Prince Varanujja dismounted from the golden peacock and went to pay respect to the rishi.

Agginetta was unable to recognize him until he inquired and the prince reminded him. He then asked, "So your father drove you away in anger. You thought of me and so came to find me."

Prince Varanujja told the truth. "I was anxious to know who my real mother and father are. A mynah bird told me that King Cetarāja is my father and Queen Subhaddā is my mother." He repeated what the mynah had told him. "I came here because I want to find my mother. Please tell me the way."

"Son, you do not yet know the arts well. Stay here and study the arts first. When you are expert, then you can go."

Prince Varanujja summoned the peacock and said, "Please go back and tell Rājaputtī that I beg to take leave to find my mother and will return once that is done." He sent the peacock off home.

On the night when the golden peacock carried Prince Varanujja away, the servant girls and nursemaids awoke and were shocked to see he was missing. They roused their friends and asked one another, "Where has the prince disappeared to?" They searched around everywhere in the residence without success, then went to tell Rājaputtī, who felt she would splinter and die. She lamented in a verse:[13]

> *"O Varanujja, most beloved, why have you abandoned me?*
> *Where have you gone on your own?*
> *Oh, this is truly some great karma I have made in the past.*
> *Perhaps you have died or been lured away*
> *or have fallen in love with someone's daughter. Why did you leave*
> *without telling me, Varanujja? I do not know if you are alive."*

She did not tell the ogre lord but grieved all throughout the city until the dawn came.

Lord Aggisikha, king of the ogres, asked the nursemaids, "Do you know what time my son Varanujja went missing? Did you hear some sound as an omen?" He raged in anger. A young girl said, "Your Majesty, at midnight I heard a faint sound, saying 'I beg to take leave of my mother and father. I will return before too long. May my mother and father be well and happy, free of illness. I will go to meet my mother and then return.'"

Lord Aggisikha, king of the ogres, overcame his sadness, thinking, "My son has gone to find Agginetta. I will follow him to the rishi's retreat."

While Rājaputtī and the ogresses were lamenting, a golden peacock flew in to attend on the ogre lord, saying, "Your Majesty, do not be sad. Your son is at the retreat of the rishi Agginetta. Once he has studied the arts, he will go find his mother and then return."

Knowing this, Lord Aggisikha ceased to sorrow. He invited Rājaputtī to go to the rishi's retreat. After they had paid respect to the rishi, they saw Prince Varanujja. Lord Aggisikha approached, embraced him, kissed his head, and said, "Why did you not tell us? You ran off and made us worried. The golden peacock told us where you are and so we came."

Prince Varanujja said, "I feared you would stop me if I told you. Please forgive me for not asking to take leave. Please give your permission for me to stay here and study the arts."

13. The Pali original has another fourteen lines of lament adapted from J543 Bhūridatta (Faussböll, *Jātaka*, VI, 189; Appleton and Shaw, *Ten Great Birth Stories*, 373–74).

Lord Aggisikha happily gave his consent and presented him with a sword, a bow, and a horse called Manomaya [made of mind]. He said, "When you go to find your mother, take this horse Manomaya to ride and be your companion." He stroked and kissed his son, took leave of the rishi, and returned to his home.

Prince Varanujja stayed at the rishi's retreat for a year until he had gained expertise in the arts. He took leave of the rishi, saying, "Sir, let me take leave to find my mother. Please tell me the way."

Agginetta examined with his divine sight and said, "Varanujja, go to the west.[14] Your elder brother Varanetta has great power. He has built a great city and rules there. He has established your mother in a position of great worship. Go there. Release the horse Manomaya to go and talk with your elder brother's horse. Your mother will hear and will come out to meet you." He saw Prince Varanujja and the horse Manomaya off.

Prince Varanujja strapped on the sword and bow, mounted Manomaya, and flew through the air from morning to evening. Seeing a great lake, they landed to stay there. He went down to bathe and happily pulled up lotus roots to eat while Manomaya went off to find grass and water, saying, "If there is any danger, think of me." After eating, Prince Varanujja went to sleep.

Lord Varuṇa, king of the *nāga*, who was ruling in the *nāga* world with Queen Vimalā, had a daughter named Samuddajā, who was sixteen years old and as beautiful as a heavenly *apsara* maiden. Lord Varuṇa came up from the *nāga* world to play in that lake. While collecting flowers to give his daughter, he looked around and saw Prince Varanujja asleep. He thought, "This is a handsome fellow, with skin like gold, very loveable, suitable to be a husband for my daughter. I will take him to the *nāga* realm and marry him to my daughter." He picked up Prince Varanujja along with his sword and bow and put him down in his palace. He said to Queen Vimalā, "I went to the human world and found this man sleeping on the bank of the lake. I brought him here in the hope of marrying him to our daughter. How do you feel about that?"

Queen Vimalā replied in a verse:

14. The Thai translator changed this to "east."

"Sire, you do not know his name, his family, or his lineage, do you?
Is he rich or poor? Why did you bring him here?
People will criticize. Both you and I will be shamed."

Lord Varuṇa replied, "Usually humans who have little merit and are born in a low family are not good-looking. Let us wake this fellow up and ask him."

They woke Prince Varanujja up. He looked in every direction and thought, "Oh, I am lost! I was sleeping alone in the forest and hills. How did I get here? What is this place called?"

He asked the *nāga* king, "What is the name of this place?"

"This is the realm of the *nāga*. I brought you here myself. What is your name?"

"Varanujja. I am the son of King Aggisikha and Queen Rājaputtī."

"Why were you sleeping alone in the forest? Where were you going?"

Prince Varanujja related the story from the beginning. When they knew, the *nāga* king and queen had great pity on him. They said, "Don't be upset. We will give you our daughter." They summoned Samuddajā and told her what had happened. Prince Varanujja and Samuddajā were anointed as husband and wife.

From then on Prince Varanujja ruled in the *nāga* realm and gave no thought to his mother or the horse Manomaya. One night three months later, he thought of his mother and grieved deeply. Samuddajā woke, saw him crying, and asked, "Why are you crying? Has someone made accusations against you? Or are you angry at me for doing something wrong?"

Prince Varanujja remained quiet, saying nothing to her. In distress, she asked him again and again. Prince Varanujja could not resist and told her the truth, "Beloved, I'm crying because I'm thinking of my mother."

"Where is she? What is her name?"

Prince Varanujja told her about the past. "My mother's name is Subhaddā. She is the major queen of King Cetarāja. When she gave birth, the jealous Queen Khemā had me placed in a pot and had a slave girl float it away. She substituted a block of wood as if my mother had given birth to a block of wood. My father the king thought my mother was inauspicious and had her floated away on a raft. As for me, I was raised by the rishi Agginetta. Later Aggisikha, king of the ogres, asked to take me as a foster child. I learned all this from a mynah bird. I did not know whether my mother was alive or dead. The mynah told me she was alive and living as a hermit on an island in the middle of the ocean. I left my foster parents and went to see the rishi Agginetta. He told me to go west. I left him, came with the horse Manomaya to the big lake in the middle of the forest, and stayed there on my own. When the horse went off to find grass and water, your father brought me down into the *nāga* realm." When he thought of the horse, he wept deeply again.

Saddened by this account, Samuddajā said, "If you wish to find your mother, I beg to go along with you." He refused. She went to her mother and father and said, "My husband is thinking of his mother and wishes to go to find her. I wish to go along with him." Her mother and father refused to allow her and Prince Varanujja to go.

Two or three days later, while Prince Varanujja was asleep at midnight, he dreamed that Agginetta the hermit came to the residence, stood on his head pillow, and said, "Prince Varanujja, you have been sleeping happily with your wife and not thinking of your mother. You fooled Aggisikha and me that you would go to find your mother, but instead you've fallen in love with this *nāga* lady." Then he disappeared.

Prince Varanujja woke up, turned to look at the hermit but saw nothing, and began to weep. "Oh, the hermit loves me so much he took the trouble to come here and lecture me." He saw Samuddajā was fast asleep. Taking his sword and bow, he left the palace. He brandished the sword over his head, making the earth split apart to create a way out. He walked through the gap in the earth up to the human world. He could not find the old road or the horse and set off on a different way. When he thought of the horse, he wept and spoke a verse:

"My life will end in disaster because, separated
from Manomaya, how can I travel through the forest?
Who will take me from this forest and point to me the direction to go?
Without Manomaya, how can I go through this forest?"

He walked on weeping until nightfall, when he slept by the roots of a tree.

When Samuddajā woke and found her husband missing and the door open, she followed his tracks to the earth without finding him. She interrogated the slave girls without getting anything and searched around everywhere without result. She went to inform Varuṇa, king of the *nāga*, who lamented along with Queen Vimalā.

Samuddajā searched in every direction without success. While walking with difficulty through the forest, she thought of the horse Manomaya and became very agitated thinking of the dangers that Prince Varanujja would be facing. She searched all over the Himavanta Forest without result. She returned to the home of Agginetta the hermit and tearfully told him what had happened.

One evening, when Prince Varanujja was walking in the forest, he saw a banyan tree. He went to stay there, ate some fruit, and fell asleep. Four wood spirits talked together, "At Mount Kālagirī [black mountain] there is a fierce lord ogre called Siṅhakaṇṇa [lion ear] who has bullied us and other spirits. He has caused us great trouble. This prince has great power of merit. He is capable of killing the lord ogre. Let us carry him into the residence of Suvaṇṇagandha [golden scent], the lord ogre's daughter. When he wakes up, he will make love with her. When her father finds out, he will be very angry. He will fight with this prince and lose his life, dying from the prince's divine arrow."

They carried Prince Varanujja along with his sword and bow, placed him on the bed in Suvaṇṇagandha's residence, and returned home.

When Suvaṇṇagandha woke up, she turned over, bumping into Prince Varanujja. She stood up and asked a slave girl, "Who is this who can come and sleep with me?"

The group of slave girls woke up in alarm and went into the room. Seeing Prince Varanujja, they said to one another, "This must be a god, or a *nāga*, or a *kumbhaṇḍa* with great power who has come to make love with Suvaṇṇagandha." The slave girls woke Prince Varanujja up and asked, "O god, where did you come from?"

Prince Varanujja looked to left and right, seeing a brilliant and beautiful residence, and thought, "This is not the roots of a tree, and this is not the realm of the *nāga*. How did I come here?"

Suvaṇṇagandha asked, "Where did you come from? Who are you—a god, a *nāga*, a *garuḍa*, or a man of some other prowess?"

"I am a human. I was lost. I went to sleep under a tree. How did I come to be sleeping here?"

"Indeed, how did you lose your way and come here?"

"I was going to find my mother."

"Is your mother living in this residence?"

"In truth, I did not come here myself. I was sleeping by a tree in the forest. I was asleep and do not know how I came to be here."

She thought, "This fellow has great merit. Perhaps he was raised by a god, who brought him here to be my husband." She told the slave girls to go away.

She asked Prince Varanujja, "Did you come here because there are some relatives of yours in this city?"

"Not a single one. What is this city called?"

"Siṅhakūṭa City."

"What is the name of the king ruling here?"

"Siṅhakūṭanta[15] ogre."

"What is your name?"

"Suvaṇṇagandha."

"I came here by mistake. Please forgive me."

She thought, "I must test him some more." She said, "Who will be your wife? Do you know?"

"I don't."

"In that case, you must leave this place. If my father and elder brother find you here, you will lose your life."

"Then help me. Tell me the way to leave here."

"You must leave by the way you came."

Prince Varanujja was beginning to fall for her. He said, "In that case, allow me to take my leave." He made as if to leave.

Seeing this, she felt that her heart would break. She said, "Usually someone who is in a hurry—whether a king, an elephant, a monk, or a woman—does not find beauty. A man who is in too much of a hurry is not beautiful in the same way. Those who are in too much of a hurry will not have good fortune."

Prince Varanujja sat still for a moment, then talked with Suvaṇṇagandha and made love to her.

From then on, Prince Varanujja stayed with Suvaṇṇagandha. Her ogre slave girls brought them additional food and drink and did not tell the secret to anyone. For over half a month, Suvaṇṇagandha did not attend on her father. Prince Varanujja reveled in the celestial food, celestial bed, and

15. Above he is named Siṅhakaṇṇa in both the Pali and Thai. From this point forward, he is Siṅhakaṇta in the Pali and Siṅhakūṭanta in the Thai.

celestial lovemaking. He forgot about the future dangers. He stayed in the residence making love to Suvaṇṇagandha for over a month.

Noticing his daughter had not come to audience for a month, King Siṅhakūṭanta asked the slave girls, "Why has my daughter disappeared? Is she sick or something?"

The slave girls acted as if they knew nothing, and sat saying nothing. That evening, Mahisakaṇṇa [buffalo ear], the younger brother of Suvaṇṇagandha, went to attend on his father, King Siṅhakūṭanta, who asked him, "Is your elder sister sick? Is that why she does not come to audience?"

"Your Majesty, I do not know."

"In that case, you must go and find out."

Mahisakaṇṇa paid respect, went to Suvaṇṇagandha's residence, and ordered the slave girls to open the door. The slave girls whispered among themselves that her younger brother had come. One ran in to tell Suvaṇṇagandha, "Your brother has come!" Prince Varanujja heard. He took his divine sword in hand and hid to one side. Mahisakaṇṇa came in and sat on a seat where he could not see Prince Varanujja. Noticing that his sister looked gloomy, not radiant, he asked, "Are you sick?"

"O brother, I have a headache."

"Our father is thinking of you. He ordered me to come and see you."

"Now you know, please go and tell our father."

Mahisakaṇṇa left the residence and went to tell their father about Suvaṇṇagandha's condition.

The slave girls talked together: "If we keep the matter secret but the king finds out that his daughter is making love with this prince, he will do something to the prince, and our lives will be up! It would be better for us to tell the king." With this agreement, they went to address the king of the ogres. "Your Majesty, a human man in his prime and of great power has come to stay in the residence of your daughter."

"Whose son is this human? What is his name? Where does he come from?"

"Your Majesty, we do not know his country, his lineage, his father, or his mother, but his name is Varanujja."

The king of the ogres was very angry, like a snake hit at the base of its tail. He said, "So this young man has great power. Why did he come alone?"

After thinking, the king sent for Mahisakaṇṇa and asked, "When you went to your sister's residence, did you see anything strange?"

"I did not."

The king told him what he had learned from the slave girls and then said, "Mahisakaṇṇa, take this pipe and blow its medicinal smoke onto this human. When he falls fast asleep, put him in an iron cage." Mahisakaṇṇa went to carry out the order and returned to report, "I have put him in a cage, sire."

The king was pleased. He said, "Tomorrow morning we will see what to do with this human." After that, he fell quiet. Prince Mahisakaṇṇa arrested the chief of the slave girls who looked after Suvaṇṇagandha's residence, and had her trussed up.

Prince Varanujja was unconscious from the smoke. Four wood spirits saw him and knew that the ogres had captured him. They discussed together, "We should help him." They went to where Prince Varanujja was. When the guards were fast asleep, two of the spirits lifted him and the cage. Another picked up the sword and bow. Another carried Suvaṇṇagandha and her bed. They placed them all close to the retreat of Agginetta the hermit, and then went away.

The next morning at dawn, the hermit came out of his retreat, saw the cage, and thought, "What is this?" He approached, saw Prince Varanujja and his wife, and tried to wake Prince Varanujja up. He was still very groggy from the smoke and would not stir. He slept all through the day and woke in the evening. Looking left and right, he thought, "How did this happen?" He woke Suvaṇṇagandha, who looked around in every direction and cried out loud, "How did we come here?"

The hermit opened the door of the cage. Seeing him, the couple paid respect. The hermit asked, "How did you two come here?"

"We don't know." They told the whole story to the hermit from the beginning to the events in Suvaṇṇagandha's residence.

The four wood spirits came to tell the hermit, "The ogre king, father of Suvaṇṇagandha, found out that Prince Varanujja is her husband and was very angry. He had the prince knocked out with smoke and put in an iron cage, and would have killed him the next morning, so we brought the couple to your retreat. Right now the city of the ogres is in uproar. The king has had the slave girls in her service arrested and tied up and will kill them." The spirits disappeared.

An ogre guard in the jail found that the prince and the cage had disappeared. In alarm he woke up his comrades. "Where has the prince gone?" They searched in every direction through until dawn without success. They went to tell Prince Mahisakaṇṇa. In alarm, he went to look in Suvaṇṇagandha's residence and found she was missing. He reported to his father, king of the ogres, "The prince and the lady have escaped." In rage, the king of the ogres ordered that the guards be arrested and executed. Then he commanded his ogre generals, "You must search for them in every direction. If you find them, come back to report."

The ogre generals reached the retreat of Agginetta and found Prince Varanujja and Suvaṇṇagandha. They returned to tell the king of the ogres. In anger, the king ordered, "You must all transform yourselves into bodies with different heads, catch him, and kill him. I will come at the rear."

The ogre generals transformed their bodies, strapped on various weapons, and all gathered to take leave of the king, who inspected the troops and sent them off. The noise of the ogre troops echoed around like the sound of the era-ending wind. The generals led the ogre army close to the hermit's retreat, then announced in a loud voice, "We have come to arrest and execute Prince Varanujja, then we will return."

Hearing this commotion, Prince Varanujja said to Suvaṇṇagandha, "Many ogre troops have come. What should we do?"

She said, "What do you think? Do as you wish."

Prince Varanujja thought of the horse Manomaya, and in an instant the horse was there. Happily, the horse asked, "Where did you go? I looked for you everywhere without success."

Prince Varanujja said, "The day we slept by the bank of the lake, a *nāga* king took me to the *nāga* realm and presented me with his daughter. I escaped from the *nāga* world. While I was asleep, some spirits put me in the residence of Suvaṇṇagandha here. In anger, her father had me arrested and placed in an iron cage. The spirits carried me and the cage to the hermit's retreat. The ogre king is after me with many ogre troops, so I called you here."

The horse replied, "Master, do not be worried. I will fight him myself." He invited Prince Varanujja to mount and soared up into the air. After inspecting the ogre armies, he said, "Your Majesty, there are huge numbers of ogres. We should hide away."

Prince Varanujja waved his sword and made a prayer, "If we are to win victory, may a mountain appear here right now." A mountain three *yojana* high appeared in front of them. Manomaya descended to land on the peak. Prince Varanujja dismounted, brandished the sword, and made another prayer: "May a great celestial wall appear surrounding this mountain completely." An imposing wall, as high as the mountain's peak, appeared instantly.

The ogre troops transformed themselves into humans with different heads—some elephants, some tigers, some rhinoceroses, some dogs, some pigs, some cattle and buffalo—all carrying various weapons such as bows, javelins, and lumps of rock. They came to the celestial wall and found they could not cross it or fly to the top of the mountain to threaten the prince.

The king of the ogres transformed his body to be one *gāvuta* tall, with ten heads and ten faces. He mounted the neck of a Nāḷāgiri elephant,[16] gripping various weapons including sword, lance, and bow. He roared out to his troops, "Capture Varanujja! Split open his chest! Cut off his hands and feet! Throw him in the ocean!" His roar echoed around like the sound of thunder. The ogre troops did not dare to approach. Instead they caused wind and rain strong enough to batter down the mountain peak. The wind and rain blew trees and clumps of forest from all directions. Prince Varanujja raised his sword and bow and blasted the wind and rain out beyond the universe.

The king of the ogres was furious. He conjured up a great cloud that spread darkness in every direction. He conjured up a rain of stones and burning charcoal. He transformed ash into *nāga* and *garuḍa*, approaching in many frightening poses from many directions. Prince Varanujja released celestial arrows, repelling everything.

The king of the ogres began to lose heart. Prince Varanujja loosed an arrow, saying, "May this arrow split open the chest of the ogre king, killing him right now." The arrow soared into the air, roaring loudly, and sped straight into the chest of the ogre king, who could not pull the arrow out. He returned to his city, lay on his throne, and died.

Among the ogre troops, some fled to the Himavanta, some flew up into the mountain peaks, some fled to hide among the forest and hills, and some fled to hide in their own homes. After the ogre king died, the sword and

16. A raging elephant tamed by the Buddha.

arrows came back to Prince Varanujja. He mounted the horse, returned to the retreat of the rishi, and told Suvaṇṇagandha all about the victory.

Seeing the defeat of his father, the ogre prince Mahisakaṇṇa was greatly dismayed. He went to his mother, Kesamālī, and said, "Mother, the husband of Suvaṇṇagandha has great powers. He has killed my father, lord of the ogres. I want revenge. Let me fight this husband of Suvaṇṇagandha."

Queen Kesamālī forbade him, saying, "Do not be angry. Cremate your father's body. Gather many ogres to pay respect and make a bier."

They were unable to raise up the corpse. The ogre troops and relatives came to help but were unable to lift the corpse. Kesamālī approached and addressed the corpse, saying, "Your Majesty, please go up on the bier." The corpse did not move. Queen Kesamālī ordered Prince Mahisakaṇṇa, "Quickly invite Suvaṇṇagandha here to help raise the corpse of her father." The prince went to bring her as ordered.

Suvaṇṇagandha said to Prince Varanujja, "Your Majesty, my father has died. My mother has sent for me. Will you come with me?"

"I will." He thought of the horse Manomaya who flew to find him. Prince Varanujja informed the horse, put on his sword and bow, mounted with Suvaṇṇagandha, and went through the air to the city of the *nāga*. They dismounted and went up into the palace. Her mother came to welcome them. Seeing her daughter, she embraced her and wept. Suvaṇṇagandha embraced her mother's feet and grieved. Prince Varanujja paid respect and sat among the ogre troops. Seeing him, Prince Mahisakaṇṇa was shocked and afraid. He paid respect to Prince Varanujja and Suvaṇṇagandha.

Queen Kesamālī said to Suvaṇṇagandha, "Please raise the corpse of your father."

Suvaṇṇagandha went to pay respect at her father's feet to ask forgiveness. She tried to lift the corpse but it did not move. Prince Varanujja went to pay respect to the corpse, saying, "You are creating karma for me. The wrong is still there. Please forgive this wrong for me." After this apology, he was able to raise the corpse, place it in an urn, and move the urn onto the bier. The ogres that had gathered there, including the queen, greatly appreciated Prince Varanujja, seeing he had the power appropriate to rule the realm. They set fire to the bier.

When the cremation was complete, Queen Kesamālī summoned the ogre generals for a discussion. "To whom should we entrust the rule of the realm from now on?"

Those at the meeting said, "The realm is yours, mistress. Please entrust the realm to whomever you think is suitable. We will not object."

She said, "Prince Varanujja, husband of Suvaṇṇagandha, was able to lift the corpse onto the bier. I will entrust the realm to him. What do you think?" The ogre generals and all the relatives unanimously gave their approval.

Queen Kesamālī had a ceremonial pavilion made and had it beautifully upholstered and decorated, with a brilliant ceiling of stars around the moon. She had people bring jewels, silver, and gold to make a heap. The next morning, the spirits and ogres came to sit in fitting places. The royal mother sat the two royals on the jeweled mound, performed the ceremony of anointment and blessing, and entrusted them with the realm. The king now called King Varanujja established Suvaṇṇagandha as his major queen, senior to sixteen thousand consorts. From then on he ruled the realm and enjoyed the heavenly treasures with his queen for three years without thinking of his mother.

The horse Manomaya saw that King Varanujja was besotted with Suvaṇṇagandha. One day, he warned him, "Your Majesty, you are enjoying yourself and not thinking of your mother."

King Varanujja thought, "The horse is telling the truth. I should go to find my mother."

He told this to Queen Mother Kesamālī and Queen Suvaṇṇagandha, who felt her heart was being destroyed. She begged him not to go. King Varanujja said to Queen Kesamālī, "Mother, I was raised by Lord Aggisikha the ogre and Rājaputtī. I wish to see the mother who gave me birth. I beg to take leave of you, and I entrust Queen Suvaṇṇagandha to you. I will go with the horse. After I have seen my mother, I will return."

Hearing this, Suvaṇṇagandha begged to go along. King Varanujja said, "You should not go. The way through the great forest is very difficult with many dangers. Once I have found my mother, I will return here and take you to attend on her."

King Varanujja consoled Queen Suvaṇṇagandha, prostrated to her mother, and took up his sword and bow. He went to the horse and said, "I wish to fly to my mother. Show me the way." He ordered the ogre troops, "Be vigilant. Protect the royal mother, Prince Mahisakaṇṇa, and Queen Suvaṇṇagandha for me." He mounted the horse, which flew up into the air, heading east. In the evening, he landed to rest overnight in the forest. On the following morning they continued the journey. After seven nights and days, buffeted by wind, sun, and rain, they passed beyond the forest and hills and various bodies of water to reach his mother's city. He thought, "This is my mother's city for certain."

He said to the horse, "This is a fine city, surrounded by a great ocean, with glittering jeweled residences inside, with gardens, lakes, and streets, rich in fruiting trees and flowering trees. The hermit had told me that my elder brother built a great city for our mother to live in. This must be it. We will land outside the city and make inquiries of the people." The horse went down to land at a pavilion outside the city.

King Varanujja asked people who came to sit and chat in this pavilion, "What is the name of this city?"

"This is a new city, built by Prince Varanetta for his mother. It is called Sākala City."

"What is the name of this royal mother?"

"Queen Subhaddā."

"Where was she before, and when did she come here?"

People related the events in order: "Queen Subhaddā is a *kinnari* princess. She was the queen of King Cetarāja. She gave birth to two sons at the same time. Another queen had her falsely accused by substituting a block of wood, taking one son to be buried in a chest and having the other son floated away in a pot. A spirit raised the buried son and gave him the name Varanetta. Queen Subhaddā was accused of being inauspicious. The king had her floated away on a raft. A spirit arranged for her to live on an island in the ocean. When Varanetta grew up, he went looking for his mother, brought her here, and built this city for her. This elder son is now called King Varanetta."

Prince Varanujja said, "I am that son who was floated away in a pot. How can I meet my mother?"

"Go to the minister and tell this to him."

Prince Varanujja stayed in the pavilion for one night. The next morning, the horse Manomaya traveled around in all directions. People tried to catch him, but none succeeded. Some went to tell King Varanetta, "Your Majesty, there is a horse outside the city that nobody can catch."

The king ordered, "In that case, have the stable master release my horse."

The people went to the stables and told the stable master, who passed it on to the horse.

The horse went out of the city, met Manomaya, and asked, "Where did you come from?"

"From the city of the ogres."

"Who did you come with, and for what purpose?

"I came with my master. He has been separated from his mother and is traveling in search of her."

"What is the name of your master?"

"Prince Varanujja."

"What is his mother's name?"

"Queen Subhaddā."

"How were Prince Varanujja and his mother separated?"

Manomaya related the story from beginning to end for the other horse to hear.

"In that case, your master must be the brother of my master. Where is he now?"

"In the pavilion over there."

"In that case, you should go to tell him, while I go to tell my master." The horse went back into the city, straight to the stable, and told the courtier looking after the horses, "Sir, go to the court and inform the king that a prince named Varanujja has come here looking for his mother. The name of his mother is the same as the king's mother, and the reason he was separated from her is the same sad story as that of our king."

The courtier went to attend on the king, and related the words of the horse. King Varanetta asked, "Where is the prince?" He rushed to the stable and asked the horse, "Where is the prince who has come here?"

"Your Majesty, Prince Varanujja, your younger brother, is at a pavilion, waiting to see you and his mother."

"In that case, please take me there right now." He decked the horse with decorations, mounted, and left the city surrounded by his courtiers. At the pavilion, he dismounted and went inside.

Seeing his elder brother, Prince Varanujja thought, "This man riding up must be my brother." He got up and went to prostrate at his feet, stirring love in his brother immediately.

King Varanetta asked, "Prince, what is your name?"

"Your Majesty, my name is Varanujja."

"What is your mother's name?"

"Subhaddā."

"What is your brother's name?"

"Varanetta. A spirit brought him up."

"And who brought you up?"

Prince Varanujja told the story from the beginning, in tears.

King Varanetta knew this was his younger brother. He embraced him, and wept also. He led him to the residence of their mother to tell her the whole story.

When she looked at Varanujja, the queen mother thought, "These two look very alike. They are certainly my sons." She embraced them both in tears, saying, "I was called inauspicious, but my sons were raised by spirits and have met together today."

King Varanetta shot a celestial arrow and made a prayer, "May a celestial residence appear." A splendid residence did indeed appear. King Varanetta presented it to his younger brother and anointed him in the position of viceroy.

After some time Prince Varanujja thought, "I have been apart from Samuddajā for a long time. I will bring her here to service my mother. Later I will fetch Suvaṇṇagandha." Next morning, he went to attend on his mother and said, "Mother, I have two wives. One called Samuddajā, the daughter of a lord of the *nāga*, lives in the *nāga* world. I fled away from there.[17] I beg to take leave to fetch Queen Samuddajā to be in service to my mother."

His mother and elder brother gave their consent. Taking his celestial bow, he went to the stable but Manomaya was not there. In fact, Manomaya had become lusty and had left the stable to go to the Himavanta Forest to roam around with the horses there. Prince Varanujja thought unhappily, "How can I go on my own?"

At that moment, there was a white elephant who had left his family and traveled by stages until he came to stay outside the city. When Prince Varanujja walked out of the city, the white elephant saw him and was pleased. He approached and asked, "Where are you going, prince?

"To the *nāga* realm."

"In that case, mount on my back and I will take you." The elephant lowered his back for Prince Varanujja to mount, then split open the earth,

17. Here the Thai translator inserted, "The other, called Suvaṇṇagandha, is the daughter of a lord of the ogres. I entrusted her to that lord." But Suvaṇṇagandha's father has already been killed.

and in a moment arrived in the *nāga* realm in front of a park. The elephant said, "This is the *nāga* realm. Please dismount."

"Why do you say this is the *nāga* realm? In truth, it's so close!"

"I know the direct route."

The prince looked around, recognized a celestial palace, and then believed the elephant. He dismounted, saying, "Please stay here." He walked to the *nāga* palace.

Young *nāga* ladies, happy to see Prince Varanujja coming, said to one another, "The king's son has come!" Some went to inform Samuddajā. Some hurried to tell the *nāga* king. Samuddajā happily came to greet him, and took him to her father and mother. Prince Varanujja paid respect to them and sat down. The *nāga* king Varuṇa asked, "Have you found your mother yet?"

"I have."

"Where is she?"

"I left the *nāga* realm here, went through the Himavanta Forest, and was sleeping by a tree. A spirit carried me and placed me in the residence of an ogre princess. When I woke up, I was shocked and tried to flee. The ogre princess caught me and made love to me. When the ogre king found out, I was captured while asleep and put in a cage. The spirit carried me and the cage to the home of the hermit. No sooner had the hermit roused me, the ogre king came in pursuit and fought with me. I killed the ogre king with a celestial arrow. The ogre queen entrusted me with the realm. Then I thought of my mother. With my horse I flew through the air, found a city, and landed outside there. My horse Manomaya met a horse from there and told him the story. The news went to my brother, the king. He took me to our mother. My brother gave me the post of viceroy. Then I thought of Samuddajā and came to find her."

Varuṇa sent King Varanujja to the abode of Samuddajā. After six or seven days, King Varanujja thought of his mother. He put on his sword and bow and took Samuddajā to attend on her father and mother. They took leave, left the *nāga* palace, and went to the elephant. The couple mounted the back of the elephant, who took them to his mother's city. After sending the elephant to the stable, Varanujja took Samuddajā to attend on his mother and father. After paying their respect, he took her to his residence. They enjoyed the pleasures of love along with a retinue of *nāga* ladies.

After some time, Manomaya returned from the Himavanta Country and went into the stables. Manomaya, the other horse, and the elephant were not locked up but left free all the time. Wherever they wanted to go, they went.

Prince Varanujja the viceroy thought of Suvaṇṇagandha. "I should bring her to stay here."

He took leave of his mother and elder brother, put on his sword, went to Manomaya, and said, "I am going to the city of Suvaṇṇagandha to fetch her here. Please decide the direction to go." He mounted the horse and headed through the sky toward the ogre city. On arrival, he dismounted and went to stay in a pavilion outside the city. Manomaya thought, "I will tell the ogres that my master has arrived." He let out a loud roar that echoed all around the city.

Suvaṇṇagandha heard the horse's call and understood that her husband had come. She summoned a slave girl to help make a jeweled throne and sweep up everything to be clean and orderly. The ogres who came to audience recognized Prince Varanujja and went to inform the king, who sent them to his queen mother and major queen. Queen Kesamālī ordered ogres to prepare a carriage to fetch Prince Varanujja. When it was done, she sent for Prince Mahisakaṇṇa and said, "Varanujja your brother-in-law has arrived. We will go out to welcome him together." Along with the queen and the elder brother, all surrounded by slaves and slave girls, they went out of the city to the pavilion.

Seeing the royal mother Queen Kesamālī coming, Prince Varanujja came out of the pavilion, paid respect, and invited them into the pavilion. Queen Kesamālī asked, "Have you met your mother?"

"I flew over the hills and forests and saw an island in the middle of the ocean where there was a great city as beautiful as Tāvatiṁsa. I went to stay in a pavilion outside the city. When people came to see me, I asked the names of the king and the king's mother. They told me the king was called Varanetta and his mother's name was Subhaddā. We talked until matters were clear. When King Varanetta knew, he came out to receive me and took me to attend on our mother. I told him what had happened from the past."

Queen Kesamālī was pleased. She said, "You fulfilled your wish." She invited him to board the royal carriage to go into the city, surrounded by ogre troops. She had the ogre troops take him up into the palace, give him food, and then return to their homes. Prince Varanujja went to sleep. A group of ogre ladies surrounded him as retinue. He enjoyed celestial happiness as joyful as Lord Sakka.

At that time there was an ogre king on Mount Kukakuṭa who had great powers. Hearing that a human was ruling in Siṅhakūṭa City, he thought, "I will go to this city, seize it, and rule there." He summoned his ogre troops and told them, "When the ogre King Siṅhakūṭanta died, a human came to rule in Siṅhakūṭa City. For this reason, I will go to seize this city, capture this king, kill him, and then rule there. Announce this to all the ogre troops. We will march in seven days."

The ogre troops acknowledged the order and informed others accordingly. After seven days, the ogre troops assembled; the king inspected them and commanded them to march on ahead. The troops cheered and shouted in uproar. On arrival they besieged Siṅhakūṭa City in seven circles. When the king arrived, he sent a missive to Queen Kesamālī, saying, "Will you hand over the realm or will you fight a war? As you are a widow, you will be my wife and you will give your daughter to my son. If you don't consent, your city will be destroyed forthwith."

Queen Kesamālī sent for Prince Mahisakaṇṇa and Prince Varanujja. "Now that King Kukakuṭa the ogre has sent such a missive, what should we do?" The princes replied, "Mother, do not be upset. We will help to fight." A reply missive was sent, saying, "King Kukakuṭa, we will fight with you. Do not take this lightly."

The two princes returned to their residences, strapped on their weapons, summoned the ogre troops, and commanded, "Ready the army." The troops prepared their weapons, and all assembled at the royal courtyard.

Prince Mahisakaṇṇa put on his weapons and inspected the troops. As commander, he led the troops out of the city, making a colossal noise. Prince Varanujja the viceroy put on his celestial sword and bow and thought of Manomaya. The horse appeared, bowed down for Varanujja to mount, and flew up to the peak of a mountain. Prince Varanujja stood firmly and shot a celestial arrow that flew with a sound like a thunderclap. The enemy troops were alarmed. The weapons slipped from their grasp, every one. King Kukakuṭa urged his troops to attack. The two sides fought together. The horse Manomaya leapt up into the air and kicked the enemy troops with his hooves, scattering them around. Some died. Some were injured. Some fled. Seeing them flee, King Kukakuṭa flew into a rage and shot an arrow that turned into a great rainstorm. Varanujja shot an arrow that turned into a gale, which swept up all the weapons and dumped them in the ocean. The ogre king shot an arrow that spurted fire from its mouth, spreading dark smoke throughout the sky. Prince Varanujja shot an arrow that spurted water from its mouth, which flooded the forest in every direction. The enemy ogres and their king were swept up by the current right back to their Kukakuṭa City. Varanujja and Mahisakaṇṇa took their troops back into the city.

In truth, when Prince Varanujja went to the ogre city to fetch Suvaṇṇagandha, the lord white elephant, who was in an auspicious pavilion for shade, was greatly stirred by lust. One night he left the elephant stable to roam in the forest, looking for a herd of elephants, until he arrived in the territory of Kāsikarāṭṭha. The elephant keepers woke up at midnight, were shocked to see the auspicious elephant was missing, and went to search throughout Sākala City without finding him. Next morning they attended on King Varanetta and said, "Your Majesty, the auspicious lord elephant has disappeared. We have searched the whole city without success."

The king commanded, "Go and search outside the city." The elephant keepers looked everywhere but did not find even one footprint. They returned to inform the king.

King Varanetta sent for the courtiers looking after horses and said, "Tell the horse Asadara that I want him to go with me."

The keeper of Asadara acknowledged the order, went to tell the horse, and took him to the king. The king went down from the palace, mounted the horse, and traveled to the Himavanta Country. He searched around all the lakes and rivers without finding the elephant, then returned to his city.

After Prince Varanujja and Prince Mahisakaṇṇa had won victory over King Kukakuṭa, they led the ogre troops back to the city. The ogre troops all drank the liquor of victory. Seven days later, Prince Varanujja said to Suvaṇṇagandha, "I am thinking of my mother. I will take leave of your mother and go to find my mother. Will you come with me or not?"

"Your Majesty, I wish to go and pay respect to your mother and elder brother. Allow me to accompany you." She went to her mother's residence and paid respect to take leave. Her mother gave her consent.

Prince Varanujja and Suvaṇṇagandha entrusted the realm to Prince Mahisakaṇṇa. Accompanied by their retinue, they left the city and traveled through the forest for three months until they reached the ocean shore. They had the ogres halt there. Prince Varanujja, Suvaṇṇagandha, and the horse Manomaya flew to Sākala City, went up into his residence, and commanded courtiers to arrange ships to fetch the ogres from the shore. Knowing they were ogres, the courtiers did not bring them to the city but had them stay in a village outside. For this reason, the sailors called that village Siṅgagama.

Prince Varanujja took Suvaṇṇagandha to pay respect to his mother, who was very happy to see her son and daughter-in-law. She gave her blessings and presented many adornments to Suvaṇṇagandha. Prince Varanujja then took Suvaṇṇagandha to attend on King Varanetta and pay respect to him and Queen Puṣapā. King Varanetta and his mother anointed Prince Varanujja to hold the post of viceroy.

One day Prince Varanujja had a dream. A great man carrying an impressive sharp sword came and cut off Prince Varanujja's feet then fled away; Prince Varanujja could not find his feet; he went to the west and met his father, who gave him his feet, which he attached as they were before. In the morning, Prince Varanujja went to attend upon his brother and related the dream. After consideration, King Varanetta said, "The feet are the elephant that has disappeared. If you look for him now, you will find him for certain."

Prince Varanujja said to the king, "I will take leave to search for the elephant. Allow me to leave my two queens with you." He attended on his mother, related the dream, and asked about his father, "What does my father look like, and what is his name?"

His mother Queen Subhaddā replied, "Your father's body is fine and perfect, with features as fine as gold. His name is Kāsika. He rules the realm in Kāsikaraṭṭha.[18] He had two queens named Khemā and Subhaddā—that is me." She related the story of how she was floated away on a raft up to the point when she was reunited with her two sons, as related above. She warned him, "What benefit can you get from wild animals? If you go to your father's home, Queen Khemā will kill you. Don't go."

Prince Varanujja paid respect, went to the residence of his two queens, and commanded them, "Ladies, be heedful. Look after my mother and brother."

18. At the start of the story he is King Cetarāja of Cetaraṭṭha. This discrepancy appears in the Pali.

He strapped on his celestial sword and bow, went down from the palace, and had a courtier harness the horse Manomaya. He mounted and said, "I am going west to the land of the humans." He ordered Manomaya to fly up into the air. They searched for the lord white elephant in the forests and hills for seven days and seven nights without success. They continued on to the territory of Kāsikaraṭṭha.

At that time there was a hunter chasing deer in the forest who saw that lord elephant in a herd. He took careful note of the hill and forest, and returned to the city to inform King Kāsika, "Sire, in the forest over there is a white elephant as white and beautiful as Mount Kelāsa, like the royal mount of an emperor, with all the features of unimpeachable beauty."

Happy to hear this, the king ordered his generals to ready troops and elephant teachers, then left the city with the hunter acting as guide. Arriving at the place that the hunter remembered, the king ordered them to surround the hill with troops and elephants in order to trap the white elephant. The elephant teachers were able to capture and train the elephant in the appointed way, without creating chaos and confusion.

At that moment Prince Varanujja was looking for the elephant from the sky. He saw the captured elephant and recognized him. He said to Manomaya, "That is our white elephant. Let us go down. When he sees us, he will come." They landed close by and called out to the elephant, who saw and recognized Prince Varanujja. He shook off his tethers and came to them. The elephant keepers saw this and shouted, "The white elephant has broken free!" They could not catch him and so went to inform King Kāsika, "Your Majesty, a man came and called out to the white elephant, and the elephant ran off to him." The king was enraged. He ordered his courtiers to arrest this man, thrash him, and lock him up at once.

The courtiers strapped on various weapons and made after Prince Varanujja. Seeing them coming to arrest him, Varanujja asked, "Why are you coming to arrest me?"

"Because you stole the white elephant, you thief. We will not spare your life."

Prince Varanujja stood brandishing his sword. The courtiers could not approach to arrest him. In fright, they ran off to inform King Kāsika, "Your Majesty, this thief has great powers. You cannot fight with this fellow."

King Kāsika took up his sword and bow, went over to Prince Varanujja, and said, "So, elephant thief, why did you come to steal my elephant?"

"It is you who are the thief. This is my elephant. He broke out of my stable. I have been searching for him for several days. Today I found him and came to catch him. For this reason, you are the thief."

"I trapped this elephant. Since you let him go, how can you say the elephant is yours? I caught him. I will cut off your head with this arrow." He shot an arrow. The arrow turned into sweets and snacks. Prince Varanujja determined to kill this king. He shot some celestial arrows, which turned into flowers, garlands, candles, and incense.

The two kings were surprised and fearful at seeing these unusual arrows. They asked after each other's name and lineage. King Kāsika asked Prince Varanujja, "What is your name?"

"Prince Varanujja. What is your name?"

"King Kāsika. And you are the son of whom?"

When speaking the name of his royal mother, Prince Varanujja raised his hands in salute and said, "My mother's name is Queen Subhaddā."

"Where do you live?"

"My mother lived in Kāsika."

"Who is your father? Where does he live?"

Prince Varanujja thought cleverly, "He thinks he is my father." He replied, "I am an orphan, separated from my father since birth. Now I live in Sākala City which my brother built for my mother."

"Why were you separated from your father?"

Prince Varanujja related the story as the mynah bird and his mother had told him in the past.

Hearing this, King Kāsika threw away his sword and bow, came to embrace Prince Varanujja, and said, "I am your father. Where is your mother at present? I do not know. I heard them say that your mother gave birth to a block of wood. I believed them without checking." He spoke further in a verse:

"I am too credulous, blinded as if all eight directions are dark.
I have done badly wrong. Please forgive your father at this time."

After begging forgiveness, King Kāsika said, "Where is your mother? I will follow you to meet her."

Prince Varanujja and King Kāsika mounted the white elephant and flew through the sky to Sākala City. The horse Manomaya flew along behind them.

Here there is a question. If the white elephant could fly anywhere, why was the king able to capture him? The answer is this. The white elephant was lost in love over a cow elephant and was not fearful of the dangers he faced. In addition, the king was able to capture him because the gods changed the elephant's mind in order that the king would meet with Prince Varanujja.

Prince Varanujja arrived at the city, left the white elephant with the keepers at the elephant stables, and took the king up into his residence. Suvaṇṇagandha and Samuddajā paid respect to their father and their husband. King Kāsika gazed at the city as beautiful, brilliant, and captivating as a heavenly city. He saw the dancing girls like heavenly *apsara* maidens and the residences like heavenly mansions. "This city is truly beautiful indeed!"

Prince Varanujja went up to the residence of King Varanetta, paid respect, and said, "Your Majesty, my elder brother, I went after the white elephant and found that our father had captured him. I did not know that he was our father. He shot an arrow at me, but the arrow changed into sweets and fruit. I shot arrows at him, but they changed into garlands, incense, candles, and flowers. For this reason, father asked whose son I was. Now he is in my residence."

King Varanetta said, "In that case, I will go to pay respect to our father." The pair went to attend on their father, paid respect, and addressed him in verse as follows:[19]

> "*Are you well, father? Are you in good health?*
> *Your queens and royal ladies, are they also?*"

King Kāsika replied to his two sons in a verse:

> "*Dear sons, I am well. I am in good health.*
> *All the royal ladies and my chief queens are so too.*"

The two sons asked further in a verse:

> "*Father, I hope you are not a drunkard, that you are not fond of liquor,*
> *and I hope you think of and delight in the dhamma, precepts, and giving.*"

19. This conventional exchange is found in several texts, including at the start of the "Great Forest" chapter of J547 Vessantara (Appleton and Shaw, *Ten Great Birth Stories*, 585–86; Faussböll, *Jātaka*, VI, 542) and in J538 Temiya (Appleton and Shaw, *Ten Great Birth Stories*, 73–74; Faussböll, *Jātaka*, VI, 23).

King Kāsika explained in a verse:

> *"Beloved sons, I am not intoxicated, and I do not drink sandal water.*
> *I am disposed to follow the precepts, the dhamma, and giving."*

The two princes asked their father further in a verse:

> *"Are your yoked animals healthy? Does your steed carry you well?*
> *Have you any illnesses or afflictions of the body?"*

King Kāsika replied in a verse:

> *"My yoked animals are healthy. My steed carries me well.*
> *I have no illnesses or afflictions of the body."*

The two princes asked in a verse:

> *"Are the inner and central troops still plentiful?*
> *Are your granaries and royal treasuries still full?"*

King Kāsika replied in a verse:

> *"The inner and central troops are still plentiful.*
> *All my granaries and royal treasuries are full."*

At that point, serving staff brought golden receptacles and placed them close to the royal group. The two princes invited their father to eat with a verse:

> *"Here is splendid food with savory dishes of heavenly taste.*
> *You are the first guest to our home. Please eat to your pleasure.*
> *This is our heavenly food, with wheat and clean accompanying dishes,*
> *complete with fruit, sweets, and snacks. Please dine."*

On this invitation, King Kāsika ate the food of many heavenly tastes and then gave his praise, saying, "This food is very delicious." When he had finished, he said to his two sons, "Please forgive me. Queen Khemā did not tell me the truth. She made me believe it was a block of wood. Though your mother and Queen Khemā were both loved by me, I told Queen Khemā to throw you away. Only later did I understand what Queen Khemā had done." After speaking thus, he asked, "Where is your mother now? Please take me to her now."

The two princes said, "We will invite her to come here."

They went to her residence to pay respect. Prince Varanujja said, "Mother, when I went after that elephant, I found he was caught by a certain king. I became angry and fought with this king. I shot an arrow but it turned into flowers. The king saw this and was amazed. He asked me, 'Whose son are you?' I told him as you had told me. He put down his sword and bow, and ran to embrace me, saying, 'I am your father.' Now he is at my residence. He wishes to meet you. I wish to invite you to go there, so I did not bring him here but came to talk to you first."

Queen Subhaddā said, "As he has traveled to this city, it is fitting that I go to pay my respect rather than he come to visit me." She got up and walked to the residence of Prince Varanujja. She went in to pay respect to her husband, embraced his feet, and lamented, "Your Majesty, while I did not see you, I survived through the power of my children, without whom I would be long dead."

Seeing Queen Subhaddā, King Kāsika was unable to control his sorrow. He embraced her, wept, and asked for her pardon, saying, "Please forgive me." The royal couple asked each other for forgiveness, back and forth. They were happily reconciled from then on.

At that time, the [Kāsika] people including courtiers and priests could not see the king and his sons. They searched around in every direction but found neither corpse, nor clothing, nor adornments. They went to tell Queen Khemā, "Your Majesty, the king was with a herd of elephants. A young man came and threatened, 'That elephant is mine,' and seized hold of it. The king and this young man shot arrows at each other. Neither found its mark. The arrow shot by the man turned into a garland of flowers, while the arrow shot by the king turned into sweets and fruit. The king and the man questioned each other for a moment and then disappeared. Whichever direction you search in, you will not find them."

Hearing this, Queen Khemā, the consorts, and governesses felt as if their feet had been cut off. They writhed around in grief beside the ocean. For this reason, the Teacher spoke a verse:[20]

20. This verse follows a pattern of repetitive description found in J538 Temiya, J546 Vidhura, and J547 Vessantara, and uses several lines from these tales (Appleton and Shaw, *Ten Great Birth Stories*, 72–73, 486-87, 550, 626–27; Faussböll, *Jātaka*, VI, 21, 300–301, 490, 579–80).

Sixteen thousand consorts, governesses, and slave girls
beat their breasts in lament: "An ogre disguised as a human
has taken the king away."
Consorts and princes, traders and brahmans,
beat their breasts in lament: "An ogre disguised as a human
has taken the king away."
Elephant drivers, army, charioteers, and infantry
beat their breasts in lament: "An ogre disguised as a human
has taken the king away."
Sixteen thousand consorts, country folk,
and city folk came together and beat their breasts in lament:
"An ogre disguised as a human has taken the king away."
Sixteen thousand consorts, governesses, and slave girls
beat their breasts in lament: "Where has the king gone?"
Consorts and princes, traders and brahmans,
beat their breasts in lament: "Where has the king gone?"
Elephant drivers, army, charioteers, and infantry
beat their breasts in lament: "Where has the king gone?"
Country folk assembled and city folk came together and
beat their breasts in lament: "Where has the king gone?"

After this lamentation, the people including Queen Khemā went out of the city to the great forest and sought around without finding him, then returned to the palace.

The seven royals, namely King Kāsika, Queen Subhaddā, the queen-in-laws, and the two princes who ruled in Sākala City, enjoyed themselves happily without thinking of their city. Prince Varanetta and Prince Varanujja went to the residence of their father and addressed him, "Your Majesty, we wish to see our city. We will go to Kāsika City."

King Kāsika acknowledged them and said, "If you truly wish to go, you must prepare the troops." The princes summoned courtiers and gave them orders in verse:[21]

"Troops of the elephant, horse, chariot, and foot divisions,
tomorrow you must prepare yourselves to assemble
on the seventh day to travel with us to Kāsika City.

21. This verse is similar to passages from J547 Vessantara and J538 Temiya (Appleton and Shaw, *Ten Great Birth Stories*, 72–73, 627; Faussböll, *Jātaka*, VI, 21–22, 579–80). The first three lines shown here were added by the Thai translator and do not appear in the Pali.

Let the citizens, priest-counselors, generals, and brahmans come,
and sixty thousand soldiers, adorned with various colors,
in white clothing, let them quickly come and assemble,
handsome to behold, adorned with various colors,
some wearing blue, some yellow,
others with red headdresses, and some in white.
Let them quickly come and assemble, adorned with various colors
just like the snowy Gandhāran mountain Gandhamādana,
which is covered with various kinds of trees
and divine plants, so it shines in all directions.
When the generals have come, let them quickly assemble,
along with elephants with girdles in gold.
The sixty thousand must ready themselves and come."

At this time, the people, including courtiers and generals, had the troops of the eighteen groups dress themselves in cloths of four colors and assemble on the seventh day. The king, his three sons, and the four royal ladies (namely, the royal mother and three daughters-in-law), surrounded by the eighteen groups of troops, left the Sākala province, crossed over the ocean through the power of the royal bow, and traveled many days and nights to reach the territory of Kāsika City.

Since the day that the king of Kāsika had disappeared, the courtiers and people of Kāsika City could not return to their city but formed themselves into an army in that territory. When they saw the troops and officers adorned in various different ways, they thought that an enemy had come. In alarm, they crowded together to watch. They saw the young troops, the four divisions, and young people like a heavenly horde. They saw the king and ascertained this was their own king, and so halted. The [other] troops also halted at that spot.

The courtiers of Kāsika came to pay respect to King Kāsika, saying, "Your Majesty, where have you been? We searched all around without finding you, and so we wept. They also informed the queen and your daughters, who wept. After you left the realm, people sought around in all directions and were distraught at not finding you. When others heard that the king had disappeared, they lamented and wept out loud."

Hearing this, King Kāsika gave orders to summon the courtiers, ministers, and slave girls of Queen Subhaddā to audience. He pointed to

Queen Subhaddā and asked, "Do you know her or not?" The generals, courtiers, and slave girls recognized her and prostrated at her feet in tears.

A daughter of Queen Khemā named Sirisobhā saw her mother had collapsed. In alarm she spoke to the governesses, who helped to revive her with water.

Then King Kāsika ordered courtiers, "Go into the city and prepare the palace for my sons and daughters-in-law." The courtiers readied three residences, then came out to inform the king, "Your Majesty, we have decorated three residences." The king took his sons and daughters-in-law along with Queen Subhaddā into the city to stay in their residences.

The consorts all came to the palace, paid respect to Queen Subhaddā, and asked, "Royal mistress, where did you go? Did you suffer from any illness?"

She replied, "The king floated me away on a raft. I floated out to the ocean, up to a certain island. Walking up from the raft, I came across a retreat, went inside, found all the monastic requisites, and became a hermit there. I was there for sixteen years. One morning when I came out of the retreat, I met a couple, man and wife, and asked where they had come from, and whose children they were. They told me they were looking for their mother. I asked what the name of their mother was. They said her name was Subhaddā, and the king of Kāsika was their father. I asked further why they had been separated. He said he had been raised by a spirit who had told him his mother called Subhaddā, a minor queen of King Kāsika, had given birth to two sons, and the major queen, called Khemā, out of jealousy had pretended that Subhaddā was inauspicious because she had given birth to a block of wood, and had a slave girl take one of the sons—meaning himself—in a chest to bury in the great forest, where he was raised by a spirit, while the other son was taken by another slave girl, floated away in a pot, and raised by a hermit. He found me and told me the same story. We three all met up and thus knew the story."

The consorts who heard this account passed it on to others. King Kāsika said, "Listen all of you, the sons of Queen Subhaddā were not a block of wood, but true humans." He pointed out the two sons. Seeing them, the people spoke among themselves, "The king has found Queen Subhaddā's two sons. They came to this city together." When the people of Sākala City knew, they spoke among themselves: "Queen Subhaddā did not give birth to a block of wood, but true humans. King Kāsika has brought Queen Subhaddā and her two sons to this city."

The slave girls of Queen Khemā were shocked when they heard the whole story. They went to inform Queen Khemā, who felt as if she would die of heartbreak. She thought, "Now I will die for sure." She could not contain her grief, and fainted immediately. Seeing this, her slave girls spoke together, concluding, "Even if Queen Khemā dies, the wrong will not disappear. Even though we had nothing to do with it, we should leave here and hide elsewhere." They ran off. Some went to tell Queen Subhaddā. Some loudly criticized all through the city what Queen Khemā had done. Queen Khemā knew all about this but lay pretending to have a fever, and did not go to court.

After seven days, when Prince Varanetta and Prince Varanujja had not seen Queen Khemā attend on the king, they asked their father, "Your Majesty, where has Queen Khemā disappeared to? We have not seen her at audience." The king sent a summons for Queen Khemā to come to audience and learned that she had a fever. He thought, "What means can I use to lure Queen Khemā?" He ordered one slave girl, "Go to Queen Khemā and tell her that the king and Queen Subhaddā are not angry. All of us have a great deal of karma attached to us from the past. The two princes have no thought of doing ill to Queen Khemā, and the two have no special power. The spirit and hermit raised them out of sympathy. Go and speak to Queen Khemā along these lines."

The slave girls went to Queen Khemā and related what the king had said. Queen Khemā was very happy at hearing this. Her fever vanished. She bathed and ate. She waited two or three days for an opportunity and then went to court and paid respect to King Kāsika and Queen Subhaddā, who presented her with heavenly adornments of great value. Queen Subhaddā said, "From this day forward, you and I will love each other as before. We forgive each other. I have no relatives, but I have much property. I will give my adornments and my wealth to your relatives. Please inform them."

Queen Khemā went to her residence, showed her relatives all the heavenly decorations and wealth, and said, "Queen Subhaddā and the king are not angry at me but have even given this treasure to my relatives. Go and fetch our relatives here." When the relatives had gathered, Queen Khemā distributed a great deal of property. Some wicked people—not relatives of Queen Khemā—who saw people receiving a great deal of property wished to have some for themselves. They gave bribes to Queen Khemā to claim they were her relatives so they could receive some property too. King Kāsika gave a great deal to everyone who came.

When he had the opportunity, King Kāsika captured those relatives who came. He had a pit dug waist-deep in the royal courtyard, had Queen Khemā's relatives sit in the pit, piled dust over them, scattered straw on top, and set it alight. When the people's skin was burnt and peeled, the king gave orders to plow over them with an iron plow, cutting those people's heads into pieces, big and small. He had the pieces fried in oil in an iron pan for Queen Khemā to eat. On top of that, he had flesh sliced from the head of Queen Khemā herself, fried in oil, and placed in her mouth to eat like eating sweets.

Queen Khemā could not bear the pain. She wept in great distress. King Kāsika had the boiling oil poured over her head, causing her death. Her relatives, about ten thousand in number, died also and were all born in the great hell. Queen Khemā was born in the Avīci hell.

King Kāsika ordered one courtier, "Have drummers go around announcing to the people that all the city folk must stop work and must help decorate the city and roads with flags, sugarcane, and banana plants, and play entertainments to their content." He ordered servants to decorate the city to be as beautiful as the Tāvatiṁsa Heaven. The people played entertainments for three months.

Prince Varanujja was anointed to rule in Kāsika City. He established Suvaṇṇagandha as his primary queen and Samuddajā, the *nāga* princess, as his second queen. King Kāsika, Prince Varanetta, and Queen Subhaddā left Kāsika City and traveled to Sākala City in a great procession, just as described above.

When they reached Sākala City, they went to the court and ruled in content. Prince Varanetta held the post of viceroy and undertook royal duties for his father and mother. He gave great donations. When his father died, he became the primary ruler, built almshouses, gave teachings to the people, and had the people established in the meditative states and precepts. The city folk who were given alms upheld the precepts and at the end of their days were reborn in the Tāvatiṁsa Heaven.

When Prince Varanetta made love with Queen Puṣapā, he had a son who was given the name of Prince Pusanetta. When he was sixteen years old and had completed his study of all the arts, his father King Varanetta entrusted the realm to him and left for the Himavanta Country, where he renounced as a rishi. He no longer followed the way of a human but perfected his wisdom and meditative attainment. At the end of his days he was reborn in the Brahma realms.

When the Great Teacher ended this teaching, he said, "O monks, I, the Tathāgata, did not help my mother through my sense of gratitude only in this birth but also when I was a bodhisatta in this way." Ending the *jātaka*, he gave the Four Noble Truths, after which eighty thousand of the followers of Buddhism achieved the way and the fruit. He then explained the birth connections: "Queen Khemā at that time was reborn as Ciñcā Mānavikā; the ogre Sīhakūṭakanta as the ogre Ālavaka;[22] Mahisakaṇṇa and the four ogre princes as the Pañcavaggiyā monks;[23] Suvaṇṇagandha as Janapada Kalyānī; Queen Kesamālī as Mahāpajāpatī; Varuṇa, king of the *nāga*, as Lord Mahānāma; Vimalā as Sumanā;[24] Prince Varanujja as Ānanda; the rishi Agginetta as the rishi Ālārudakā;[25] the spirit Pālita as Mahā Kassapa; the king of the swans as Mahā Sāriputta; the ogre Aggisikha as Mahā Moggallāna; Lord Sakka, king of the gods, as Anuruddha; King Kāsika as Siri Suddhodhana; Queen Subhaddā as Queen Mahāmāyā; Queen Puṣapā as Queen Bimbā; other people as the followers of Buddhism; and Prince Varanetta as I, the Tathāgata."

22. An ogre reformed and converted by the Buddha.
23. The five monks to whom the Buddha preached the first sermon: Kondañña, Bhaddiya, Vappa, Mahānāma, and Assaji.
24. A daughter of the king of Kosala who brought five hundred royal maidens to question the Buddha on giving.
25. In the Pali, Kālārudakā; neither is identifiable.

APPENDIX I

COLLECTIONS OF THE FIFTY JĀTAKA

Showing the tales from the Thailand National Library collection found in other collections.

		Thailand National Library	Cambodia National Library	Luang Prabang (Finot)	Yangon "Zimme"/ Chiang Mai	Wat Sung Men, Phrae
1	**Samuddaghosa**	1	1	1	6	1
2	**Sudhana**	2	2	3	11	2
3	**Sudhanu**	3	3	2	20	3
4	**Ratanapajjota**	4	4	14	23	13
5	**Sirivipulakitti**	5	5		19	30
6	**Vipula Rāja**	6	6		26	39
7	**Siri Cuḍāmaṇi**	7	7	48	17	48
8	**Candarāja**	8	8		21	
9	**Subhamitta**	9	9	5	5	
10	**Siridhara**	10	10	38	9	38
11	**Dulaka Paṇḍita**	11	12	11	2	10
12	**Āditta**	12	13	43	1	43
13	**Dukammānika**	13	14	18	46	
14	**Mahāsurasena**	14	15	47	28	47
15	**Suvaṇṇakumāra**	15	16		40	31
16	**Kanakavaṇṇarāja**	16	17			
17	**Viriyapaṇḍita**	17	18	42	25	42
18	**Dhammasoṇḍaka**	18	19			

		Thailand National Library	Cambodia National Library	Luang Prabang (Finot)	Yangon "Zimme"/ Chiang Mai	Wat Sung Men, Phrae
19	**Sudassana**	19	20		50	
20	**Vattaṅgulīrāja**	20	21		37	
21	**Porāṇakapilarāja**	21	22		43	
22	**Dhammikapaṇḍitarāja**	22	23		8	
23	**Cāgadāna**	23	24		7	
24	**Dhammarāja**	24	25			
25	**Narajīva**	25	26	27	12	26
26	**Surūpa**	26	27	44	14	44
27	**Mahāpaduma**	27	28	46	27	46
28	**Bhaṇḍāgāra**	28	29			29
29	**Bahalāgāvi**	29	30	25	33	24
30	**Seta Paṇḍita**	30	31	10	30	9
31	**Puppha**	31	32			
32	**Bārāṇasīrāja**	32	33	16	24	15
33	**Brahmaghosarāja**	33	34	36	29	36
34	**Devarukkhakumāra**	34	35			
35	**Salabha**	35	36			
36	**Siddhisāra**	36	37	28	48	27
37	**Narajiva's kathin**	37	38			
38	**Atidevarāja**	38	39			
39	**Pācittakumāra**	39	x			
40	**Sabbasiddhi**	40	11	19		18
41	**Saṅghāpatta**	41	x		10	
42	**Candasena**	42	x			
43	**Suvaṇṇa Kacchapa**	43				
44	**Sisora**	44				
45	**Varavaṃsa**	45				
46	**Arindama**	46		41	4	
47	**Rathasena**	47				

		Thailand National Library	Cambodia National Library	Luang Prabang (Finot)	Yangon "Zimme"/ Chiang Mai	Wat Sung Men, Phrae
48	**Suvannasirasa**	48				
49	**Vanāvana**	49				
50	**Bākula**	50				
51	**Sonanda**	51	x	15		14
52	**Sihanada**	52	40			
53	**Suvaṇṇasaṅkha**	53	41	6		6
54	**Surabha**	54	42			
55	**Suvaṇṇa Kacchapa**	55	44			
56	**Devandha**	56	43			
57	**Supina**	57	45			
58	**Suvannavamsa**	58	46			
59	**Varanujja**	59	47			
60	**Sirasā**	60	48	4	38	4
61	**Candagadha**	61	49	7		7

x = available in a different Cambodian collection.

Source: Fickle, "An Historical and Structural Study," 16; Terral, "Samuddaghosajātaka," 339–41; Skilling, "*Jātaka* and *Paññāsa-jātaka*," 171–73; *Chiang mai panyat chadok.*

APPENDIX II
SUMMARIES OF ALL SIXTY-ONE TALES

1. SAMUDDAGHOSA

Prince Samuddaghosa of Brahmapura, the Bodhisatta, is exceptionally handsome and talented. Hearing of his reputation, Princess Vindumatī of nearby Rammapura makes a prayer at the city-spirit shrine to become his husband. Learning of her beauty, Samuddaghosa travels to Rammapura. On seeing him, her father betroths them immediately. They worship at the city-spirit shrine in thanks. A year later, in the royal park, they nurse a wounded *vijjādhara*, who rewards them with a sword giving the power of flight. They fly to the Himavanta Forest and tour its sights. Another *vijjādhara* steals the sword, stranding them. They set off across the ocean on a log, but a storm breaks the log in two and they are parted. She reaches Maddaraṭṭha City, sells a ring, and builds a rest house decorated with murals on their story. He is rescued by the goddess Maṇi Mekhalā, who gets Indra to force the *vijjādhara* to return the sword. Samuddaghosa travels to Maddaraṭṭha, finds the rest house, and recognizes the murals. He and Vindumatī are reunited and return to rule in both their cities.

2. SUDHANA

A rival king plots to kill the *nāga* who is the source of abundance for North Pancala City, but a hunter helps to save the *nāga*. When this hunter is entranced by seven *kinnari* sisters bathing in a pond, the *nāga* lends him a *nāga*-noose with which he captures one, Manoharā. Admitting she is too beautiful to keep for himself, the hunter presents her to the king's son, Sudhana, the Bodhisatta. They are married and love each other greatly, but the king's priest-counselor plots against Sudhana. While Sudhana is away at war, his father the king has a dream. The priest-counselor claims the dream foretells great disaster, which can be averted only by sacrificing all kinds of creatures, including a *kinnari*, of which only Manoharā is available. Just before she is to be taken for sacrifice, her mother-in-law returns her wings, enabling her to escape. Before returning to her home at Mount Kelāsa, she instructs a rishi to dissuade Sudhana from following her, as the way is not for humans, but she also gives the rishi a mantra and other equipment in case Sudhana insists. Sudhana makes the epic journey, taking seven years, seven months, and seven days. Manoharā's father sets him several tests of strength and skill, including identifying Manoharā among her seven sisters, all dressed to look alike. Indra assists by transforming himself into a golden fly and flying round her head. Sudhana and Manohara are married again and return to live in the human world.

3. SUDHANU

Because the king of Bārāṇasī has no heir, Sakka sends the Bodhisatta Sudhanu down. At the moment of his birth, a horse is also born. When his father dies and Sudhanu is about to succeed, the horse abducts Sudhanu, flies up into the air, and takes him to Seta, where he helps Sudhanu get into the bedroom of the beautiful Princess Cirappa. When Sudhanu is discovered, her father holds an archery contest in which he proves he is a suitable son-in-law. After a time, Sudhanu pines for his mother. On their journey home, the horse is captured by an ogre king, and the couple are separated in a shipwreck. Cirappa reaches Indapatta and sells her jewelry to build a pavilion with murals of her relationship with Sudhanu. Sudhanu reaches the ogre realm, meets his cousin, who is a captured servant there, and makes love with her, with the ogre king's twelve daughters, and with the ogre's sister. He gets possession of his old horse and escapes. At Indapatta, he sees Cirappa's murals and they are reunited. They return to Bārāṇasī, where he becomes king. He travels to the ogre realm, persuades the ogre king to follow the precepts, and brings back all his loves.

4. RATANAPAJJOTA: THE SHINING GEM

While pregnant with the Bodhisatta, the queen of Meghavatī has a dream that predicts a massive flood. The king and queen escape on a boat, but it breaks apart and they are separated. The queen lands at Mount Canda, where Indra provides the wherewithal for an ascetic existence and where she gives birth to the Bodhisatta. One day while she is gathering fruit in the forest, the queen is captured by an ogre. The Bodhisatta finds her and offers the ogre his heart in exchange for his mother's life. After the Bodhisatta cuts out his own heart, his mother makes a prayer of truth. Impressed by the gratitude to his mother, Indra arrives to restore him to life and return mother and son to their home, where the Bodhisatta rules for a month but then leaves to become an ascetic in the Himavanta Forest.

5. SIRIVIPULAKITTI

An evil king attacks Campāka City knowing that its king will not resist because he faithfully follows the precepts. The king and already pregnant queen flee to an ascetic life in the forest near Mount Vipula. They shelter a lost hunter, who returns to Campāka and reveals their whereabouts. Troops come and take away the king. The queen gives birth to the Bodhisatta. After a time, he goes to Campāka to rescue his father, who is about to be executed. The evil king agrees to execute the Bodhisatta in place of his father, but the executioner's sword shatters to dust, all other methods of killing him fail, and the evil king is swallowed up by the earth. Father and son return to the forest to fetch the mother, but she has wasted away to death. At her cremation, the Bodhisatta lies on the pyre but again is unharmed. At her Mount Vipula retreat, he builds a village as a memorial to her.

6. KING VIPULA

King Vipula, the generous king of Sucivatti, wishes to give internal alms, meaning some form of self-sacrifice such as giving his own flesh and blood or his own wife and children, to advance his progress toward enlightenment. Sakka comes down to help him by transforming himself into a sequence of three brahmans who ask for his daughter, his wife, and his realm respectively. The gods applaud tumultuously. At the end, Sakka reveals himself and returns the gifts.

7. SIRI CUḌĀMAṆĪ

The Bodhisatta is a devout king of Bārāṇasī who wishes to give internal alms, meaning his own body, to advance his progress toward enlightenment. To assist the king in this endeavor, Lord Sakka comes disguised as a brahman with only half a body and begs for some of the king's body. When the king makes a prayer of truth, two ogres appear with a saw, and the king instructs them to saw him in half from head to feet. After the ogres complete the task, the king, who is miraculously still alive, presents one half to the brahman. Sakka puts the two pieces of the king back together and leads a great celebration in his praise.

8. KING CANDA

The Bodhisatta is born as the son of a trader in Bārāṇasī. At age sixteen, he accompanies merchants on a trading expedition by junk. At markets along the way, he buys various animals. The traders tell him he is foolish as he will waste his capital, but he disagrees. He releases all the animals at a mountain occupied by a rishi-monk. The junk is wrecked, and the Bodhisatta is rescued by the goddess Maṇī Mekhalā, who deposits him on a stone slab, where he is identified by a flower-chariot to become king of Suvaṇṇabhūmi. Various animals bring him eighty-four thousand of various articles each day as reward for him releasing one of their kind earlier. He holds another great donation, and Sakka comes down to praise him.

9. SUBHAMITTA

When his younger brother is about to launch a coup, King Subhamitta of Campā (the Bodhisatta) flees into the forest with his wife and two sons. While crossing a river, the four are separated. The two sons are brought up by fishermen. The queen is taken as a wife by a junk captain but resists his advances. Subhamitta becomes king in Takkasilā after being identified by a flower-chariot. The two sons are presented to him as royal servants, but he does not recognize them. When the junk captain visits Takkasilā, mother and sons are reunited, but Subhamitta almost has the sons executed on a misunderstanding before they are all reunited.

10. SIRIDHARA

Siridhara, the Bodhisatta, is a rich man in Bārāṇasī. When a Pacceka Buddha visits his house, he offers him food and prays that he may receive the beneficial result of this almsgiving immediately. His house is instantly replaced by a palace. Limitless celestial food appears. The gods shower him with wealth. Siridhara increases his almsgiving and is reborn after death in the heavens.

11. DULAKA PAṆḌITA

When thirty-three Buddhist monks arrive in Cina, the brahman priest-counselor, fearing the king's patronage will be transferred from the brahmans to the monks, tells the king they are robbers in disguise. The king orders the monks arrested, caned, and executed. The Bodhisatta, Dulaka Paṇḍita, son of a rich man, offers to buy their release. The king asks for the weight of each in gold. The gold donated by Dulaka's mother is enough to redeem only thirty. Mortgaging Dulaka's wife and children saves two more, leaving only a young novice. Dulaka offers himself in place of the novice. Dulaka's father returns from a trading trip just in time to redeem his son from execution. The thirty-three monks meditate to become *arahant*, then appear in the sky over the city. In alarm, the king sends for Dulaka, who calls the monks down. Their leader lectures the king on consorting with good or bad people. The king becomes a devotee, drives away the brahman priest-counselor, and appoints Dulaka as minister.

12. ĀDITTA

After a dream, the Bodhisatta, king of Jetuttara, resolves to give his own body, wife, child, or realm as internal alms. Sakka appears before him as an old brahman and asks for food. When he then throws the food on the ground, the king is unmoved. Sakka appears again as a young brahman and asks for his wife. She consents. He gives her. Sakka reveals himself and praises both of them.

13. DUKAMMĀNIKA

The Bodhisatta is advised by his merchant father not to marry a woman who has been married twice already, not to befriend a man who has disrobed three times, and not to associate with a king who makes rash decisions. After his father's death, he tests this teaching. He marries a twice-married woman, befriends a thrice-disrobed man, and traps the king's golden swan alive but tells his wife he has killed and cooked it. She informs on him to get a reward and to be free to marry a new lover. The thrice-disrobed friend takes his clothes. The king condemns him to execution without trial. On hearing this, the gatekeepers at the four city gates refuse to let the executioners take him out for execution, and each tells a story about the consequences of rash decisions: a snake that kills a child but a pet mongoose is blamed and killed, a pet hawk that saves its master from a snake bite but is killed, a princess who is speared by a man but whose pet dog is blamed and killed, and a dog that is wrongly accused of theft and killed. Summoned back to court, the Bodhisatta reveals that the golden swan is still safe, and lectures the king, who promptly offers to make him viceroy. He refuses, in keeping with his father's advice not to associate with a king who makes rash decisions, and travels to another city, where he is discovered by a flower-chariot and made king. When his former wife and former friend, now married, arrive to beg alms, he drives them away.

14. MAHĀSURASENA

King Mahāsurasena of Bārāṇasī, tired of normal almsgiving, wishes to give internal alms, meaning his own body. Learning of this, Indra appears before him as a headless mendicant. Despite the pleading of his queen and people, the king cuts off his own head to give to the mendicant. Indra reveals himself, and the king's head is restored. The Buddha gives a sermon on the benefits of offering the eight requisites and other alms to monks.

15. SUVAṆṆA KUMĀRA: THE GOLDEN PRINCE

The young Bodhisatta, born as the son of a king of Bārāṇasī, wishes to see the ocean. The royal party travels to the coast. In honor of the Bodhisatta, the *nāga* and guardian spirits of the ocean provide him with a white elephant that walks on the water so he can view the gems and other wonders in the ocean. The spirits also invite the retainers to carry away gems. The gods offer still more gems. The city is full of them. Merchants spread this news to the king of Sīhala, who threatens to attack. The Bodhisatta leads a magnificent army to Sīhala. Sakka provides him with a magical bow and arrows with which he terrifies the king and people of Sīhala. The king of Sīhala submits and is treated to a lecture on good and bad friends. The king of Sīhala travels to Bārāṇasī with the Bodhisatta in a magnificent procession. The spirits and *nāga* again provide every convenience and service as they cross the ocean. The Bodhisatta rules in Bārāṇasī as a king of immense power and splendor. All other kings gather to be lectured on the practice of dhamma, which accounts for the Bodhisatta's splendor.

16. KING KANAKAVAṆṆA

The king's priest-counselor predicts a terrible drought in Kanakavatī twelve years hence. King Kanakavaṇṇa orders everyone to plant and store rice, which he buys and keeps in granaries. When the drought comes, stores are soon exhausted and people die of starvation. In the palace, the queen cooks the last coconut-shell of rice for the king. A Paccekka Buddha, seeing the pitiful state of the world, resolves to help the king-Bodhisatta along the path to Buddhahood. He appears before the king to beg alms. The king gives him his last meal. Great clouds appear and pour down not only rain but flowers, food, clothing, and wealth.

17. VIRIYA PAṆḌITA

The king of Mahāraṭṭha has a Buddha image inscribed on a gold sheet and sent to the king of Pañcāla in the hope of curing his wrong thinking. Miracles occur as the image crosses the sea. The recipient king is inspired to devotion, orders the carving of a Buddha image from sandalwood, and invites people to cover it with gold leaf. A pauper, Viriya Paṇḍita, the Bodhisatta, plans to sell himself to pay for gold leaf. His wife implores him to sell her and their child instead, which he does. On arrival at the image pavilion, Viriya Paṇḍita is told he must wait for the king to affix gold leaf first. Viriya Paṇḍita attends on the king and asks permission to go ahead. To tease him, the king tells Viriya Paṇḍita to ask the Buddha image and obey the response. After Viriya Paṇḍita makes a prayer, Indra and the gods invest the image and make it respond, giving permission. He affixes gold but does not have enough to complete the job. He makes another prayer for someone who can convert his flesh to gold. Indra appears as a goldsmith who promises to do so. Viriya Paṇḍita cuts off own flesh, which Indra converts into gold leaf that is used to complete the task. On death, Viriya Paṇḍita goes to the heavens and after many more lives is reborn as Gotama Buddha and achieves enlightenment.

18. DHAMMASOṆḌAKA

The king of Bārāṇasī offers a reward for anyone who can teach him the dhamma. When no such teacher can be found, he wanders in the forest. Indra appears as an ogre and offers to teach the dhamma in return for being allowed to eat the king's flesh. They haggle over which should happen first, the teaching or the eating. Indra proposes that the king leap from a mountain into his mouth, and he will teach him the dhamma during the descent. The king agrees. When the king leaps, Indra catches him in his arms, takes him to the heavens, teaches him the dhamma, tells him he will be Gotama Buddha in the future, and then returns him to the human world and restores him to his kingdom.

19. SUDASSANA

The Bodhisatta, son of a rich man in Bārāṇasī, comes upon an ascetic monk in the forest. Seing an opportunity to make merit, he builds a hut for the monk, provides all the monastic requirements, and supports him throughout his life. After death, the Bodhisatta is reborn as King Sudassana of Kusāvatī and is blessed with eighty-four thousand of everything as the beneficial result of his services to the ascetic in the previous life. His city prospers and he enjoys enormous longevity.

20. KING VAṬṬAṄGULĪ

King Pasenadi of Kosala asks the Buddha's permission to make a Buddha image to be worshiped when he is not there. The Buddha consents. On completion the king asks about the reward for making a Buddha image, and hence the Buddha relates a past life. A merchant who repairs the damaged finger of a Buddha image is reborn as the Bodhisatta, a prince of Bārāṇasī, with a powerful finger. After he succeeds as King Vaṭṭaṅgulī and rules by the precepts, the city is attacked by a massive army led by 101 rulers who believe he will not resist. The king only points his finger and they are routed. The king, able to remember the past life, explains the origin of his power. The Buddha explains the rewards of making or repairing Buddha images.

21. THE KING OF OLD KAPILA

The Buddha lectures Sāriputta on the beneficial results of producing the teachings of the Buddha, describing the enormous benefits not just for writing but also for supplying the paper, pen, bookends, oil lamp, and other materials. The Buddha then tells a story of the past about a noble in old Kapila who had the teachings written down and was reborn as a prince-Bodhisatta who had whatever he wanted in terms of property, places, and attributes.

22. KING DHAMMIKA PAṆḌITA

King Dhammika Paṇḍita of Bārāṇasī makes a great almsgiving, prompting Sakka to come down and conduct him up to Tāvatiṁsa Heaven. Sakka explains that the occupants of the splendid heavenly palaces are there as reward for performing various services for the religion, including making Buddha images and feeding monks. The king chooses to return to the human world in order to earn merit in the same way. He describes the heavens to his people and advises them to make merit.

23. CĀGADĀNA: THE GREAT GIVING

In a long story of the present, Moggallāna gives a sermon that induces the queen of Ajita and sixteen thousand consorts to offer him expensive cloths just given them by the king, who is currently away at war. Phra Moggallāna flies back to the Buddha with the cloth all floating behind him. When the king returns from war and asks after the missing cloth, he is overjoyed to hear what happened. He invites the Buddha, who teaches him on the fruit of almsgiving. The king, queen, and consorts offer him cloth, which floats behind him on his return to the monastery, to the astonishment of the monks. The Buddha tells them this is not unique, and thus tells the *jātaka*.

A bodhisatta who sees a robber stripping the robes from a Pacceka Buddha rushes to fashion a temporary covering from leaves while he makes his own clothes into a robe. The Bodhisatta prays for a beneficial result, and the Pacceka Buddha gives his blessing. Divine wind blows leaves into thousands of pieces of cloth. Sakka throws down a cloth that multiplies into thousands of pieces that fall at the Bodhisatta's feet. He offers all the cloth to the Pacceka Buddha, but the pieces float behind the Bodhisatta on his return home. Seeing this wonder, the king and court shower him with gifts.

24. DHAMMARĀJA

Realizing all property is the result of past karma, King Dhammarāja of Jambūdīpa builds a pavilion, distributes alms, and prays this will help him toward enlightenment. Sakka comes down, takes him to the heavens, and invites him to stay. The king declines on grounds that only self-made merit has true benefit, and returns to the human world.

25. NARAJĪVA

Narajīva the Bodhisatta is born in a poor family in Bārāṇasī. After his father dies, he grows rice. During harvest, his mother is bitten to death by a snake. Sakka appears as a brahman who undertakes to revive Narajīva's mother in return for the son's heart. After Narajīva cuts out his heart and dies, his revived mother makes a prayer of truth for his life. Narajīva revives. Sakka reveals himself.

26. SURŪPA

King Surūpa of Indapattha, the Bodhisatta, becoming aware of impermanence, wishes to hear the dhamma but cannot find a teacher, however much he offers. Sakka appears as an ogre, offering to teach the dhamma in return for a meal of human flesh. Before the king can offer himself, the queen offers herself. Sakka feigns eating her, then announces he is not full. The king's son offers himself. When Sakka announces he is still not full, the king promises to offer himself after the teaching. The ogre gives a lecture on the four wrong courses, then Sakka reveals himself and returns the king's wife and son.

27. MAHĀPADUMA

When a rival king brings an army to seize his queen, the king of Aṅgavatī refuses to fight and leaves for the forest. The queen prefers to accompany him rather than be left as a "widow." On the journey, their raft splits apart and they are separated, but she makes a prayer of truth that reunites them. Sakka provides a hut and the wherewithal for an ascetic life. She does all the work. He dies of sickness. Their son, the Bodhisatta, is born. While collecting food in the forest, she is bitten to death by a cobra. The Bodhisatta prays to offer his body in exchange for his mother. Sakka arrives disguised as a brahman and tells him she will revive if the son cuts out his own heart and puts it in his mother's mouth. She revives and makes a prayer for her son, and Sakka revives him too.

28. BHAṆḌĀGĀRA: THE TREASURER

The Bodhisatta is born to the queen of Mithilā. Sakka sets the king ten questions with a deadline of seven years, seven months, and seven days, and a penalty of death for failure. He cannot answer, nor can the queen. In anger he orders the royal treasurer to execute her. Instead the treasurer shelters her and the Bodhisatta, born soon after, in his own house. At the expiry of the deadline, the king is desperate to find someone to answer the questions. The seven-year-old Bodhisatta volunteers. The eleven questions are on the basics of Buddhism (What is one but not two? —Mount Meru; etc.). At each correct answer, Indra and gods rain down flowers, the people cheer, and the king presents the Bodhisatta with more wealth, eventually giving the whole kingdom. At the end, Sakka appears and grants the Bodhisatta four wishes. He wishes to uphold the precepts and rejoice in giving. The treasurer reveals that the Bodhisatta is the king's own son. The king is reunited with the queen, and the treasurer is rewarded.

29. BAHALĀGĀVĪ

When a cow, the Bodhisatta, is cropping grass in the forest, a tiger proposes to eat her. The cow begs to be allowed to feed her calf first, promising to return. The tiger consents. The cow returns to her calf, who insists on being eaten by the tiger in place of the mother. When the tiger hears the calf's plea to be eaten instead, the tiger announces that he will eat neither of them. Lord Sakka installs all three in the heavens as reward for this display of sincerity, forbearance, gratitude, and appreciation of the virtue of others. The Buddha repeats this sentiment in a longer sermon, detailing the benefits that accrue to those who display these four virtues.

30. SETA PAṆḌITA

In Bārāṇasī, the Bodhisatta is born as a white mouse that observes the precepts, bringing great wealth to its brahman owner's household. After a quarrel the mouse flees to the forest, and the brahman's wealth ebbs away. The mouse returns to find the brahman destitute and homeless. He instructs the brahman to sell him in the royal court. The king agrees to a high price, which restores the brahman's wealth. The mouse becomes a teacher of the dhamma. To test him, Indra appears and asks for his flesh. The mouse throws himself into a pit of burning charcoal but is caught by a giant lotus. Indra takes him on a visit to the Tāvatiṁsa Heaven.

31. PUPPHA

When Usabha, an elder, visits Visāla, King Vijaya offers him scented water to bathe, washes the monk's feet, and makes a prayer to have a great reward, including becoming a Buddha in the future, in return for this act. In his next life he is reborn as Prince Puppha of Siribhanda. On the day he is being anointed as king, a gem elephant, gem woman, and gem general appear along with many offerings as a result of the merit of bathing the monk. He lectures the 101 attending kings on devotional practice. The Buddha confirms the immense benefits that accrue in later lives as a result of simple acts of merit-making, such as bathing a monk.

32. THE KING OF BĀRĀṆASĪ

A woman prays to be reborn in all future births as a male with her husband as her brother. After several births, the pair are born as swans with two heads and their bodies fused. A hunter captures them and presents them to the king of Bārāṇasī. The queen wants to split them apart. A courtier achieves this by inducing the couple to distrust one another, argue, and fight. When the king hears how the division was achieved, he is distraught that this was done to a loving couple. The courtier is banished. The king lectures his people on the importance of friendship, trust, and thoughtfulness. After several more lives, he becomes the Buddha and, remembering his earlier life in Bārāṇasī, gives sermons on the same theme.

33. KING BRAHMAGHOSA

King Brahmaghosa, the Bodhisatta, rules well in Kusuma. To test him, Sakka comes down from the heavens with his charioteer disguised as a dog and himself as the dog owner. When the dog barks, Sakka suggests the king feed him rice. After he barks a second time, he suggest the king get others to feed him rice. After the rice is exhausted and the dog barks a third time, Sakka suggests the king feed all unrighteous people to the dog. After that is done, the dog falls quiet, and Sakka gives a sermon stating that the king should feed sinful and unrighteous people to the dog. Sakka makes a thousand celestial palaces full of *apsara* maidens appear in the sky and gives a second sermon, stating that those who live a righteous life will go to these palaces.

34. DEVARUKKHA KUMĀRA

Devarukkha Kumāra, the Bodhisatta, is a poor man in Purinda. While in the forest collecting grass and firewood to sell, the Bodhisatta comes across a Buddha image at the foot of a tree. He worships the image and prays for good fortune. A poor widow comes across the same image and prays to be married to a bodhisatta. They meet and are married. Sakka sends down Vissukamma to make a residence for them. People and animals appear in thousands for them. The king is at first angry and then impressed at the fruit of their merit. The Bodhisatta teaches the king on the fruits of merit-making.

35. SALABHA: THE GRASSHOPPER

When a crow is about to eat a worm, the worm says the crow must first answer four questions, and if his answers are wrong and he still tries to eat the worm, the crow's head will break into seven pieces. After the crow gives his answers, the worm gets the crow to ferry him to the Buddha at the Jeta Grove. The Buddha gives different answers to the questions, and the crow agrees not to eat the worm. The Buddha then tells a similar story of when he was a bodhisatta born of a merchant family and living as a hermit. A *garuḍa* planned to eat a grasshopper but the grasshopper put the same conditions, the hermit showed the *garuḍa*'s answers were wrong, and the *garuḍa* agreed not to eat the grasshopper. The hermit's answers explain the excellence of the Buddhist path toward *nibbāna*.

36. SIDDHISĀRA

Siddhisāra the Bodhisatta, son of the queen, and Puññasāra, son of a rich man, are expelled from Bārāṇasī for rowdy behavior. Along the road they meet two tree spirits, who recognize their merit and advise them how to find various magical articles. Siddhisāra goes to Mithila, where he is discovered by a flower-chariot and made king. Puññasāra goes to Kusumapura and is married to a princess. When her father discovers that jewels spill from Puññasāra's mouth, they take him to the royal park and poison him. Three ogres plan to eat him, but another tree spirit recognizes his merit and tells the ogres to give him magical articles. When he returns to the city, his father-in-law plays another trick to steal the articles and strand Puññasāra in the forest. Another tree spirit gives him magical fruits. He goes to Mithila, is reunited with Siddhisāra, and succeeds him.

37. NARAJĪVA'S KAṬHINA

Narajīva, the Bodhisatta, is born into a poor family in Haṃsāvati. When hired to guard a merchant's rice fields, he advises the merchant to give alms to earn merit. Among the merchant's four friends, only one agrees, while the others are not interested. When the two make offerings of *kaṭhina* robes to the Padumuttara Buddha, a boy, girl, and rich man also join in. Narajīva becomes wealthy and on death goes to the Tusita Heaven. The merchant is reborn as a spirit of the place at Mount Gandhamādana. The three who refused to join the *kaṭhina* are reborn as a tiger, a kingfisher, and an ogre. The friend who helped in the *kaṭhina* is reborn as a merchant but with a deformed body. He meets his old friend, now the spirit of the place, who gives him seven jewels that enable him to grow wealthy. He marries the beautiful daughter of a rich man. Other jealous men tell her father that his new son-in-law grew rich by theft and abduct him to the Himavanta Forest. There he again meets his old friend, now the spirit of the place, who gives him two branches from a magic tree. By eating one, he loses his deformity and becomes handsome. He returns to his wife and tricks those who abducted him into eating the other branch, which turns them into monkeys. He becomes rich and famous. The spirit of the place is reborn as Sakka.

38. KING ATIDEVA

King Vicitra of Aññavatī invites the Koṇḍañña Buddha to spend the rains retreat in his royal park and summons people from all over the Jambu Continent to make a massive *kaṭhina*. The king makes a wish to become a Buddha in the future, and the Koṇḍañña Buddha predicts that he will become Gotama. When he is later reborn as King Atideva of Kusāvatī, equipped with all the gem elements, he gives alms in all four continents. He enjoys many fine rebirths before achieving enlightenment as Gotama. The Buddha explains that this was the result of the *kaṭhina*.

39. PRINCE PĀCITTA

The Bodhisatta, Prince Pācitta of Brahmabandhu, rejects all candidates for marriage and sets off to seek a partner himself. As the astrologer predicts, in Bārāṇasī he comes upon a heavily pregnant lady plowing a paddy field and sheltered by a parasol. He offers to plow the fields in return for the hand of her daughter, Arabimba. Sixteen years later they are married. When Pācitta returns to visit his parents, the prince of Bārāṇasī seizes his beautiful wife. When Pācitta comes in search of her, she kills the prince with his own sword, and Sakka helps them escape to a forest. A hunter shoots Pācitta dead and abducts Arabimba, but she kills the hunter with his own sword. Sakka provides her with some medicine that brings Pācitta back to life. While the couple are crossing a river, a novice abducts Arabimba, but she tricks him into climbing a tree while she escapes. By a prayer of truth, she makes her breasts disappear and takes on the appearance of a man. At Campāka City, she uses the medicine given by Sakka to bring the king's daughter back to life, refuses the king's offer of his daughter and realm, is ordained as a monk, and becomes the city's patriarch. She has a pavilion constructed and decorated with paintings of her story with Pācitta. He arrives and sees the paintings. The patriarch tells him he must be ordained as a monk in order to find his wife. After a time the patriarch reveals the truth to Pācitta and makes a prayer of truth for her breasts to reappear. They disrobe and return to rule in Brahmabandhu.

40. SABBASIDDHI

When kings flock to ask for the hand of his beautiful daughter, the king of Siribhaja tells them to queue up to talk to her through the night and promises to give her to the first one who gets her to reply. All fail. The Bodhisatta, born as a prince of Alika, goes to Takkasilā to study how to remove a heart and replace it. Hearing of the beautiful princess, he travels to Siribhaja and is given the same challenge. He takes a courtier up into her palace, removes the courtier's heart, and addresses four riddles to the heart. The first riddle asks which of four men who contribute to saving a queen should become her husband. When the courtier's heart offers one answer, the princess speaks up and offers a different answer. The three subsequent riddles produce a similar result. At the last, where the question is, "which feels softer, kapok or a woman," the courtier's heart answers "kapok," but the princess interjects, "A husband who has a soft heart without any hardness feels softer than either kapok or a woman." The Bodhisatta and the princess are married. They return to Alika to reign.

41. SAṄGHĀPATTA

The Bodhisatta is born as a prince in Yasa and is named because of a mark like a conch on his palm. After an exchange of pictures on gold plate, he is betrothed to his cousin, a princess of Lomāna. En route there, he is shipwrecked. A companion survives and returns to Yasa with the news. Omens tell that the Bodhisatta will survive. Another companion reaches Lomāna, where the news causes great distress, especially to the betrothed princess, who attempts suicide. The Bodhisatta reaches land. A brahman addicted to gambling steals two betrothal rings from the Bodhisatta and puts out his eyes. The Bodhisatta is found and cared for by two hunters. Later he is discovered by the princess and identified by the conch on his palm. Her father presents the princess to the Bodhisatta. Through a misunderstanding, he doubts her loyalty. After the princess makes a prayer of truth about her devotion to the Bodhisatta, one of his eyes reappears. When he makes a prayer of truth that he was not angry at the brahman, the other eye reappears. The brahman has been captured and blinded, but the Bodhisatta makes another prayer of truth that restores his sight. The Bodhisatta rewards the two hunters. He is married to his cousin, and they rule in Lomāna.

42. CANDASENA

When the Bodhisatta, a pauper, comes across a Buddha image damaged by rainfall, he repairs it with clay. To decorate the image with gold leaf, his wife agrees to be sold into slavery. At the end of his life, the Bodhisatta is taken by the gods to Tusita heaven, and is subsequently reborn as Prince Candasena in Bārāṇasī. At age sixteen, he rejects all potential brides and sets out on his own search. Meanwhile Princess Upalava of Ambaṅga is pining for a husband. Her father designs an archery contest, which all suitors fail. A hunter tells Candasena of the contest and lends him a bow. He succeeds. He and the princess are married. After some blissful time, they travel to visit his parents. An ogre accosts them. Candasena promises to return and be eaten after visiting his parents. On seeing the Bodhisatta's splendor, the ogre renounces flesh eating. Candasena rules well. In old age he renounces and goes to the Himavanta Forest.

43. SUVAṆṆA KACCHAPA: THE GOLDEN TURTLE

The Bodhisatta is born as a giant turtle with a golden shell living in the ocean. When five hundred merchants are shipwrecked, he ferries them to an island. Seeing they are weak from lack of food, he suggests they kill him, roast his flesh to eat, and use the shell as a boat to escape. The merchants refuse. The turtle climbs up a mountain and hurls himself down. As he begged in a prayer, his flesh is split into pieces but the shell is intact. The merchants feed on his flesh and sail home to Bārāṇasī in the shell. The king erects the golden shell as a monument.

44. SISORA

King Sisora of Ananta, the Bodhisatta, is a great king. When he has a dream, brahmans predict the planet Saturn will cause him trouble. The king flies into a temper and departs alone for the Himavanta Forest. Because of karma made in the past, his crown turns into a basket, which some peasants believe he has stolen from them. Similar things happen with his sword and horse. Each time he is beaten up. He takes refuge in a temple, where the monks nurse him back to health. He begs to be ordained there. While dyeing his robes outside the temple, he is again mistaken for a thief and beaten up but is rescued and nursed by the monks. He travels further and stays overnight in an old couple's house, but his jewels turn into seeds stolen from the couple. He becomes a mendicant in Acala City. When priests predict that the king of Acala's daughter will marry a pauper, the king has her expelled to live outside the city. She meets the Bodhisatta and there is mutual attraction because of a relationship in previous lives. She tests him by seeing how he eats food and how he responds to her slave girls' flirtation, and realizes he is high born. They become a couple. She becomes pregnant and gives birth to a son. Her father is captivated by the grandson but plots to get rid of the father, Sisora. Once they meet and talk, however, the king realizes his quality, and Sisora reveals his identity. Now that his karma has improved, his crown, sword, and horse return to their old form and are returned by the peasants. Sisora pardons the peasants who beat him and rewards the monks who helped him. Sisora and his queen return to his capital to rule.

45. VARAVAṂSA

Varavaṃsa, the Bodhisatta, and his elder brother Vaṃsuriyāmāsa, sons of the king of Bhūsa, are condemned to execution through the machinations of the king's minor wife and her son. Their mother bribes the executioner to enable them to escape. They eat two magic cocks who promise to give them excecptional powers. At Ayamā, where the reigning king has just died, Vaṃsuriyāmāsa is identified as the successor by a flower-chariot. Varavaṃsa gets separated from him and is captured by a rich trader who robs him and plans to kill him, but he is saved by the trader's daughter, Gāravī. The trader takes him to Khura, where he kills an ogre terrorizing the city, marries the king's daughter Makuṭa, and becomes king. The guardian spirits give him a jewel for flying. He takes Gāravī to go in search of his brother, but they are robbed by a rishi, chased by an ogre, and then shipwrecked and separated on the ocean. Varavaṃsa arrives in Ayamā, where his brother has made a pavilion with paintings showing their story, and they are reunited. He returns to Bhusā to fetch Makuṭa. Meanwhile in the forest, Gāravī is nearly shot by a hunter and then suspected of adultery by the hunter's wife, who maltreats her and tries to sell her as a slave. When Gāravī gives birth to a son, the hunter's wife tosses the son away, but luckily he is discovered by courtiers from Ayamā. Gāravī eventually finds the same pavilion and is reunited with her son and husband. Varavaṃsa and Vaṃsuriyāmāsa return to Bhusā with a massive army. They kill the son of the evil minor wife, who poisons herself. They rebuke their father for his bad judgment but forgive him and are reunited with their mother.

46. ARINDAMA

King Arindama of Sucīravatī resolves to give internal alms. Sakka comes disguised as a mendicant brahman to help him perfect his merit. To the people's dismay, the king hands over the realm to the brahman and leaves the city. Sakka appears as another brahman who asks for their carriage and horse. Finally the king sells himself and the queen into slavery to give alms. While staying in the porch of a rich man's house, the queen delivers a stillborn son. The rich man's wife throws her out at midnight with rain falling. She begs the gatekeeper for help. Arindama, who is the gatekeeper, initially refuses until he recognizes her. To revive their son, the king makes a prayer of truth, recounting his observation of the precepts. The son stirs. The queen also makes a prayer of truth, citing her acceptance of being sold for alms, and the son revives. Sakka reveals himself and returns the family to rule in Sucīravatī.

47. RATHASENA

A rich man who is ruined after having twelve daughters abandons them in a forest. They are adopted by an ogress, Sandhāmāra, but escape to Kutāra. After they are found in a banyan tree, emitting a golden aura, the king of Kutāra makes all of them his queens. Sandhāmāra enraptures the king, is made his major queen, and persuades him to pluck out the twelve queens' eyes, leaving only the youngest with sight in one eye. The eleven others become pregnant. Sakka sends down the Bodhisatta Rathasena to be conceived by the youngest. The king has all twelve imprisoned in a cave. When the eleven give birth, they share their babies' flesh as food. The youngest gives birth to Rathasena. On growing up, Rathasena appeals to Sakka to provide them with cloth and ornaments and to teach him to gamble.

To feed the twelve, Rathasena gambles—first with cowherds and later with the king. When the king learns that this remarkable boy is his own son, Sandhāmāra maneuvers to have him sent to the ogre realm carrying a note instructing her daughter to eat him. On the way Rathasena meets a rishi, who changes the note. On Rathasena's arrival, the ogress's daughter falls in love with him, and he is anointed with her to rule the realm. After a dalliance, he takes her to the royal park, gets her drunk, learns from her the means to restore the sight of the twelve sisters, and escapes. On failing to follow him, the ogress's daughter dies of a broken heart. On seeing him return, the ogress Sandhāmāra dies of defeat. Rathasena restores sight to the twelve, who again become queens.

48. SUVAṆṆASIRASA: THE GOLDEN HEAD

The Bodhisatta is born in a poor family in Bārāṇasī, and his father dies before his birth. In the womb, he determines to conceal his beautiful golden body inside his head and is thus born as a golden head. When his mother goes herding, he emerges from the head and does the chores and cooking. At age seven, he persuades his mother to borrow money from the headman and departs on a trading voyage. Spotting a sandy island, he asks to be put off there. Two *nāga* girls who playfully damage his garden compensate him with great wealth. The traders pick him up on the way back. Aged sixteen, he wishes to marry a princess. The king sets a test for the Bodhisatta to prove his merit by building a golden bridge, which he does through a prayer of truth and help from Sakka. The king's first two daughters refuse him, but the third agrees. After some time, a minister proposes that the Bodhisatta is an unsuitable royal son-in-law and should be executed or banished. The king agrees. Sakka comes down, poses four riddles to the king, and promises death if someone does not answer them and play polo with him in the skies within seven days. At the last minute, after being reminded of the Bodhisatta's earlier act of merit, the king sends for the Bodhisatta, who extracts his body from the head, answers the riddles, and plays polo with Indra. The king presents him with the realm.

49. VANĀVANA

When Valikā, first queen of King Komala of Koṭi, gives birth to the Bodhisatta, the jealous second queen has the child buried in the forest, shows the king a log of wood, and tells him that Valikā gave birth to this log. The king sends Valikā to be a kitchen slave. The second queen gives birth to a son destined to succeed. Valikā's son is rescued and brought up by a tree spirit under the name Vanāvana. When the boy is seven, the tree spirit relates his origins and advises him to study the arts with a rishi. On his way to Koṭi, he is captured by an ogre couple but escapes being eaten by teaching them the dhamma. At the next city, Kāsikaraṭha, where the king has just died, he is discovered by a flower-chariot, anointed as king, and adopted by the dowager queen. The jealous chief priest lures him up a mountain and throws him into a ravine, but he is rescued by two spirits. Resuming his journey, he drinks from a lake owned by a *kinnara*, who imprisons him for three years. He is released when the *kinnara* can find no one else to teach the dhamma, and the Bodhisatta gives a sermon on the benefits of observing the precepts. He is married to the *kinnara's* daughter, Suvaṇṇagīrī. The *kinnara* equips him with wings to continue his journey with Suvaṇṇagīrī. While staying with a rishi on the way, their wings are burned when the rishi's hut catches fire. They continue on foot and are separated when chased by an ogre, but meet again at another rishi's hut. They reach Kāsikaraṭha again. Suvaṇṇagīrī infiltrates the court as a singer in order to contact the dowager queen. The chief priest who threw him down the ravine is punished and Vanāvana becomes ruler again. He goes to Koṭi and is reunited with his mother, Valikā. Suvaṇṇagīrī and the dowager queen send three riddles to King Komala. The Bodhisatta answers them correctly, takes his mother to Kāsikaraṭha, and returns to attack Koṭi with a great army and many supportive spirits. He defeats his half-brother in an elephant duel and tells King Komala about the deceit over his birth. The king executes the rival queen. The Bodhisatta relates three stories emphasizing that bad deeds always have consequences, and returns to rule in Kāsikaraṭha.

50. BĀKULA

The Bodhisatta is born in Bārāṇasī to a rich man in decline. At death, his father tells him to keep his skull and use it to identify a plot of land to till. The skull identifies a piece of unpromising upland, but Indra comes to help clear it. When the Bodhisatta pines for a wife, Indra sends down a divine lady, who is born as a daughter of King Sattakuṭa. When she is fifteen, Sakka places her in the Bodhisatta's hut in a giant egg. He discovers her and they live happily. After seeing her beauty, the village headman encourages the king of Bārāṇasī to acquire her. The king sets a series of contests where the winner will get the wife, but she produces from her egg a fighting cock, horse, and elephant that enable Bākula to defeat the king's contestants. The king sends a spy who discovers she is allergic to egg and then tricks the Bodhisatta into eating egg. She has to leave Bākula and return to Sattakuṭa. He follows after her, assisted by divine relatives descending from heaven. At Sattakuṭa, her father the king sets Bākula a series of tests, which he passes with help from Sakka. They return to Bārāṇasī to take revenge on the king and village headman, and then reign there.

51. SONANDA

In Bārāṇasī, a rich man and poor man get into a dispute over things borrowed and not returned. When asked to adjudicate, the king orders the rich man's son to marry the poor man's daughter. One day, the husband makes an unfair accusation against the wife. She makes a prayer of truth that her child be born through her mouth. Sakka arranges this and has the child, Padumāvatī, brought up by a rishi in the Himavanta Forest. When the Bodhisatta, Prince Sonanda of Bārāṇasī, comes to hunt deer, a tree spirit arranges for him to meet Padumāvatī. They make love. After a few days, Sonanda returns to Bārāṇasī to tell his parents, who go to the forest to ask the rishi for his daughter's hand. The couple are married. Kālakaṇṇī, who is married to Sonanda's brother but would prefer Sonanda, kills her own husband with poison, maneuvers to have Padumāvatī exiled on suspicion of being a water spirit, and marries Sonanda. By another prayer of truth, Padumāvatī conjures up a garden in the forest and a pavilion with two talking parakeets. When the royal party comes to visit, the parakeets reveal Padumāvatī's origins and Kālakaṇṇī's plot. Kālakaṇṇī confesses, poisons herself, and goes to hell. Padumāvatī and Sonanda are married. When the king finds a white hair and decides to renounce, they inherit the realm. When Sonanda later finds a white hair, he and Padumāvatī follow suit.

52. SĪHANĀDA

Suñbhāgī is the daughter of a Brahmavati merchant fallen on hard times. After her parents die, she begs land from the headman to plant rice. Sakka has an elephant trample her fields so that she will give chase, drink water from the elephant's footprint, and thus become pregnant with the Bodhisatta. When Suñbhāgī and the young Bodhisatta are digging a pond, an ogre threatens to eat them. The Bodhisatta quells the ogre and makes him promise to stop eating humans. Impressed by the Bodhisatta's power, Suñbhāgī names him Sīhanāda (lion's roar). At age fifteen, Sīhanāda sets off to find his elephant father. Along the way, he challenges two strong fellows to a trial of strength and recruits them as companions. They come across an ogre who, once subdued, begs to be released from rebirth as an ogre. The Bodhisatta lectures him to uphold the precepts. The ogre gives him a walking stick that can kill or bring back to life. With this, they kill the ogre, open his stomach, and return life to the bones of humans and animals that the ogre had eaten. Traveling onward they reach two cities, each deserted because of a marauding ogre, whom they kill; then they revive the victims' bones in the same way. Leaving his companions to rule these two cities, Sīhanāda travels to Bārāṇasī, where the king has pacified an ogre for fifteen years by feeding him condemned criminals and recent corpses but has now run out of supply. The king's daughter intends to give herself to the ogre to save her father. The Bodhisatta rescues her and discovers this is the same ogre that he had encountered as a child. He lectures him to follow the precepts so that he may be reborn better, then kills him with the walking stick, and revives the bones of the ogre's prey. The princess offers herself in marriage, but the Bodhisatta insists he is too low-born. The king of Bārāṇasī marries them and entrusts them with the kingdom. His birthplace, Brahmavati, and the territories ruled by his old companions become his dependencies.

53. SUVAṆṆASAṄKHA: THE GOLDEN CONCH

The king of Brahmapura has two queens. After a seer predicts that Queen Candā Devī will have a beautiful son, her jealous rival queen and an evil minister maneuver to have her driven away from Brahmapura. The Bodhisatta, conceived by Candā Devī, decides to be born in a golden conch. When his mother sees his golden body outside the shell, she smashes the shell. Hearing about his son, the king has them brought back, but the rival queen and minister maneuver to have them expelled again. The raft on which they are floated away breaks up in a storm, and they are separated. His mother reaches the shore and becomes a cook for a rich man. After help from a *nāga* and a rishi, the Bodhisatta is adopted and brought up by a doting ogress queen. In her palace, he finds magic shoes and a negrito suit, which he uses to escape. The ogress chases after him and dies of a broken heart when he refuses to return. Still dressed in the ugly negrito suit, the Bodhisatta becomes a cowherd for a village headman. He wins a contest for the hand of a princess of Bārāṇasī. Six rival sons-in-law conspire to have the king execute him, but he survives due to his superior merit and some mantras given him earlier by the doting ogress. Sakka intervenes, threatening the king with death unless he or his delegate can answer two questions and win a polo game against Indra in the sky. The Bodhisatta performs the tasks and removes the negrito suit in the process. He is anointed king and reunited with his mother. Hearing of the splendor of Bārāṇasī under his rule, his father invites him back to Brahmapura. The rival queen and evil minister trick another king into attacking Brahmapura, but the Bodhisatta defeats them, helped by a magic sword he fetches from his ogress stepmother in the heavens. He rules justly in Brahmapura.

54. SURABBHA

Surabbha the Bodhisatta, elder son of the king of Theyya, renounces and leaves for the Himavanta Forest. At a lake he protects the fish and turtles against fishermen. He resolves a case where two men have brought false accusations against each other. To instruct the two men, he starts telling stories to show the importance of consorting with good people. A self-exiled king travels with a strong man, judge, goldsmith, and learned man who help him overcome difficulties. The judge resolves a case of deception. The learned man finds the weight of an elephant. A flower-chariot identifies the learned man as the next king, but he installs another king instead.

The Bodhisatta then introduces another set of stories about a junkmaster on a trading expedition who finds an ingenious way to recover the merchants' property and helps the king to avoid attack by answering riddles. After the junkmaster's death, his son returns to the same city, unravels a web of false accusations, answers yet more riddles on behalf of the king, marries the king's daughter, and succeeds him.

The Bodhisatta then tells of a dancing girl who avoids the violent attentions of a cruel prince by telling him moral tales all night, including one with the same plot as P40 Sabbasiddhi, another about a queen bringing her dead husband back to life, another about an errant king who is saved from the machinations of prostitutes by a loyal courtier, and another about a prince who becomes a robber in order to be reunited with his estranged father. The meaning of all the dancing girl's stories is that a king should associate only with good and clever people. At the end of the night of storytelling, the cruel prince makes the dancing girl his queen and rules well from then on.

The Bodhisatta now continues on his journey to the Himavanta but is waylaid by another case where two men steal from each other and call on him to give judgment. After this, he finally reaches the Himavanta, where Sakka provides him with a retreat. Nearby, a crow tries to catch a golden crab. The crab challenges the crow to answer twenty questions on what is the most insufferable, happy, needy, beautiful, ugly, big, high, hot, cool, fine, dark, bright, fragrant, foul-smelling, strong, distant, fast, excellent, substantial, and delicious thing. The crow gives answers mostly about eating, displaying his real interest in the crab. The crow and crab seek out Surabha, who gives answers illustrating the dhamma.

55. SUVAṆṆAKACCHAPA: THE GOLDEN TURTLE (2)

In Rājagaha, the Bodhisatta is born as a golden turtle that is adopted by a childless old couple. From his knowledge of astrology, the turtle predicts a flood and advises the couple to make a raft. When the waters rise, the turtle advises the couple to be generous to wild animals but wary of humans. While the turtle is underwater guarding the raft's anchor rope, the couple provide shelter for a tiger, cobra, and monkey, and later (forgetting the turtle's advice) for a human courtier. After the waters recede, the animals repay the couple by providing meat and other articles from the forest. The tiger eats a royal servant, and gives the golden casket in his possession to the couple out of gratitude. The courtier they sheltered reports them for stealing the casket, and the couple is jailed. The cobra engineers their release by blinding the princess and giving the couple the medicine to cure the blindness. The old man becomes a minister at court. The golden turtle gives him long lectures on the beneficial results of observing the precepts and doing good works. Sakka comes down and addresses five riddles to the king. When he cannot answer them, he summons the golden turtle, who can. The answers reaffirm the benefits of observing the five precepts, and the turtle completes the teaching with another lecture on the same theme.

56. DEVANDHA

Devandha, the Bodhisatta, is born as son of King Kāsika in Bārāṇasī. While visiting the forest, King Kāsika is eaten by Nanda, an ogre. To save himself, the king's horse persuades the ogre to return to the city in the guise of the king and eat humans secretly at night. Devandha and his sister Jandana discover the truth and flee at night with the horse. The ogre chases after them and eats the horse's head, but Sakka arrives and revives him with a new head from a lion.

Devandha and Jandana find a deserted city where the people had all been eaten by an eagle. Jandana discovers Prince Abhaya hidden in a drum. They become lovers. She gets pregnant. To shield the fact from Devandha, the couple send Devandha on dangerous missions in the Himavanta Forest in the hope that he is killed. He survives each time, on one occasion by delivering the *kumbhaṇḍa* a lecture on the precepts, and gains a retinue of monkeys, bears, and *kumbhaṇḍa*. Devandha discovers Prince Abhaya but forgives him. Devandha leads his retinue to Bārāṇasī, exposes the impostor ogre Nanda, and kills him in a great battle.

Devandha is anointed king, rejects the 101 princesses on offer, and sets out to find a gem woman. A hermit guides him to Suvaṇṇa Kesarā of Kosiya. After overcoming ogres and many other obstacles on the way, he finds Suvaṇṇa Kesarā; they become lovers and return to Bārāṇasī. When Devandha leaves Suvaṇṇa Kesarā outside the city while he informs his mother, an ogress comes upon Suvaṇṇa Kesarā, throws her in a river, and impersonates her in order to become queen. Suvaṇṇa Kesarā is saved by an old couple. Devandha sees through the ogress's guise and sets off to find Suvaṇṇa Kesarā. She identifies herself by winning a contest to preach the dhamma. They return to Bārāṇasī with his old forest retinue, expose the ogress, and give her to the *kumbhaṇḍa* as a shared wife.

When Suvaṇṇa Kesarā becomes pregnant, she sets out to visit her mother but gives birth on the ocean to one son and later in Kosiya to another. Before long, the two princes go off to study the arts, defeating ogres and acquiring princesses along the way. In old age, Devandha and Suvaṇṇa Kesarā retire to the Himavanta Forest as rishi.

57. SUPINA

Supina, the Bodhisatta, is abandoned by his rich but mean father and brought up by a royal monk. When he has a dream predicting he will become king, the king of Kosambī has him arrested. When the king lusts after Princess Padumāvatī of Khommaraṭha, he sends Supina to fetch her, planning to kill him afterward. Helped by an albino monkey chief, Supina meets the princess in the royal park and they fall in love. Boarding a ship to take her away, he falls into the water and they are separated. A courtier takes the princess back to the king of Kosambī.

On the monkey's advice, Supina embarks on a quest. He first obtains a jewel that enables him to fly or walk on water, then uses this device to trick four kings into handing over their magic articles including a staff that can kill or revive and a drum that can conjure up anything. When Supina returns to Kosambī, the king tries to have him killed, but Supina destroys his attackers with the staff and conjures up a magnificent new city with the drum. Realizing he cannot win, the king of Kosambī marries Supina to Princess Padumāvatī and hands over the realm.

When the parents of Princess Padumāvatī discover that she was abducted to Kosambi, they propose to attack the city but are dissuaded by merchants who know of Supina's power. When Padumāvati becomes pregnant, she and Supina travel to visit her parents. Supina apologizes to Padumāvati's parents for abducting her, and they are reconciled. Supina and his queen have two sons. When the younger goes on a quest to find a wife, Supina gives him some of his magical kit. The son acquires the daughter of a *kinnari* and fends off royal rivals.

58. SUVAṆṆAVAṀSA

Suvaṇṇavaṁsa the Bodhisatta is born as the only son of the king of Jeyyavaṁsa. On his father's death, he concedes the throne to his evil uncle and goes to hunt elephants in the forest. Princess Pūraṇī of Ariṭṭha flees from her drunken father to stay with a rishi, who gives her a magic sword and mantra, with which she evades ogres. A tree spirit arranges for her to meet Suvaṇṇavaṁsa. They marry.

Hoping to seize Pūraṇī, the evil uncle sends Suvaṇṇavaṁsa off on a mission to the *nāga* world. On his journey, Suvaṇṇavaṁsa comes upon three abandoned cities, kills their evil forces, and marries their three princesses. The last of these, a *nāga*, escorts him to complete his mission in the *nāga* world, after which they tour the Himavanta Forest, where a *vijjādhara* steals their magic sword. Frightened by a *garuḍa*, the *nāga* princess flees back to the *nāga* world.

Sakka returns the magic sword to Suvaṇṇavaṁsa, turns himself into a horse for Suvaṇṇavaṁsa to ride in return for lectures on the dhamma, and takes him to the heavens, where Suvaṇṇavaṁsa marries an *apsara*. On return to the human world he is reunited with the *nāga* princess.

Back in Jeyyavaṁsa, Suvaṇṇavaṁsa's wife Pūraṇī is still being pursued by his wicked uncle. She flees into the forest, is adopted by a group of ogresses, and gives birth to a son. Alerted by Sakka, Suvaṇṇavaṁsa hears of the threat to Pūraṇī and returns to Jeyyavaṁsa, accompanied by his four wives, causing his evil uncle to die in an accident. Suvaṇṇavaṁsa finds Pūraṇī in the forest, but a water spirit floats her away on the ocean and impersonates her. The water spirit is discovered on return to the city, as Suvaṇṇavaṁsa's *nāga* wife can see through her disguise. Pūraṇī is found.

Suvaṇṇavaṁsa is anointed as king and married to his cousin, the evil uncle's daughter, as a sixth wife. He leads an army to intimidate the drunken father who drove Pūraṇī out, and they are reconciled. Suvaṇṇavaṁsa and Pūraṇī have a son, Pūraṇavaṁsa, who starts to follow in his father's footsteps. He enters the forest and marries a lady born in a milkwood flower and raised by a rishi. He defeats an ogre lord and marries his daughter, who has a powerful magic ring. He returns to rule in Ariṭṭha with his two queens.

59. VARANUJJA

Subhaddā, a *kinnari* princess, is stranded in the forest when a hunter takes her wings. A wood spirit arranges for her to meet and marry King Cetarāja of Videha (later he becomes King Kāsika of Kāsi). When she gives birth to twins, his jealous senior queen Khemā has one buried in the forest and the other floated away, and tells the king that Subhaddā gave birth to a block of wood and is thus inauspicious. The king has Subhaddā floated away. She arrives at an island, where she lives as a hermit. The first son, Varanetta, the Bodhisatta, is brought up by a wood spirit and the second, Varanujja, by a hermit.

Aged sixteen, Varanetta sets out to find his mother. At a rishi's retreat on the way, he meets and marries Puṣapā, a divine princess born in a lotus flower. With a bow and sword provided by the rishi, and a horse from the heavens, the couple travel to enjoy the Himavanta Forest. Worried they are loitering too long, a spirit transports them to his mother, Subhaddā. With a prayer, Varanetta creates a magnificent city on the island. Named Sākala, the city attracts many people.

Varanujja is adopted by an ogre lord, Aggisikha. Aged sixteen, he becomes curious about his origins. Knowing this, Sakka appears as a mynah bird, tells him the story, and provides a peacock to take him back to his rishi foster father to study the arts before searching for his mother. When the ogre lord learns of this, he sympathizes and provides Varanujja with a bow, sword, and horse. While asleep on the first night of his journey, Varanujja is abducted to the *nāga* world by a *nāga* king, who marries him to his daughter, Samuddajā. After Varanujja leaves without her, he is abducted to the palace of an ogre king, where he is seduced by the ogre's daughter. When he is discovered and in danger, wood spirits transport him back to his hermit patron. An ogre army comes after him but is defeated in a great battle and the ogre king killed. At the cremation, Varanujja shows his powers and is selected to rule the ogre realm. When the horse reminds him that he is neglecting his mother, he resumes his quest and is soon reunited with his mother and brother in magnificent Sākala City. He goes to fetch his *nāga* wife with the help of a white elephant. On the expedition to fetch his ogre wife, he helps to defend her city from a rival ogre army.

Varanujja sets off to find the white elephant, which has wandered off, and to locate his father. By chance, his father has just trapped the white elephant, so the two missions coincide. Varanujja forgives his father for the events of his birth and takes him to Sākala City. All are reconciled. The father returns to his city and brutally punishes the evil Queen Khemā and her relatives. Varanujja becomes ruler in Kāsika and Varanetta in Sākala.

60. SIRASĀ

Sirasā the Bodhisatta is the seventh son of the king of Pupphavatī. Because of his mother's vow, he is born through her mouth. At eight months, the infant magically hides himself in a chest. An evil brahman persuades the king that Sirasā is inauspicious and must be expelled on a ship. His mother goes with him. The city becomes quiet and gloomy. An old minister, Ayyaka, returns to the city on a visit and discovers the cause of the gloom. He lectures the evil brahman and his accomplices on the proper conduct of royal servants, returns to his home, and leads prayers and merit-making intended to bring Sirasā there. The ship arrives and there is great rejoicing. Sakka sends down fragrant rain, which spreads to Pupphavatī. Sirasā's brother rides out to investigate. After finding Sirasā, he fetches the other brothers, their father, and some citizens. There is a great celebration.

The evil brahmans are driven away. Sirasā gives sermons on good and bad people. Sakka invites him up to the heavens, but after he leaves his mother collapses and the people weep at this loss. Out of sympathy for his mother and the people, Sirasā returns to the human world, accompanied by a panoply of gods and angels, in the body of a twenty-year-old. The gem elements appear, and he becomes a splendid wheel-rolling emperor.

61. CANDAGĀDHA

In Campaka, after a girl becomes pregnant from drinking tiger's urine in an elephants footprint and gives birth to an admirable son, Kunjara, other women emulate her by having children out of wedlock, provoking a drought, famine, and epidemic of crime and disease. The king starts to punish the loose women, but Kunjara intercedes to make him stop.

Suriyagādha and Candagādha (the Bodhisatta) are sons of a poor family. During the drought and famine, their parents drive them out, forcing them to live by begging. When they wander into the forest, Indra comes down and provides them with a medicine that can bring the dead back to life. They revive a crow, who becomes their guide but then shops them to an ogre who plans to eat them. The ogre relents after the boys use the medicine to revive the ogre's recently deceased wife. Other ogres still want to eat the boys, but they escape.

When Sujāta-tiṁsa, daughter of the king of Kāsī, dies of a snake bite, the two brothers bring her back to life, and the king marries her to Suriyagādha. The two brothers decide to visit their parents. They distribute bamboo canisters of wealth to people who helped them when they were begging and to their parents, but do not reveal themselves to the parents. On return to Kāsī, the king dies and Suriyagādha succeeds.

Candagādha revives a boy bitten to death by a tiger and is adopted by his merchant father. At Indapatta, the merchant learns that Princess Devadhi Saṅka has died and arranges for Candagādha to come to treat her. He cures her and is married to her. While returning to visit his parents, their ship sinks and the couple is separated. Devadhi Saṅka reaches land and is sheltered by an old woman. A prince, Sudassana Cakka, sees her, falls in love, and floats his recently married queen Brahmacārī away on a raft. Her angry retainers stage a revolt that fails. Devadhi Saṅka becomes a nun to protect herself from the prince.

After Candagādha reaches land, he revives a dead *nāga*, who gives him a jewel with extraordinary power of sight. He also helps a wounded *vijjādhara*, who gives him a magic sword and shoes but warns him their powers will disappear if he goes with a woman.

Three merchant's daughters get lost and chance upon Candagādha. Although they flirt with him, he does not respond. He leads them home in an epic quest, using his magic devices to help people along the way and to defend them from robbers and ogres. On arrival home, their parents marry him to all three, but he leaves after a week with each.

Candagādha comes upon the floated-away queen, Brahmacārī. She is reluctant to return home but he takes her there, resisting her advances along the way. Impressed by his celibacy, her parents marry them and present him with the realm. An envoy arrives from a neighboring king, asking for Brahmacārī's hand, but is rejected rather brusquely. The slighted king mounts a massive attack but cannot match the magic of Candagādha and Brahmacārī, who has been trained by her stepmother, an adept. She even holds her own in an elephant duel.

Using his magic sight, Candagādha locates Devadhi Saṅka and travels to see her. She leaves the sisterhood of nuns. When Sudassana Cakka learns that she has left the order but gone with another man, he demands a massive ransom, which Candagādha provides through his magic devices.

Brahmacārī leads an army to take revenge on Sudassana Cakka for floating her away. After an epic siege by female troops, she takes the city. Sudassana Cakka is captured and condemned to carrying away urine and feces. He dies within three days. Candagādha and Devadhi Saṅka are installed to rule the city, which prospers under their rule.

Soon after, Princess Uttama Dhānī arrives, expecting to be married to Sudassana Cakka, who has already died. Candagādha takes her instead. Her father's city is attacked by a king slighted in his request for Uttama Dhānī as his queen. The father appeals for help. Candagādha dispatches an army while he himself flies on ahead and initially is treated with suspicion until the astrologer identifies him. He defeats several waves of attack using a lot of magic. After three years he returns to Anūpama and his three queens. He has a son by Uttama Dhānī. He leaves her and the son to take Devadhi Saṅka back to Indapatta, where he rules, while paying occasional visits to the cities of his other queens.

A backstory explains that in a previous life, Candagādha was a noble's son who repaired a Buddha image, and that six women who helped in this project became his six wives in this life.

His son Duggata Khattiyavaṃsa rejects countless candidates to become his queen but finally wins a princess by defeating her brother in a contest and abducting her. Her father intends to make war in revenge but is persuaded that friendly relations would be better.

GLOSSARY

(P) = Pali. For proper names not found here, consult the *Dictionary of Pali Names* at www.palikanon.com/english/pali_names/dic_idx.html

akkhohiṇī (P) อักโขเภณี, *akkhopheni*, a number with 42 zeroes.

Amarinda อมรินทร์, *amarin*, a name for Indra.

Anāthapiṇḍika อนาถปิณฑิกะ; see Jeta Grove.

anchan อัญชัน, *añjana*, *Clitoria ternatea*, butterfly pea, a creeper with a deep blue flower.

Anotatta อโนดาต, *anodat*, a lake in the Himavanta.

antaravāsaka (P) อันตรวาสก, *antarawasok*, the "inner" robe of a monk, generally called a *sabong* in Thai.

apsara อัปสร, *apson*, accharā, celestial maiden, angel.

asaṅkheyya (P) อสงไขย, *asongkhai*, a crore (ten million) to the power of ten, or just an incalculably long period.

ascendant ลัคนา, *lakhana*, lagna, the planet rising on the eastern horizon at the time of birth, the most influential planet in a person's horoscope.

asura (P) อสูร, *asun*, a class of malevolent deities or demons.

Avīci อวิจี, *awiji,* avīci, the lowest of all the eight great hells, described in the Three Worlds cosmology as "the great hell of suffering without respite." It is surrounded by iron walls nine *yojana* thick and has constant fire that torments but never kills. This hell is the destination of those who break the five precepts and commit major crimes such as killing their own mother or father.

baldachin บุษบก, *busabok*, a canopy or booth over a throne or pulpit.

Bamboo Grove เวฬุวัน, *weluwan,* Veḷuvana, a park near Rājagaha bestowed on the Buddha.

camara, camari (P) จมร, จมรี *jamon, jamari*, a yak, and a form of regalia based on its tail.

Cātumahārajika จาตุมหาราชิก, *jatumaharachika*, the first level of the heavens, the realm of four great kings" appointed by Indra to be the guardians of the world.

Chaddanta ฉัททันต์, *chatthan*, (1) a lake in the Himavanta, (2) a great elephant in the Himavanta and his lineage of elephants; a symbol of strength.

cīvara (P) จีวร, *jiwon*, the principal robe of a monk.

crore โกฏิ, *kot*, koṭi, ten million.

demon มาร, *man*, māra, a class of beings, among the most malevolent, with the power to fly and to transform their bodies infinitely.

dhutaṅga (P) ธุดงค์, *thudong*, ascetic practices, especially of an itinerant monk.

Erāvana เอราวัณ, *erawan*, the elephant mount of Indra.

fig มะเดื่อ, *maduea*, udumbara, *Ficus lacor* and related trees.

financier เศรษฐี, *seṭṭhī*, a wealthy person, a financier, often of the king.

five irons เครื่องจำห้าประการ, *khrueang jam ha prakan*, term for a form of restraint with an iron collar, handcuffs, leg irons, a chain around the waist, plus a cangue or yoke around the neck.

flower-chariot บุสสรถ/บุษยะรถ, *putsarot/putsayarot*, pussaratha, flower-chariot, a self-propelling device for identifying a new king (pus—means to blossom, and pussa is the constellation Prasesepe in Cancer, which has five stars seen as a flower garland).

four-limbed army จตุรงค์, *jaturong*, caturaṅga. The four divisions of an army: elephant troops, cavalry, chariots, and infantry.

Four Noble Truths อริยสัจจ์, *ariyasat*, *ariyasacca*. The truth of suffering; the truth of the cause of suffering; the truth of the end of suffering; the truth of the path leading to the end of suffering. The core of Theravada Buddhis teaching; in summary: in the world there is suffering, which is caused by craving but can be overcome by attaining *nibbāna* (release) through following the eightfold path of Buddhist discipline.

gandhabba (P) คนธรรพ์, *khonthan*, gandharva, celestial beings, benign, often musicians.

Gandhamādana คันธมาทน์, *khanthamat*, "intoxicating with fragrance," a mountain range beyond the seven ranges, inhabited by Pacceka Buddhas.

garuḍa (P) ครุฑ, *khrut*, a mythical creature based on an eagle; rivals of the *nāga*; mount of Vishnu.

gāvuta (P) คาพยุต, *khaphayut*, a measure of distance; a quarter of a *yojana*, about four kilometers.

gem-jewel mantra มนต์มณีจินดา/จินดามณี, *mon manijinda/jindamani*, cintāmaṇimanta, a general-purpose incantation to ask for assistance, mentioned in many literary works, now used by fishermen to lure their catch.

Great Being มหาสัตว์, *mahasat*, mahāsatta, epithet of the Bodhisatta.

hatthaliṅga (P) หัสดีลิงค์, *hatsadiling*, a mythical animal with the head, wings, and tail of a duck and the tusks and trunk of an elephant.

Himavanta หิมพานต์, *himaphan*, "snowy mountains," a wild territory beyond the area of human habitation, populated by wild and mythical creatures; a mythologized version of the Himalayas.

holy-day precepts อุโบสถศีล, *uposathasin*, uposatha sīla, a set of eight precepts observed on the holy days in the lunar month.

Indra พระอินทร์ *phra in*, often known as Amarin; king of the gods, presiding over Tāvatiṁsa, the heaven of the thirty-three gods; the most prominent of the Hindu gods in Thai tradition, closely associated with kingship, able to intervene directly in the world.

Jambu Continent ชมพูทวีป, *chomphuthawip*, jambudīpa, southernmost of the four continents, originally meaning the Indian subcontinent; Jambu is often identified as the rose apple but more likely was a black plum, *Eugenia jambolana*.

Jeta Grove เชตวัน, *chetawan*, Jetavana, a grove outside Sāvatthī, dedicated to the Buddha by a merchant, Sudatta, dubbed Anāthapiṇḍika, "giver of alms to the unprotected."

jiam เจียม, a mat made from animal hair.

kahāpaṇa (P) กหาปณะ, *kahapana*, a coin; the Thai translators sometimes rendered this as *tamlueng*.

kammajavāta (P) กัมมัชวาต, *kammatchawat*, a wind that blows in the womb to start delivery.

Kassapa กัสสปะ, *kassapa*, the Buddha preceding Gotama.

kinnara, kinnari (P) กินนน (usually กินนร กินรา) /กินรี, *kinnon/kinnari*, a creature from the Himavanta Forest with the lower body of a bird and the head and upper body of a human.

Kosiya โกสีย์, *kosi*, a name for Indra.

Kubera *See* Vesavaṇa.

kumbhaṇḍa (P) กุมภัณฑ์, *kumphan*, a class of mythical beings, often malevolent, sometimes portrayed as dwarfish and pot bellied.

lalang หญ้าคา, *ya kha*, *Imperata cylindrica*, a coarse grass.

Maghavā มัฆวาน, *makhawan*, a name for Indra, possibly based on his name as Magh in an earlier life.

maṇḍapa (P) มณฑป, *mondop*, a pavilion for housing an image or other purposes, usually with a peaked roof.

masang มะทราง, มะซาง, *Madhuca pierrei*, a tree, mahua.

Mātali มาตลี, *matali*, Indra's charioteer.

members of the Buddhist Council สังคีติกาจารย์, *sangkhitikajan*, saṅgītikācariya, alluding to the early convocations of monks that settled the content of the Buddha's teachings.

Meru, Sineru พระสุเมรุ, *phra sumeru*, in Buddhist cosmology, the center of the universe.

nāga (P) นาค, *nak*, a mythical snake, modeled on a cobra.

nakkhatta (P) นักษัตร, *naksat*, a constellation, especially one used in astrology.

Nandana นันทวัน, *nanthawan*, the main park and lotus lake in the Tāvatiṃsa Heaven.

ogre ยักษ์, *yak*, yakkha, a non-human being, attendant on Kubera/Vessavaṇa. In some contexts they are benign, but in the *jātaka* tales they feed on human flesh. They have no specific form or appearance but seem to resemble humans and to be capable of adopting a human likeness.

Pacceka Buddha พระปัจเจกโพธิ, *phra patjek phothi*, one who achieves awakening by himself at a time when there is no fully awakened Buddha.

Paṇḍukambalasilā ปัณฑุกัมพลศิลา, *panthukamphonsila*, "yellowish blanket stone," Indra's throne.

Pārichattaka ปาริ(ก)ฉัตร, *pari(ka)chat*, a wishing tree in the Tāvatiṁsa Heaven.

priest-counselor ปุโรหิต, *purohit*, purohita, a brahman serving as chief advisor to a king.

Principles of Harmony สังคหวัตถุ, *sangkhawatthu*, *saṅgahavatthu*, a set of four: generosity, good speaking, helpfulness, and consistency; with a variant for rulers, comprising shrewdness in promoting agriculture, shrewdness in managing officials, shrewdness in promoting commerce and employment, and kind and convincing speech.

residence ปราสาท, *prasat*, pāsāda, a building, usually tall, for gods or royalty.

Sakka สักกะ, *sakka,* the usual name for Indra in the *jātaka*.

sal สาละ, *sāla*, the tree *Shorea robusta,* translated to Thai as ต้นรัง, *ton rang*, *Shorea siamensis*, a closely related dipterocarp tree.

saṅghāṭī (P) สังฆาฏิ, *sangkhati*, one of the three robes of a monk, an outer shawl, worn folded over the shoulder during ceremonies.

sapphire อินทนิล, *inthanin*, indanīla.

Satta Paribhaṇḍa สัตบริภัณฑ์, *sattaboriphan*, seven mountain ranges surrounding Meru.

sen เส้น, forty meters.

swan หงส์, *hong*, haṃsa. This mythical animal is modeled on a Brahmany Goose but is considered an epitome of beauty, hence is translated as "swan" since "goose" in English lacks the symbolic meaning.

Tathāgata ตถาคต, *tathakhot*, "thus-gone-one," "thus-come-one," an epithet of the Buddha.

Tāvatiṁsa ดาวดึงส์, *dawadueng*, heaven of the thirty-three gods, presided over by Indra.

Ten Royal Virtues ทศพิธราชธรรม, *thotsaphit ratchatham*, dasabidharājadhamma, a code of conduct for kings, as configured by Buddhist tradition. The ten virtues are munificence, moral living, generosity, justice, compassion, absence of bad ambition, suppression of anger, non-oppressiveness, and upholding the dhamma or Buddhist teachings.

Thousand-Eyed One ท้าวสหัสนัยน์, *thao sahatsanai*, the god Indra. According to the *Mahabharata*, Indra seduced the wife of the sage Gotama, and Gotama cursed Indra to have female sex organs all over his body but later relented and changed these into a thousand eyes. According to the *Ramayana*, Indra was always thousand-eyed, but after Indra seduced his wife, Gotama cursed Indra to lose his testicles and later relented and replaced them with those of a ram. According to the Mala Sutra, Indra was given this name because he could see a thousand things in an instant.

Tipiṭika ไตรปิฎก, *traipidok*, "three baskets," a collection of Buddhist texts grouped in three categories: monastic codes (*vinaya*); discourses and teachings of the Buddha (*sutta*); and scholastic texts (*abhidhamma*).

tree of plenty กัลปพฤกษ์, *kalapaphruek*, kapparukkha, "tree [that fulfills] wishes," a wishing tree with fruit of anything desired.

Triple Gem พระรัตนตรัย, *phra rattanatrai*, ratanattaya; the Buddha, the Dhamma, and the Sangha.

Tusita ดุสิต, *dusit*, the fourth of the six levels of heaven, where a bodhisatta is born in the life prior to his final birth in the human world.

usubha (P) อุสุภ, *usup*, a measure of length, often 120–140 cubits, 60–70 meters.

Vejayanta เวชยันต์, *wetchayan*, the name of Indra's palace and chariot.

Vesavaṇa เวสวัณ, sometimes กุเวร, Kubera, Kuvera, guardian of the north, served by the *yakkha* ogres.

viceroy อุปราช, *uparat*, uparājā, a second or deputy king.

vijjādhara (P) วิทยาธร, *withayathon*, "holder of knowledge," especially supernatural knowledge; a being resident in the Himavanta with the ability to fly and a reputation for mischief; they are usually represented in human form.

vimāna (P) วิมาน, *wiman*, here a mobile palace, capable of flight.

vipassanā (P) วิปัสสนา, *wipatsana*, "clear sight," a form of insight meditation.

Vissukamma วิสสุกรรม, *witsukam*, Visvakarman, Indra's craftsman.

water spirit รากษส, *raksot*, rakkhasa, a malevolent spirit that lives in water, appears at night, and eats humans.

wood-apple มะขวิด, *makhwit, Feronia limonia.*

yāgu (P) ยาคู, *yakhu*, unripe rice boiled with sugar.

yojana (P) โยชน์, *yot*, a measure of distance, about sixteen kilometers.

Yugandhara ยุคันธร, *yukhanthon*, one of the Satta Paribhaṇḍa.

BIBLIOGRAPHY

The first printings

Panyat chadok prachum nithan nai prathet ni tae boran 50 rueang: phak thi 1 samutthakhot chadok kap suthon chadok [Paññāsa Jātaka, collection of 50 old tales from this country: Volume 1; Samuddaghosa and Sudhana]. Printed for the cremation of MR Lek Siriwong na Krungthep. Wachirayan Library seal on title page. Bangkok: Sophon Piphathanakon, 1924.

Vol. 2 (P3), 1924
Vol. 3 (P4–P8), 1924
Vol. 4 (P9–P14), 1924
Vol. 5 (P15), 1925
Vol. 6 (P16–P18), 1925
Vol. 7 (P19–P24), 1925
Vol. 8 (P25–P30), 1925
Vol. 9 (P31–P35), 1925
Vol. 10 (P36–P40), 1926
Vol. 11 (P41–P44), 1926
Vol. 12 (P45), 1927
Vol. 13 (P46–P47), 1927
Vol. 14 (P48), 1927
Vol. 15 (P49), 1928
Vol. 16 (P50), 1930
Vol. 17 (P51), 1929
Vol. 18 (P52), 1928
Vol. 19 (P53), 1928
Vol. 20 (P54), 1931
Vol. 21 (P55), 1929
Vol. 22 (P56), 1930
Vol. 23 (P57), 1930
Vol. 24 (P58), 1930
Vol. 25 (P59), 1930
Vol. 26 (P60), [1930?]
Vol. 27 (P61), 1935.

Sources

Appleton, Naomi. "Jātaka Stories and Paccekabuddhas in Early Buddhism." In Naomi Appleton and Peter Harvey, ed., *Buddhist Path, Buddhist Teachings: Studies in Memory of L. S. Cousins*, Sheffield: Equinox, 2019.

———. *Jātaka Stories in Theravāda Buddhism: Narrating the Bodhisatta Path*. London and New York: Routledge, 2016.

Appleton, Naomi, and Sarah Shaw. *The Ten Great Birth Stories of the Buddha: The Mahānipāta of the Jātakatthavaṇṇanā*. Chiang Mai: Silkworm Books, 2016.

Arthid Sheravanichkul. "Self-Sacrifice of the Bodhisatta in the Paññāsa Jātaka." *Religion Compass* 2, no. 5 (2008): 769–87.

Beal, Samuel, trans. *Si-yu-ki: Buddhist Records of the Western World*. Translated from the Chinese of Hiuen Tsiang [Xuanzang, Hsüan-tsang]. Delhi: Oriental Book Reprint, 1969.

Bizot, François. "La consécration des statues et le culte des morts." In *Recherches nouvelles sur le Cambodge*, edited by François Bizot, 101–27. Paris: EFEO, 1994.

Chiang mai panyat chadok. Translated by Chanin Sukhakesi and Prasit Saenthap. Edited by Prasit Saenthap. Bangkok: Fine Arts Department, 1998.

Cowell, E. B., ed. *The Jātaka or Stories of the Buddha's Former Births*. 6 vols. Cambridge: Cambridge University Press, 1907.

Crosby, Kate. *Theravada Buddhism: Continuity, Diversity, and Identity*. Chichester: Wiley Blackwell, 2013.

Damrong Rajanubhab, Prince. "Kham athibai" [Preface]. Printed in all Thai editions of the Fifty Jātaka since 1924.

Faussböll, V., ed. *The Jātaka Together with its Commentary, being Tales of the Anterior Births of Gotama Buddha*. 6 vols. London: Trübner and Co., 1877–96.

Fickle, Dorothy M. "An Historical and Structural Study of the Paññāsa Jātaka." PhD diss., University of Pennsylvania, 1978.

Fine Arts Department. *Panyat chadok* [Paññāsa Jātaka]. 2 vols. Bangkok: Fine Arts Department, 2000.

Gombrich, Richard F. "Kosala-Bimba-Vaṇṇanā." In *Buddhism in Ceylon and Studies on Religious Syncretism in Buddhist Countries*, ed. H. Bechert, Göttingen: Abhandlungen der Akademie der Wissenschaften, 1978, 281–303.

GSB [Government Savings Bank], *Panyat chadok: phak phasa thai-pali*. 4 vols. Bangkok: Mulniti omsin phuea sangkhom [Government Savings Bank Foundation for Society], 2011.

Horner, I. B. and Padmanabh S. Jaini, trans. *Apocryphal Birth-Stories (Paññāsa-jātaka)*. 2 vols. London: Pali Text Society, 1985–86.

Hudak, Thomas John. *The Tale of Prince Samuttakote: A Buddhist Epic from Thailand*. Ohio: Ohio University Press, 1996.

Ingersoll, Fern S., trans. *Sang Thong: A Dance-Drama from Thailand written by King Rama II & the Poets of His Court*. Rutland, VT: Charles E. Tuttle Company, 1973.

Jaini, Padmanabh S. "The Apocryphal Jatakas of Southeast Asian Buddhism." *The Indian Journal of Buddhist Studies* 1, no. 1 (1989): 22–39. Reprinted in Jaini, *Collected Papers on Buddhist Studies* (Delhi: Motilal Banarsidass, 2001), 375–98.

———, ed. *Paññāsa-jātaka or Zimmè Paṇṇāsa (in the Burmese Recension)*. 2 vols. London: Pali Text Society, 1981, 1983.

———. "The Story of Sudhana and Manoharā: An analysis of the texts and the Borobudur reliefs." *Bulletin of the School of Oriental and African Studies* 29, no. 3 (1966): 533–58.

Jones, J. J., trans. *The Mahāvastu*. Vol. 3 (Vol. 19 of *Sacred Books of the Buddhists*). London: Luzac, 1956.

Khoroche, Peter, trans. *Once a Peacock, Once an Actress: Twenty-Four Lives of the Bodhisattva from Haribhaṭṭ's "Jātakamālā."* Chicago: University of Chicago Press, 2017.

McDaniel, Justin T. *Gathering Leaves & Lifting Words: Histories of Buddhist Monastic Education in Laos and Thailand*. Chiang Mai: Silkworm Books, 2008.

Niyada Lausunthorn. "Panyat chadok: Kan sueksa choeng prawat" [Historical study of the Fifty Jātaka]. In *Phinitwannakam: ruam botkhwam wichakan dan wannakhadi lae phasa* [Literary analysis: Collected articles on language and literature]. N.p.: 1992.

———. *Panyat chadok: Prawatisat lae khwam samkhan thi mi to wannakam roi krong khong thai* [Paññāsa Jātaka: Its genesis and significance to Thai poetical works]. 2nd edition. Bangkok: Lai kham, 2015 [1995].

Notton, Camille, trans. "Chronique de Suvaṇṇa K'ôm Khăm." In *Annales du Siam*, Vol 1, 82–135. Paris: Imprimeries Charles Lavauzelle et Cie, 1926.

Nyalankar, Lakshmi Narayan, trans. *The Hitopadesh: A Collection of Fables and Tales in Sanscrit by Vishnusarma*. Calcutta: Shastra Prakasha Press, 1830.

Pali Manuscripts Research Project. *Paññāsajātaka: Thai recension nos. 12–18, 22–39 kept in the Otani University Library, transliterations from manuscripts in Khmer*. Kyoto: Shin Buddhist Comprehensive Research Institute, Otani University, 2004.

Panyat chadok. 2 vols. Bangkok: Fine Arts Department, 2000.

Phap kiao kap wannakhadi thai [Pictures associated with Thai literature]. Prepared by Waldemar C. Sailer, Niyada Lausunthorn, et al. Printed for the cremation of Somdet Phra Phuthajan (Sangiam Janthasirimahathera), Wat Thepsirin, December 17, 1983.

Phojani Phengplian. "Kan sueksa wannakam isan rueang suwannasangkuman" [Study of the Northeastern Story, Prince of the Golden Conch]. MA thesis, Silpakorn University, 1989.

Prachum phongsawadan phak thi 72 tamnan mueang suwannakhomkham [Collected chronicles part 72, legend of Suwanna Khomkham]. Bangkok: Wiswakon, 1939.

Rattanaphon Chuenka. "The Journey of Nang Sip Song (The Twelve Sisters) or Phra Rot Meri in South East Asia: From Folktale to Regional Tale and Modern Ritualistic Belief." Presentation at the 13th International Conference of Thai Studies, Chiang Mai, July 17, 2017.

Santi Pakdeekham, ed. and trans. *Piṭakamālā, 'The Garland of the Piṭaka.'* Bangkok: Fragile Palm Leaves Foundation; Lumbini: Lumbini International Research Institute, 2011.

Skilling, Peter. "Jātaka and Paññāsa-jātaka in South-East Asia." *Journal of the Pali Text Society* 28 (2006): 113–73.

———. "Reflections on the Pali Literature of Siam." In *From Birch Bark to Digital Data: Recent Advances in Buddhist Manuscript Research*, edited by Paul Harrison and Jens-Uwe Hartmann, 347–66. Vienna: Österreichische Akademie der Wissenschaften, 2014.

———. "Romance and Riddle: Buddhist Narratives of Siam." In *Imagination and Narrative: Lexical and Cultural Translation in Buddhist Asia*, edited by Peter Skilling and Justin Thomas McDaniel, 161–86. Chiang Mai: Silkworm Books, 2017.

Skilling, Peter, Jason A. Carbine, Claudio Cicuzza, and Santi Pakdeekham, ed. *How Theravada is Theravada? Exploring Buddhist Identities*. Chiang Mai: Silkworm Books, 2012.

Terral, Ginette. "Samuddaghosajātaka. Conte pāli tiré du Paññāsajātaka." *Bulletin de l'Ecole française d'Extreme-Orient* 48, no. 1 (1956): 249–351.

Trongjai Hutarangkura, ed. *Upathawathotsamat khlong dan: Wannakam phet nam ek haeng phranakhon si ayutthaya* [Through All Twelve Months: A Major Work of Ayutthaya Literature]. Bangkok: Sirindhorn Anthropology Center, 2017.

Unebe, Toshiya. "Three Stories from the Thai Recension of the Paññāsa-jātaka: Transliteration and Preliminary Notes." *Journal of Sanskrit Literature* 3 (2007), 1–23.

Velder, Christian, and Katrin A. Velder. "The Striped Tiger Prince and Pahala: The Portly Cow." Translated into German from the 1956 Thai edition by Christian Velder, and into English by Katrin A. Velder. *Tai Culture* 5, no. 1 (2000): 135–39.

Wannakam samai thonburi lem 2 [Thonburi-era literature, vol. 2]. Bangkok: Fine Arts Department, 1990.

Wyatt, David K., and Aroonrut Wichienkeeo, trans and ed. *The Chiang Mai Chronicle*. Chiang Mai: Silkworm Books, 1995.

Yamamoto, Kosho, trans. *The Mahayana Mahaparinirvana-Sutra*. 3 vols. Tokyo: Karin Bunko, 1973.

www.ingramcontent.com/pod-product-compliance
Lightning Source LLC
Chambersburg PA
CBHW051249300426
44114CB00011B/956
* 9 7 8 6 1 6 2 1 5 1 2 7 9 *